Women in the Great European Revolutions

Women in the Great European Revolutions

Gender, Culture, Class, and the State

Bailey Stone

BLOOMSBURY ACADEMIC

NEW YORK • LONDON • OXFORD • NEW DELHI • SYDNEY

BLOOMSBURY ACADEMIC
Bloomsbury Publishing Plc, 50 Bedford Square, London, WC1B 3DP, UK
Bloomsbury Publishing Inc, 1359 Broadway, New York, NY 10018, USA
Bloomsbury Publishing Ireland, 29 Earlsfort Terrace, Dublin 2, D02 AY28, Ireland

BLOOMSBURY, BLOOMSBURY ACADEMIC and the Diana logo are trademarks of
Bloomsbury Publishing Plc

First published in the United States of America 2025

A catalogue record for this book is available from the British Library.

A catalog record for this book is available from the Library of Congress.

ISBN: HB: 9798765153239
Paperback: 9798765153222
eBook: 9798765153215
ePDF: 9798765153246

Typeset by Deanta Global Publishing Services, Chennai, India
Printed and bound in the United States of America

For product safety related questions contact productsafety @bloomsbury.com.

To find out more about our authors and books visit www.bloomsbury.com
and sign up for our newsletters.

CONTENTS

ACKNOWLEDGMENTS

It is my pleasant task to acknowledge here a few of the individuals without whose personal support, professional advice, and/or notable contributions to revolutionary and women's studies I could not have possibly conceived, researched, and (ultimately) written this book.

Recognition is due first to Professor of History Emeritus Thomas E. Kaiser, now successfully "relocated" from the University of Arkansas to academic pursuits in the vicinity of the University of Maryland. Tom and I have become intellectual companions-at-arms over the decades as we have come, from different perspectives, to share a fascination with the intersection of women's history and the more traditional diplomatic history of ancien régime and revolutionary France. As Chapter 3 in this study will most strikingly demonstrate, I have profited immensely from Tom's erudition and advice relating to the life of France's ill-fated revolutionary Queen Marie-Antoinette.

I also owe much to the long-standing support of Professor Jack A. Goldstone, sociologist of comparative revolutions and demography in the Schar School of Policy and Government at George Mason University. Jack has over the years helped to clarify for me the myriad ways in which history and sociology can serve as mutually reinforcing disciplines, notably in the realm of the comparative analysis of past and present revolutions.

I furthermore must acknowledge the timely support of George Lawson, a professor in the Department of International Relations at The Australian National University. Professor Lawson took valuable time out of his teaching and research schedule in late 2024 to read over my manuscript and to write up a detailed and invaluable critique of it. His perspective on the comparative analysis and typologies of modern revolutions has enriched my work in many respects.

In recent months I have also benefited from the advice tendered to me by Jennifer N. Heuer, Professor of French History at UMass (Amherst). We share a commitment to the intersectionality of questions of gender, family, revolution, citizenship, and war, and I have found Jennifer's suggestions regarding (most notably) the documentation requisite for Chapters 4 and 5 of this book to be helpful and enlightening in all respects.

In addition, I am grateful for the access I have had in recent years to the collections in the libraries of the Five Colleges Consortium here in western Massachusetts. In that connection, I should especially acknowledge the help afforded to me by Jason Fuller, curator of the Five Colleges Library Repository Collection in Amherst, MA, and by A. J. Menon, chief librarian at LITS, the Mount Holyoke College Library in South Hadley, MA.

I have also profited from acute criticism of my work offered to me on several memorable occasions by male *and, particularly, female* members of the Five Colleges International Relations Seminar hosted formerly by the University of Massachusetts at Amherst. Special thanks, in this connection, go to Political Science Emeritus Professor Eric Einhorn for inviting me to attend the sessions of that seminar as an "outsider." Collegial commentary can be of such enormous benefit when one is engaged in preparing a major work of synthesis and reinterpretation.

I should also acknowledge the editorial support, over a period marked by pandemic-related crises, of Susan McEachern, erstwhile senior executive editor for History, International Studies, and Geography at Rowman & Littlefield Publishers in Boulder, Colorado, and of her current successor, Ashley Dodge, editor for Bloomsbury Academic Publishers.

Finally, yet surely not least, grateful thanks are due, as ever, to certain special individuals in the private corridors of my life. As always in the past, so now, they know exactly who they are.

Introduction

Women in the European Revolutionary Experience

In 2014, Cambridge University Press published what was, up to that point, my most ambitious work, *The Anatomy of Revolution Revisited: A Comparative Analysis of England, France, and Russia*.[1] In that study, I explained how the climactic stages of revolution in mid-seventeenth-century England, late-eighteenth-century France, and early-twentieth-century Russia "unavoidably left in their wake legions of disillusioned citizens, to some extent on the Right but [also] on the Left—from embittered Levellers and 'saints' in England to defiant *enragés* and *Hébertists* in France to 'Left' SRs and Bolsheviks and soldiers, sailors, workers, and peasants in Russia."[2] What I failed to emphasize at that point in the book—though I did at least briefly raise the subject later—was the fact that *women,* who were among the "disillusioned citizens" conjured up on those pages in 2014, had played a variety of key roles in all three European revolutions, and—very notably—had done so both on the left *and* on the right sides of the political spectrum. In the present work, I will try to remedy that deficiency by drawing upon traditional and more recent literature (and upon some original sources) to study women's involvement in all the phases of these sociopolitical upheavals. In this Introduction, I will spell out several specific and, I surely hope, persuasive arguments for writing such a book, and then cursorily outline my overall approach to the subject.

There is, first, the undeniable fact that those laboring in the vineyards of women's studies quite properly insist that we view women in revolutionary situations, much as we would view menfolk, not as monolithic, but rather as profoundly diversified and "conflicted" in their concerns. For instance, women petitioning on behalf of (male) Levellers in revolutionary England, Patricia Higgins has maintained, "did not abandon their customary deference to men and to a male-dominated society," even though they *did* "tentatively put forward justifications for the involvement of women in politics based on the equal rights of men and women."[3] Higgins's compatriot Ann Hughes has likewise rejected any simplistic views on this subject, pointing (for example) to "incoherencies" in Leveller rhetoric on gender issues "indicating some of the instabilities and tensions surrounding early modern understandings of women."[4] When it comes to revolutionary France, Olwen Hufton has sounded a similar theme. Not only has she cited divisions in *urban* settings between highly politicized women and those of their sisters primarily exercised by urgent economic problems, she has also acknowledged the preponderant numbers in the First Republic's *rural* hinterland of traditionalist peasant women "who boycotted the mass of the constitutional priest, who in the hard years of 1793–4 organized clandestine masses, who continued to slap a cross on the forehead of the newborn, who placed a Marian girdle on the stomach of the parturient, and who gathered to say the rosary and taught their children their prayers." Far indeed were such women—in both geographical *and* psychological terms—from the purportedly "liberated" working women of the great insurrectionary *journées* of Paris and of other cities in 1793–4.[5] Revolutionary Russia, too, furnishes us with numerous examples of the complicated (and not necessarily class-centered) roles played by women in the turmoil of 1917 and subsequent years. Even most *Bolshevik* women, Barbara E. Clements has insisted, "were in fact less radical than the proclamations that applauded their coming," and a vast majority of their urban and rural sisters would have had little or no sympathy for Alexandra Kollontai's advanced notions about "companionate sexual relations," socialized child-rearing, and the like.[6] Clearly, in the most critical days of revolution in Russia, just as in those occurring earlier in England and France, women played complex roles and exposed complicated concerns and perspectives that make it impossible for us to assign them any more reductively than we could assign men—or, more generally, male-dominated groups—to some ideologically pre-ordained position on the "far left" of the political spectrum.

A second justification for this book lies in the fact that women's studies today play an ever more strategic role in scholarly efforts to interpret the causes, process, and outcomes of the classic European revolutions as well as of more recent social upheavals in the greater world beyond Europe.[7] As I have tried to demonstrate in my most recent book, *Rethinking Revolutionary Change in Europe,* much of the current literature on this subject takes the form of exchanges between *structuralists* emphasizing the importance of international politics, state formation, and state/class articulations, and *postmodernists* (or post-structuralists) prioritizing textual "deconstruction," discourse/ideology, national identity, and—most pertinently for us—gender.[8] As we will see in greater detail in Chapter 1, scholars such as Iranian-American sociologist Valentine Moghadam and British theorist Beverley Southgate have long advocated for a prominent role for gendered and feminist perspectives in revolutionary analyses of a more or less postmodernist bent. For instance, Moghadam, as far back as 1997, was observing that "feminist studies have revealed the significance of gender dynamics and their links to political, economic and ideological processes, including constructions of national identity, in times of social transformation." She was also, by the same token, reminding her readers that "research should also attempt to situate gender issues in the various stages of a revolution," therefore including "prerevolutionary conditions, proximate causes, the course of the revolution, and its short-term and long-term outcomes."[9] Moghadam continues today to explore the "decentering" implications of gender issues—here, with a specific reference to events in the Middle East and North Africa—in a study coauthored with Shamiran Mako.[10] Southgate, for his part, having "deconstructed" such standard building blocks of structuralist revolutionary analysis as Marxism, "statism," and geopolitics, has gone on to interrogate revolutionary feminist and gendered narratives in provocative ways. For this theorist, it is not merely a question of challenging patriarchy by championing "women's studies," but also a question of fundamentally rethinking the *very terms of analysis* habitually employed in such studies. "Even the central roles of male/female need to be historicized," according to Southgate, "and their contingency and heterogeneity recognized." The "centers of our [revolutionary] histories," he concludes, must thus be "once more destabilized."[11] While not all women's scholars would reconceptualize the practice of history in such a radical fashion, we will see throughout this book many examples of how such scholars have turned concerns raised by postmodernists to good use in studying women's perspectives and political roles in the major European revolutions.

A final argument for a book of this kind derives from both the interpretative exchanges between structuralists and postmodernists briefly treated in this Introduction and the concept (much debated by feminists and others) of *intersectionality*. This last term, introduced into social studies by Black feminist Kimberlé Crenshaw in a pair of essays dating from 1989 and 1991, alludes to factors such as race, class, ethnicity, religion, sex, gender, and so forth to explain "how groups' and individuals' social and political identities result in unique combinations of discrimination and privilege."[12] Although intersectionality has won plaudits in some quarters over the years for widening the scope of "first wave" and "second wave" feminist studies to include Black women and other women of color, immigrant women, and some other marginalized groups and individuals in traditionally white- and male-dominated societies, it has also—unavoidably, perhaps—been caught up in various controversies in those same academic quarters.[13] We will be returning to intersectionality when we discuss, in Chapters 1, 4, and 5, the theorizing of *gender* in revolutionary situations and women's radical *and* conservative roles in the English, French, and Russian Revolutions. For the moment, we mention intersectionality only to point out that the analytical factors or "systems of discrimination" that it identifies can be found in traditional historiographical terms under the headings of both postmodernism *and* structuralism as we have defined those terms on these pages. (Hence, if *gender, religion,* and *race* are often subjects of postmodernist analysis, *class* and *statism* are perhaps more characteristic of structuralist inquiry). What all this amounts to is yet another reason for studying women in European revolutions: to follow the dynamic, shifting interactions among such factors as gender, religion, class, national identity, statism, and—where applicable—*race/ethnicity.*

Having thus spelled out at some length our reasons for undertaking this project, it only remains for us to discuss briefly the general content of each of the five chapters that, when taken together, will constitute the main body of the book to follow.

In Chapter 1, "Theorizing Gender in Revolutionary Situations," we reassess theoretical aspects of gender (and associated issues) against the background of revolutionary upheavals, not only in early modern/modern Europe, but also in the greater world beyond Europe. We will do this by posing three basic questions. First, how have historians, sociologists, and other social scientists dealt in conceptual terms with gender, sexuality, and patriarchy? Second, enlarging on what we have already said in this Introduction concerning the scholarly literature on revolutions in general, we ask: What roles do gender (and women's studies) currently play in the confrontation (in historical/sociological writing) between structuralist and postmodernist (or "post-structuralist") explanations of revolutionary change? Finally, we inquire: To what extent (and in what *specific ways*) are prominent feminist scholars optimistic or pessimistic about the prospects for favorable *gendered outcomes*—outcomes propitious, that is, for women—in modern revolutionary situations? We can hope that pondering these questions will provide us with a theoretical grounding for the ensuing inquiry into élitist and "ordinary" women's experiences in the revolutions that in earlier centuries convulsed England, France, and Russia.

Heeding as we must Valentine Moghadam's reminder that *gender* is "an integral dimension of the revolutionary process,"[14] and realizing at the same time that readers unfamiliar with the English, French, and Russian Revolutions need to have a more specific sense of *how they actually unfolded,* we turn, in Chapter 2, "A Brief Sketch of the English, French, and Russian Revolutions," to the basic chronologies of those three upheavals. We start with the events attending the transitions from old regimes to full-blown revolutions in England (1637 to 1640), France (1787 to 1789), and Russia (1916 to 1917); move on from there to what we might term the "honeymoons" marking the early, more or less conciliatory phases of revolution in the three countries; proceed next to the social and political radicalization that blighted earlier hopes for reconciliation in all three situations; then recapitulate the climactic, "terrorist" phases of the three upheavals; and, finally, sum up developments in the so-called Thermidorian or post-Terrorist stages of revolution in England, France, and Russia.

Chapter 3, "Unsuccessful Consort Queens in the European Revolutions," reappraises the relative importance ascribable to *gendered/cultural* and *statist* factors in the disastrous revolutionary careers of three "consort queens": namely, Henrietta Maria of England, Marie-Antoinette of France, and Alexandra Feodorovna of Russia. Whatever the tendency in feminist scholarship to stress the role played by gender and related cultural issues in these women's misfortunes, we set forth, in this chapter, a kind of *counter-case* by showing how Henrietta Maria's, Marie-Antoinette's, and Alexandra's ineptitude in *political matters* contrasted so stunningly with the leadership displayed earlier in England, France, and Russia, respectively, by three recognized (or de facto) "queens regnant": that is, Elizabeth I, Cathérine de Médicis, and Catherine II. In other words, we have here, in *postmodernist* and *structuralist* terms (*and* in terms of intersectionality) a *test case* involving the relative significance of *gender, religion, national identity*, and other *cultural dynamics*, on the one hand, and *statism* (above all, *state security*) on the other hand. For all six women mentioned above, this last factor seems to have been decisive.

Chapter 4, "Women's Emancipatory Roles in England, France, and Russia," discusses how, in Europe's three classic cases of countrywide revolutionary upheaval, women who were no longer content with their customary relegation to powerless roles in society took advantage of politically dynamic situations to express their grievances and voice their aspirations in public and novel forums. In England, women delivered petitions to male politicians, published treatises, and played unprecedented roles as prophetesses and preachers. In France, women rioted in the streets to voice pressing economic concerns and displayed "modern" patters of sociability in political clubs and societies. Finally, in Russia, *élitist* women embraced suffrage and other feminist causes and even interacted with proletarian sisters who were more urgently moved by basic economic concerns. Furthermore, as Chapter 4 demonstrates in detail, the dynamic of *gender* interacted—indeed, sometimes actually clashed—in all these women's revolutionary activities with other dynamic factors, including religion, secular ideology, class, and—at times—*political* issues including the requirements for, and rights and duties of, citizenship.

Chapter 5, "Disillusioned and Traditionalist Women Confronting Revolution," follows through on our determination to review in this book reactionary/traditionalist as well as emancipatory roles of women in revolutionary England, France, and Russia. We will be encountering here women who, in all three revolutionary situations, were forced to question their initially progressive philosophies of change, as well as women who, from the start, were predisposed *on principle* to defend established ways of faith and tradition. We will, moreover, explore in Chapter 5, much as we explored in preceding chapters, how *gendered* considerations involving women could interact and, sometimes, clash sharply with other elements of intersectionality such as *religion* (notably in England and France) and *class* (in France and, likely most commonly, in Russia). Finally, here, as before, we will review the *statist* component in intersectionality as we show how disillusioned and traditionalist women in these three countries were affected by—and at times reacted against or even identified with—statist forces that, like other forces, loomed behind these periods of political and sociocultural change.

Conclusion: Race/Ethnicity and Statism as Women's Revolutionary Problematics. In this brief conclusion, we summarize the main lines of argumentation in this book and then have some additional things to say concerning *race/ethnicity* and *statism* as outstandingly problematic issues in any comparative study of women's roles and perspectives in the three classic European revolutions.

1

Theorizing Gender in Revolutionary Situations

"The woman question," so feminist historian Karen Offen has observed, opens "a window into the heart of a politics of gender . . . which, like the better-documented politics of religion, race, and class, [offers] issues of central importance to the historian who would hope to comprehend the processes of sociopolitical change at their most elemental level."[1] Sociologist Valentine Moghadam has held forth in similar fashion, but has placed the issue of gender within a framework of more explicitly *revolutionary* research. "Two sets of scholarship," Moghadam has contended, "have examined revolutionary change. In one set, standard social science studies have emphasized the international context as well as class, status, and power within a given society, but . . . ignored gender as an analytic category in revolutionary transformation. In the other set, feminist studies have revealed the significance of gender dynamics and their links to political, economic, and ideological processes, including constructions of national identity, in times of social transformation." No wonder, then, that this Iranian American scholar would conclude by proclaiming that "gender is indeed an integral dimension of the revolutionary process and should be accorded conceptual value by sociologists of revolution."[2] Yet what applies here to sociologists applies to professional historians just as well: they, too, must be prepared to theorize this aspect of the modern revolutionary experience. Indeed, this has been an agenda item for historians ever since Marx, Engels, and others writing in the classic socialist tradition first raised the "woman question" for their readers.[3]

In Chapter 1, we will reassess theoretical aspects of gender (and associated issues) against the backdrop of revolutionary upheavals, not only in Europe, but also in the developing world. We will do this by posing three questions. First, how have scholars dealt in *theoretical terms* with gender, sexuality, and patriarchy? (Although gender and sexuality can, undoubtedly, be regarded as conceptual gateways to "men's history" and to LGBT/queer studies[4] as well as to women's history, in this book, on women in revolution, they are to be taken principally as openings to women's experiences.) Second, what kind of a role (or roles??) does gender play in the confrontation (in historical and sociological writing) between structuralist and postmodernist (or "poststructuralist") explanations of revolutionary change? Third, to what extent (and in what *specific ways*) are prominent feminist scholars optimistic or pessimistic about the prospects for favorable *gendered outcomes*—outcomes propitious, in other words, for *women*—in modern revolutionary situations? To raise and explore these questions is—if done with sensitivity and care—to provide ourselves with some theoretical context for the ensuing discussion of women's lives in the three full-fledged revolutions that in earlier centuries convulsed England, France, and Russia.

Gender, Sexuality, and Patriarchy: Some Theoretical Issues

Successfully theorizing issues like gender, sexuality, and patriarchy surely involves (among other things) consulting the informed literature to pose, and answer, queries such as the following. Are we to conceptualize gender and sexuality as *separate* or as *intimately related* phenomena? If we concede that *gender inequality* that still privileges *males* over *females* in so many societies can be properly designated as *patriarchy*, how then do we assess the *relative utility* of gender and patriarchy as analytical constructs? How have the *origins* of, specifically, *patriarchy* been diversely interpreted by those specialists studying male/female relationships in modern societies? How impressed (or, perhaps, unimpressed) are feminist sociologists and other experts by arguments stressing the *universality* and the likely "staying power" of patriarchy in the modern world? Finally—to return to gender— how are we to react to scholarly claims that gender is really an outdated "category of historical analysis?" Such are the questions that we must consider in detail in this initial section of Chapter 1.

On the first of these issues, the tendency to differentiate sharply between *gender* as a cultural construct and *sexuality* as a biological construct seems now to hold less water among feminists than it used to. According to the general editors for Joan Acker's 2006 book *Class Questions: Feminist Answers,* this turn of events was discernible as far back as the late 1980s. They noted that when sociologists Beth Hess and Myra Ferree introduced their pioneering anthology *Analyzing Gender: A Handbook of Social Science Research* back in 1987, they identified three phases in the study of men and women since 1970. "Initially," Hess and Ferree had argued, "the emphasis was on sex differences and the extent to which such differences might be based on the biological properties of individuals." In the next phase of this process, the focus had shifted "to . . . individual sex roles and [to] socialization, exposing gender as the product of specific social arrangements, although still conceptualizing it as an individual trait." Yet in the third and final phase of this process, gender (so Hess and Ferree had held) was coming to acquire an ever more pivotal role in basic social analysis: "The hall-mark of the third stage," they had asserted, "is the recognition of the centrality of gender as an organizing principle in all social systems, including work, politics, everyday interaction, families, economic development, law, education, and . . . other social domains." It was surely possible, Beth Hess and Myra Ferree had added, that gender might function in *race-specific* and *class-specific* ways; still, their essential conclusion here (again, as recorded in 1987) had been that gender is indeed "pervasive in society and operates at multiple levels."[5]

This posited shift toward new evaluations of the sex/gender distinction seems to be reflected in subsequent work on the subject. In 1999, for instance, feminist historian Joan Wallach Scott, despite insisting on interpreting *gender* in fairly radical post-structuralist terms—terms that we will have to reevaluate later on in this chapter—admitted no less that, in the 1970s and 1980s, "it had been crucial" for feminist writers like herself "to separate biology from culture and to justify change as an aspect not of radical social engineering, but of history." The term "gender," Scott continued, had done "important theoretical work in those days; the word itself . . . was disturbing."[6] Evidently, however, by 1999 Scott was questioning the need "to separate biology from culture." Several years later, feminist historian Merry Wiesner-Hanks, in a study entitled simply *Gender in History*, spoke similarly of a major shift of emphasis in the scholarly writing on this contentious issue. Women's historians, she recalled, in the early 1980s "differentiated primarily between 'sex,' by which they meant physical, morphological, and anatomical differences (which are often called 'biological differences') and 'gender,' by which they [usually] meant a culturally constructed, historically changing, and often unstable system of differences." But with the coming of the early 2000s, Merry Wiesner-Hanks detected a change in the way specialists approached the assumed distinction between sexuality and gender. Even as some scholars and their students clung to the gender/sex distinction, she wrote, "that distinction became contested." Indeed, Wiesner-Hanks continued, "some scholars wondered whether social gender and biological sex are so interrelated that any distinction between the two is meaningless."[7] She then proceeded to postulate and discuss four factors complicating the significance of the long-accepted sex/gender distinction: (1) "biological issues" involving ambiguous markers such as internal chromosomes and hormones and external genitalia; (2) "anthropological issues" involving the comparative ethnography of differing systems and orderings of gender in different societies; (3) psychological issues involving "gender dysphoria," that is, the shifting gender identities and sexual orientations of some individuals; and (4) "women's history" issues usually involving the "deconstruction" or "destabilization" of previously accepted gender categories in society. These factors, according to Wiesner-Hanks, had in recent times increasingly led historians and others "to denaturalize sexuality, that is, to emphasize its social construction and historical variability."[8]

The third of these complicating factors is perhaps most outstandingly exemplified by work done in the field of LGBT/queer studies. Developments appertaining to trans history, for instance, have been aptly summarized on the pages of the American Historical Association's newsmagazine *Perspectives on History* by associate editor Kritika Agarwal, who defines scholarship in this area as dealing with "people who move away from the gender they were assigned at birth."[9] Of the greatest pertinence to us in this chapter is the fact that at least *some* trans historians interrogate gender—and, thus, by indirection, the traditional distinction between gender and sexuality— in the kind of deconstructionist fashion habitually associated today with postmodernism. As Agarwal presents the question, those unsatisfied with simply studying people in the past *as trans*, instead "think of trans more abstractly, as an analytic with which to study change." Viewed in this light, *trans* "destabilizes gender itself as a category." This interpretation shifts the scholarship "away from a search for trans people in the past and towards using trans as a lens through which to see the world. It permits one to ask new questions about gender categories and other forms of human difference."[10] A similar line of thought is taken up by historian Regina Kunzel regarding queer studies. Rather than simply attempting to locate "subjects who might identify or be identified as queer," Kunzel writes, "historians increasingly deploy 'queer' as a critical lens to investigate challenges to normative modes of gender and sexuality." Hence, some scholars have found "queer" useful as "both a critical and a descriptive tool"; they are impressed by its "troubling of sexual identity, its . . . reach across a range of non-normative sexual and gender subject positions," and even, possibly, by its capacity "to expose taken-for-granted assumptions, institutions, and arrangements beyond the realm of sexuality and gender."[11] Here, then, we see arresting examples of how modern research continues to complicate the distinction once conventionally (and simplistically?) drawn between gender and sexuality.

Yet it is also no more than fair to point out, in this connection, that radical Marxian feminists—for their own reasons—have been rejecting the idea of an uncomplicated gender/sexuality distinction since at least the 1980s. Exemplifying this tendency was author Maria Mies, who (in 1986) decried the "well-known dualistic pattern of dividing 'nature' from 'culture'" because it—arguably—placed all too vulnerable women in all societies "on the side of 'nature,'" where they could be objectified, exploited, and "colonized" by those whom Mies characterized disgustedly as "idealistic patriarchal philosophers and scientists." This theorist of feminism summed up her feelings on the subject in this way:

> But let us not fool ourselves. Human sex and sexuality have never been purely crude biological affairs. Nor has the female or male body been a purely biological affair. "Human nature" has always been social and historical. Human physiology has throughout history been influenced and shaped by interaction with other human beings and with external nature. Thus, sex is as much a cultural and historical category as gender is.[12]

Interestingly, Mies coupled this critique of notions of a gender/sex duality with a critique of "cultural feminism," which she blamed (at least in part) for this duality in the first place; and she did this—with unknowing irony, it would seem—even as "cultural" or postmodernist feminists like Joan Scott and her confederates in academia were in the process of moving, in analytical terms, *away* from such a duality! For Maria Mies, it is nevertheless obvious, a "purely cultural feminist movement" would never be able to "identify the forces and powers" obstructing women's progress in the world, let alone enable such women to "develop a realistic perspective of a future society free of exploitation and oppression."[13]

All of these arguments having been discussed here, two women's historians of modern France have in recent times tried to reformulate issues in a way that preserves both the *separate identities* of gender and sexuality *and* the linkage between them. For Anne Verjus, sexuality "is a practice, a playful demonstration of human inventiveness that is a matter of free choice of the private individual," while gender "is the system by which the world of men and women is divided, in other words, which invents sex as the natural criterion of division of the social world so as to order it hierarchically." Hence, if we believe Verjus, "gender and sex are commonly linked," and indeed gender *requires* sexuality, or rather its "particular" manifestation, *heterosexuality*, so that in patriarchal societies (i.e., the great majority of *studied* societies) the "public space" could be preserved for men and the "private" or "domestic" space reserved to women. "We had to wait for the feminist scholarship of the 1970s," Verjus has noted with reference to developments in France, for these matters to be "interrogated and qualified."[14] A similar message has come from Karen Offen: "I will speak of 'the sexes,' she has announced, "to connote male and female, and will use the term gender when I discuss the sociopolitical constructions of 'masculine' and 'feminine' that pervade the French debate on the woman question, as indeed it does elsewhere as well."[15] This method of defining issues, then, just might provide for us a middle-of-the-road, conciliatory "way out" of the eternally debated gender/sexuality question.

In the meantime, Anne Verjus's invocation of patriarchal societies in this connection reminds us that reconsidering *gender* sooner or later means reconsidering *patriarchy* as well. Certainly, the British sociologist Sylvia Walby, whose *Theorizing Patriarchy* remains a standard reference work in the field, has long emphasized patriarchy's conceptual interrelationship with gender.[16] "The concept of patriarchy," she has said, "has been defined . . . usually with two similar core elements. Firstly, there is the core notion of gender inequality. Secondly, there is a degree of systematicity in that the different aspects of gender relations are connected in some way." Sylvia Walby has, in fact, stated even more categorically that "It is not theoretically useful to tie the concept of patriarchy to anything other than gender inequality. It is unnecessarily restricting, and at times highly misleading, to tie it either to a specific household form, or to a dominant structure, such as the economy."[17] A few years later, Merry Wiesner-Hanks, in *Gender in History*, reaffirmed unequivocally the idea of a linkage between gender and patriarchy:

> Searching . . . for the origins of patriarchy first involves . . . forgetting what biology, anthropology, psychology, and history have all revealed about the instability and ambiguity of dichotomous gender categories. Despite the presence of third and fourth genders, physical hermaphrodites, and transgendered individuals, most of the world's cultures have a system of two genders in which there are enormous differences between what it means to be a man and what it means to be a woman.

Wiesner-Hanks's insistent invocation of a "gender hierarchy in which men are dominant and women are subordinate, what is normally called patriarchy," is widely shared by feminist social scientists and social workers (notably, if not exclusively, in underdeveloped countries) as well as by feminist historians.[18]

Before we move on to revisit scholarly differences over the *roots* and *permanence* of patriarchy, however, we might say a few words concerning the *relative utility* of gender and patriarchy as analytical constructs. Specialists in the field, perhaps not so surprisingly, have in recent decades clashed at times over this matter. The previously mentioned Joan Wallach Scott, for instance, in her provocative *Gender and the Politics of History* (1999), implicitly deemphasized the centrality of patriarchy by portraying it as only *one* of three possible approaches (along with Marxism and psychoanalytical theory) to the analysis of gender. "Theories of patriarchy," she protested, "do not show what gender inequality has to do with other inequalities." Moreover, any theorizing of patriarchy, for Scott at least, relies excessively upon the "single variable of physical difference" and thus unjustifiably assumes "a consistent or inherent meaning for the human body . . . and thus the ahistoricity of gender itself."[19] Here, transparently, she was exposing a post-structuralist perspective that (as we will have occasion to stress later on) has continued to loom large in the perdurable debate over the causes of major sociopolitical revolutions. Suffice it to add here that Scott's ideas on the relative *analytical value* of gender and patriarchy have in recent decades been enthusiastically endorsed by Tristan Bridges and James Messerschmidt, writing for the online *Feminist Reflections* publication. "Patriarchy," so they have alleged in this forum, "is a concept that is less used today in feminist social science than it was in the late 1970s and 1980s." The term, according to Bridges and Messerschmidt, "has a slippery and imprecise feel"; it has been used so frequently and "uncritically" as to forfeit its erstwhile status as "a generally useful *analytical* concept."[20]

But is this in fact true? Intriguingly, as Bridges and Messerschmidt themselves admitted in this online article, which was offered as a professional tribute to the recently deceased feminist sociologist Joan Acker, Acker herself years before had cautioned against the danger of too hastily "abandoning the project of patriarchy." "In the move to gender," so Acker had warned, "the connections between urgent political issues and theoretical analysis, which made the development of feminist thought possible, may be weakened. Gender lacks the critical-political sharpness of patriarchy and may be more easily assimilated and coopted than patriarchy."[21] Although Acker herself continued in later years to concern herself more, in her analytical work, with gender than with patriarchy, a number of historians, sociologists, and other social scientists, often focusing upon women's issues in "developing world" countries, have found it necessary to use patriarchal concepts in dealing with the deleterious impact of the male/female binary upon women's all-too-precarious existence in such countries. Valentine Moghadam very likely spoke for many of these scholars when (in 1996) she emphasized how convincingly Sylvia Walby's theoretical work had "salvaged [patriarchy] as a conceptual tool and inspired many feminist researchers perplexed by the intractability of gender subordination."[22]

Yet, at the same time, those specialists sharing these concerns have frequently differed in their explanations of the *origins* of patriarchy and in their appraisals of its durability in today's world. On the former point, Gerda Lerner famously took issue with nineteenth-century theorists like Friedrich Engels. For Engels, patriarchy (whose existence he had never denied) had emerged out of a two-stage process leading originally from matriarchy to patriarchy. Engels wrote very extensively about what he called the "world-historical defeat of the female sex," something that followed from the advent of the "agricultural revolution," the appearance of private property, the development of the nuclear family, and the rise of the bureaucratic—or at least proto-bureaucratic—state.[23] More recently, Gerda Lerner has "reversed Engels's narrative" by arguing that the subordination of women— seen, for instance, in the emergence of patriarchy enforced by legal codes in the ancient Near East—had actually *preceded* the appearance of private property, class society, and early statist power, there and elsewhere. Women, in effect, *were* the primordial property, exploited for their procreative power by men through marriage, prostitution, and slavery; gender hierarchy came *before* the more complicated arrangements of "civilization."[24] Yet Lerner's ideas have in turn been challenged on a number of grounds: for instance, materialists of one persuasion or another have rejected her symbolic readings of the past and her prioritization of gender hierarchies over class hierarchies, while classicists have at times found fault with her interpretation of prostitution and other practices in the ancient world. Without pursuing this matter any farther into the weeds of informed debate, we might conclude, with Merry Wiesner-Hanks, that "Most scholars . . . see the development of patriarchy as a complicated process, involving everything that is normally considered part of 'civilization:' property ownership, plow agriculture, the bureaucratic state, writing, hereditary aristocracies, and the development of organized religion and philosophy."[25]

Of greater significance for a majority of feminists is what is happening to women in the world's myriad and diverse societies *today*. For such scholars, the germane questions are: How *universal*, or at least *common*, is the phenomenon of gender inequality, or patriarchy; and how pessimistic or optimistic should they be regarding its *ultimate demise*? On both questions, unsurprisingly, there has been much (at times heated) disagreement. Back in the 1980s, Maria Mies, proceeding (as we noted earlier) from Marxist assumptions, deplored the "fact" that so many of her colleagues in the West, abandoning their "former internationalist orientation," had accepted the argument that "we Western feminists have no right to criticize [developing] countries, that we do not know enough about what is happening there, that culturally and historically these societies are so different from Western societies that our criticism would amount to yet another manifestation of paternalism or Eurocentric cultural imperialism," and so on. At the same time, however—and this is noteworthy—Mies was equally unimpressed by assertions that "women in socialist countries," having already advanced so far toward their own "liberation," were "better equipped to bring about full liberation for women" than were feminists in "capitalist" societies. Arguing from this somewhat complicated position on feminist issues, Maria Mies urged women of both West *and* East to realize *in common* how cruelly they are kept apart by a "capitalist patriarchy that has integrated the whole world into a system of global exploitation and accumulation."[26]

It is true that Mies was in turn taken to task by Sylvia Walby for placing "too much explanatory emphasis upon changes in capitalism" when attempting to define patriarchy in global terms.[27] At the same time, Walby *did* agree with Mies that most theorists of patriarchy (unlike Mies herself, and unlike other staunchly Marxist feminists) have come to define patriarchy in the universalist language of racial, ethnic, and cultural diversity. True, Walby also sympathized (somewhat) with those "cultural feminists" who insisted that "cultural differences" were insufficiently grasped by the term "patriarchy." In the end, however, she accepted the "universalist" conception of patriarchy, insisting only that the surest way to comprehend this phenomenon lay, not in advocating the kind of sweeping dialectical analysis of "global exploitation and accumulation" favored by Marxist/feminist theorists such as Maria Mies, but rather in *reimagining* patriarchy as a "system" composed of interrelated and "globally relevant" elements such as domestic female labor, industrial female labor, the patriarchal state, and male violence.[28]

Nevertheless, doubts among feminist scholars about the universal appropriateness of the term *patriarchy* have continued to roil the field of women's studies in these early decades of the twenty-first century. Such doubts have been aired and thoughtfully discussed, by (among others) feminists of color in the academy—as, for instance, in a fascinating exchange between Beverly Guy-Sheftall and Evelyn M. Hammond put out in an anthology edited by Joan Scott in 2008.[29] For all of that, Beverly Guy-Sheftall, bell hooks, Leslie McCall, and an array of other feminist writers, by endorsing, like Kimberlé Crenshaw, the notion of intersectionality in women's affairs, have done much to solidify the concept of patriarchy as a *global* system of "privilege and discrimination" commingling the effects of race, ethnicity, gender, sex, and other social/analytical factors.[30] Indeed, the late American sociologist Joan Acker, in her final book, *Class Questions: Feminist Answers* (2006), probably summed up the frustrations felt by many such writers in the "bad" old days of "first wave" and "second wave" feminism:

> Feminist scholars of color and Third World feminist scholars in . . . Britain and the United States had made clear for years that much feminist theorizing ignored race and ethnicity and thus helped to perpetuate racism. Feminists of color argued that, in practice, most (white) feminist theorizing assumed a white, middle-class woman similar to the women doing the theorizing, and that theories about this . . . woman do not represent the experiences of women in other racial and class situations. Although white feminists recognized that race should be part of their analyses, they did not appreciate how deeply a white racial perspective was built into their analyses.

Yet Acker, for all her sensitivity on this subject, still confessed to being less interested in theorizing "the interconnections among race, gender, and class" in today's world than in focusing *by preference* upon *class* and *capitalism* as "thoroughly gendered and racialized" phenomena.[31]

Joan Acker's works, along with those of Maria Mies and certain other feminists, underscored the durability of class-oriented renderings of gender and patriarchy. Yet her reliance upon class analysis left her open to the criticism that, like many of those other theorists, she had largely left out of her account the *structuralist* issue of *political power* and its impact on women in modern societies. Cultural historian Laura L. Downs has, tellingly, broached this issue in her recently updated survey *Writing Gender History*. Assuredly, Downs is quick to acknowledge the reservations of more than one feminist of color regarding any Western-inspired, universalist conception of patriarchy; indeed, she goes so far as to charge on one occasion that "western feminists have constructed their own (collective) identity at the expense of their non-western 'sisters' through the creation of a deceptively universal analytic tool: patriarchy." Still, we may find it to be of even greater relevance that Downs has insisted on highlighting the kinds of *political questions* too often deemphasized by feminists of *all* persuasions. "The post-structuralist vision," as she has posed the issue, "is rife with problems of its own, notably . . . that the textualization of social relations tends to obscure the fact that these relations (of gender, race, or class) are also relations of *power*. For historians of women and gender, this is not a minor point."[32] Plainly, for this feminist, *any* "resistance to and critique of an existing patriarchal order" must call for the kind of scholarly analysis that inevitably will raise questions of a profoundly *political* nature.

But to debate the *universality* of patriarchy is, almost inevitably, to debate as well the question of its *ultimate fate* in today's (and tomorrow's) world. How hopeful or pessimistic, that is to ask, should those revisiting women's issues be regarding the likelihood of patriarchy's *demise* anytime soon? If we were to judge entirely from the remarks of United Nations research/development official Mihály Simai in Helsinki, Finland—remarks prefacing Valentine Moghadam's 1996 anthology *Patriarchy and Economic Development*—we would expect patriarchy, in one form or other, to persist for at least the near future. "In certain parts of the developing world," Simai held, "patriarchy has changed . . . little, and still assumes cruel forms." He acknowledged the *variations* in patriarchy "which exist between certain countries and regions at the end of the twentieth century." Nonetheless, Simai also concluded somberly from existing "trajectories" of patriarchy and development, that, as a general rule, and "in spite of the improvements in the social and economic position of women, some of the fundamental characteristics of . . . patriarchal societies" continue to exercise "a major influence on the possibilities for [women's] full participation in, and on the outcomes of, the development process."[33] Simai's dampening conclusion was seconded by Sylvia Walby, contributing to the same anthology. Walby spoke on this occasion—as she already had in her famous 1990 study *Theorizing Patriarchy*—about the transition in the West from so-called "private patriarchy," based traditionally upon "household production," to what she termed "public patriarchy," under whose aegis the "expropriation of women" is "segregationist" and "collectivist" in nature and is carried out increasingly in *public* as well as in *private* "arenas." For Walby, the "concept of patriarchy" was *still* "indispensable to the macro-level analysis of changes in gender relations." As she summed up her stance on the subject:

"Systematically interrelated forms of gender inequality do not stop when the household-based form of private patriarchy diminishes. Rather, we see new forms."[34]

These were, surely, pessimistic predictions as to the likely durability of patriarchy in the modern world. Some feminists in the social sciences have striven to temper them, at least somewhat. Valentine Moghadam, for example, was clearly concerned that Sylvia Walby's "emphasis on industrial exploitation—like [her] argument that the system of patriarchy is highly stable, pervades all social structures, and is responsible for the negative aspects of women's engagement in paid work—obscured not only some of the positive changes effected by certain aspects of the development process (principally education and employment for women), but, more crucially, women's *agency*."[35] Still, on the other hand—and of a special interest to any historians of women's roles in *European* revolutions—Moghadam *herself* turned pessimistic when it came to women's prospects in *certain European societies*. "The current situation of women in eastern Europe and in the former Soviet Union," she readily confessed, "provides compelling evidence that the elimination of patriarchy requires equity and empowerment in the spheres of both production and reproduction, and political organization to effectively counter backlashes." Women in these regions, Moghadam affirmed unequivocally, still labored under an exhausting "double burden" of private/domestic and public/industrial disadvantages.[36] Her colleague Tuovi Allén reached very similar conclusions for women in the "Nordic" (i.e. Scandinavian) welfare states.[37] And though the jury on this question may still be "out," with area studies yielding varying appraisals of the *persistence* of patriarchy, Korean-born sociologist John Lie has still discovered much truth in the so-called "female marginalization thesis." This thesis holds that (in Lie's words) "the incorporation of women into the capitalist economy has further oppressed women; they are exploited in the workplace, while burdened by patriarchal rule and domestic duties at home."[38]

Finally, in this initial section of Chapter 1, we need to return, at least briefly, to the question of gender—and, specifically, to the controversy over the continued usefulness of gender as a "category of historical analysis." We earlier referenced Joan Wallach Scott's provocative *Gender and the Politics of History*; what we did *not* reference at the time was the fact that, in the revised 1999 edition of the book, Scott suggested that gender might have outlived its analytical value for women's historians. Perhaps, on this endlessly debated issue, we should let Scott speak at some length for herself:

As the 1990s draw to a close, "gender" seems to have lost its ability to . . . provoke us. It has, in the United States, become an aspect of "ordinary usage," routinely offered as a synonym for women, for the differences between the sexes, for sex. . . Books that purport to offer a "gender analysis" . . . rarely examine how . . . meanings of "women" and "men" are discursively established. . . . Indeed, many feminist scholars who use the term "gender" do so while explicitly rejecting the premise that "men" and "women" are historically variable categories. This has had the effect of denying "gender" its radical . . . agency. It is, these days, a term that has lost its critical edge.[39]

Or so, at least, Joan W. Scott contended. Yet many writers who are *still* warmly supportive of women's studies today would surely find her critique of the analytical uses of gender to be problematic at best. To begin with, those specialists studying the condition of women in the underdeveloped world whose research findings can be consulted in anthologies such as *Patriarchy and Economic Development*—and they include some of today's most highly regarded political scientists, sociologists, demographers, anthropologists, economists, and so on—would *necessarily* have to resist such an argument. Insofar as such area studies experts associate patriarchy with gender inequality due to their familiarity with the glaring disparities between women's and men's status in underdeveloped societies existing all over the world, they would, for obvious reasons, insist upon the *a priori* objective reality of "gender" itself.[40]

Additionally, others teaching and writing in somewhat more traditional, Western-oriented areas of women's studies have continued to chant the praises of gender as an essential tool of analysis. Take, for example, Laura Lee Downs, whose trenchant *Writing Gender History* we earlier encountered. Downs went out of her way to speak of "the very centrality of gender to so much recent historical scholarship," even as she granted the paradoxical fact that "the operations of gender as a tool of critical analysis have become less visible even as it is being incorporated into ever wider realms of research." But Downs also remarked, in a transparent allusion to Joan Scott:

> the success of gender does not necessarily imply that it has "lost" its critical edge; far from it. A widely diffused tool of historical analysis can always become banal or routine in the hands of scholars who choose to treat gender as an interpretative device that permits the rediscovery[only?] of the same old binary oppositions. But such scholars...are precisely [those] refusing to use gender for explicitly critical purposes.[41]

And Downs went on to praise once again "the critical force of gender." A few years later, in 2016 (as we noted earlier), Tristan Bridges and James W. Messerschmidt, even as they were celebrating Joan Acker's scholarly achievements in *Feminist Reflections*, paid their own compliments to what Laura Downs had so recently termed "the operations of gender as a tool of critical analysis" in women's affairs.[42]

We will set this issue aside for now, but in the next section of Chapter 1 we will eventually have to return to Joan Scott's provocative thesis that "the meanings of 'women' and 'men' are discursively established." To argue in this fashion is to accept one of the cardinal premises of postmodernism (or, as Scott would term it, "post-structuralism"). It will then be our task, as historians of women *in revolution*, to reconsider the postmodernist "turn" and the theorizing of gender—but to do so in the more tangible context of the ongoing debate over the causes of modern sociopolitical revolutions.

Gender in the Current Debate over Revolutionary Causation

"A paper that I wrote in 1989 and circulated in 1990," recalled feminist Valentine Moghadam in 1997, "attempted to theorize gender in a structuralist vein, situating gender in the realm of culture and showing its links to politics and the economy. After this was critiqued by several friends and colleagues, I took a different approach, one that was premised on the social reality of gender and its integral role in production and reproduction." Although Moghadam here was not explicitly pitting structuralism against postmodernism, her accompanying declaration that, in revolutions, "women and gender issues figure prominently in political discourses, state ideologies, legal policies, and in the construction of . . . national identity" placed her, it would appear, in the postmodernist camp of revolutionary theorists.[43] In fact, scholarly writing on revolutionary origins these days seems increasingly characterized by complex and (at times) polemical exchanges between structuralists accentuating statist formation, geopolitics, and state/class interactions, and postmodernists prioritizing textual deconstruction, the explanatory power of revolutionary discourse/ideology, national identity, and (of special interest to us) gender.[44] Here, we might cursorily review this debate between structuralists and postmodernists, and in doing so suggest *in detail* how issues of gender and women's history have come to find a place (or places?) within it. Of course, the origins of revolution—especially of the European kind—were not always caught up in a greater exchange between specialists identifying themselves as structuralists and scholars flying the banners of postmodernism or post-structuralism. In the post–Second World War years, those engaged in English and French revolutionary studies, taking their cue from imposing figures such as Christopher Hill, Georges Lefebvre, and Albert Soboul—to say nothing of more distant authorities such as Karl Marx and Friedrich Engels—saw the upheavals in mid-seventeenth-century England and late-eighteenth-century France as having arisen basically from struggles between economically regressive (feudal) aristocracies and economically progressive (capitalist) gentry and/or bourgeois *élites*. In both cases, so the narrative usually ran, the entrepreneurial-minded élitists, desiring both a greater degree of status recognition and a more meaningful role in public affairs, and benefiting from the support of laboring folk of city and/or countryside, prevailed over their aristocratic enemies *and* over absolute monarchies that were insolvent in their finances, inefficient in their bureaucratic operations, and stubbornly resistant to social change. Unsurprisingly, this explanatory paradigm also informed what social scientists in the postwar USSR had to say about Russia: for them, the events of October 1917 remained the inevitable consequence of class confrontation between capitalists and workers—a confrontation in which Lenin's selfless Bolsheviks, the very incarnation of revolutionary vanguardism, had unerringly blazed the path to the world's first truly socialist society.[45]

Yet this Marxian interpretation of revolutionary causes, however influential in bygone decades, has long since fallen into disfavor owing to a combination of factors—the archival research of a younger generation of historians, the theorizing of postwar political scientists, a "real-world" context of changing post–Cold War East–West relations, and so forth. From the 1950s on, revisionist historians in the United Kingdom and the United States such as Alfred Cobban, George Taylor, and Conrad Russell (predictably dubbed "Anglo-Saxons" by their French colleagues) largely rejected long-term revolutionary causation and viewed the European upheavals as originating in fortuitous convergences of more immediate factors and as unfolding on the basis of unpredictable contingencies.[46] At the same time, other social scientists approached the issue of revolutionary origins from angles not usually explored in historians' works. "Structural/ functional" or "systems/value consensus" analysts like Chalmers Johnson, for instance, suggested that revolutions in general have occurred when "disequilibrated" social systems, weighed down by accumulating "multiple dysfunctions," and destabilized further by their intransigent, isolated, and incompetent governing élites, have been propelled toward fatal breakdowns by triggers of various types—triggers such as defeats in war, the emergence of truly revolutionary parties, the appearance of charismatic leaders, and so on.[47] Again, a number of theorists—most notably, Ted R. Gurr and James C. Davies—found ways to prioritize, in their scholarship, *psychological* dynamics, focusing either on the discontents, politicization, and public roles of *individual protagonists* in revolutionary situations or on what sociologist Michael S. Kimmel has called "the *aggregate social psychology* of mass discontent that leads to revolutionary mobilization."[48]

To one extent or another, the Chalmers Johnsons, Ted Gurrs, and James C. Davies of the social scientific literature—and many of their fellow-travelers as well—drew inspiration from the established historical literature on the classic European (as well as other) revolutions. And so have those scholars writing more recently in what we have come to identify as structuralist or postmodernist veins. At this point, we need to define both structuralism and postmodernism in theoretical terms, explaining briefly how each of these perspectives has tended to split into two primary sub-tendencies. Only then will we be able to situate gendered issues, as discussed conceptually earlier in this chapter, in the framework of the larger debate over revolutionary causation.

Michael Kimmel, whose *Revolution: A Sociological Interpretation* usefully reviews much of the twentieth century's sociological literature on revolution, has identified the "three structural elements that compose a theory of revolution" as the "international context," "class struggle," and the "state." Revolutions, he has argued, are "at their core, *about* capitalist industrialization and state centralization, and these processes provide the framework for structural theories." What may be most noteworthy in Kimmel's discussion, however, is his *Weberian* rather than *Marxian* take on the entity that is, in fact, so central to structuralist revolutionary theory today: namely, the *state*. "Paying attention to the state as an active agent in revolutionary struggles," according to Kimmel, "means treating [it] as an analytically distinct category from either the class structure upon which it is based or the social values that it may embody."[49] Accepting this final assertion means endorsing Kimmel's overall formulation that the state, although never standing "entirely above society," preserves at all times a certain irreducible measure of autonomy from both socioeconomic interests *and* societal values.

Michael Kimmel's emphasis upon both "capitalist industrialization" *and* "state centralization" in his initial discussion of structural theories of revolution also reflects what has become a very significant split within the structuralist family—between what we might call Marxist/Leninist "capitalism-centered structuralism" and Weberian/Hintzian "state-centered structuralism." We will not be detained too long here by the first of these two sub-tendencies: it is likely fair to say that most sociologists and other social scientists who have written theoretically on revolution over the past several decades have gravitated to state-centered rather than to capitalism-centered structuralism. Still, we certainly should acknowledge that some modern theorists of revolution—most impressively, Immanuel Wallerstein—*have* premised their theories upon the Marxian assumption that "the affairs of state and of capitalism are inextricably interrelated, that they are only two sides, or aspects, of . . . the same historical development," and that, consequently, statist interests historically have *ultimately* mirrored, and thus been largely reducible to, the dynamics of international economic development.[50] Wallerstein—to revisit his theory in brief—has, over the years, postulated the cardinal importance of a "capitalist world system" developing since early modern times and deeply conditioning both the contours of interstate competition—that is, geopolitics—and the likelihood for localized outbreaks of revolution. For Wallerstein, revolutions have customarily been most characteristic of regions situated on the "periphery" or the "semi-periphery" of the capitalist "world system," subject to the tug-and-pull of competing state-imperialist systems.[51] Other proponents of capitalism-centered structuralism, if not necessarily as prolific as an Immanuel Wallerstein, have still made significant contributions to this scholarly literature on revolutionary origins.[52]

This having been said, we must concern ourselves here chiefly with the state-centered strain of structuralism, which has figured so centrally in the revolutionary writing of modern times. As we noted earlier, the theoretical roots of this approach to revolution lie largely in the seminal studies of German sociologist Max Weber and his compatriot, historian Otto Hintze. Unlike Marx and Lenin, who conceived the state largely through the prism of socioeconomic class struggle, Weber and Hintze saw in the state, and especially in its *administrative* and *bureaucratic* aspects, "processes that cannot be reduced to class analysis and that [despite this] are directly relevant to the study of revolution."[53] A "compulsory political organization with continuous operations will be called a state," Weber wrote, "insofar as it successfully upholds the claim to the *monopoly* of the *legitimate* use of physical force in the enforcement of order."[54] Consequently, for Max Weber, revolutions were logically to be seen as events primarily brought on by breakdowns in the ability of certain old regime states to administer the means of such "physical force," both *internally* (via police repression of domestic opposition) and *externally* (via the sustained military capacity to defeat foreign adversaries.)In other words, we can already begin to divine, with Weber, a theoretical linkage of *statist* analysis with *revolutionary* analysis. Such a theoretical linkage was then taken even farther by Otto Hintze. As Michael Kimmel has observed, the "kernel of Hintze's theory of revolution" lay in that it "describes how political opposition is first set in motion by autonomous states pursuing distinctly political interests in the global arena."[55] And undeniably such "political opposition," once "set in motion," *can* lead to genuine revolution. Thus, Max Weber and (even more explicitly) Otto Hintze reconceptualized the state as a semiautonomous *geopolitical* as well as *sociopolitical* entity, and, in doing so, associated issues of state formation with matters of international politics and revolutionary causation. In accomplishing all this, they were unwittingly anticipating most subsequent state-centered structuralist explanations of revolution.

Of all those explanations, the most influential—if, at the same time, controversial—has perhaps been Theda Skocpol's 1979 *States and Social Revolutions.* In this major study, Skocpol set out what she termed a "comparative historical analysis" of the French, Russian, and Chinese Revolutions. Essentially, she maintained, full-blown "social-revolutionary transformations" of all three countries occurred when catastrophic failures in statist foreign and domestic policies dialectically interacted and then *explosively converged.* The inability of Bourbon France, Romanov Russia, and Qing China to compete militarily (and, in addition, economically) with Great Britain, Germany, and Japan, respectively, not only subverted the international prestige and security of these old regime states but also subverted their control over their domestic societies by compromising the status of "dominant class" feudal/landholding interests facing increasingly restive peasant elements in the countryside. Loss of control over the rurally oriented class structures *within* these countries, reinforcing as it did a failure of strategic/economic outreach abroad, permitted what Skocpol called "societal political crises" in all three cases to blossom unexpectedly into full-fledged sociopolitical revolutions. In all three situations, moreover, Skocpol saw *postrevolutionary states* eventually emerging which proved more successful than their old regime predecessors had been at implementing foreign and domestic policies on the basis of administrative and economic reforms.[56]

It might be helpful at this point to discuss briefly how even theorists continuing to work within the parameters of state-centered structuralism (as well as certain other scholars) have attempted to modify and thereby move in suggestive ways beyond Skocpol's provocative but too narrowly conceived structuralist approach to state-related issues. Of special interest for some readers of this book may be the emergence, in this connection, of certain historians' and sociologists' *gender-related* insights.

To begin with, criticisms of *States and Social Revolutions* have often involved placing a greater emphasis upon human motivation, social/demographic change, and the roles of ideas/ideologies in the outbreak (and further development) of revolutions. Thus, for example, historian and sociologist Charles Tilly contributed substantially to the discussion by including in his own structuralist analysis of revolution a healthy admixture of what Skocpol had largely dismissed as "voluntarism." That is, he highlighted the issue of *personal agency.* "Revolutionary action becomes likely," he contended, "when, in the presence of vulnerable power-holders, potential opponents of those power-holders communicate with each other sufficiently to recognize that they have the collective capacity to overturn the existing structure."[57] And Tilly would return to this argument later on by alluding to "the appearance of contenders, or coalitions of contenders" advancing "competing claims to control of the state" in revolutionary situations, and by referring as well to the stark inability or unwillingness of *ancien régime* rulers to suppress such claims.[58] The question of the role of *individual actors* in revolutionary outbreaks also preoccupied sociologist Eric Selbin, who, contributing in 1997 to a major anthology of articles on revolutionary theory that we have already encountered, insisted (in a clear swipe at Theda Skocpol) that "We must . . . bring people back in . . . . Revolutions do not come, they are made." For Selbin—as for many others in the field—both "leaders" *and* "the people" testify in their own ways to the significance of *agency* in revolutionary upheavals.[59]

Structuralists have likewise insisted at times upon the revolutionary implications of *demographic change* in societies destined—so it would seem—for major sociopolitical upheaval. Especially of interest here have been the arguments of Jack Goldstone. In his breakout monograph, *Revolution and Rebellion in the Early Modern World*, Goldstone accentuated *population dynamics* in original ways. His theory, so he proclaimed, "synthesizes the 'new' history of demographic and social history with the 'old' history of revolutions and state crises by mapping the diverse links between them."[60] Goldstone has elaborated upon this insight over the years. Contributing, for example, to an important anthology of articles on the causes of the French Revolution coedited (in 2011) by historians Thomas Kaiser and Dale Van Kley, he adduced "underlying demographic and economic trends" in the eighteenth century that, in combination with "conflicts over religion and shifts in public opinion," helped to bring about a conjuncture of forces capable of overthrowing the ancien régime. Specifically, the first of four major factors Goldstone cited here involved *demographic dynamics*, including population growth and changes in the *distribution* of population "across cities and the countryside, across age groups, across social and economic and legal divisions, and across regions."[61] For this structuralist, then, as for so many of his peers, state-centered explanations of revolution, however enlightening in *general terms*, are not adequate if they do not take into account the social and demographic dimensions of prerevolutionary situations—as well as of actual revolutionary situations themselves.

The other critical issue frequently raised by Skocpol's fellow structuralists involves the lack of a sustained *cultural* or *ideological* analysis in her work. Jeff Goodwin, for example, admitted that "statist analysis," as he called it, *does* suffer from the "fundamental problem" of not adequately theorizing some "nonstate or nonpolitical" factors making for revolution—and one of these factors is "collective beliefs and discourses." This is, Goodwin regretfully confessed, "a significant problem indeed."[62] His associate Timothy P. Wickham-Crowley was inclined to agree with this, although he added a provocative wrinkle—namely, a suggestion that a prospective scholarly division of labor might best have "structural" theorists focusing upon the long-term and immediate *origins* of revolutions, and "cultural" theorists concerning themselves with "what the revolutionaries do to society once in power." After all—so, in any case, this particular sociologist hypothesized—"the powers of ideology to remake the social order seem greatest when disorder reigns and both [revolutionary] state and society are *already* in flux or chaos."[63] At the same time, it is crucial to note that most structuralists, even while faulting *States and Social Revolutions* for its general neglect of cultural or ideological analysis, have concurred with Skocpol that *ideas* must be thoroughly *contextualized* in their times. As Misagh Parsa, the author of a comparative monograph on upheavals in Iran, Nicaragua, and the Philippines, phrased it in 2000: "Analyses that attribute sweeping powers to ideology fail to account for the social origins of ideologies and their relations to the social structure. Ideologies do not emerge in a vacuum and should always be understood in their social and historical context."[64] Sociologist John Foran had already written something along rather similar lines in 1997: "Culture must be rigorously linked to social structure and imaginatively synthesized with political economy and international contexts."[65]

Yet, insofar as structuralism emphasizes the issue of *state formation*, we should also note that certain historians and sociologists have seen this latter phenomenon as, at least in part, a *familial* and *gender-related* process. Historian Sarah Hanley, for instance, in a major discussion of what she termed "family formation" and "state building" in early modern France, has held that the French state, rather than emerging as "some kind of political outgrowth of western political thought" or as a byproduct of representative institutions, was "engendered" by a "Family-State compact" and its "attendant family model of authority." As such, this "state" generally adumbrated for modern times a model of "political power wedded to male authority."[66] Sociologist Julia Adams, writing subsequently in a similar vein, has deplored the fact that "sociological theories of state formation" have remained stubbornly "resistant to specifically feminist concepts, observations, and insights." "Gender and family," for Adams as (it seems) for Hanley, have been "neglected constituents of the development of state power and institutions" in early modern Europe."[67] Hence, we have here the "patrimonial" or "familial" state, with its *gendered* characteristics, as defined by various theorists of state-oriented structuralism.

In the final analysis, nevertheless, most structuralist theorists of revolution would also be likely to rally to one of Charles Tilly's defining arguments: "The point is . . . that relations *among* states affect the locus, likelihood, character, and outcome of revolutions. . . . To know which states are liable to revolution, we must examine not only their domestic politics, but also their locations in [prevailing sets] of relations among states."[68] To this extent, then, the structuralism employed in much revolutionary theorizing still arguably comes with a discernible emphasis upon *international affairs* analysis.

But what of those scholars in the postmodernist or "post-structuralist" camp? This includes, we argue, those strongly committed to women's studies, and who—like Valentine Moghadam—have found their research on gender and revolutionary change forcing them to disavow initially structuralist assumptions. There are, of course, canonical reference-points here in the earlier writings of Michel Foucault and Jacques Derrida,[69] and, as we will see below, other specialists have also elaborated on the subject. More recently, however, postmodernist theorizing on revolution, much like the structuralist literature on the subject, has tended to split into two strains. Modern German historian Richard J. Evans, notably, has explained this bifurcation as a distinction between what he termed "moderate" postmodernism and something altogether more "extreme." In its "more moderate guise," Evans conceded, postmodernism "has encouraged historians to take the irrational in the past more seriously, to pay more attention to ideas, beliefs and culture as influences in their own right, to devote more effort to framing our work in literary terms, to put individuals, often humble individuals, back into history, to emancipate ourselves from . . . a constricting straitjacket of social-science approaches, quantification, and socioeconomic determinism."[70] Radical postmodernism, on the other hand, insisted Evans, is less defensible: it "takes its cue from another post, post-structuralism, roughly speaking the idea that language is arbitrarily constructed, and represents nothing but itself, so that whenever we read something, the meaning we put into it is necessarily our own and nobody else's, except of course insofar as our own way of reading is part of a wider discourse or set of beliefs."[71] For Richard Evans, such a *discursive* kind of postmodernism has a corrosive impact on the historical discipline: it forecloses any possibility that scholars could ever agree on what historical documents and/or artifacts actually *mean*, and therefore makes commonly shared interpretative findings all but impossible.

Richard Evans's arraignment of what he called radical postmodernism—or post-structuralism—has, predictably, drawn heavy fire from advanced postmodernist authors. Exemplifying this tendency, British postmodernist Beverley Southgate saw Evans as hypocritical: "Having acknowledged the force of postmodernism," Southgate opined, "Richard Evans continues to write against it and in defiance of it." He followed this up with a laundry-list of analytical sins that Evans had (purportedly) committed in his feckless defense of what Southgate disparaged as "modernist" history.[72] We will soon have to take up again Southgate's advocacy of radical postmodernism. Yet, in fairness to Richard Evans, we should first point out that others in the field have also differentiated between "moderate" and "radical" strains of postmodernist analysis. For example, respected social scientist Pauline Marie Rosenau held that radical post-structuralists "remain uncompromisingly anti-empirical whereas [moderate] post-modernists focus on the concrete in the form of . . . daily life, as an alternative to theory." Beyond this, Rosenau argued that what she termed "skeptical" post-structuralism all too often prescribed "a pessimistic, gloomy, negative assessment" of life, and that it viewed the "post-modern age" as "one of fragmentation, disintegration, malaise, meaninglessness . . . and societal chaos." Yet we should note also that Rosenau, much like Evans and other scholars, readily conceded the *usefulness* of moderate or (to use her other term) *affirmative* postmodernism, which "often provides fascinating insights . . . across a wide range of topics because it . . . focuses on what is nonobvious, left out, and generally forgotten in a text and examines what is unsaid, overlooked, understated, and never overtly recognized." The insights derived from *this* postmodernism, Rosenau was consequently quick to reiterate, are "innovative and stimulating."[73]

Alas, however, radical postmodernists would regard such a careful distinction drawn between two strains of postmodernism with utter contempt. In this connection, we once again refer to Beverley Southgate. Not for him, the cautionary statements and definitions hazarded by "faint-hearts" such as Richard J. Evans and Pauline Marie Rosenau! For Southgate—and in this he very likely spoke for many another postmodernist (or post-structuralist) as well—history should have a deliberately "destabilizing" and "decentering" function. In Southgate's words:

> postmodernist history's function becomes to *destabilize*—endlessly to question all certainties, reveal alternatives, and provoke reassessments... . In a situation where the certainties of meaning are deliberately "shaken," and where that "shaking" itself is seen as a positive virtue, and as a legitimate aim for history, there can be no going back to [the] confident "modernist" belief in history as "a search for truth and the construction of *knowledge* about the past," built on a core of "factual information."

The "prospect of such finalities and closures," announced Southgate with palpable relish, "has been lost in postmodernity."[74] It can therefore scarcely surprise us that, in championing this kind of approach to history, Southgate should unhesitatingly deconstruct such classic building blocks of structuralist analysis as Marxian class economics, the state, and interstate relations.

It is also unsurprising that Southgate should interrogate *feminist* and *gendered* forces of change in equally radical ways. "In the case of feminism," he wrote, "it [isn't] just a question of unearthing and utilizing a few more texts by women authors, and disinterring . . . evidence of women's contributions to existing narratives. Feminism, rather, [comes] to imply a complete rethinking of the past." A genuinely "open-minded" approach to women's history, Southgate insisted, "extends to definitions of femininity (and masculinity) itself. For femininity (and gender) can themselves be historicized, and they change over time . . . they are contingent and could (and will) be different from what they now appear to be."[75] Thus, Southgate was quite prepared to leave traditional "women's history"—and hence, by implication, even patriarchy as well—behind, and to explore new realms of "destabilized" history involving women (and, indeed, men).[76] In this, he was but restating Joan Scott's post-structuralist message—a message that she had formulated earlier, in the 1980s and 1990s—on matters involving *gender* and *sexuality*.

> These questions [Scott had written] do not assume the abiding existence of a homogeneous collectivity called "women" upon which measurable experiences are visited. Rather, they interrogate the production of the category "women" itself as a historical or political event, whose circumstances and effects are the object of analysis. . .. This approach seems to me to be well within the purview of feminist concerns.

And so, for the Southgates and Scotts of the profession, *fixed notions* of "gender" and "sexuality" had to give way before *changeable notions* of these concepts, which were (in Scott's words) "articulated by language," and, as such, had always "changed over time and across cultures."[77]

It would appear, then, that for radical theorists of gender and sex such as Southgate and Scott, history *as a discipline* in a sense *retreated* (as Southgate put it) "from being a truthful representation of a single reality to [having] a problematic, multi-layered . . . textuality, having at best a tenuous connection with the elusive actuality that it purport[ed] to describe."[78]Such a striking postmodernist description of history as having a "problematic, multi-layered . . . textuality" is obviously critical, for it takes us directly back to Jacques Derrida's emphasis upon *texts* and *deconstruction* in the processing of history. And for "texts," why not substitute "scripts"? This is precisely what Joan Scott's fellow-Francophile Keith Baker tried to do in relation to the 1789 revolution, in an article written over thirty years ago.[79] Recently (in collaboration with Dan Edelstein) he has suggested extending this kind of iconoclastic textual approach to revolutions *in general*. As Baker and Edelstein presented the argument:

> In politics, as in the theater or on the screen, scripts generate events. They do so in the obvious sense that a script suggests positions to be taken, actions to be carried out, incidents to be anticipated. They do so, less obviously, in the sense that positions that have been taken, actions that have been carried out, or incidents that have occurred are necessarily configured (or reconfigured) to give them meaning within a script— or within competing scripts. . . . Competition to impose a script, or to control a script that has been imposed, is a fundamental fact of politics, though perhaps never more . . . than in a situation that has been declared revolutionary.[80]

"Scripts generate events," we suspect, is, in essence, the old radical postmodernist or post-structuralist wine being poured into (superficially) "new" bottles. Moreover, the preoccupation in such a perspective with the *textuality* of "scripts" and, thus, of history—in the present case, the history of gender, sexuality, and women—takes us naturally enough back to Joan Scott's advanced uses of post-structuralism in the ever-contentious field of women's (and especially women's *revolutionary*) studies.

Scott's discursive stance on gendered and (specifically) women's issues has ensured that, over the years, she has remained conspicuously involved in the arguments pitting post-structuralist scholars like herself against feminists (and others) of a somewhat less advanced persuasion. For example, her acknowledgment that some of the same (praiseworthy) feminists who had "resisted the consolidation of 'women' into homogeneous categories" had, at the very same time, "launched political appeals in the name of 'women' [!]" has left her open to a charge of intellectual inconsistency, if not of outright dishonesty.[81] Still, for Joan Scott, such an inconsistency (she preferred to call it "tension") has always been "the source of feminism's most creative political interventions." But this has assuredly *not* been an argument accepted by all of Scott's contemporaries. As we shall see now, her critics have included (1) eminent revolutionary historians, and (2) some of Scott's fellow feminists in the social sciences.

Among the former group, the late Charles Tilly was especially noteworthy. In *Roads From Past to Future* (1997), Tilly readily conceded that he, too, like other social scientists, advocated "historicizing social analysis and informing it with a clearer understanding of culture"—a transparent nod to "cultural" feminists like Joan Scott. But this was as far as he would go on this issue, as he launched into a scathing critique of what he considered to be a species of "skepticism" run amuck:

> At a time when literary models of analysis have gained [a] wide popularity among graduate students and junior professors in North American social science, we run the risk of excessive skepticism. Virtuous vilification of cant skids over into careless condemnation of the entire social-scientific enterprise. Criticism that appears to identify weaknesses in particular theories and empirical claims actually embodies profound doubts concerning the existence of coherent social processes . . . and . . . the accessibility of social processes to systematic knowledge.

And, lest his readers find this critique overly *general,* Tilly went on to target specifically "deconstruction and other forms of literary theory" employed by post-structuralists "to define our supposed knowledge of social life as a set of constructed—or even fabricated—texts almost infinitely susceptible to multiple, changing interpretations." In this connection, Joan Scott herself came in for some caustic criticism:

> Scott challenges the very possibility of reliable knowledge. In the human sciences, she claims, "as in society as a whole, contests about knowledge are contests for power; labels of good and bad, objective and prejudiced, are but weapons in the contests. Social science then is not about 'truth,' but [is] about knowledge and its relationship—critical or subservient—to power". . . . This second step [Tilly thus concluded here] takes us into the abyss of radical skepticism.[82]

Charles Tilly, we must emphasize, wholeheartedly supported scholarship in the field of women's history; what he patently could *not* stomach was a *purely discursive* approach to the subject, an approach which, he felt, risked "deconstructing women away" as "real" human beings fully comprehensible in the various contexts (which, for him, frequently meant the *revolutionary* contexts) of the historical past.

Other historians who have distinguished in like fashion between *empirical* and *purely discursive* conceptions of women include Roger Chartier and the aforementioned Richard J. Evans. Chartier, who cut his teeth initially on the debate over the intellectual/cultural origins of the French Revolution, has gone on to wrestle with the related challenge posed to the historical profession by discursive forms of postmodernism.[83] In refuting what he has called "the most radical formulations of the 'linguistic turn'" in historical writing, Chartier has insisted that "the processes by which discourse constructs interests or events are themselves socially rooted and determined. . . . Thus those processes refer to objective social properties external to discourse that are characteristic of each of the groups, communities, and classes that make up the social world."[84] Logically, therefore, Chartier could not help but accept the objective realities of "gender," "gender inequality," and—thus—the systems of *patriarchy* predicated upon those realities, and he has alluded to them in discussing revolutionary and other aspects of women's history:

> One major objective of the history of women is thus to study the varied mechanisms, on every level, that guaranteed (or were calculated to guarantee) that women would consent to the dominant representations of the differences between the sexes in such matters as women's juridical inferiority, the schools' inculcation of gender roles, the [gendered] division of tasks and spaces, and the exclusion of women from the public sphere.

"Sexual difference," reiterated Chartier, is without any doubt "embodied in practices and events," but those practices and events "are in turn rooted in social positions and interests calculated to guarantee the subjection of women and the domination of men."[85]

Meanwhile, Richard Evans seized upon a polemical exchange (in 1993) between Joan Scott and Laura Downs to articulate a sharp critique of postmodernist theory—and of its deployment in women's history—that more or less echoed what Roger Chartier was saying on the subject. Some historians are unfortunately tempted, so lamented Evans, "to shift their attention from the empathetic reconstruction of the history of the oppressed groups they identify with to the linguistic analysis of the concepts which they perceive as having structured that oppression: from women, for instance, to gender." But this, he remarked regretfully, could "have its pitfalls"—as was evidenced most arrestingly, for Evans at least, in the work of discursive postmodernists like Scott.[86] Other historians have subsequently voiced similar reservations about such theorization (i.e., post-structuralism) taken too far in the realm of social—here, that is, women's—history.[87]

But the differences between post-structuralist and less radical stances on women's issues have been most hotly debated in specifically *feminist* circles. Here, to begin with, it is only fair to note that a post-structuralist like Joan Scott has had her outspoken defenders. Denise Riley, for example, writing in 1989, defined "women" (and, by implication, other gendered categories as well) in terms that were as "anti-essentialist" as those popularized by Scott. The term "women," according to Riley, "is historically, discursively constructed, and always relatively to other categories which themselves change; 'women' is a volatile collectivity in which female persons can be . . . differently positioned . . . while for the individual, 'being a woman' is also inconstant."[88]Meanwhile, feminist historian Catherine Hall, holding forth in a similar vein, expressed her frustration with her British compatriots for *not* being—as Joan Scott *was*—sufficiently "theoretical" in their work. "There is tremendous resistance within the discipline," so Hall complained, "to thinking theoretically." "Only post-structuralism and deconstruction," she proclaimed, "can provide a way forward."[89] It is also true that some feminists concentrating on "developing world" systems of patriarchy, and utilizing Foucauldian analysis, have (in the words of Jane L. Parpart) talked up "the postmodern critique of the modern, and the crucial relationship between power and language," all the while rejecting "analysis that draws primarily upon macro-economic data and broad generalizations" concerning male/female relations in far-flung parts of the world.[90] Then, again, feminists more recently associated in academia with Joan Scott—including, for instance, Judith Butler and Elizabeth Weed—have added their thoughtful commentaries to this post-structuralist literature emphasizing the *discursivity* of the "woman" category in historical analysis.[91]

But there has also been a growing reaction against this way of conceptualizing women's issues. Speaking as one of a number of social scientists studying "developing world" systems of patriarchy, for example, Elizabeth Dore in the 1990s disapproved of "self-consciously postmodern authors" who, as she claimed, tended toward overtly rejecting "the structural and systematic nature of women's oppression." The "*sine qua non* of feminism," declared Dore, "is that men's oppression of women characterizes most societies." One unfortunate result of rejecting theories of patriarchy, and focusing instead on the social construction of gender, Elizabeth Dore went on, "is that the political objective of women's emancipation is diffused, or lost entirely." (We can surely take "focusing instead on the social construction of gender" to mean postmodernism as we have already encountered it.[92]) French revolutionary scholar Lynn Hunt and colleague Victoria Bonnell made almost the same point soon thereafter. Writing in 1999—just as Joan Scott's revised *Gender and the Politics of History* was appearing—Hunt and Bonnell avowed: "[we]have all been profoundly influenced by the cultural turn; nevertheless, we have 'refused to accept the obliteration of the social that is implied by the most radical forms of culturalism or poststructuralism. The status or meaning of the social may be in question. . .but life without it has proved impossible'."[93]

This determination to move "beyond the cultural turn," as Hunt and Bonnell put it in 1999, has resurfaced repeatedly in the feminist literature. Merry Wiesner-Hanks has noted how, for many of the feminist critics of the "culturalist" or post-structuralist turn in women's studies, accentuating issues of *textuality* and *discursivity* has had the ironic (and, quite possibly, inadvertent) effect of denying women *personal agency* in critical historical situations. As Wiesner-Hanks has recapitulated the issue:

> The linguistic turn . . . elicited harsh responses from many historians, including many who focused on women and gender. They asserted that it denied women the ability to shape their world—what is usually termed "agency"—in both past and present by positing unchangeable linguistic structures. Wasn't it ironic, they noted, that just as women were learning they *had* a history, and asserting [that] they were *part* of history, "history" became just a text and "women" just a historical construct?[94]

Moreover—if certain politicized feminists were correct—denying women *agency* had obvious *political* implications, too. According to Robyn Wiegman, the "theoretical considerations" so often emphasized by radical post-structuralists allowed less of a "public political voice" for women, and "feminism's ability to define and inhabit social change" was thereby "jettisoned in favor of academic insularity."[95] If Laura Downs managed to avoid such political polemics in her *Writing Gender History* (rev. ed., 2010), she no less insisted that Joan Scott and her allies acknowledge "the fact that gender, understood as a purely discursive construct, cannot in and of itself explain change." "Without some way of linking discursive process to social experience," Downs continued, "historians cannot account for the changing meanings of masculine and feminine. This is . . . the most serious problem . . . left to historians of gender."[96]

Where, then, does all of this theoretical disputation leave us as we look to establish a context for studying the roles of women in the great European revolutions? We can see that issues of gender *have*, at long last, found acknowledged roles in the greater debate over structuralist and postmodernist explanations of revolutionary change. While, clearly, gender must have its place in structuralist analysis of state formation, gender, and women's studies in particular, should be especially evaluated within the subfield of "moderate" postmodernism as it has been defined in this chapter. Assuming, therefore, the *objective existence* of *women*, and hence of *patriarchy*, we can not only investigate women's issues as part of the political culture of old regimes about to be transformed by revolutionary change, but also turn to account research findings about the actual day-to-day experiences of "real" women caught up in the English, French, and

Russian Revolutions. Yet having in this way located gender *theoretically* and women's experiences *in particular* within the greater debate over revolutionary change, we might also find it enlightening, in the final section of this chapter, to examine how some feminist social scientists have ventured to theorize the *gendered outcomes* of major sociopolitical upheavals.

Feminist Theorizing of the Gendered Outcomes of Revolution

Passing over for the time being the roles played by women in the *stage-by-stage unfolding* of revolution—a subject we will eventually confront in connection with the English, French, and Russian Revolutions—we will concentrate here upon feminist efforts to theorize the gendered *consequences* of modern sociopolitical upheavals. In doing this, we may notice in the relevant scholarship a not entirely unexpected parallel to the progression, in the theoretical literature on revolutionary causation, from class-centered to state-centered to postmodernist perspectives. We may also discover that feminists considering the gendered outcomes of modern revolutions from a class-oriented point of view have tended to reach relatively pessimistic conclusions on the subject, whereas feminists striving to cast off the fetters of a strict class analysis have drawn somewhat more optimistic inferences from their work.

One of the so-called "dual systems" (i.e., feminist/Marxist) scholars writing extensively about gendered revolutionary outcomes since the 1970s has been Sheila Rowbotham. In her pathbreaking study *Women, Resistance, and Revolution* (1972), for example, Rowbotham came up with ambivalent appraisals of how women had fared in (to go no farther) the major *European* revolutions. In the case of seventeenth-century England, she readily conceded, Puritanism had at least "effected a species of moral improvement in the position of women. Within a very confined sense it allowed women a certain restricted dignity. It provided an impetus for a more humane conception of relationships between the sexes." Again, Rowbotham credited the English Revolution with fostering a tradition of "radical-puritan democracy" pivoting, at least in part, on "the idea of the individual as the independent owner of his own person and capacities, with the right to resist invasion and violation." And this, wrote Rowbotham, also carried implications for *women*: "Within Puritanism . . . was the assumption that women, as human beings, had certain inalienable rights to civil and religious liberty."[97] Yet, alas, for this Marxist historian as well as for other left-leaning feminists, *ideological/political* realities seemingly boding well for women in this revolutionary situation were ultimately subsumed in less favorable *economic/developmental* realities:

> Puritanism assumed . . . the small independent concern, either farm or family business, in which the family worked side by side and the wife could well be a partner, although still an inferior partner. But this ideal of self-sufficient independence was rapidly ceasing to represent the new reality. . . . The roles of husband and wife were more specifically differentiated. The external world of work became the sphere of the man exclusively, [while] the internal world of the family and household was the proper business of the woman.

And this tendency, argued Rowbotham, sorted all too easily with the fact that, even in *puritan* attitudes toward political authority, there were significant "ambiguities." Except for millenarians and for other extreme visionaries in the seventeenth-century English upheaval, revolutionaries inevitably associated patriarchy in government with patriarchy in the family; "the idea of participation in government," added Rowbotham bluntly, "was restricted to those who owned property and to men."[98]

Ambiguity also aptly described for this feminist/Marxian scholar the French Revolution's legacy for women. Rowbotham could undeniably rejoice over "indications of a great acceleration of [women's] activity and consciousness" in the political events that brought down France's *ancien régime* in the late eighteenth century; on the other hand, she could not help but detect "considerable ambiguity in 'liberty, equality, fraternity' towards women" in those events. Moreover, like so many other "dual perspective" scholars, Rowbotham also saw what she called the "bourgeois radical feminism" of revolutionary France as an ideology "still in the phase of moral exhortation, before there was either the possibility of a radical and socialist movement from below, to which the revolutionary feminist could relate, or a movement like that of suffragettes, of privileged women for equal rights with bourgeois man." (Not unexpectedly, she also contended here that the best that could be said for Jean-Jacques Rousseau—often identified as the intellectual godfather of the 1789 upheaval—was that he had hazarded "a justification for women's place in the organization of capitalist society which [was] at once more effective and more sophisticated than puritanism's religious homilies.")[99] In the final analysis, Rowbotham concluded, women remained, in the wake of the French Revolution, much as they had remained in the aftermath of the earlier English Revolution—namely, "identified as part of nature," and best educated "to nourish and serve men, not to act of [their] own accord."[100]

But did the advent of Marxism in the nineteenth century, and of allegedly "communist" forms of upheaval in the twentieth century, leave Rowbotham with a buoyant sense of optimism where women's aspirations were concerned? It hardly appears so. Although she could state that "As a Marxist and as a feminist I cherish the elements in bourgeois humanism which Marx incorporated and transformed in his thinking," this in no way blinded her to the abject failures of the Russian revolutionary experience. "The Soviet Union, so long important as the model of a revolutionary alternative," Sheila Rowbotham could lament even before the actual implosion of that state, "had retreated from the creative experiments of the twenties" and hence had repeated "the tragic and faltering earlier attempts, specifically, to connect female aspirations with revolution." Indeed, she drew an unflattering picture of Marxists and "women's liberationists" as inhabiting two starkly different worlds:

> Marxists have in general assumed that the overthrow of capitalist society will necessitate a fundamental transformation in the organization and control of production and social relations which come from the capitalist mode of production. Women's liberation implies that if the revolutionary movement is to involve women, not as supporters or attendants only, but as equals . . . the scope of production must be seen in a wider sense and cover also the production undertaken by women in the family and the production of self through sexuality.[101]

It is clear as well from her work that Sheila Rowbotham, disillusioned by the "dual failures" of modern socialism *and* "advanced capitalism" to deal adequately with women's problems, joined some of her scholarly feminist sisters in (somewhat nebulously) advocating "a movement of working-class women . . . alongside black, yellow and brown women struggling against racialism and imperialism [and] . . . class, colonial and sexual oppression."[102]

Similar leftist/feminist indictments of the modern revolutionary tradition's historic shortcomings have come from scholars whom we have already encountered, such as Maria Mies (1986) and Margaret Randall (1992). Mies was notably obsessed by what she saw as the nefarious operations of a "capitalist patriarchy" which—in spite of dramatic episodes like the Bolshevik Revolution in Russia—has integrated the entire world into a "system of global exploitation and accumulation." According to Mies, feminists would always be challenged to analyze and condemn an "international division of labor" under whose auspices housewives in the West and exploited, poorly compensated female workers in the developing world are held in a kind of global, patriarchy-sanctioned bondage.[103] Even though (as we noted earlier) theorists of patriarchy such as Sylvia Walby have found such an analysis, portraying "house-wifization" in the West and exploited female labor in the "Third World" as mutually reinforcing evils in a worldwide "patriarchy/capitalism" system, to be simplistic and somewhat inaccurate, they have at the same time concurred with Mies (and with historians like Sheila Rowbotham) that feminists today need to question relentlessly as to *why* upheavals of "national liberation" in the twentieth century have *not* automatically led to genuine and durable "women's liberations."[104]

Such a *parti pris* patently motivated Margaret Randall as well. Writing in the dramatic aftermath of the collapse of communism in Russia and in Eastern Europe in the early 1990s, this "dual perspective" feminist dismissed the comforting fiction that "what [had] happened in the Soviet Union and in Eastern Europe [was] simply part of the ongoing process of creating socialism." Considering these "reverses" to be, in fact, "real reverses that, although undoubtedly part of the process, also pushed that process back generations," Randall described the key to such failures (in Russia and elsewhere) as *feminist* in nature:

> I believe that in each of the revolutionary experiments the failure to develop an indigenous feminist discourse and a vital feminist agenda impeded the consolidation that would push an otherwise more humane society forward. Again and always, the men had their way. It was obviously too frightening to have to confront the unleashed power of women, silenced for centuries. Easier [for these men] to pay lip service to "women's rights," while being careful not to allow them to become a priority or to threaten male power.[105]

For sure, Randall—like most of her colleagues in the field—was too sophisticated *not* to admit into her analysis other factors as well. As she put it, "race relations, cultural diversity, sexual difference, critical thought, certain individual freedoms, and the nature of power itself" had all played their various roles in "tearing these [socialist] experiments apart."[106] Yet, in the final analysis, Randall invariably returned to an argument that she found most congenial—namely, that only through the adoption of an activist, critical, and well-informed feminism could women realize their "full potential *as women*" and thereby force a still-exploitative, still-capitalist, "postrevolutionary" world to serve *their* interests.

Yet not *all* feminist scholars have characterized the gendered outcomes of modern revolutions in the darkly pessimistic, class-oriented terms employed by the likes of Sheila Rowbotham, Maria Mies, and Margaret Randall. Maxine Molyneux, Mary A. Tétrault, and Valentine M. Moghadam, for example, have all dealt with this contentious question in post-Marxian ways that are more nuanced, that allow (in other words) for varying degrees of optimism regarding women's postrevolutionary prospects.

Sociologist Maxine Molyneux would be the first among such specialists to admit that women in "existing socialist countries certainly have not achieved full equality, let alone emancipation." She was particularly careful (writing in 1986) *not* to gloss over what she viewed as the problematic "operations of patriarchy" in such countries. But she also insisted that these realities be treated in an *empirical* rather than in an *ideological*—and, hence, by implication, *simplistic*—fashion:

> Male power, whether institutionalized or interpersonal, and the essentialist . . . arguments which legitimize it, do play a part in . . . women's continuing subordination after revolutionary upheavals; but the importance of such factors should not be exaggerated. Nor should the achievements of these revolutions be underestimated, or the real material constraints . . . they have faced be left out of account. To recognize the importance of these constraints is not to provide an apologia for the failings of postrevolutionary society but [rather] to establish more realistic parameters for comprehending the underlying and persistent causes of gender inequality.[107]

And, indeed, there is no doubt that feminist chroniclers of (for instance) the Russian Revolution, all too painfully aware of the major developmental challenges faced by female—and male—revolutionaries in the newly created Soviet Union, would endorse Molyneux's call for "realistic parameters" in accounting for the phenomenon of postrevolutionary "gender inequality."

But Molyneux went farther than this in her discussion of the gendered consequences of modern sociopolitical upheavals. Feminists often erred, she asserted, not only by overstating the role played by patriarchy and understating the importance of "real material constraints" in such situations, but also by *oversimplifying the question of "women's interests"*—a question which, she wrote, is "far more complex than is frequently assumed." To begin with, Molyneux argued, since "women are positioned within their societies through a variety of different means—among them class, ethnicity, and gender—the interests which they have as a group are similarly shaped in complex and sometimes conflicting ways." It is hence difficult, if not altogether impossible, to generalize about "the interests of women." And Molyneux, at this point, delved even more deeply into the matter by postulating a distinction for which she has since become widely known in women's affairs—that is, the distinction between broadly conceived "women's interests" and more narrowly conceived "gender interests."[108]

For Molyneux, "gender interests" may be either "strategic" or "practical" in nature. "Strategic gender interests" can be deduced from women's *systemic subordination* in society, and viewed in terms of what women "strategically" need, such as "the abolition of the sexual division of labor, the alleviation of the burden of domestic labor and childcare, the removal of institutionalized forms of discrimination, the establishment of political equality, freedom of choice over childbearing, and . . . adoption of adequate measures against male violence and control over women." On the other hand, so Molyneux maintained, "practical gender interests" are more *immediate* interests, "formulated by women themselves" and thus usually involving "a response to an *immediate* perceived need"; they do *not* ordinarily entail "a strategic goal such as women's emancipation or gender equality." "Practical gender interests," in so many words, "do not in themselves challenge the prevailing forms of gender subordination, even though they do arise directly out of them." For this scholar, the term "feminism" most properly attaches to "strategic" rather than to "practical" gender interests; in fact, she opined, "it is the politicization of . . . practical interests and their transformation into strategic interests that women can identify with and support which constitutes a central aspect of feminist political practice."[109]

Nonetheless, Maxine Molyneux's *larger* point here was that feminist political practice, however useful it might be to women in some situations, could in the end founder upon the shoals of class, race, and other divisive social forces. This, in turn, is why Molyneux feared that feminist criticisms of socialist (i.e., postrevolutionary) regimes could sometimes rest, simplistically and thus *unfairly*, "on an implicit or explicit assumption that there is a given entity, "women's interests," which is ignored or overridden by policymakers." To redefine the problem: women's *general* interests, unlike "strategic" and "practical" *gender* interests, must acknowledge societal dynamics such as class and race. And Molyneux stressed that this was most acutely the case in *revolutionary* and *postrevolutionary* situations:

> In such situations, gender issues are frequently displaced by class conflict, and this is principally because although women may suffer discrimination on the basis of gender and may be aware that they do so, they nonetheless suffer differentially according to their social class. These differences crucially affect attitudes toward revolutionary change, especially if this is in the direction of socialism.[110]

Since, in conclusion, women's interests—as defined by Molyneux—are significantly *broader* than gender interests in that they must accommodate class and race along with gender and other factors, they must be adequately addressed by the revolutionary/postrevolutionary state. This was, in sum, one feminist's way of calling for a critically informed awareness of the *sheer complexity* of interests affecting women in revolutionary situations; such an awareness ideally should serve "to guard against any [overly] simple treatment of whether a state is or is not acting in the interests of women," and thereby guard against what might *otherwise* be unduly facile—and negative—assessments of postrevolutionary regimes.[111]

The late international relations theorist Mary Ann Tétrault, on the other hand, tried to deal with the gendered outcomes of modern revolutions, not so much by emphasizing the *complexity of women's interests* in the eyes of the postrevolutionary state, as by emphasizing the historic significance, for those interests, of *familial institutions* within that state. To begin with, Tétrault (like her contemporary Theda Skocpol) had a structuralist sense of the *statist aspects* of revolutions, whether those revolutions were of bourgeois or socialist inspiration. It might be true, Tétrault conceded, that, as a rule, "revolutionaries acting together seek to end political regimes they see as oppressive." Still, also as a rule, *women* were unlikely to be among the chief *political beneficiaries* of such campaigns, whatever their contributions to them might have been. Tétrault anatomized this process in structuralist terms:

> revolutionaries compete among themselves to control the outcomes of their revolutions, not only in terms of the designs of new regimes but, perhaps even more, [in terms of] the identity of the individuals and groups who will dominate them. . . ..Those groups whose pre-revolutionary power was greatest . . . also dominate afterwards. . . . Once the victors [have] added the resources of the state to their arsenals, they [are] strong enough to fend off potential rivals with more thoroughgoing social aims. In Theda Skocpol's terms, this is the outcome of political revolution, and it is unlikely to include women *as women* among the victors.[112]

"Paying your dues," Tétrault resignedly commented in a similar vein a bit later on, "does not necessarily guarantee permanent membership as an autonomous actor in a post-revolutionary society and political economy. Women's entitlements to freedom and equality can be erased in a number of ways." Again, Tétrault, like many of the feminist writers whom we have already encountered, was also quite willing to see patriarchy, or, as she described it, "sanctified patterns of authoritarianism and exploitation," as lying in wait at all times to "contradict revolutionary principles."[113]

Yet if this political scientist was willing to invoke that *bête noire* of feminists, patriarchy, in her analysis of the gendered outcomes of revolutions, and to recall as well historic socialist indictments of that bourgeois institution *par excellence* the privatized family, she could also—surprisingly, perhaps—assert that "the personal life that has grown up inside the bourgeois family is a life shared by women and men as equal partners in intimacy." And from *this* general observation it was but a small step for Tétrault to *this* normative statement regarding the best possible revolutionary outcome for women:

> The kind of revolution that is best for women is one that results in a regime based on personal liberty, equal rights for women and men, and laws [that are] enforced in the home as well as in the street and the marketplace. . . . A new regime unwilling or unable to extend equal protection to women and men *in their family lives* as well as in the parts of their lives . . . lived in the separate realm of the public space denies them both liberty and equality.[114]

Whatever the inconsistencies in her argument, then, Mary Ann Tétrault, like Maxine Molyneux, had her own way of transcending reductionist Marxian distinctions between bourgeois and socialist revolutions when characterizing the gendered outcomes of modern revolutionary upheavals.

Finally, we have the thought-provoking theorizing of gendered outcomes of revolutions offered in 1997 by sociologist Valentine Moghadam— theorizing doubtlessly intended to improve upon both the Marxism and the state-oriented structuralism of earlier feminist social scientists. Moghadam made her contribution to this vigorous controversy by distinguishing between two models of revolution: first, the "woman-in-the-family" or patriarchal model of revolution and, second, the "women's emancipation" or modernizing model. The former model, so Moghadam explained, "conformed to events in revolutionary France" (and elsewhere), whereas the latter model applied to the events that transpired later in (among other countries) revolutionary Russia.[115]

Moghadam went to considerable lengths to explain what she meant to convey by associating major modern revolutions—and, above all, their gendered outcomes—with these two models. Thus, here is her description of the "woman-in-the-family" model:

> This type of revolution excludes or marginalizes women from definitions and constructions of independence, liberation, and liberty. It frequently constructs an ideological linkage between patriarchal values, nationalism, and the religious order. It assigns women the role of wife and mother, and associates women not only with family but also with tradition, culture, and religion . . . . [Here] the family is exalted and women's role within it made paramount.

And then, by the same token, we also have her description of the "women's emancipation" model:

> The women's emancipation model holds that the emancipation of women is an essential part of the revolution or project of social transformation. It constructs Woman as part of the productive forces and citizenry, to be mobilized for economic and political purposes; she is to be liberated from patriarchal controls expressly for that purpose. Here the discourse is more strongly that of sexual equality rather than [that of sexual] difference.[116]

Clearly, Moghadam to some extent borrowed from Maxine Molyneux's work in this area by suggesting that, whereas "emancipatory" revolutions serve at least some "strategic and practical gender interests" and in addition address many if not all "women's interests," the "woman-in-the-family" model is, by its very nature, "inimical to the strategic gender interests of women, though it may address some practical gender needs and the specific interests of some groups of women."[117]

Moghadam's theorizing of gendered outcomes of modern revolutions was undoubtedly useful. Her association of *specific revolutions* with one or the other of these two models showed that, at least, she, too, was quite capable of transcending the tired paradigmatic distinctions between bourgeois and socialist upheavals. Specifically, she viewed not only the late-eighteenth-century French Revolution but also the upheavals in twentieth-century Algeria, Iran, and Eastern (formerly Soviet-dominated) Europe as *patriarchal* in nature, whereas she saw bourgeois Kemalist Turkey, much like Russia, China, Vietnam, Yemen, and Nicaragua, as having had an *emancipatory* revolution. However, Moghadam betrayed some conceptual confusion when she contrasted the French Revolution, which "despite its many progressive features, had an extremely conservative outcome for women," with a Russian Revolution which—so she claimed—*still remained*, in hindsight, "the avant-garde revolution *par excellence*" for women.[118] First, Moghadam—like a number of other feminists—failed to differentiate adequately between *conservative* and *radicalized* women in *both* revolutionized polities. Second, she failed in both cases to differentiate adequately between the *sequential phases* of *unfolding* revolution and the *consequences* of revolution. Taken all in all, however, Moghadam's ideas, like those of Molyneux and Tétrault, leave us with much to ponder concerning the gendered outcomes of modern revolutions. But at the same time, they may also leave us (especially, but not exclusively, if we are *Europeanists*) no less determined to examine in much greater detail how ordinary—as well as some not-so-ordinary—women fared as full-fledged revolutions unfolded *phase-by-phase* in mid-seventeenth-century England, in late-eighteenth-century France, and in early-twentieth-century Russia.

In Chapter 1, we have attempted to reappraise theoretical aspects of gender (and related issues) against the backdrop of modern revolutionary upheavals both in Europe and in the larger world beyond Europe. One advocate of *masculinity* and of *men's studies*, admittedly, has insisted on the impossibility of understanding "the culturally constructed sets of attributes and behaviors considered appropriate in males and females without reference to each other."[119] Still, we *have* seen on these pages how many a feminist social scientist has in modern times wrestled theoretically with issues of gender, sexuality, and patriarchy. We have, in addition, gained a sense of how *gender* has come to play a role in the debates over revolutionary causes that, these days, seem ever more to pit theorists of a structuralist persuasion against those of a postmodernist (or post-structuralist) orientation. If, on the one hand, gender can be viewed as an essential constituent of the "patrimonial state," and hence as significant in state-centered structuralism, it should be regarded as just as critical to feminist aspects of postmodernist theory. Finally, we have seen how feminist historians and other specialists have arrived at differing conclusions about the prospects for favorable gendered outcomes (i.e., favorable specifically for *women*) in modern revolutionary situations. We can only hope that Chapter 1 has thereby furnished us with an adequate theoretical grounding for what will *really* concentrate our minds in the chapters that follow—namely, a carefully informed and sympathetic discussion of women's experiences in the three historic revolutions that, in earlier centuries, convulsed England, France, and Russia.

2

A Brief Sketch of the English, French, and Russian Revolutions

There are legitimate theoretical as well as purely practical reasons for briefly chronicling in this chapter the successive stages of the three principal European revolutions. In practical terms, certainly, it would be helpful to those readers attracted to the subject of women's experiences in revolutionary England, France, and Russia, but not necessarily that familiar with those upheavals as a whole, to have from the beginning a more specific sense of how significant events actually unfolded in them. Beyond this, however, there is also the theoretical question of how scholars have evaluated the *significance of issues of process* in revolutionary studies. For instance, critics of Theda Skocpol's comparative analysis of the French, Russian and Chinese Revolutions have often faulted her for stressing issues of *causation* and (to some extent) *consequences* at the expense of issues of *process*. As I noted in an earlier book, it is not surprising that social historians such as Lynn Hunt, playing up the importance of how revolutions actually *unfold*, would perceive tautological, lockstep characteristics in Skocpol's analytical model which conflate the causes, process, and results of revolution and thus (arguably) make it difficult to assess the contingencies and personalities of revolutions in their own right.[1] Of greater significance, though, is the fact that some of Skocpol's fellow social scientists have seized upon the same issue. Chalmers Johnson did so in his revised (1982) edition of *Revolutionary Change,*[2] and Michael Kimmel did so just as well in 1990, maintaining that "although [Skocpol] has a great deal to say about the causes and consequences of revolution (and the correlations between them), she devotes scant space to the *process* of revolution, to how human beings actually make a revolution."[3] Most relevant for us, however, is feminist Valentine Moghadam's insistence that *gender* is "an integral dimension of the revolutionary process," and should therefore be granted "conceptual value" by those studying women's roles in revolutions.[4]

Accordingly, for both practical *and* theoretical reasons we turn now, in Chapter 2, to the basic sequences of developments in the revolutions that convulsed mid-seventeenth-century England, late-eighteenth-century France, and early-twentieth-century Russia. We start with the events attending the "breakthroughs to revolution" in England (1637–40), France (1787–89), and Russia (1916–17); move on from there to what we might term the "honeymoons" of early revolution in the three countries; proceed next to the processes of radicalization that followed in all three situations; then sum up developments in the climactic, terroristic phases of the three revolutions; and then, finally, recapitulate the Thermidorian or post-Terrorist stages of revolution in England, France, and Russia.

Transitions: Breakthroughs to Revolution

The crumbling of Stuart, Bourbon, and Romanov absolutism during the years 1637–40, 1787–9, and 1916–17, respectively, is, in a strict chronological sense, uncomplicated enough, and it has been the subject of countless works of history. In the case of England, Charles I's attempt to impose the Anglican Book of Common Prayer on Presbyterian Scotland in 1637 led to a national uprising there the following year, which during 1639–40 (in the so-called Bishops' Wars) the English were unable to quell. The king's multiplying difficulties eventually forced him—for the first time since 1628—to consult parliament. The abortive "Short Parliament" of April 1640 was followed by the convocation, in that November, of what is still known as the "Long Parliament," fated to endure (with notable interruptions, to be sure) for almost twenty years; and the English Revolution was underway. In the case of France, governmental insolvency forced Louis XVI to appeal, first (in 1787) to an Assembly of Notables, and eventually (in 1788–9) to the historically prescribed Estates General to rescue his government from bankruptcy and all that it implied. Stalemate in the latter body over a variety of issues led to popular intervention in this heretofore largely élitist quarrel: the upshot was the July Days (seizure of the Parisian Bastille) and then the October Days, which secured the early revolution by removing both royal family and legislature from Versailles to the capital. In the case of Russia, everything happened in (comparatively) breakneck fashion: foods riots at St. Petersburg (patriotically renamed "Petrograd" in wartime) triggered in late February 1917 a week of spreading proletarian unrest which terminated with Nicholas II's abdication, first on his own behalf and then on that of his only son Alexei. Tsarist Russia thus—abruptly—became a revolutionary republic.

Hence, we have the bare bones of chronology. Palpably, however, we need to put at least *some* substantive flesh on those bare bones. We can do that by concentrating, in all three cases of transition to revolution, on four cardinal factors: (1) statist/fiscal and economic issues; (2) constitutional/political developments; (3) military questions; and (4) the political-cultural context of events. It seems logical to proceed here in "real chronological time," that is to say, from developments in mid-seventeenth-century England to those in late-eighteenth-century France to those in early-twentieth-century Russia.

The precariousness of Charles I's finances in the late 1630s has appeared increasingly evident to modern-day scholars. According to the late Kevin Sharpe, it is true, Charles apparently felt in early 1639 that the existing surplus in his treasury, reinforced by county militia contributions and feudal obligations newly exacted from the peerage, would see him through the anticipated confrontation with the defiant Scots, and (crucially) enable him to avoid recurrence to Parliament.[5] Yet most authorities on the subject would likely agree with G. E. Aylmer's prior—and sobering—assessment that "Charles I was able to keep going without recourse to parliament [only] so long as he kept out of war." If the "Bishops' Wars" did therefore make the reconvening of parliament a "financial necessity," Aylmer speculated, this was so, in part, owing to "grave weaknesses in the administrative system" that impeded the logistics of Charles I's military preparations in 1639 and 1640. It was due as well, Aylmer held, to the fact that royal revenues were "anticipated" in such a fashion as to make it impossible for the Crown to balance its books. The Crown, after all, could not *as of yet* be sustained through the workings of a "fully-fledged credit system, such as began to come into existence [only] during the 1690s."[6]

But Stuart finances at this perilous time were most strikingly deficient in the *larger context* of a foreign policy that had *always* to reckon with the ultimate possibility of warfare waged not only on land (as, for instance, in Scotland) but also on the seas. Yet even regarding naval affairs *alone*, Conrad Russell has argued, and even assuming the (unlikely) eventuality of "compliant and well-satisfied Parliaments," *any* English monarch would have found *regular peace-time subsidies* to be hopelessly inadequate. Even the government's recourse to the widely hated Ship Money assessments of the late 1630s, which had at least made extensive naval rearmament possible for the time being, highlighted, in Russell's words, "the growing gap between the maximum weight of taxation the King's subjects were likely to consent to and the minimum sum on which a King could preserve solvency and national security."[7]

This latter point reminds us how inseparable, ultimately, were *fiscal* from *political/constitutional* matters. Charles I was a ruler, noted Mark Fissel damningly but correctly, "who eschewed the ruled. He made few progresses in the shires, thwarted the gentry's petitioning by secluding himself, and trimmed the aspirations of the nobility. . . . He seems to have taken for granted the allegiance of his subjects, save for a favored few, and showed little interest in the complications of government." In the end, concluded Fissel dismissively, Charles "had succeeded in isolating himself from the political nation, but at his peril." Even when the expenses of war finally forced the king to summon Parliament in early 1640, he did so for *financial* reasons alone. "Discussion of policy or redress of grievances were not even to be considered. The opinions and reactions of the ruled were irrelevant."[8] Yet, clearly, such an attitude was hopelessly unrealistic, given the resentments that had been festering most notably (if hardly exclusively) in gentry ranks during the Personal Rule of 1629–40—resentments bound to boil over speedily in any reconvened parliament. That even in the abortive Short Parliament of April 1640 John Pym and several of his more contumacious associates were already advancing radical prescriptions for constitutional reform augured very poorly indeed for prospects of cooperation between Crown and Parliament.[9]

That Charles I had to face this looming constitutional crisis in a state of near-isolation became starkly evident when, in a futile effort to avoid recourse to Parliament, he sought last-minute financial aid from the City of London; and his isolation was even more stunningly demonstrated by the results of elections for both the Short and the Long Parliaments in 1640. On the former point, the refusal of the Londoners to subsidize royal policies was dictated by the *lack of security* for desperately needed loans; how, after all, could such loans be safely made to the king, given Crown finances that lacked legitimacy in the absence of representative government?[10] On the latter point, Lawrence Stone has remarked (with reference to the elections in early 1640 to the Short Parliament) that "a more crushing demonstration of the collapse of royal authority before an aroused electorate could hardly be imagined." And things only went from bad to worse in elections, later in the year, to the Long Parliament: only 11 percent of its members, Stone has informed us, were to consist of "courtiers, officials and hangers-on," representing "a smaller proportion than in any previous Parliament of which we have record." Hence, by November 1640, Stone could easily enough conclude, "Charles found himself almost alone."[11]

Charles I's *constitutional* isolation in 1640 endangered him all the more in that he could *not* rely on military coercion to engineer some sort of coup de force against his multiplying opponents. However much consternation there may have been on this score among Londoners in early 1640, some of whom saw the king's troops as designed more surely for action against themselves than against Scottish forces in northern counties, those who have studied these issues most assiduously have found the English units inferior to the Scots in ways that resemble unflattering comparisons between the Russian and German armies in the First World War. Take, for example, the question of *personnel*. "With the exception of Sir Jacob Astley," Mark Fissel has observed, "the officers of the First Bishops' War were inexpert and uninspiring. In contrast, the [Scottish] Covenanters selected what appear to have been able commanders." Officers chosen by court connection, on the English side, had to confront officers sought out for professionalism, on the other. Moreover, the situation for the English was probably even worse in the Second Bishops' War, given the "extraordinary turnover in officer corps personnel" and the lack of junior officers; the latter problem plagued the English much as a lack of NCOs would bedevil Russia's military in 1916–17. Charles's failure to call out the cream of the local militia to fill rank-and-file positions meant, Fissel has affirmed, that "the royal army would largely approximate to the riff-raff of an overseas expedition, with similar results."[12] Inadequate financing, administrative inefficiency, and bottlenecks in the procurement of supplies of all sorts only aggravated the king's personnel problems in both 1639 and 1640.[13] Military problems, then, helped mightily to render Charles I's *political* situation untenable in 1640.

Yet it was probably the *political-cultural* aspects of Charles's dilemma that made it, in the end, so intractable. In more specific terms, the conspiratorial mentality of those who for historical reasons feared and hated continental and Irish Catholicism irredeemably isolated Charles I and his unabashedly Catholic wife Henrietta Maria in (increasingly Puritan) England. The king, by turning his back at this time on Cardinal Richelieu's (indirectly?) pro-English policies in France, spurning the Protestant Dutch and the Protestant Danes, conceding unparalleled influence to Henrietta Maria and to several of her Jesuit and Spanish supporters at Court, scheming for Spanish, Irish-Catholic, and even papal support in his struggle against the defiantly Presbyterian Scots, and permitting passage of Spanish troops across England while refusing to challenge Madrid's navy in "his" Channel, played perfectly—and ruinously—into the hands of affrighted subjects who saw in him the ultimate nightmare of an English monarch given over to "popish" and, hence, treasonous machinations against his own country.[14] It was all very well for Charles, egged on in this by his advisers, to believe in a "counter-conspiracy" welding together French intriguers, Dutch and Swedish Protestants, Scottish Covenanters, and his own insubordinate Puritan subjects, all of whom were supposedly threatening his sacrosanct role as God's anointed sovereign in the British Isles.[15] The fact remained that anti-Catholic paranoia and conspiracy-mindedness attracted greater support than did conspiratorial thinking on the "other side" in early Stuart England; and it was in these severely polarized circumstances, immensely dangerous to Charles I and to the regime he was striving in 1640 to uphold, that he was forced to confront parliamentarian representatives of his apprehensive and angry subjects at Westminster Palace in London.

In the case of France, state finances (and broader economic realities) were again one of the four primary factors in the transition to revolution. By 1787–8, many of the *financiers* on whose short-term advances (*anticipations*) of capital the crown had increasingly come to live day by day were using both public and private funds to speculate as never before on the Paris stock exchange; and they themselves were, often, on the verge of or in actual bankruptcy at this time. A "severe general crisis" in financial circles was apparently shaking public confidence in the fiscal system.[16] This general crisis, in turn, may have owed some of its severity to a larger economic recession of the post-1778 period which has long been described by E. Labrousse and those following in his wake. Producers' hardships in this supposed "inter-cyclical recession" may have driven them to resist royal tax collectors' demands; this, in turn, may have adversely affected financiers who depended in part upon income from the indirect taxes levied on such producers, and thereby accelerated the trend toward bankruptcies, and, ultimately, governmental insolvency.[17] At the very least, it *does* appear likely that the French economy *was* encountering major difficulties on the eve of the Revolution. Furthermore, we know that other factors were also militating against increasingly desperate efforts by Louis XVI's ministers to stave off bankruptcy. Gail Bossenga has summarized much of the research in this area by citing four of these complicating factors: (1) the partial internationalization of French long-term debt; (2) changing official attitudes toward (disproportionately expensive) maintenance of so much *short-term* debt; (3) tendencies in the influential Paris Parlement toward endorsing the reconvening of the country's historic Estates General for the purposes not only of approving new taxation but also of guaranteeing government loans; and (4) changing attitudes in society concerning what some financial historians have called the "sanctity of the national debt."[18]

And here, too, as in the prior English situation, a fiscal crisis blossomed soon into a *constitutional* crisis. Eleventh-hour efforts by Louis XVI's ministers to ram badly needed structural reforms (including a modernized system of taxation) through, first, an "Assembly of Notables" and, then, the privileged and powerful Paris Parlement only elicited from those bodies—and from an ever more politicized citizenry—repeated calls for the convening (for the first time since 1614–15) of the kingdom's Estates General.[19] As early as August 1787, Jean Egret tells us, "everyone was calling for the Estates General, and some daring journalists were already speculating about its potential composition . . . and about the task it would have to accomplish."[20] Attempts by the government to carry out a coup de force against the Paris Parlement and other institutions opposed to its edicts in May 1788 only provoked widespread outrage in society. In such circumstances of almost complete isolation—recalling, of course, those of Charles I in 1639–40—Louis XVI had little choice but to retreat. By early July 1788, his government in a Counciliar decree was inviting "all Frenchmen, through provincial Estates or assemblies, to make known their opinions on the appropriate rules to be followed" in the summoning of the Estates General. On August 8, a royal edict informed the nation that the Estates General would reconvene on May 1, 1789, and on August 16 still another decree, effectively announcing the state's "temporary" bankruptcy, also promised the crown's creditors that the upcoming national convocation would *permanently* secure their investments. Soon after having thereby associated fiscal and constitutional issues indissolubly in the eyes of the nation, the finance minister, Loménie de Brienne, gave way to Swiss financier Jacques Necker. Absolutism in France was now (like English absolutism 150 years earlier) signing its own death warrant.[21]

The French government's inability to suppress the opposition in 1788—or to stem the tide of popular agitation the following summer— also reflected in part the state of the army. Here, with the third of our four analytical factors, we discover yet another element common to all three revolutions. True, French forces had not been shattered by defeat in the late 1780s, as Charles I's army had been by 1640, and as those forces fighting for tsarist Russia would be by 1917. Still, Louis XVI's troops were no better prepared to crush domestic dissent than were those of the besieged Stuart and Romanov rulers. In a season of "peace" imposed by looming national bankruptcy, Louis XVI convened a special council of war to promulgate badly needed military reforms. Yet, however much the resultant measures laid the groundwork for spectacular French triumphs in battles soon to come, in 1788–89 they tended only to exacerbate tensions within officered ranks, pitting court aristocrats, provincial squires, newly created nobles, and ambitious, affluent commoners against each other.[22] Moreover, deterioration of morale among the officers must have had implications for the army's efficacy as an instrument of social control in 1788–89. On more than one occasion during this period, officers hesitated to order their troops into action against rioters, or the soldiers themselves proved reluctant, even under orders, to march against their countrymen. When we factor into the equation how aristocratic officers and military commoners alike wore themselves out policing the countryside in a time of subsistence crisis, and were frequently underpaid and hungry themselves, it becomes even easier to understand the increasing unreliability of the French army as a weapon of domestic social repression in 1788–89.

Finally, there was for Louis XVI, as there had been for Charles I, the *political-cultural* context, in which all other problems took on enhanced significance. By fusing in the eyes of the state's multiplying critics "foreign" issues of state security and geopolitics with domestic issues of "ministerial despotism," Austrophobia and Anglophobia did for the French what anti-Catholic paranoia had done for the English. Austrophobia in French minds centered increasingly on the activities (real or imagined) of the Austrian-born queen Marie-Antoinette, sister to Austrian ruler Joseph II. The consensus of scholars such as John Hardman, Munro Price, and Thomas E. Kaiser is that Marie-Antoinette's political influence at Versailles, however questionable in the early years of her husband's reign, had become something to reckon with by the late 1780s.[23] At Court, her widely rumored role in the appointment of finance minister Loménie de Brienne and her advocacy of a hard line against the Paris Parlement and other law-courts attacking the government's eleventh-hour reforms helped to earn for her the unenviable sobriquet of "madame Déficit." In European affairs, the queen's reported efforts to divert French funds needed at home to her brother's military campaign against Turkey showed (so Kaiser has maintained) "that Marie-Antoinette was undermining the entire thrust of French foreign policy, which, as regards the defense of Turkey, enjoyed great public support." By 1787–8, then, it would appear that, through the queen's agency, "'despotism' at home had now become fused representationally with 'despotism' abroad."[24] As for Anglophobia in prerevolutionary France, it operated much as did Austrophobia to erode the regime's prestige and basic credibility by conjoining domestic and geostrategic issues in the eyes of Louis XVI's increasingly caustic critics. We know this notably in connection with the abortive Dutch revolution, in the course of which France's "Patriot" protégés were driven from power by the same Anglo/ Prussian coalition which had drubbed French forces so humiliatingly in the Seven Years' War. France, haunted already by the specter of bankruptcy, could do absolutely nothing for its Dutch allies; hence, the same observers bent upon condemning "ministerial despotism" at Versailles delighted in scorning France as "the plaything of the will of others."[25] And so Louis XVI, like Charles I before him, isolated at home and badly diminished abroad, had to face a revolutionary reckoning in an historically weakened condition.

That tsarist Russia's economic weaknesses had become critical by 1916–17 can best be seen by placing them in an *international context*. Wartime inflation, to begin with, though hardly unique to this polity, *did* in Russia go "far beyond the experience of any other country." The "decline of the ruble on foreign exchanges," Norman Stone has written, "the rise in basic costs such as transport, shortages that could be exploited by profiteers, the need for firms to obtain relatively scarce skilled labor by offering higher and higher wages, monopolies' tendency to go for quick profits in an era of uncertainty, all made for inflation's being more marked in Russia than in other countries."[26] Yet, as all experts on this issue also stress, problems such as runaway inflation, overtaxed railroad networks, lagging coal, pig iron, and steel production, strategic isolation from markets and sources of wealth and industrial commodities in the West, and so on—all these weaknesses ultimately had an effect more *directly* lethal to Nicholas II's regime in the undersupplied food markets of urban Russia. "There was more than enough grain to feed everyone in Russia in 1916," W. Bruce Lincoln has written, "but Russia's peasants . . . refused to sell their grain at the low prices fixed by the government while the cost of rapidly disappearing consumer goods soared."[27] In other words, the failure adequately to integrate urban and rural sectors of the economy in wartime Russia may have done even more than (for instance) lagging output in key industrial sectors and lagging labor productivity to spell doom for the Imperial regime by early 1917.

That the ministers in place so hopelessly botched management of the economy points to the second of our four key transitional factors—namely, the incompetence and *constitutional isolation* of Nicholas II's regime in this season of supreme national testing. In the final seventeen months of the old regime, Orlando Figes has noted, "Russia had four Prime Ministers, five Ministers of the Interior, three Foreign Ministers, three War Ministers, three Ministers of Transport and four Ministers of Agriculture. This 'ministerial leapfrog' . . . not only removed competent men from power, but also disorganized the work of government since no one remained long enough in office to master their responsibilities."[28] The tsar's dismissal of War Minister A. A. Polivanov had been bad enough, depriving Russia of its last champion of sustained military reform; now, the Prime Ministry of Boris Stürmer insured utter failure in the official effort to cope with an urban food crisis that most directly threatened the political status quo.[29] Even worse, in the early weeks of 1917, and as if to spite his government's multiplying critics, Nicholas II "replaced every minister who had a shred of talent or independence with men whose cause Aleksandra had pleaded" in recent days. In doing so, he (and his wife) "recklessly destroyed the last pillars of their political support."[30] The Imperial couple (it goes without saying) had long held at arm's length even timorous liberals in élitist society such as Paul Miliukov and Prince Georgii Lvov—let alone more legitimate representatives of Russia's laboring (and now often militarily mobilized) masses.[31]

Regarding military mobilization: Nicholas II—like Charles I and Louis XVI before him—could no longer depend in a pinch on the *unconditional* support of his own army. Here, the critical issues by late 1916 to early 1917 seem not to have been so much a lack of munitions, weapons, and other war matériel, nor failures in distribution of medicine, clothes, and other nonmilitary necessities, but rather questions of *changing personnel, deteriorating morale,* and the *larger political context* in which the soldiers at the front had to operate. New military recruits at all levels, according to military historian Allan K. Wildman, were "hastily assembled and badly trained peasant youths and over-forty *ratniki* who bitterly resented being torn away from their families and plots." The newest officers may have identified with the Allied cause for the most part; however, "they were also susceptible to political ideas and negatively disposed toward the tsarist government." But for historian Wildman, the really "dangerous new element" now was "the interaction of the mood at the front with the deteriorating political situation in the rear. . . . The replacements infected the front-line troops with their laxer discipline and civilian concerns, while the latter . . . communicated their battle traumas and utter despair to replacements."[32] The Imperial Army, it is admittedly true, did *not* actually disintegrate as an institution in the critical early weeks of 1917; still, retrospective analysis (and subsequent events at Petrograd) suggest that, by now, its efficacy, not only as a weapon of war against the Central Powers, but also as a *usable instrument of counterrevolutionary repression,* may have passed the point of no return.

Finally, we have to reconsider here, as in the two earlier transitions to revolution, the *cultural context* of events. In this connection, the association of rumored "dark forces" at Court and in general élite society with Imperial Germany and its formidable armies was especially fatal to Nicholas II and his family and, therefore, to the dynasty and old regime as a whole. This would have been true, it is well to stress, even if the tsar, tsarina, and Court elements had not also by now been tarred with the brush of sexual scandal associated with Rasputin.[33] The cultural phenomenon of Germanophobia—in a time of national humiliation administered by German arms—was significant above all in that it (momentarily) *united all social, professional, economic, and ethnic elements in society against the existing regime,* thus helping mightily to remove the inflexible and isolated Romanov couple from power. As Boris Kolonitskii and Orlando Figes have truly written: "Fear of the 'dark forces' (Black Hundred, Monarchist, Rasputinite and German) temporarily united diverse political groups (constitutional monarchists and republicans, liberals and socialists) behind February as a national revolution."[34] Hence the deadliness of references to Alexandra as the "German Woman," and of contemporary discourses linking the Imperial family, the bungling ministers, Rasputin's faction at Court, and others with unnamed (but presumably omnipresent) German "spies." Hence, as well, the danger posed for the government by ordinary soldiers at the front, who, Wildman tells us, were becoming ever more "convinced of the 'German stranglehold,' the treason of government figures, and the German sympathies of the tsarina," and were thus ever more prepared to ask: "What's the use of fighting if the Germans have already taken over?"[35]

Having thereby briefly recapitulated the "breakthroughs" to revolution in England, France, and Russia, we should now move on to reconsider the early, "honeymoon" phases of these three upheavals. We will swiftly discover how easy it was to be for individuals and groups across the political spectrum in these crises to agree on what they detested most about their countries' benighted *ancien régimes*—and yet, by the same token, how incredibly difficult it was to be for them to find any consensus in laying the secure foundations of their new, revolutionized states and societies.

Revolutionary "Honeymoons"

There was a hopeful sense of new beginnings in the earliest days of all three of our revolutions, even if, we must allow, it lasted longer in England (about a year or so) and in France (almost two years) than it did in war-ravaged, economically devastated Russia (scarcely two months!). In England (in

1640), Lawrence Stone tells us, "even so cautious a man as Sir Edward Hyde, the future royalist leader," spoke "rapturously" of "a dawning of a fair and lasting day of happiness to this kingdom," while as late as the summer of 1642 a Yorkshire gentleman could still share with an MP his "hearty desires for a thorough reformation both of Church and Commonwealth," and his view of the Parliament as being "able if need require to build a new world."[36] In 1789, the British ambassador to France wrote to inform his home government that the recent popular seizure of the Bastille heralded a relatively bloodless "revolution" that would curb the powers of the French king and inaugurate a new régime of social equality; and one of his compatriots glowingly assured his wife that he had witnessed "the most extraordinary revolution that perhaps ever took place in human society."[37] Finally, in Russia in February 1917, poet Alexander Blok marveled that "A miracle has happened, and we may expect more miracles," while Prince Georgii Lvov, fated to be the first prime minister in revolutionary Russia, observed ecstatically: "I believe in the vitality and the wisdom of our great people, as expressed in the national uprising that [has overthrown] the old regime."[38] In retrospect, however, we are likely to discern in such euphoria little more than fragile hopes for conciliatory change ultimately dashed on the jagged reefs of political reality.

Perhaps we can best grasp the futility of these honeymoon stages of revolution by carrying out two tasks. First, we touch on the dynamics of sociopolitical polarization and initial radicalization which, almost from the very start, worked to jeopardize the early, moderate revolutionaries' reformist efforts. Second, we focus on three revealing "points of no return" in these three upheavals—that is, traumatic developments pointing *irreversibly away* from consensus politics and toward more violent, *prolonged processes* of radicalization. These traumatic developments, specifically, were Charles I's abortive entry into Parliament in January 1642 and later departure from London; Louis XVI's ill-fated attempt to flee Paris (the "flight to Varennes") in June 1791; and Foreign Minister Paul Miliukov's precipitation of the "April Crisis" in 1917 over diplomatic/geostrategic issues inhering in the First World War. We may reasonably expect to find here, not, for sure, perfect uniformities, but at the very least a generalized sense of early legislative achievements imperiled and of early hopes for social reconciliation proven premature.

Polarization was clearly at work early on in revolutionary England. On the parliamentary side, John Pym and his adherents in the Commons, in striving to reach some sort of stable accommodation with King Charles, were haunted by the potential linkages between the Thirty Years' War still raging on the Continent, the presence of Scottish and English armies in northern England that had, somehow, to be paid off, and their fears, never far from the surface of events, of scarifying "popish plots" against English security.[39] Their anxieties on all these (interrelated) fronts help to explain the ferocity with which they went after the king's strong-arm lieutenant Thomas Wentworth, earl of Strafford, who was executed (on a bill of attainder) on May 12, 1641. Nor did the shedding of Strafford's blood in any way appease Pym and Company, who continued into 1642 to be driven by the same fears that had animated them earlier. Indeed, "for the whole of the first session of the Long Parliament," Kevin Sharpe insisted, "the papist scare dominated the agenda and coalesced the Commons. More than anything else, it was the solvent that eroded trust in the king."[40] For his part, Charles I, however gracious he might appear in discussions with members of Parliament, never really forgave Pym and the other leading oppositionists for Strafford's execution (and the incarceration of his other principal adviser, Archbishop William Laud). The death of the earl of Bedford on May 9, 1641, robbed both sides of a valuable intermediary; and it seems that, henceforth, the king increasingly relied on advice from his (inflexible) wife Henrietta Maria and the equally uncompromising Marquis of Hamilton and duke of Lennox.[41] Tensions between the two sides were only exacerbated in late 1641 to early 1642 by the Irish Rebellion. This sanguinary uprising of Anglo-Catholic landlords and peasants against English protestant settlers came at the worst imaginable time in that, as Lawrence Stone argued, "the plain need to crush it made necessary the resurrection of central power in its most extreme and dangerous form, an army."[42] But how was that army to be raised and (most critically of all) who was to control it? For Pym and his allies, already fearing royal retribution for their "murder" of Strafford, parliamentary control over such an army (and of critical state ministries) was clearly essential; for Charles and *his* supporters, the grim news filtering out of Dublin pointed just as surely to the opposite conclusion, namely, that royal control in these areas *must not* be surrendered.

The "point of no return" that, in the English case, brought an end to the honeymoon phase of revolution was the king's bungled attempt, by entering Parliament in January 1642, to arrest five MPs and one Peer on charges of treason; their timely withdrawal into a City of London now predisposed in favor of the parliamentary cause may well have saved their necks.[43] A disillusioned Charles I and his family soon left London; the monarch was not to see his capital again until he was remanded there as a prisoner following his defeat in the Civil War. In February–March 1642, first, the Commons, and then, somewhat more hesitantly, the Lords passed (without royal approval) the Militia Ordinance, drafted to place the militia, that is, the home defense forces, under the control of Westminster. The king's countering promulgation of Commissions of Array to raise the militia in *his* defense further polarized the situation without really advancing his cause. It was, indeed, on the specific issue of control of the militia, left by the breakup of the army as the sole military force within the country, that the Civil War formally began. Desultory negotiations between the two sides (and fiery exchanges of oratory and pamphlets) dragged on over the summer; but by

August the king, effectively burning his boats behind him, had raised the banner of civil conflict at Nottingham. He knew by this time that he had also lost his capital; anxieties boiling up over Ireland, "Papist" plots, and rumored Catholic machinations on the Continent had helped foment a pro-parliamentary upheaval at London even before the end of 1641.[44] By August 1642, then, the revolutionary "honeymoon" (if such it was) undoubtedly was breaking down in England, foundering above all upon the punishing rocks of competing ideological and geopolitical myths, conspiratorial fears, and mutual and unconquerable hatred and distrust.

In France, too, the honeymoon phase of revolution was undermined by polarization from the very start. As early as 1789, Louis XVI reacted to decrees forced through the Constituent Assembly on the tumultuous night of August 4—decrees that curbed seigneurial and particularist privileges in the kingdom—by writing angrily to the Archbishop of Arles: "I will never consent to the spoliation of my clergy or of my nobility. I will not sanction decrees by which they are despoiled."[45] Furthermore, he condemned all concessions wrung from him during that memorable summer in a pronunciamento sent surreptitiously both to his Spanish cousin, Charles IV, and to his Imperial Austrian brother-in-law Joseph II soon after the October Days had removed the royal family from Versailles to Paris. Louis XVI recorded his "solemn protest against all the acts contrary to my royal authority extracted from me by force since 15 July of this year"—thus for the people's historic seizure of the Bastille!—even while (rather lamely) reaffirming his "determination to fulfill the promises" he had made at a notorious and divisive *séance royale* of the National Assembly on June 23.[46] Again, much as Charles I's position had been weakened from the start by his French/Catholic queen's intriguing, so Louis XVI's general credibility in the eyes of his most politicized subjects was affected for the worse from early on by the antics, real or rumored, of his Habsburg Austrian wife Marie-Antoinette.[47] Hence, when we reappraise political dynamics within the National Assembly during 1789–91, we find them dominated—much as the analogous dynamics had been dominated in John Pym's Parliament during the early 1640s—by burgeoning distrust of a monarch who was clearly out of touch with, and falling farther behind, new (and evolving) revolutionary realities. By the early months of 1791, in fact, the dialectic of distrust between the king and his legislature—and the forces of latent radicalization *within* that legislature—acquired even sharper edges. The Assembly, viewing matters through the prisms of conspiracy, national security needs, and the overarching nexus (as powerful in France as earlier in England) between domestic and international affairs began to take concrete steps on its own initiative to ensure the safety of a kingdom whose king appeared increasingly unreliable. That it could do so was made possible by the same kind of shift of political forces toward the Left as had aided Pym and his parliamentary allies in the early years of the English Revolution.[48]

The "point of no return" terminating the honeymoon in France was the royal family's "flight to Varennes" on the night of June 20–21, 1791.[49] Louis XVI's attempt to escape from a capital that had become steadily less congenial to him in recent months was thwarted by the vigilance of local citizens at several points in far northeastern France; he, his wife, and their children were in the next few days transported back to Paris, a city now grown ominously silent and suspicious. Louis would "temporarily" be suspended from his regal functions by a Constituent Assembly still deeply involved in completing its labors on what was soon to be known as the "Constitution of 1791." After a period of prolonged (and increasingly divisive) discussion in the Assembly about how to deal with this would-be fugitive monarch, Louis XVI was finally reinstated on the precarious understanding that he would definitively endorse the constitutional document soon to emerge from the representatives' work. Still, his endorsement of the completed Constitution of 1791 in September, it must be said, rang rather hollow in light of the defiant manifesto he had left behind him at the Tuileries Palace on June 20, excoriating his "rebellious" subjects and condemning their "subversive" works of innovation. The newly elected Legislative Assembly would have to deal as best it could with this ticklish situation starting in October 1791. Louis XVI, we may note, was obviously in no position to emulate Charles I by raising the standard of civil war in some bastion of provincial royalism. But the political crisis in the summer of 1791 ignited by the "Flight to Varennes" no less dispelled any lingering illusions about the king's and queen's acceptance of the Revolution, and thus put paid to the (relatively) optimistic, consensual "honeymoon" atmosphere of 1789.

In the case of Russia, the "honeymoon days" were swept away (as Trotsky might say, "into the dust bin of history") in little more than ten weeks. Why the brevity of this honeymoon—if such it was? Two reasons for this come immediately to mind. First, the total, irredeemable collapse of the monarchy in February 1917 completely transformed the political dynamics of the situation: the huge concentration of power in autocratic tsardom gave way to both *dvoevlastie*—a highly fluid, unstable division between *formal* state power in the newly emergent Provisional Government and increasingly *real, coercive* state power in the newly emergent Petrograd Soviet—and what Orlando Figes has called *mnogovlastie*, the draining away of genuine state power to proliferating centers of power and legitimacy at the *local level*.[50] Second, the situation in Russia, to a much greater extent than those in the two earlier upheavals, was dominated from start to finish by the seemingly insoluble dilemma and myriad domestic complications of total war. In this case, the forces of polarization destroyed the legitimacy of the leader most closely identified with exhausted Russia's continued involvement in the First World War—that is, foreign minister Paul Miliukov—and did so at both the national and the local levels.[51] This meant that polarization poisoned not only relations between liberals and socialists at Petrograd—the usual story retailed in textbooks—but also relations *within each* of these factions, as well as those within moderate and radical factions contesting for power in provincial Russia.[52] The main point for our purposes, however, is that, with the ever more costly continuation of Russian involvement in a seemingly endless war, the initiative even in these early days of 1917 was shifting away from liberals and moderates in the Petrograd government toward more radical, even socialist, individuals. Paul Miliukov, War Minister Alexander Guchkov, Prime Minister Prince Lvov, and other leaders of their ilk found themselves increasingly challenged by slightly more militant individuals such as Alexander Kerensky, Nikolai Nekrasov, and M. I. Tereshchenko, who had been present at the creation of the new Russian regime—not to mention émigrés arriving later on the scene such as Irakli Tsereteli, Victor Chernov, and (of course) V. I. Lenin.[53] Hence, polarization and radicalization commenced especially early on in Russia's revolutionary cataclysm.

The "point of no return" marking the transition, in Russia, from its abortive (and largely illusory) honeymoon to a more sustained course of radicalization came with Miliukov's "covering note" sent to the Allies on April 18, 1917, and designed to reinterpret Russian foreign policy objectives in a way that would preserve Miliukov's stress upon traditional tsarist geostrategic interests while at the same time reassuring the Western governments of Petrograd's undiminished adherence to the Alliance.[54] But the publication of Miliukov's note, with its predictable and provocative insistence on the prosecution of the struggle against the Central Powers to a "decisive victory," infuriated Tsereteli, Chernov, and the other militants in the Petrograd Soviet, led to clashes in the streets between anti-Miliukov and pro-Miliukov crowds, and raised for protagonists on both sides of the Petrograd *dvoevlastie* the dread specter of civil war. The upshot was a political compromise coopting leading socialists into the government on May 5 but excluding the two most prominent conservative figures: Foreign Minister Miliukov and War Minister Guchkov. Thus was born, out of the chaos and frenzied political maneuvering of the April Crisis, the first of three moderately socialist Coalition Governments that tried to direct public affairs in Russia prior to the more decisive Bolshevik coup d'état of October 1917. What seemed clear by early May 1917 was that the Russian authorities had turned their backs on Miliukov's last, desperate attempt to preserve some of the continuities of the old—and by now hopelessly discredited— Romanov policies; what was *not* so clear was whether the moderate Socialist Revolutionaries (SRs) and Mensheviks who now were ensconced precariously in power would be able to tackle forthrightly and successfully the monstrous issue of the war, so that they could then go on to deal with Soviet Russia's burning *domestic* problems—above all, the questions of land redistribution and urban workplace reform.[55]

One thing that made the ultimate failure of these three revolutionary honeymoons so tragic was that, in all of them, politicians had been able to achieve or at least work toward useful reforms—and this had even included, in the case of Russia, debates that would lead ultimately to the historic concession of female suffrage on July 20, 1917.[56] But everything was soon to be thrown again into question, in each of these countries, as the discredited days of honeymoon illusions gave way to perilous days of sustained radicalization lying just ahead. It is to that dramatic and yet very instructive story, the "radicalization of the revolutions," that we must next briefly direct our attention.

Radicalization of the Revolutions

The stages of radicalization in these three revolutions that were (at least in part) touched off by the stunning miscalculations of two monarchs and a foreign minister proved even more unequal in their duration than were the "honeymoons" to which they succeeded. In England, radicalization extended all the way from the initiation of civil war hostilities in the summer of 1642 to the execution of Charles I and the abolition of both monarchy and House of Lords in January 1649. In France, the comparable process extended only from the "Varennes crisis" of June–September 1791 to the Jacobin seizure of power after the *journées* of May 31–June 2, 1793. In Russia, the revolution radicalized even more swiftly—from the formation of the First Coalition Government on May 5, 1917, to the Bolsheviks' seizure of power in late October of the same year. Such a pronounced *acceleration of the pace of radicalization* suggests that, as we advance from England to France to Russia, we find sociopolitical change occurring under ever greater exogenous and endogenous pressures on governance; stated somewhat differently, we confront an *ever tighter nexus* between external and internal events driving the process of revolution in the three polities under review. In each revolutionary situation, we can cursorily analyze two aspects of the radicalization process: (a) the essential dialectic between *war* (civil or foreign or both) and élitist factional struggles for state power; and (b) the growing tendency of those contending for power to accommodate and even (in some respects) *champion aggressively* the interests of the urban and/or rural masses.

Granted everything we already know about the schizoid and polarizing tendencies in the English political culture of the early 1600s, we would find it difficult *not* to conclude in retrospect that Charles I, in risking civil war against his most inspired foes starting in 1642, was in reality digging his own personal grave. In the final analysis, Anthony Fletcher has noted, "Charles's cause lacked ideological momentum. Indeed many were probably left wondering who they were expected to fight against. The tale that there was a parliamentary design against the kingdom was simply not as persuasive as the contrary story that the nation's enemies were papists and their malignant friends at court."[57] The first politician to turn the well-grounded parliamentary fears about Charles I to account was John Pym, whose ascendancy among his peers at Westminster seems to have been fairly consistently maintained until his death in late 1643. Under Pym's leadership, the parliamentary forces cultivated close ties with Puritan interests in London and nearby counties, formed a "committee for the defense of the kingdom," and eventually brought the Scots into the war (the *Solemn League and Covenant*).[58] After Pym's death, and as the war dragged on, the MPs increasingly divided into those in the so-called "war party," insistent on fighting the king to the bitter end, and those in the "peace party," whose fear of sociopolitical radicalization stemming from this struggle inclined them, ever more desperately, to seek some kind of settlement with the royalists.[59] In the end, Charles I's obdurate refusal to deal straightforwardly with his adversaries led to a coalescing of "Independents" in what became (by 1645) the New Model Army, in the House of Commons, and in the most fervent Puritan congregations; and it was these Independents, whose moving spirits were Oliver Cromwell and the other "Grandees" in the New Model Army, who achieved the decisive defeat of the royalist forces in the civil war.[60] But a "second" civil war had then to be (briefly) waged in 1648 against a king who *still* stubbornly refused to accept either his opponents' battlefield victories or the legitimacy of their cause. By now, however, Cromwell and the other radicalized Independents had had their fill of this monarch's endless duplicity and intransigence. Although specialists remain to this day divided over the eagerness of the generals (and others) to march an unrepentant Charles I to the scaffold, this was in the end the history-making course of action to which they were driven.[61] The generals occupied London in December 1648, removed 100 "unreliable" MPs in "Pride's Purge," and then put the king on trial for his life before the "rump" of the Commons. Charles I was executed on January 30, 1649, as a traitor to his people; and both the monarchy and the Lords were abolished *as institutions*.

From the very start, it is clear, the parliament's resolution to levy war against Charles I carried implications of *social* subversion that were certain to trouble some influential Englishmen. If, as David Underdown has observed, the "harsh pressures of war" conferred "positions of power and influence" on Puritan zealots such as Sir Henry Vane, and younger, doctrinaire republicans such as Henry Marten, the same pressures eventually drove other MPs (such as Denzil Holles) to regret their initial defiance of the king.[62] Hence, the desperate desire of "Presbyterian"—and even some "Independent"—MPs to come to almost *any* terms with Charles I in the later stages of the war. Insofar as there *was* any élitist attempt to accommodate "popular" aspirations in the topsy-turvy 1640s, it occurred through the agency of the New Model Army. Certainly this "godly" army, with its stress on evangelism and lay preaching, religious iconoclasm, spiritual equality, and the reformation of manners, to say nothing of promotion by merit in the officered ranks, could provide for those who fought under its banners an experience unique by the standards of the day. In these senses, the New Model was (within limits) a sort of "revolution within a revolution."[63] It is also true that substantial links existed in time between "agitators" in military ranks who desired further army reforms and the London-based radicals known to history as the "Levellers."[64] Yet however much Cromwell and his peers in the army may have used the popular energies unleashed by agitators and Levellers to their own purposes in their struggle with the king in the late 1640s, there is no evidence that Cromwell (as a lesser East Anglian gentleman himself) ever viewed his victorious army as an engine of general sociopolitical revolution in a *modern* sense. Even the urban-based Levellers, no matter how advanced some of their political and economic notions might have been, had (in the words of G. E. Aylmer) "little to offer the landless peasants, or those whose holdings were simply too small for them to subsist upon."[65] It is surely obvious, then, that even in the days leading to the regicide of 1649, the politics of *social advocacy* in the English Revolution were severely limited at the very best.

In the French Revolution, the dialectic between warfare abroad and the struggle for power at home involved *two successive legislatures* (the Legislative Assembly and National Convention) during 1791–3. In the short-lived Legislative Assembly (1791–2), the primary factions battling for supremacy were the "Feuillants" and the "Brissotins." In essence, the Feuillants (Duport, Barnave, Alexandre de Lameth, etc.) held the initiative early on in the new legislature but could not maintain their colleagues' support for a centrist policy of irenic constitutional royalism. However much this policy was sabotaged from the beginning by the king's and queen's intrigues, and by the obstructionism of the Far Right in the Assembly, it was undermined just as much by dissension among the Feuillants themselves. In particular, the flamboyant Marquis de Lafayette, trying to preserve royal authority (and his own prestige), fatefully endorsed a growing move toward jettisoning the 1756 Austrian alliance and—possibly—going to war with Vienna.[66] But the most formidable threat to Feuillant moderation came from the partisans of J.-P. Brissot on the Left. For Brissot and his cronies, consummating what they regarded as an "incomplete" revolution neatly involved their own accession to power, and achieving both of these objectives meant overthrowing the Feuillant ministers by raising a national demand for war with the Austrians. In this design the Brissotins (helped along by others) were successful: by April 1792 both king and Assembly were stampeded into a declaration of war against Vienna.[67] But if Brissot had been clever enough to use his fellow deputies' patriotism to further his own agenda in 1791–2, he failed to anticipate how the wages of war would require ever more centralization of government and a concomitant democratization of politics at Paris and in the provinces. In the end, it was the "Montagnard" faction of Jacobins, closely associated with politicians like Maximilien Robespierre in the popularly elected Convention during 1792 and 1793, who profited from Brissotin (Girondist) mismanagement of the war effort (and from Brissot's ruinous attempts to save the life of a "treasonous" Louis XVI put on trial in the newly declared Republic) to assume power during the most advanced period of the Revolution.[68] In the popular *journées* of May 31–June 2, 1793, just four months after the execution (January 21, 1793) of Louis XVI, the Jacobins came to power by purging most Girondists from the government.

Regarding the élitist advocacy of plebeian interests in revolutionary France, we *do* find, not only a growing degree of *military meritocracy* far exceeding what we encountered in the case of England, but also—at least for some time—a deliberate élitist outreach to middle and lower strata of society largely lacking in England's less cataclysmic upheaval. In the case of the army, the compelling need to replace aristocratic (*émigré*) officers meant new opportunities for thwarted NCOs, soldiers of fortune, ambitious provincial nobles, and commoners with heretofore limited military experience. Again, with the famous *levée en masse* of August 23, 1793 came the massive reality of conscription, and a plethora of reforms designed to secure soldiers' adherence to the new Republic.[69] Then, there was the alliance struck for a time between politicians contending for power in Paris and other towns and the artisanal *sans-culottes* (analogous in some respects to revolutionary England's Levellers); this led to a variety of unprecedented reforms. For instance, the abolition of the distinction between "active" and "passive" citizens extended voting to most (male) *domiciliés* over the age of twenty-five; legislation of August 1792 and July 1793 abrogated the seigneurial regime which had oppressed the French peasantry for centuries; the deputies outlawed the hoarding of "necessities," requisitioned grain for Paris, and eventually passed the *Maximum général* (price controls) on a wide range of commodities; and (most relevantly for us) the deputies accorded new rights to women in some marital and familial areas of the law.[70] Still, wartime expediency, for all of this, lurked behind a lot of the "altruism" on these (and other) matters. Even in revolutionary times, France's leaders were not about to throw over socioeconomic interests anchored in existing relations of property holding and production; nor were most *men* about to surrender too many rights anchored in patriarchal relationships that had prevailed since time out of mind. Yet *some* of the reforms promulgated in these perilous times *did* prove to be lasting; admittedly, therefore, the process of radicalization in France did give a new meaning to the revolutionary phrase "politics of social advocacy."

In the Russian Revolution, the dialectic between the waging of war and the struggle for power at home proved (as in the earlier upheavals) to be politically decisive. In this case, of course, the military storm in which the moderate revolutionaries were caught up had been raging for several years and had already swept from power both the old regime's last monarch and the first group of his successors. All scholarly analysis today suggests that the moderates who desperately strove to control the destabilizing forces unleashed by revolution in Russia from very early May until late October 1917 were so hopelessly ensnared in a web of diplomatic and domestic contradictions as to make their eventual ouster by more single-minded extremists a virtual certainty. More specifically: Tsereteli, Kerensky, Tereshchenko, Lvov, Chernov, and the others wanted simultaneously to promote peace through a Stockholm conference—the "soviet policy"—and to seek a revision of Allied war aims via traditional diplomatic channels—the official government policy.[71] They were, in the end, frustrated on both of these fronts. As the year wore on, one "Coalition Government" gave way to another as these liberals and moderate socialists failed to extract spent, bleeding Russia from a war increasingly viewed both within military ranks *and* behind the lines as subordinating Russian needs to those of the Western Powers. Discernible signposts of radicalization along the way included Kerensky's disastrous "June Offensive" against the Central Powers, the (premature) "July Days" at Petrograd, General Lavr Kornilov's abortive right-wing *coup* in late August, and the Bolsheviks' capture soon thereafter of the strategically situated soviets in both Petrograd and Moscow.[72] By September and early October, Kerensky's Third Coalition Government, cobbled together in haste, was increasingly discredited abroad and isolated at home. By late October, it was largely yielding control of the Petrograd military garrison to the so-called Military Revolutionary Committee (MRC)—and, as Orlando Figes has observed, it was this body that *institutionally* made the Bolshevik insurrection-to-come possible.[73] On October 24–25, 1917, Lenin persuaded the effective radical majority in the Second All-Russian Congress of Soviets to declare the Provisional Government defunct and to sanction the formation of a new, all-Bolshevik government (*Sovnarkom*) in the capital. Radicalization in Russia, as earlier in England and France, had triumphed.

In the case of Russia, we may have to abandon the term "politics of social advocacy" altogether (unless we apply it to the surging Bolsheviks!) and stress instead how the soldiers and sailors, workers, and peasants seized the initiative from the moderate leaders in this deepening revolution during 1917. The galling inability of the Provisional Government to extricate the country from the world war, and to tackle domestic issues by convening its long-promised Constituent Assembly, permitted radicalization in military, proletarian, and peasant ranks to proceed apace. As the year dragged on, polarization in the army between élitist officers and soldiers' committeemen, on the one hand, and rank-and-file troops, on the other, intensified. For the average troops of the line, craving peace, the Revolution promised a new distribution of lands back home, a process of distributive justice in which these peasants/soldiers ached to participate. Expectations were every bit as revolutionary among the peasant/sailors in naval ranks, at Kronstadt and elsewhere.[74] Then, again, soldiers and workers often mobilized together in the country's factories, mills, and mines as 1917 wore on. They came to focus their conspiratorial anxieties (and, of course, their waxing sense of socioeconomic injustice) on Russia's "bourgeois" industrialists, managers, foremen, and technicians—especially in the wake of Kerensky's failed "June Offensive" and the Kornilov Affair in August.[75] Meanwhile, a parallel process of radicalization was taking place on an even vaster scale in rural Russia. Here, "the collapse of the old authorities, and the new government's inability to create a viable new administrative structure in their place, left a vacuum which the peasants themselves . . . made haste to fill." As John Keep and others have convincingly argued, this led, not only to the many violent scenes of peasant expropriation of isolated and powerless gentry so often detailed in textbooks, but—even more dangerously to the authorities—to a withdrawal of peasant produce from urban and military markets.[76] Ultimately, then, the structural "disconnect" between the urban/consuming and rural/producing economies would help to sink Kerensky and Company in 1917 much as it had already helped to doom Nicholas II and his ineffectual ministers at the start of that same year.

What this brief summary of revolutionary radicalization may leave us with, above all, is a visceral sense of impending tragedy in all three of these upheavals—the tragedy of popular aspirations about to be (at best) very fleetingly acknowledged, but then shattered irrevocably upon the jagged rocks of harsh new Terrorist (and post-Terrorist) realities.

Reigns of "Terror and Virtue"

In his pioneering comparative analysis of the three great European revolutions, Crane Brinton spoke of their climactic "reigns of terror and virtue" as being characterized by a "set of variables . . . all woven together in a complicated pattern of reality." Especially salient factors in this "set of variables," according to Brinton, were, as follows: the "habit of violence" in countries "conditioned" by history "to expect the unexpected"; the "pressure of a foreign and civil war"; an "acute economic crisis"; a "class struggle" manifesting itself in one fashion or another; an ideological belief system, whether spiritual or secular in nature; the "jamming" of untested governmental machinery in the hands of impatient and authoritarian leaders; and, finally, the increasingly lethal competition for power waged by these rather extraordinary individuals. In all of this (and in keeping with much of the sociological writing of the early twentieth century), Brinton continually played up the notion of elements "in constant interaction one with another, a change in one effecting complex corresponding changes in all the others, and hence in the total situation."[77]

Although wondering—inevitably—whether Crane Brinton, if writing today rather than in the late 1930s, would approach this subject at all differently, we will summarize these especially critical phases of the English, French, and Russian Revolutions against the (by now) familiar backdrop of historiography currently caught between "structuralist" or state-oriented interpretations of terror and "postmodernist" interpretations stressing political culture, psychology, and the laboring masses (most relevantly for us, women). In the former connection, we sum up state-sanctioned campaigns of terror in these upheavals as responding, chiefly, if not exclusively, to *circumstances*—that is, to interrelated external and internal threats to the rule of Independents, Jacobins, and Bolsheviks, respectively.[78] In the latter connection, we observe that revolutionary climacterics in England, France, and Russia left in their wake legions of disillusioned ultra-radical men and women, to some extent on the Right but most poignantly on the Left—from Levellers, agitators, and Puritan "saints" in England to Parisian *enragés* and *Hébertistes* in France to soldiers, sailors, workers, and peasants in Russia.

It is certainly arguable that the English Commonwealth, during 1649–53, had to defend itself as ruthlessly against all comers, domestic and foreign, as would French and Russian terrorists in the later revolutions—even if (unlike the Jacobins and Bolsheviks) the Cromwellians never actually *theorized* their "terror." Ronald Hutton has noted that, in the wake of Charles I's execution in January 1649, "Scotland was passively, and most of Ireland actively, hostile. The royalists still held privateer bases in the Scilly Isles, Jersey and the Isle of Man, and a powerful fleet operating out of Irish ports. Not a single foreign state came forward to recognize the Commonwealth, and most were shocked by the unprecedented act of the King's execution."[79] Charles I's eldest son, immediately styling himself "Charles II," would for the next decade serve as a rallying point for pro-Stuart conspiracies interweaving, at intervals, all varieties of dramatic events within and beyond English borders.[80] Indeed, in a manner adumbrating what would transpire later on in revolutionary France and Russia, events *outside of* revolutionary England interacted dangerously with political developments *within* the newly established republic. To begin with, the new government's decision to mobilize militarily against the Irish in 1649 revived Leveller agitation in a New Model Army still unhappy over its arrears of pay and over many other issues as well; the upshot was the crushing (in May) of the last in a series of military mutinies at Burford in Oxfordshire.[81] Then, again, the New Model Army's need to move against the Scots the following year reflected the geostrategic issue of links between the Presbyterians at Edinburgh, who deplored the alleged lack of ecclesiastical discipline and growth of sectarianism in England, and English Presbyterians, whether in parliamentary or merchant careers. This matter would only be settled definitively on the battlefield at Worcester (in September of 1651).[82] Finally, the resolution of Henrietta Maria, Charles II, and other royalist exiles flocking together in France and the Low Countries to overthrow the Commonwealth and thus avenge Charles I's execution meant further international and domestic headaches for Oliver Cromwell and his comrades. The result, unsurprisingly, was that Cromwell and all others charged with defending the Commonwealth resorted at times to acts of what later revolutionaries would formally theorize as revolutionary "terror."[83]

At the same time, these turbulent years elicited from humble Englishmen and Englishwomen an array of complaints concerning the tribulations in their daily lives. John Lilburne and the other Levellers, for instance, having already risen to prominence by proposing radical reforms in the late Civil War days, returned to the attack in the aftermath of the 1649 regicide by launching a series of increasingly strident attacks upon the institutions of the Commonwealth. Most dangerous were their pamphlet indictments of Cromwell's New Model Army. Taking the side of army "agitators," Lilburne and Company insisted (in Ian Gentles's words) that "the soldiers must have the uninhibited right to petition parliament, while the exercise of martial law must be sharply curtailed. Officers and men were to be on an equal footing. . . . indeed, it was the soldiers who were the essential part of the army, the officers being 'but the form or letter.' The soldiers therefore had the right to control and overthrow the officers if they threatened their life, liberty, or freedom." This was truly, Gentles has written, "a quixotic and inherently anarchistic vision of the army."[84] Again, radicals *within* army ranks were simultaneously petitioning the Rump Parliament with their own grievances. To the standard litany of complaints about arrears of pay and other professional issues they added a Leveller-like call for the abolition of tithes, liberty of conscience, freeing of prisoners for debt, and relaxation of the existing code of martial law, and they invoked as well the cause of "the poor of this nation, whose miseries cry aloud in our ears for redress."[85] Crackdowns on such agitation, however, led to even more remarkable actions, including proclamations of "gender equality" framed in strikingly modern terms by hundreds of *women* also mobilized to petition the Rump Parliament about the more conventional socioeconomic issues.[86] Yet although the regime in the end had little trouble in suppressing male (and female) revolutionary ferment such as this, the Cromwellians were further embarrassed (in the July–December 1653 sessions of the so-called "Barebones Parliament") by calls from "respectable" Englishmen for such reforms as ending tithes and lay patronage to churchly livings, codification of English law, and abolition of the court of Chancery.[87] And along with all of this *secular* agitation came the millenarian preaching of innumerable sectarian groups in society.[88]

In the case of France, the external and internal pressures menacing the Revolution were of an even greater magnitude and intensity. In hindsight, they seem to have reached their apogee in the late summer and fall of 1793. On the international front, Britain and Austria, abetted by other members of what was becoming the "First Coalition," appeared to be closing in on the revolutionaries. In August, in fact, Vienna's seasoned diplomat Florimund Mercy-Argenteau argued that the time had come for a final assault on France, as the Republic's institutions had by now been so gravely weakened.[89] In the same month, the key Mediterranean port of Toulon fell to the British; moreover, Prime Minister William Pitt's naval forces were simultaneously threatening France's other coasts. (At London, as at Vienna, war was a policy grounded in hard-nosed considerations of national security experienced in ideological as well as in strategic/territorial terms.[90]) For the embattled French, of course, the coordinated campaign of the British and Austrians posed an all-absorbing threat; and this threat was all the more pressing in that, by this time, it appeared also to be catching up *domestic insurrection* in its toils. In Normandy and Brittany to the northwest, in the Vendée to the west, and in many provincial regions of the South wracked by "federalism," the Republic's Jacobin leaders felt they were fending off a counterrevolutionary assault encouraged and in some measure aided by the First Coalition states.[91] Yet if the *general* question in these areas of provincial France was one of rallying to or rejecting unprecedented statist interference in people's daily lives, the *specific* issue providing the cutting edge to the debate (because it involved by late 1793 the *very survival* of the Revolution) was the issue of *war*. "In practical terms," P. M. Jones has flatly concluded, "it was the war emergency consequent on the formation of the First Coalition . . . that brought the Terror to every peasant's doorstep."[92] As we all know today, the French responded to all of this with the Jacobin Terror of 1793–4. The Terror (Richard T. Bienvenu has held) began in earnest only on September 5, 1793, when the beleaguered National Convention, reacting to circumstances, declared "that punishment and coercion were to be the sole policy of the government toward its enemies." This likely was, indeed, "the psychological turning point in the evolution of the Terror" as national policy.[93]

And, in the case of France as in that of England, only to a much greater extent, the outbreak of statist terror was accompanied by a groundswell of popular activism—some (but not all) of it endorsed by the embattled Jacobin leadership. Even as the Girondists and Jacobins were locked in their death struggle in the Convention in early 1793, for instance, a loosely assembled "*enragé* party" of Parisian radicals—including, most notably, Jacques Roux, Théophile Leclerc, Jean Varlet, Pauline Léon, and Claire Lacombe—championed a program summed up by R. B. Rose: "the rigorous repression of food-hoarding and money speculation by legislation and intimidation; the intensification of . . . political Terror against . . . counter-revolutionaries, and against the potentially counter-revolutionary classes of aristocrats, priests, and bourgeois; and a purge of the 'counter-revolutionary classes' from the army and the administration in favor of patriotic sans-culottes."[94] The alliance at this time between *male* and *female* radicals was notably striking: both Pauline Léon and Claire Lacombe, for example, as *enragées* and as members of the Parisian Society of Revolutionary Republican Women, repeatedly petitioned the ruling Convention for implementation of political and economic Terror.[95] Although the *enragés* found their energy (and some of their program) coopted in coming months by the consolidating Robespierrist regime, a revival of the popular movement briefly challenged the Jacobin government in 1794. Still, its leaders—J.- R. Hébert, A. F. Momoro, C.-P. Ronsin, F. N. Vincent, P. G. Chaumette, and so on—were, essentially, "men without ideas, living by mere confusion. They had no solution for the economic crisis on which they thrived."[96] Indeed, even those historians sympathetic to the overall *sans-culotte* movement in revolutionary France have conceded that, in the end, it succumbed as much to internal political, economic, and *gendered* contradictions as it did to a Robespierrist and post-Robespierrist government increasingly eager, once it had defeated the First Coalition, to get back to legislative and economic "business-as-usual."[97] That government, to be sure, had—under the pressure of the war emergency of 1793. . .4—granted far more in the way of socioeconomic concessions to laboring Frenchmen and Frenchwomen than had ever been granted by the Cromwellians to their English subjects; still, the end result was that "the Revolutionary Government [in France] had no intention of driving the "aristocracy of merchants" from the state which it was laboring to establish."[98]

As for the Bolsheviks from 1917 to 1921: they, too, confronted a major international/domestic emergency. The cataclysm within Russia itself, David Foglesong has aptly written, was but part of "an international struggle . . . in which not only Russians and Ukrainians but also Latvians, Estonians, Czechs, Germans, Americans and many other nationalities fought and died; a war waged not only behind the lines in Russia but also in the parliaments and streets of foreign countries; a struggle between Reds and Whites not only to mobilize the bodies and sympathies of Russian peasants but also to win the hearts and open the purses of foreign sympathizers." The *immediate* background to events in Russia was, of course, the war of 1914–18, which (again quoting Foglesong) had originated in part in "the global rivalry of European powers for territory, markets, natural resources and political dominance."[99] For Russia, the results of involvement in this war were disastrous: defeated on the Eastern Front by Imperial Germany, it lost (under the Carthaginian treaty of Brest-Litovsk) 34 percent of its population, 32 percent of its arable lands, 54 percent of its "industrial undertakings," and—amazingly—89 percent of its coal capacity![100] But even worse, perhaps, the Western Powers, still engaged in the struggle with Berlin and its allies, tried desperately to intervene in (now Soviet) Russia— initially for *geostrategic* reasons, to restore the eastern military front against the Central Powers, but also for *ideological*, anti-Bolshevik reasons. The upshot of all of this was that, by August 1918, the Bolsheviks' situation seemed as desperate as that of the Jacobins had been in August 1793. Lenin and his comrades were caught between still-dangerous German forces in western Russia and British, French, American, Japanese, and Czech forces gathering just about everywhere else.[101] Again, foreign and domestic threats to revolutionary governance interacted as perilously in Russia as they had previously in England and France. In this case, Left Socialist Revolutionary (SR) insurrection and peasant uprisings on the Volga and elsewhere in the provinces especially seemed to jeopardize the Bolsheviks' already tenuous hold on power.[102] In response, Lenin and his comrades, assuming (in what we might call Robespierrist fashion) a nefarious collusion between foreign and domestic enemies of the revolutionary cause, unleashed the soon-to-be-dreaded brigades of Felix Dzerzhinskii's *Cheka* upon all those in Russian society deemed to be suspect in Communist eyes. The Red Terror of 1918–21 was the result.[103]

Moreover, in Russia, as earlier in England and France, the revolutionary climacteric was marked by agitation—and subsequent disillusionment—on the Far Left. Probably the most spectacular revolt against the Bolsheviks' (or Communists') ever-tightening rule was the massive uprising of "sovietized" sailors at Kronstadt in March 1921; it capped several years of growing unrest among far leftist SRs and Bolsheviks, workers, peasants, and military men, and forced upon Lenin an agonizing reappraisal of his entire revolutionary strategy.[104] The Left SRs had long since been alienated both by Lenin's (reluctant) decision to make peace with Imperial Germany and by his stance on a variety of domestic issues.[105] As for ultra-leftists within Lenin's own Bolshevik (or Communist) Party, they challenged what was rapidly becoming Party orthodoxy on a variety of issues. Most germane for our purposes is the key role played in the ultra-leftist Bolshevik faction known as the "Workers' Opposition" by radical feminist Aleksandra Kollontai. In 1920, Kollontai coalesced with Aleksandr Shliapnikov, S. P. Medvedev, and other idealists to champion trade unionists and other proletarian elements within the new Soviet state; still, she is best known to posterity for her advocacy of Russian women's issues over the years.[106] But possibly the most vexing challenge to Bolshevik rule in the "terror" phase of the Russian Revolution came from "ordinary" men and women of the laboring classes. At Moscow, Petrograd, and in the other metropoles of Soviet Russia, workers striking over increasingly desperate economic conditions—conditions only exacerbated by the new government's disastrous "War Communism" policies—were, in the end, controlled with a combination of judicious concessions, threats, and (where necessary) outright military suppression.[107] But it was above all in the countryside where the Bolsheviks, as doctrinaire Marxists out of touch with the solidarities and complexities of age-old peasant society, found themselves opposed on a wide array of issues. "By the autumn of 1920," Orlando Figes has written, "the whole of the country was inflamed with peasant wars."[108] Ultimately, the peasants (much like the workers, for that matter) were not only protesting economic hardships but also bridling against Communist rule. Finally, the desire for *genuine* and not merely formulaic "Soviet democracy," embraced with deadly seriousness at the Kronstadt naval base on the Gulf of Finland by sailors and other elements of local society, led (in March of 1921) to an uprising that the affrighted Soviet authorities put down with what we can only call sickening ferocity.[109]

Summing up these "reigns of terror and virtue" in England, France, and Russia leaves us with a sense of revolutionary leaders determined (when necessary) to lash out ruthlessly against foreign and domestic adversaries but also with a sense of tragic *ruptures* between élitist politicians (Cromwellians, Robespierrists, Leninists) and their erstwhile ultra-leftist supporters claiming to represent the masses. Our logical next step will be to touch upon the ways in which the politicians, activists, and just ordinary folk who survived their countries' most lethal days of revolution managed the challenges they inevitably inherited from those dangerous—if, at their best, inspirational—times.

"Thermidor" in the Three Revolutions

Even trying to summarize briefly the final (Thermidorian) phases of the three classic European revolutions can immediately involve us in controversies and contradictions. There is, to begin with, the simple question: how to define "Thermidor"? Periodization may not be too much of a problem in the English and French cases: we can easily enough agree that revolution in England ended with the Stuart Restoration of May 1660, that it ended in France with the Bonapartist *coup* of November 1799, and, hence, that Thermidor in these two cases coincided roughly with the English Protectorate of the late 1650s and the French Directory of the late 1790s. In the Russian case, however, things are a bit more complicated: whereas Robert V. Daniels equated Thermidor with the "New Economic Policy" era of the 1920s, his colleague Sheila Fitzpatrick has regarded it as more a phenomenon of the 1930s than of the 1920s.[110] For the sake of argument, we will accept Daniels's periodization, seeing, as he did (and, indeed, as Crane Brinton customarily did), a Russian Thermidor extending from 1921 to 1928 or even 1929.

But beyond the issue of *defining* Thermidor, there is the more substantive question of how best to understand its complexities and contradictions in its actual English, French, and Russian revolutionary settings. We will address this matter on the next few pages by depicting Thermidor, first, as a reaction against the immediately preceding phase of statist "terror," and, second, as an attempt—unsuccessful or successful, depending upon the specific country in question—to overcome a *crisis of governmental legitimacy* in the twilight stage of revolution.

We start here with the French, for whom "Thermidor" still signifies the month (July to August 1794) during which the Robespierrists fell from power. Certainly the "Thermidorian Reaction" in this country took on many political, economic, and social guises.[111] After the Robespierrists' downfall, the Convention took critical steps to reverse what it now saw as a dangerous overconcentration of power in the executive agencies of government. Those agencies were purged; the notorious Revolutionary Tribunal at Paris (and its provincial counterparts) were significantly weakened; thousands of prisoners were released in the capital and in provincial communities; the Paris Jacobin Club and its sister societies in all local venues were hobbled or silenced altogether; and those designated as "notorious terrorists" who had survived Robespierre and his closest confidants were marked out for prosecution. And along with drastic relaxation of the political Terror came relaxation of the economic terror and a pronounced shift in social "manners and mores."[112] In the former connection, the deputies eventually abolished the *Maximum général* (price and wage controls), lifted restrictions on trade, closed down the armaments workshops in the capital, winked at speculation and hoarding, and did little or nothing to prevent the debasement of the paper currency (*assignats* and *mandats territoriaux*). In the latter connection, we can just as easily point to dramatic signs of the post-terror times.[113] To begin with, the massive prison releases in the wake of 9 Thermidor meant the recirculation, in "polite" society, of many nobles and affluent bourgeois whose thoughts (naturally enough) turned to class vengeance, including outright political thuggery. The Thermidorian Reaction at Paris was threateningly personified in the *jeunesse dorée* ("Gilded Youth")— dandyish toughs who beat up Jacobins, harassed other ex-revolutionaries, and rejected the whole culture of Spartan modesty and simplicity hitherto associated with the Terror.[114] But, arguably, the shift in "manners and mores" was most revealingly reflected in the contradictory roles of women, both at Paris and in the provinces. While Thérèse Cabarrus might set fashions at Paris for the pampered *nouvelles riches* of the post-Robespierrist era, hundreds of her less fortunate sisters (at Paris and in provincial France) were beggared by hoarding, speculation, and inflation, ever more restricted in their political activism, and formally denied familial rights by legists tacking to the Right in this period. Meanwhile, women in rural localities, Olwen Hufton has argued, wanted above all "a warm, comforting, personal and familial religion . . which endorsed the family . . . and gave the hope of salvation through Christian burial of the dead."[115] Such, then, were the myriad forms of reaction in post-Terror France.

More fundamentally, however, the Directory (1795–9) never really secured total acceptance in what should have been its key middle-class constituencies.[116] Its financial policies alienated its creditors, military and civilian pensioners, government employees, and ever-influential *rentiers*; its eternal warring with London cost it the support of shipbuilders, insurances agents, merchants, and refiners stifled by the British blockade; its recourse to massive military conscription sowed widespread fear and hatred among young men in the provinces; and its increasingly intolerant stance toward Catholicism could only turn away the (traditionally Catholic) masses. Though there may have been a final, dramatic efflorescence of leftist political enthusiasm in 1799 due to the crisis of the War of the Second Coalition, changes in the ruling personnel of the Directory—above all, the elevation to executive power of the abbé Emmanuel Joseph Sieyès, still celebrated for his crucial role in the early days of the Revolution—pointed to a basic revision of constitutional arrangements in France.[117] Early in the Revolution, observers as ideologically dissimilar as Edmund Burke and Maximilien Robespierre had foreseen the possibility of a military finale to this upheaval. Napoleon himself may not have been inevitable; yet, given all that had occurred up to this point in revolutionary France, someone very much like him was, by this time, unlikely to be avoided. In the final analysis, the Thermidorian years in France were years of failed governmental *legitimacy*.

We can draw a like picture for Protectoral England, even if the Thermidorian Reaction was not, in this case, quite as clear-cut a phenomenon as it would be later in France. Many a conservative, Austin Woolrych suggested, "must have found it comforting that the constitutional balance between Protector, Council of State, and parliament" called for in the wake of the "Barebones" fiasco "bore a recognizable resemblance to the old trinity of king, privy council, and parliament"; and many others were "relieved that the ancient common law of England was no longer under threat."[118] Moreover, the purgative and prosecutorial aspects of the 1649–53 Commonwealth were toned down, if not altogether eliminated. "In fact," Woolrych conceded, "there were . . . remarkably few political prisoners under the Protectorate . . . no one suffered death for a political offence unless he planned or engaged in armed rebellion or conspired to assassinate Cromwell."[119] Again, no loyalty pledge for administrative, judicial, and clerical personnel was established to replace the old 1649 "Engagement" of loyalty to the Commonwealth. It is also true that something of a *social* reaction set in with the dissolution of "Barebones" in December 1653. It was undeniable, one of Cromwell's biographers has held, that the great man "as Protector often looked and acted like a king." The Protectoral Court soon took on the ceremonial trappings of royalty; the Protector himself came to be addressed as "Your Highness" by English courtiers and European ambassadors alike; and by 1656 (if not before), people were slipping into the old habit of referring to the Council of State as the "Privy Council."[120] Meanwhile, in London society at large, Christopher Hill has written, "the oligarchy came back to power. . . . John Evelyn first saw women painting themselves in May 1654; by August of that year it even seemed safe to address a bishop by his title, 'the times now being more open.'" Yet at the same time, for plebeian subjects "the excise was extended to many hitherto untaxed objects of popular consumption."

The poor complained bitterly but (of course) in vain.[121] The scandalous fashions and *mores* of Restoration society (and the associated degradation of women's status, especially in "polite" society) had not yet settled in; but they were, in some respects, prefigured in the late 1650s.

Moreover, in England as in France later, those Thermidorian years of revolution were years of squandered opportunities for state legitimacy. We can see, today, that Oliver Cromwell had, from late 1653 until his death in September 1658, three realistic chances to make his government acceptable in the eyes of the gentry, the "natural rulers" in mid-seventeenth-century England. Those opportunities were available to him in connection with the First Protectorate Parliament (1654–5), the major generals (1655–7), and the Second Protectorate Parliament (1657–8). Yet Cromwell failed to legitimize his rule in all three of these situations. Roger Howell explained something of this when, in reviewing *the role of the army* in this era, he wrote that "the weapon that had won the revolutionary war made the peaceful settlement of it impossible." So long as the army could intrude into the Protectorate's domestic politics, Howell said, "it both stood in the way of the legitimation of the government via the parliamentary route and heightened the level of the politics of frustration and confrontation within Parliament itself."[122] A similar conclusion, with its stress on the delegitimizing role of the New Model Army, has been drawn by most Cromwellian biographers. Peter Gaunt spoke for most of them: however generously he credited Oliver with "doing God's will" as best he comprehended it and with "working for the greater good of the nation and its people," Gaunt could not, in the end, avoid the harsh conclusion that "the Protector and his entire regime were always an imposition, ultimately surviving only through army backing."[123] Again, historians such as David Smith and Patrick Little who have studied the relationship between *both* Oliver and his son Richard Cromwell and the people's representatives at Westminster Palace have essentially come up with the same conclusion—as has Christopher Durston, the most recent specialist writing on the experiment involving the major generals.[124] If, then, the Directors in Thermidorian France forfeited the support of what should have been their essential constituencies in "bourgeois" ranks of society, the Protectoral regime in late-revolutionary England, by the same token, could not overcome the resistance of the (largely genteel) "natural rulers" to its provocative and unprecedented mix of fiscally oppressive militarism and heterodox ecclesiology.

Finally, there is the Russian Thermidor of the 1920s—and here, in some respects, we may have a revolutionary finale plowing *truly new ground*. In the first place, the reaction against Terror in Soviet Russia occurred mainly in economic and social spheres, and *not* in *politics* or *government*. Thermidor in this country, that is, was much more *schizophrenic* than it had been in England and France, much more sharply *split* between a theorized *tactical retreat* in economics and in society, on the one hand, and an ongoing *strategic advance* toward totalitarian *politics*, on the other. In this latter connection, decisions were taken at the Tenth Bolshevik Party Congress in Moscow in 1921 to ban the Workers' Opposition and all other "deviations" within the Party and to ensure the concentration of power *within* Bolshevik ranks—starting with the Central Committee and its more specialized subcommittees (the Politburo, the Orgboro, and the Central Control Commission).[125] Stalin, of course, would be the major beneficiary of all of this—in the wake of Lenin's premature death in January 1924. Yet, at the same time, a reaction *against* the Bolshevik Terror of 1918–21 surely *did* occur in nonpolitical areas. Most obviously, the New Economic Policy (NEP), a temporary (?) retreat from the requisitions, quotas, and emergency measures of "War Communism," gave Russians a "breathing spell" in their historic march toward a fully socialized economy and society; as part of the effort to restore productivity to the economy, the NEP replaced the wartime requisitioning of agriculture with a tax in kind, and tolerated (at levels below the "commanding heights" of the economy) the revival of free exchanges of goods and services between the city and the countryside.[126] Then, again, we find in society at large the same extremes of wealth and poverty (and the same post-Terror pressures placed upon women) that we have encountered in the earlier instances of Thermidor. At one extreme were the "Nepmen," middlemen profiting from the exchanges between city and countryside: they were "a walking symbol of this new and ugly capitalism," men who "dressed their wives and mistresses in diamonds and furs" and "drove around in huge imported cars."[127] At the other extreme were "men, women and children with pinched faces and hungry eyes" who "stood about gazing into the windows" of stores stocked with luxury goods that only Nepmen and their newly affluent ilk could afford.[128] And, as in the earlier Thermidors, so also in this one, *women* all too often bore the brunt of the new socioeconomic inequalities via unemployment, abandonment, and prostitution.[129]

But if Thermidor in the Russian Revolution meant a mixed verdict in political and socioeconomic affairs, at least for a time, it eventually conferred a certain *legitimacy* on late-revolutionary government that had eluded the French and English in *their* upheavals. After all, Lenin's successors in the NEP era had, in a sense, to look *beyond* NEP altogether: they had to engage in an acerbic debate over economic and developmental strategies reflecting both Russian insecurities in global affairs *and* growing domestic disillusionment in idealistic Communist Party ranks. The actual debate over issues of industrialization and over the "modernization" of Soviet Russia has, of course, been the subject of countless studies.[130] What we need specifically to underscore here, instead, is the fact that the leaders of the new Russia, casting about desperately for a secure *social base* for their ambitious plans to make their country more competitive in a perilous world, located that base, not in the already-decimated gentry and bourgeoisie, nor in the rural peasantry, but rather in a newly cast proletariat. These "young, committed workers," so Hiroaki Kuromiya has written, "were mainly young urban males who had experienced the revolution and the civil war in their teens or younger, first entered industrial work shortly after the revolution, and . . . had had several years of work experience and some skills by the late 1920s." These "new forces" pressed for ever higher tempos of production in the factories, exposed "class aliens" in the apparatus, and, "hopeful of tomorrow's gratification, endured today's difficulties." Such were the workers who, "dissatisfied with NEP ideologically, emotionally, and perhaps also materially," would come into their own as the primary *popular* advocates for Stalin and his modernizing adherents.[131] Sheila Fitzpatrick has interpreted this new phenomenon of Thermidorian legitimacy, Russian-style, somewhat more subtly—that is to say, in *cultural* and *psychological* as well as socioeconomic terms. By excoriating wealthy peasants (*"kulaks"*) and various "bourgeois elements," she has hypothesized, Stalin and his henchmen provided *Komsomol* (Communist youth) laborers and others with a way to *redefine* themselves, that is, to establish their own identities more securely in a world turned upside down by the recent storms of world war, revolution, and civil war.[132] And young women in particular, as we will demonstrate in detail later, would have a variety of significant roles to play in this process of the *popular legitimization of revolution*—even if (as we will also see) women *in general* were destined to manifest highly ambivalent attitudes toward new political, socioeconomic, and cultural realities in the early Soviet Russia of the 1920s.[133]

In conclusion: Chapter 2 has attempted to provide for those readers intrigued by the subject of women's experiences in the English, French, and Russian Revolutions a *sense of context*, an awareness of the broad sweep of events—and of institutional developments—to which women in various stations of life in these upheavals had to react. It has also endeavored to address the more specific concerns of those specialists in the field of revolutionary studies for whom issues of *process* remain as significant as questions of *causation* and *consequences*. In the chapters that follow, we move on to reconsider how some *specific women*—whether ensconced in the seats of power and privilege or *not* so empowered or privileged—responded to their revolutionary and postrevolutionary times.

3

Unsuccessful Consort Queens in the European Revolutions

Gender, Culture, and "Strategic Politics"

When historian Thomas Kaiser suggested that Marie-Antoinette's alleged "usurpation of power" in old regime France was *especially* resented "because it was undertaken to advance causes the French people found repugnant and threatening,"[1] he was, in a way, harkening back to basic tensions between structuralist and postmodernist interpretations of revolutionary change. By choosing, that is, to frame his argument with reference to the queen's role in *her adopted kingdom's foreign policy*, Kaiser was (if unknowingly) inviting us to revisit, in Chapter 3, the contentious question of the relative importance to be ascribed to *gendered/cultural* and *political* issues in the disastrous revolutionary careers of not only Marie-Antoinette but also English Queen Henrietta Maria and Russian Empress Alexandra Feodorovna. Whatever the tendency in feminist scholarship to emphasize the roles played by gender, religion, and sundry other cultural issues in these women's misfortunes, the pages that follow will develop a partial "counter-case" by demonstrating how strikingly Henrietta Maria's, Marie-Antoinette's, and Alexandra's ineptitude in matters of *strategic politics* contrasted with the pragmatic leadership displayed earlier in England, France, and Russia, respectively, by three uncommon stateswomen: that is, Elizabeth l, Cathérine de Médicis, and Catherine II ("the Great"). The purpose here would *not* be to deny the importance of gender and related aspects of culture, but rather to reassert the significance of *strategic politics* in the revolutionary equation—an equation involving, here, the woes of three monarchs' wives. By doing so, such a discussion may well reaffirm the relevance, in revolutionary analysis, of statist structuralism.

To be sure, there were discernible differences between so-called "queens regnant" (and *ruling* female regents) at the heart of state power in nonrevolutionary eras and "queens consort" subordinate to regally empowered husbands on the thresholds (and in the early stages) of full-fledged sociopolitical revolutions. We will briefly explore some of those differences immediately below; but we may suspect in advance that, in fact, those differences were somewhat overshadowed by the *strategic* roles of these highly situated (and highly visible) women in both nonrevolutionary *and* revolutionary situations. This should make it all the easier for us to draw *direct* and therefore useful comparisons between the queens regnant and queens consort introduced above, and thus in the end to underscore in structuralist fashion the *stunning policy-related failures* of Henrietta Maria, Marie-Antoinette, and Alexandra Feodorovna.

Queens Regnant and Queens Consort: A Distinction without Too Much Difference?

A Wikipedia entry differentiating between regnant queens and consort queens leaves us with something less than a clear-cut distinction between these two categories of powerful women. "A queen regnant," we are informed, is "a queen in her own right with all the powers of a monarch, who (usually) has become queen by inheriting the throne upon the death of the previous monarch." By contrast, we learn, "a queen consort" is merely "the wife of a reigning king" but "usually shares her husband's social rank and status. She holds the feminine equivalent of the king's monarchical titles, but historically, she does not share the king's political and military power." Nevertheless, at this point some qualifications begin to muddy the waters. "Often the queen consort of a deceased king (the dowager queen or queen mother) has served as regent if her child, the successor to the throne, [is] still a minor." Complicating matters still further, our Wikipedia entry goes on to affirm (quite accurately, we must allow) that "there have been many examples of queens consort being shrewd or ambitious stateswomen."[2]

According to this schema, three of the women introduced earlier—Henrietta Maria of England, Marie-Antoinette of France, and Alexandra Feodorovna of Russia—were undeniably consort queens (or, in one case, a consort empress). But what of their predecessors, Elizabeth l, Cathérine de Médicis, and Catherine II (i.e. "the Great")? There can be no question that the first and last of these individuals fully qualified as "regnant" monarchs—Catherine II in particular succeeding to an assassinated husband, Tsar Peter III. But what of Cathérine de Médicis? "Salic Law" in France incontrovertibly denied the status of a queen regnant to a "mere" woman.[3] Still, there is a burgeoning literature on female regents (and on queen mothers) in early modern France that, emphasizing as it does their historical significance, allows us to regard Cathérine de Médicis, as we would naturally regard Elizabeth I and Catherine the Great, as cardinally involved in state policymaking. Every historian of sixteenth-century France knows well that Cathérine de Médicis was a widowed queen mother for the last thirty years of her life, from July 1559 to January 1589, and also served as Regent of France during 1560–3 and (for a time) in 1574.[4] Thus, to review briefly here the scholarship on regents and queen mothers in the French ancien régime should help us to contextualize our later discussion of Cathérine's troubled, but significant, years in power.

Historians have naturally enough chosen to treat the "regency/queen mother question" from differing points of view. Fanny Cosandey, for instance, has stressed juridical aspects of the issue. "In the framework of a monarchy founded upon dynastic continuity," she has written, "the participation of a woman is absolutely necessary for monarchical operations." For if, "by virtue of the Salic Law, there can be no queen without a king, the opposite is equally true: no queen, no king, the transmission of the royal patrimony depending in the final analysis upon the wombs of these ladies." For Fanny Cosandey, therefore, "the maternal function of the royal spouse seems every bit as necessary as the warmaking prowess and political skills of those [male rulers] who have benefited exclusively from the statutory rules . . . governing access to the throne." As for *la régente* in particular: "she reinforces the State by her actions, but also helps it to wax in power by bringing to the crown her own political and cultural gifts."[5]

Meanwhile, other scholars have had other ways of historicizing female regents and queen mothers in France. Ironically, perhaps, Katherine Crawford did so by invoking an ill-fated consort queen—namely, Marie-Antoinette. After all, Crawford asserted, Louis XVI's spouse was someone "out of a past in which queen mothers could be regents, and regents kept the monarchy powerful." What Crawford referred to as the "competing collective imaginations born during the Revolution" attributed to Marie-Antoinette "the power of queen mothers past. The revolutionaries had to destroy the potent tradition that Marie-Antoinette represented. The modern Médicis had to be the last of her kind." Analogizing Cathérine de Médicis and Marie-Antoinette, therefore, testified to the lasting potency of regents and queen mothers in the French political imagination—even in times of revolution.[6] But if Crawford likened Cathérine to a future queen consort, Susan Doran likened her to a notable contemporary queen regnant. "The English State Papers," noted Doran, "make clear that Queen Elizabeth and her ambassadors took Cathérine very seriously indeed as a major political player, especially during the reigns of her younger sons, Charles IX and Henry III." In their missives to England, "Elizabeth's envoys reported time and again on Cathérine's informal power at court, and especially her influence over her sons." Though ambassadorial judgments at times "may have exaggerated Cathérine's role," allowed Doran, the envoys' reports "do demonstrate that she was treated in the English court as a figure who needed to be understood and courted."[7] Yet, significantly, historian Mack Holt had anticipated all of these scholarly assessments of Cathérine in 1986 when he concluded that, throughout the 1559–89 period, "the queen mother lurked behind the throne, attempting to provide the acumen and leadership that her sons so sadly lacked as monarchs."[8]

For our purposes, then, we can safely rank Cathérine de Médicis alongside England's Elizabeth I and Russia's Catherine II in this relatively exclusive "club" of female state decision-makers. We can also reiterate that consort queens, unlike queens regnant and regents/queen mothers, had (i.e., in terms of executive power) to defer to their husbands. Beyond these points, however, what do specialists on this subject tell us about the functions usually attributed to consort queens? Have such experts arrived at anything like a consensus on this question?

There does appear to be a developing consensus, at least in English historiography, that there was no wide "influence chasm" yawning between queens regnant and queens consort in early modern times. "In particular," Caroline Hibbard has maintained, "the nature of Elizabeth's political role as the final arbiter of policy has meant that the political influence of consorts is usually, and usually unfairly, derided." Rejecting as she has all purportedly "anachronistic views of what constituted the 'political,'" Hibbard has suggested that a "new paradigm" is starting to address the hitherto overlooked question of "the public import of apparently 'private' royal activities."[9] Indeed, if we are to believe Hibbard, the very nature of the (Caroline) court needs to be interrogated anew:

> The peacetime Caroline court before 1638 . . . can only partially be understood in terms of faction defined around policy. . . . Some of the structures of the court...deserve more attention: the court as marriage market, advancing dynasties and creating alliances; the court as a cosmopolitan site of consumption and display, where large resources are deployed and controlled; the court as the fount of honor, where there is constant jostling for the appointment, the "place," that carries both tangible and intangible rewards.

"In this perspective on the court," Hibbard concluded, "the consort's role would loom a great deal larger than it traditionally has."[10]

Several of Hibbard's colleagues have also dwelt upon the influence of early modern consort queens. Malcolm Smuts, for instance, has commented that Henrietta Maria, unfazed by the rude slings and arrows of misogyny and xenophobia, was "a woman who, like all powerful queen consorts, wielded [her] power through court networks that largely circumvented established institutions such as the Privy Council. Hers was a form of the politics of intimacy dependent on access and informal contacts rather than [on] formal decision making in the proper forums." In addition, Smuts insisted, the "permeable" nature of the seventeenth century's national borders—that is, borders over which *international* forces of dynasticism, confessional allegiance, aristocratic connection, and military recruitment practices could easily flow back and forth—produced a European world "within which women as well as men wielded significant power through their skill in managing human relationships."[11] Yet, again, Henrietta Maria's modern biographer, Michelle White, has even more carefully enumerated the queen consort's roles in early modern England. First, she must "produce a male heir, or, failing a son, a daughter." Second, she must ideally conform to "socially accepted female behavioral standards" by being "obedient, passive, submissive, chaste, pious, kind and deferential." Third, discharging her roles as social leader, she must exercise "a significant influence upon moral values, recreations, and tastes in the fine arts." Finally, according to White, a consort queen was expected to play "a formal, symbolic, and ritualistic role" at court, even while "staying out of the business of government." She did not hold "sovereign authority," in other words, even if she admittedly enjoyed something of a "special legal position."[12]

Yet whatever this last, dampening observation may have suggested, English consorts (assuredly including Henrietta Maria) found it difficult to remain altogether out of politics, whatever the strictures on their behavior might in theory be. Indeed, Michelle White herself conceded that during Charles I's "Personal Rule" (1629–40), his wife's "behind-the-scenes" role in helping to staff the court, and thereby exercise her powers of patronage, irritated Puritan observers of Stuart policies. "The trouble, as far as her [Puritan] detractors were concerned, was that the queen had overstepped . . . her proper bounds; the personal had been made political."[13] Moreover, Frances Dolan has even argued that Henrietta Maria's biological "fecundity" worked against her in Protestants' minds: "the birth of so many children" to this very militantly Catholic consort queen "advertised to the nation the extent of Charles's and Henrietta's intimacy," thereby underscoring yet again the queen's (at least potentially) threatening influence.[14]

But what of consort queens (or empresses) in the later cases of Bourbon France and Romanov Russia? Should we assume that, in the cases of Marie-Antoinette and Alexandra Feodorovna, *personal status* would *not* have its political implications, as it clearly did in the earlier case of Charles I's consort queen? Probably not, respond those who have most assiduously studied these two women. In part, of course, this was a *juridical* matter. Even without a prescribed political function, Fanny Cosandey would remind us, Marie-Antoinette shared in royal sovereignty as the king's consort and as the mother to the royal children in a monarchy "cast in dynastic terms."[15] But there was yet another aspect to the matter in this particular case. As Thomas Kaiser has noted, Louis XVI's unusual (for

France) decision *not* to take a mistress meant that, of necessity, his wife wound up performing both a mistress's customary role of "fashion- and taste-setting" *and* the more traditional role of wife-and-mother. Yet this likely made her appear to her multiplying critics as something of a political menace—all the more so in that the normal sites of her private life—such as the Trianon Palace at Versailles—conjured up for many contemporaries the specter of her native Habsburg Austria. And this in an era when, for those selfsame French subjects, their country had been humiliatingly "played" by Vienna for its own geopolitical purposes! Additionally, persistent (if unfounded) rumors concerning the queen's debauchery, as well as her involvement, even in the prerevolutionary years, in ministerial politics seemed to make her private life "far more politically threatening than that of recent queens."[16]

And if personal status held its potentially destabilizing political implications in the case of Louis XVI's consort queen, it most certainly did so as well in the case of Emperor Nicholas II's wife. Another way of putting this would be to say that Alexandra Feodorovna, while fulfilling the first two roles of consort deportment as defined by Michelle White— that is, those concerning "fecundity" and "pious, kind, and deferential" female behavior—did not fulfill the last two prescribed roles, those involving practices of sociocultural leadership and the avoidance of politics. On the one hand, Orlando Figes has written, Alexandra "gave the impression of resenting the public role which her position obliged her to play. She appeared only rarely at court and social functions and . . . [she] adopted a pose of reserve . . . which made her seem awkward and unsympathetic. She gained a reputation for coldness and hauteur, two very un-Russian vices." On the other hand, Figes has noted that, "in her bossy way," the ill-fated German-born Empress consort "set out to organize the state as if it was part of her personal household" and pushed her husband "this way and that according to her own ambitions, vanities, fears and jealousies." As this historian and countless biographers have ironically remarked, Alexandra liked to compare herself with Catherine II, whereas, in reality, "her role was much more reminiscent of Marie-Antoinette."[17]

A wealth of evidence, therefore, appears to justify two chief conclusions up to this point. First, we can without too much difficulty assimilate Cathérine de Médicis to the exclusive "society" of female policymakers that also included England's Elizabeth I and Russia's Catherine II; and yet, second, we can simultaneously point to sufficient *political* similarities between these three very powerful women and royal consorts like Henrietta Maria, Marie-Antoinette, and Alexandra Feodorovna to make comparisons between them (i.e., in each national case) meaningful and, thus, valuable.

Elizabeth I and the Ill-Conceived Revolutionary Statecraft of Henrietta Maria

Caroline Hibbard, as we recall, has argued that, because of Queen Elizabeth I's role as the "final arbiter of policy" in late sixteenth-century England, the political influence of consort queens has been "usually, and usually unfairly, derided."[18] Yet however this may be, it remains true that, in the realm of geopolitics and in the specific case of Charles I's spouse Henrietta Maria, comparisons between an earlier queen regnant and a seventeenth-century queen consort appear overwhelmingly to favor the former over the latter. This fact, admittedly, has not exempted Elizabeth I from the cut and thrust of academic debate, including feminist exchanges: on the one hand (for instance) historian Allison Heisch has seen in this Tudor queen an all-too-typical "token" woman who accepted "male notions of how the world was or should be organized," whereas Susan Bassnett has contrariwise eulogized Elizabeth as a role-model, as "a symbol of active female assertiveness for future generations."[19] For the moment, we may prefer the cautionary judgment of Elizabethan scholar Susan Doran, for whom "there has perhaps been too great a tendency in recent years to impose on the past a feminist perspective ... which judges [this monarch] by today's standards of political correctness."[20] But our paramount purpose here must still be to explain how Elizabeth I achieved the kind of success in international affairs that would elude Henrietta Maria (and, necessarily, her kingly husband) a half-century later.

Certainly England's geostrategic situation at the time of Elizabeth's accession in 1558 was far from enviable. European high politics were dominated then—as, indeed, they would be well into the next century—by the power struggle between the Austro-Spanish Habsburgs and the Valois, and later Bourbon, rulers of France.[21] Weaker states on the periphery of this vast continental struggle had, of necessity, to navigate between the warring Habsburgs and French without unduly antagonizing either of the parties—and this, at a time when all such states had also to deal with the unprecedented forces of polarization unleashed by the Protestant and Catholic Reformations. For Elizabeth in particular, this meant managing specific issues within the general framework set by English strategic interests. It may be "fashionable" in some quarters "to claim that Elizabeth had no foreign policy and merely reacted to the problems that beset her," Susan Doran has said, but—much like R. B. Wernham before her—she insisted that this was *not* in fact the case: "she did pursue consistent general aims and objectives and in this sense had a foreign policy." True, her goals were "primarily defensive and . . . she entertained no dreams of expansion in France, the Americas or the Indies." Hence, her defensive posture meant that Elizabeth I (in Doran's words) "was prepared to use force to keep the

French out of Scotland and the Spanish out of Ireland." Yet, always with a mind to prevent a joint invasion by the Catholic powers, the Queen "tried to keep on amicable terms with both France and Spain for as long as humanly possible; and when she quarrelled with the one [power] she made political overtures to the other [power]."[22] R. B. Wernham had anticipated Doran's analysis when (in 1980) he stressed how "Elizabeth had made use of the internal difficulties, political and religious, of both Spain and France in a way that had kept them both too preoccupied at home to risk adventures at home." Like Doran, Wernham marveled at how the queen had done this "without irritating" either power "into open hostility." She had "shaken off dependence upon either Spain or France and had brought both to seek her friendship."[23]

Yet the diplomatic situation on the Continent as viewed from London in those years was always worrisome, and indeed, as time went on, increasingly perilous. This was due above all, perhaps, to the way the religious passions fostered by the international warfare of Protestants and Catholics worked to transform politics *within* Habsburg Spain and Valois France, thus undermining the tenuous balance of power maintained between the two kingdoms. If Wallace T. MacCaffrey is to be believed in this connection, two transformations were at work here—one further consolidating Spanish power and the other severely weakening the French. Spain, once (under Charles V) little more than "a dynastic confederation ruled by a very peripatetic lord . . . not especially identified with any part of his scattered dominions" had, after 1556, become a "highly centralized . . . empire" ruled by Philip II, "the immobile bureaucrat at Madrid." But both this first "transformation," consolidating Spain, and the second one, dangerously weakening Valois France, had been helped along by the religious dynamic:

> The decisions of [the Council of] Trent had given to Catholicism a rigidly dogmatic definition. . . . Philip weighed in on the side of Catholic orthodoxy, not for merely . . . worldly considerations but as a principled believer. The second transformation was also a product of the Reformation; if revived Catholicism provided a focal point of principle for the Spanish monarchy, it was fatally divisive for the French kingdom. Here the Protestants were highly organized, both politically and militarily; the dynasty remained officially Catholic but its power to maintain national unity was eroding rapidly.

"For England," MacCaffrey concluded, "these changes posed awkward and painful choices."[24] By the early 1580s, to be specific, the queen and her advisers probably sensed that they might have to choose between intervention and nonintervention in European conflicts such as the burgeoning anti-Spanish revolt of the Dutch Netherlands and the internecine "civil wars of religion" heating up in Cathérine de Médicis's already imperiled France.

Although scholars (Charles Wilson among them[25]) have often criticized Elizabeth for her lack of consistency on English policies regarding such matters, it seems plain to most specialists today that she had complicated and ever-shifting realities to deal with. "Throughout these years," as Susan Doran has observed, "the dominant European problem was the Revolt of the Netherlands with its dual threat of an unconditional victory for Spain and expansionist opportunities for the French. Elizabeth and all her councillors recognized . . . that England's security depended on the freedom of the Netherlands from both Spanish military rule and French aggrandizement. The difficulty lay in establishing ways to prevent both these occurrences."[26] It was probably not the queen's fault that, in the end, circumstances forced her to intervene directly in the anti-Spanish turmoil in the Netherlands. This policy, which also entailed collaborating to a certain degree with Huguenot (i.e., Protestant) forces in a strife-torn and temporarily crippled France, would eventually precipitate war between Tudor England and Philip II's Spain.

Yet the Anglo-Spanish conflict dating from the late 1580s, caught up most often in the popular mind by England's "providential" defeat of Philip II's *Gran Armada* in 1588, has too often been depicted simplistically as an "inevitable" confrontation between two strong-minded individuals, the English and Spanish monarchs, each out to defeat (and, conceivably, destroy) the other. The weight of evidence currently provides us with a more nuanced view of the situation. For one thing, Wallace T. MacCaffrey (anticipating in this judgment more recent revisionism) emphasized in his follow-up study of 1992 the palpable apprehension with which Queen Elizabeth regarded a possible head-on war with Philip's Spain. "After nearly 30 years of struggle in which she had striven . . . to preserve England in peace," MacCaffrey wrote, "events too mighty to be mastered forced her hand and drove her reluctantly to war." Her goal was "to mobilize French cooperation in a diplomatic offensive that would persuade Philip II to restore the status quo of his father's time in the Low Countries. In such a regime the Spanish presence would be too weak to allow the use of the provinces as a base for aggression across the North Sea, but strong enough to check French ambitions in that direction." Sadly enough, however, these efforts "had not prospered, and between 1581 and 1585 England and Spain drifted towards war."[27] During the last two decades, Susan Doran, Pauline Croft, P. E. J. Hammer, and others have enlarged on this general theme. Indeed, Croft has even argued for a radical recasting of the Anglo-Spanish relationship of the 1580s:

British historians have tended to neglect the complex pan-European dimensions of Spanish policy and over-emphasized the importance of England. In consequence, the conflict of 1588 has been depicted as a bilateral fight between two sworn enemies. Spanish historians have sometimes concurred, writing of the "dual antagonism" of Philip and Elizabeth, both 'semi-legendary' figures in their own lifetimes. Yet the evidence supports neither the 'inevitabilist' nor the bilateral view. Both monarchs presided over courts and councils in which multiple strategies were debated. Each contained . . . a peace-leaning and an aggressive party, so policy was shaped not least by whichever of the two factions was temporarily in the ascendant.

And if Elizabeth was hardly bent upon war, neither was Philip. "Despite his occasional thoughts about intervention and his frequent irritation with Elizabeth," contended Croft, he "did not seriously consider an invasion until 1585, thirty years after his accession to the Spanish throne. His strategy in 1588 was multilateral, aiming above all to restore Spanish control over the Low Countries."[28] MacCaffrey's and Croft's countryman P. E. J. Hammer has reconceptualized late-sixteenth-century Anglo-Spanish relations in a similarly revisionist fashion.[29]

If the overall scholarly verdict on Elizabethan foreign policy has long been a mixed one, it does appear to be largely positive today. Thirty years ago, Wallace T. MacCaffrey allowed that "England had survived unscathed" from its epic battle with Philip II's Spain and agreed that "the Continental balance, the perpetual rivalry between Spain and France, which had been the best guarantor of English safety in the past, was re-established." At the same time, however, he asserted that the Dutch and French had been more instrumental than the English in "halting Spanish power," and argued as well that Elizabeth had (in *Irish* affairs) "bequeathed to her successors an unwanted burden, which would weigh heavily on their shoulders for generations to come." For MacCaffrey, this Tudor queen could more appropriately be dubbed "Elizabeth the Fortunate" than (as her admirers have long insisted) "Elizabeth the Great."[30] Yet Susan Doran has left us with what is perhaps a more balanced conclusion on this subject:

> Overall, ... despite the queen's own personal weaknesses and the limitations of her military machine, she made an important contribution to the international war effort against Spain. By her death, moreover, her main objectives were fulfilled: England's borders were secured; the Spanish presence was removed from France; France was kept out of Flanders; the power of Spain was 'impeached' but not destroyed; the [Dutch] United Provinces were free from the threat of Spanish military rule; and Protestantism was tolerated in France and supreme in the United Provinces.

It was perfectly true, Doran conceded, that "Elizabeth's policies were not solely responsible for these outcomes, but they undoubtedly helped." There was, then, more than a kernel of truth in what this historian good-naturedly termed "the myth of the glorious Elizabethan war against Spain, as promoted in swashbuckling Hollywood films and old-fashioned nationalistic texts."[31] Above all, a reasonable (if always tenuous) balance conducive to English security was maintained, under this Tudor queen regnant, between the Spanish (and their Guise adherents within French borders) and the temporarily weakened forces of Valois/Bourbon France itself.

Yet the reference to "nationalistic texts" also reminds us that Elizabethan *aficionados* continue to reevaluate the relative importance of "non-strategic" factors—for instance, *ideological* and *cultural* forces—in promoting this queen's policies. Prominent in this connection were gendered and patriotic appeals. As we saw earlier, feminists such as Allison Heisch and Susan Bassnett differed sharply back in the 1980s over the gendered aspects of Elizabethan rule; and they have been joined by many colleagues in what has now become a wide-ranging debate over this subject.[32] In a somewhat less polemical vein, Christopher Haigh broke new ground by identifying (in 1988) three key gender-related challenges that this queen had to confront. First, she had to settle a succession question naturally complicated by her failure either to marry or to designate, early on, a successor. Second, she had to overcome her initial inexperience in geostrategic matters and fight to compel her (male) councilors to obey her orders and accept her policies, especially in *military* affairs. Third, she had unavoidably to find ways (as would *any* stateswoman) to acknowledge constraints imposed by socially constructed gender roles—even while fashioning "an image of monarchy that was appropriate for a woman yet which invited obedience."[33] This last point has since been persuasively seconded by Susan Frye and Carole Levin: their research has reaffirmed the notion "that Elizabeth had to work much harder than her male predecessors to mitigate deeply embedded social antagonisms to female rule" and to construct and valorize "representations of appropriate modes of female rule for public consumption." This challenge, if we accept Charles Beem's additional commentary on the subject, occupied this queen's entire reign, and "overlay all of the major problems identified in conventional political histories."[34]

Yet however stimulating such gendered reflections on Elizabeth I may be, we may find them in the end inadequate—certainly by themselves—as explanations for the evolution of her foreign policy. Take, for example, the critical issue of *warfare*. In a coauthored article, Charles Beem and Carole Levin have conceded the obvious point that this queen, "like her sister Mary, tread warily upon the military aspects of kingship, and made no effort to inhabit the role of a military leader . . . in the field." Elizabeth, then, was "constrained to watch the periodic successes and more frequent disasters of her armies and navies from the safety of fortress England." Yet, as Beem and Levin acutely observe, more was involved here than the frustration of a queen unable to control her masculine commanders in the field:

Elizabeth, in fact, placed little faith in the utility of warfare and only authorized military deployments when she felt she absolutely had to. Whether this was because she was a woman has been endlessly debated, but it is just as plausible that her reasons were similar to those of her grandfather, Henry VII, who also saw little reason for hemorrhaging England's limited resources for the uncertainties of armed conflict.

Indeed, princes on the Continent might customarily adhere to "male-gendered expectations of kingly military leadership by leading armies in the field"; yet Elizabeth could just as easily (and usefully) craft "spectacles for both domestic and foreign consumption" that could resoundingly celebrate England's capacity for warfare.[35] Susan Doran had previously made very similar points concerning the queen's leadership in wartime; in addition, however, she had also raised the issue of Elizabeth's advancing age in the late 1580s and 1590s—by which time many of her advisers and generals considered her to be out of touch with military realities—and also accentuated inadequacies in England's military infrastructure and finances that would equally plague four *very male* Stuart monarchs in the century to come.[36]

Moreover, *English patriotism* may have overshadowed *gender* as a cultural factor conducive to Elizabethan success in European affairs. Charles Beem and Carole Levin, certainly, have been quick to embrace this very point, observing that "unlike her sister Mary, the daughter of a foreign consort who married outside of the realm, Elizabeth emphasized her position as entirely or "merely" English, being the daughter of both an English father and mother." As Beem and Levin go on to explain, this kind of self-justification could only enhance this monarch's stature in popular eyes:

Elizabeth was emulating the worldview of her subjects. This was sound policy; unlike her sister or her cousin Mary Queen of Scots, Elizabeth could not count on the support of powerful foreign relations to bolster her position in England—she literally had no choice but to court the popularity of her own subjects. This process began with her coronation procession of January 1559, in which Elizabeth's active engagement of the people of London . . . set in motion the creation of a widespread perception that she loved her people.

Hence, this position, going hand-in-hand with Elizabeth's reported lack of any desire to travel *outside* the realm, could be "fully consistent with the desires of her increasingly xenophobic subjects at large—feelings exacerbated by the religious polarization of the later sixteenth century."[37] Feminist Anna Whitelock has also emphasized along these same lines how, for the English, there was such a stunning contrast to be drawn between a Queen Mary viewed as "a tool of the Spanish" and a Queen Elizabeth perceived as having defended her country against those same Spanish in the Armada Crisis of 1588. Such a victorious monarch, according to Whitelock, was likely in future generations to be lionized not only for having "exceeded the traditional expectations of her gender" but—even more, perhaps—for having served her people as "a vehicle of English nationalism."[38]

But if, when it came to Elizabeth I, cultural factors likely reinforced what most historians now regard as a more or less successful foreign policy, did something similar happen a half-century later in the case of Charles I's consort queen, Henrietta Maria? Unfortunately, this does not appear to have happened, since what Jessica Bell has called the "contradictory strands in her loyalties" placed a curse on Charles I's consort from the very start.[39] Henrietta Maria, youngest daughter of French Bourbon King Henri IV by his second wife, Marie de Médicis, was married (at 14) to Charles I on June 13, 1625, soon after her arrival in England from France.[40] This union—like the later marriages of Louis XVI with Marie-Antoinette and of Nicholas II with Alexandra, it is true—would flourish as time went on; yet it was to be abruptly terminated on January 30, 1649, by Charles I's execution at the height of revolution—a social and political *dénouement* to which Charles's consort queen, it must be regretfully conceded, contributed quite substantially.

In Henrietta Maria's case, the "contradictory strands in her loyalties" lay in the irreconcilable demands of politics and religion. Those conflicting demands were foreshadowed in a letter presented by the now widowed Marie de Médicis to her daughter prior to her departure for England in June 1625. As one of Henrietta's biographers has written, the letter "contained detailed instructions as to how she was to behave towards her husband, his subjects, her retainers and towards God." In her morning and evening devotions, the letter ran on, the young queen-to-be "was to remember that without God she would be nothing, and that she had been placed in the world to do a great and glorious task." Happily born "a Christian and a Catholic," Charles's young spouse "must remember that she had been sent into a foreign country expressly to help the Catholics who had suffered for so long. After God and religion, her first duty was to her husband—she was . . . to love him as such, and to honor him as a king, while praying each day for his conversion." Although she was of course enjoined additionally to "care for her husband's subjects," Henrietta Maria was especially counseled by her diplomatically minded mother to "foster good relations between England and France."[41]

In this letter's insistence that *only* "after God and religion" was the new consort to construe her "first duty" as being "to her husband" there lay an insoluble problem for the royal couple—given, that is, the larger diplomatic context of Charles I's reign. After all, England was still witnessing in this era, as it had under Elizabeth I, the great continental power struggle pitting France against the Austro-Spanish Habsburgs. In the Thirty Years' War which spread across western-central Europe from 1618 to 1648, that struggle would be approaching its climax—but only after making Englishmen and Englishwomen fear for their country's political and religious security. Historians of political culture tell us today that early Stuart England was increasingly riven between rival conspiracy theories tying together religious, constitutional, and state/security issues and prescribing radically different remedies for the kingdom's ills. The "popular" conspiracy theory, Ann Hughes has said, "explained political conflict in terms of an authoritarian popish plot to undermine English laws and liberties as well as true religion, a plot which had alarming support from evil counselors at court." On the other, traditionalist side, Charles and his closest aides naturally saw such views as a "subversive attempt to undermine his God-given authority: 'popularity,' not popery, was the great threat to the stability of English (and British) subjects." Such all-encompassing theories were, in Hughes's well-chosen words, "mutually reinforcing."[42] Given such extreme polarization in English society, how, we might easily ask, could the presence of a notoriously *Catholic* queen *not* have added significantly to Charles I's problems?

History's heavy hand only made the problem worse. It ensured that any attempt by the Stuart party to tar its critics with the brush of "popular" sabotage, of plebeian revolt jeopardizing the divinely ordained ranks of social hierarchy and prerogatives of monarchy, was likely to be trumped in the eyes of many English subjects by opposition tactics tarring Charles I (and Henrietta Maria) with the far more damning brush of "popery." After all, "popery" conjured up for most contemporaries such traumatic events as the Marian persecutions of the 1550s, the treason of Mary Stuart and the Spanish Armada of the 1580s, the Gunpowder Plot under James I, and all of the bloody Catholic assassinations martyring Protestants on the Continent—not to mention the *current* efforts of the Habsburgs to roll back (in the Thirty Years' War) a century of Protestantism in European theaters of action not all *that* distant from England's still-imperiled shores. Modern research appears to show convincingly how difficult it would be to overestimate the early-seventeenth-century tendency, in *all* ranks of English society, to detect priests and other "papists" under every bed, and to detest and fear Ireland (and, to some extent, even Scotland) as prospective avenues for papist infiltration of embattled, evangelical England.[43] Could, then, the presence of Henrietta Maria in England after 1625 have failed to aggravate such anxieties?

Not that the newly celebrated royal marriage immediately blossomed into a warm personal relationship; nor, early on, did it afford the still youthful consort queen much scope for influencing the king in public matters. George Villiers, duke of Buckingham, held inordinate sway over Charles I in the domain of policymaking until his assassination in 1628. Yet, tellingly, Venice's ambassador to England was recording within two weeks of Buckingham's death the popular conviction that "the queen would henceforth have great influence," and followed this up soon thereafter by noting that "every day, she concentrates in herself the favor and love that was previously divided between her and the duke."[44] That Charles reportedly reciprocated his wife's devotion in full was only confirmed with the successful birth of the future Charles II on May 29, 1630. (This "especially fecund marriage," as White has called it, would eventually produce nine offspring, six of whom would survive childhood.) Yet another important event in the consolidation of the marriage was the death, in March 1635, of the Lord Treasurer, Richard Weston, with whom Henrietta Maria had never gotten along. As the queen's most recent biographer has stated, Henrietta had "resented the Lord Treasurer's enforcement of laws which prohibited English Catholics from attending mass at her chapels; she begrudged his tight control over royal expenditure; and she regarded him as a competitor for influence with the king."[45] With figures such as Buckingham and Weston now safely consigned to the past, and with her own "fecundity" reinforcing her unique role as consort queen, Henrietta was, by the late 1630s, firmly ensconced in Charles's affections.

It is admittedly true that, at least until the late 1630s and early 1640s, the queen's entourage included Protestants as well as Catholics; only with the onset of the Scottish "Prayer Book" rebellion, the Bishops' Wars, and, finally, the early stages of the Civil War did Henrietta (and her royal husband) irrevocably cast their lot with domestic Catholics and those Catholics abroad generally identified with the Habsburg cause on the war-torn Continent.[46] Still, the queen's basic lack of pragmatism, and of an understanding of English interests in the larger world of European geopolitics, had manifested itself as early as 1630, when she was drawn into Bourbon family quarrels in her native France and conspired *against* Cardinal Richelieu. Such machinations made no sense: Richelieu advocated an anti-Habsburg coalition of Protestant *and* like-minded Catholic states in Western Europe—a policy which the English queen (and her husband) would have done well to endorse.[47] Yet, once again, during the late 1620s and most of the 1630s Charles's consort queen—contrary to what many a scholar has traditionally averred—could claim Protestant as well as Catholic friends at court. As Malcolm Smuts has somberly commented, however, "all of this changed" between 1638 and 1640:

> the queen identified herself with a pro-Spanish foreign policy, the rigorous prosecution of wars against Scottish Presbyterianism, more aggressive Catholic proselytizing at court, and the political interests of anti-Puritan ministers like [the Earl of] Strafford. The possibility that Charles might try to use Spanish or Irish Catholic troops further darkened the political landscape. So did his willingness to fight the Scots without parliamentary support and the queen's willingness to sponsor a voluntary levy among English Catholics to help fund the war effort.

As Smuts has further observed, Henrietta's persistent quarrels with her royal brother Louis XIII and his principal minister Richelieu "meant that she had effectively become an *opponent* of French policies. Although a French queen [by birth], she had become a supporter of Spanish interests."[48]

And so by the time Charles I, having been militarily humiliated by the Scots and constitutionally defied by John Pym and others in the Long Parliament, raised the standard of civil war at Nottingham in August 1642, the queen was all too ready to play a leading role in what became known as the "Cavalier" cause. This could have surprised no one: when Charles I had vainly attempted to arrest the defiant Five Members in Parliament on January 4, 1642, his wife had reportedly urged him to "go and pull the rogues out by the ears or never see her again." At about the same time, Henrietta had courteously but firmly insisted to the Venetian ambassador that "she considered it impossible to re-establish her husband's authority in any other way."[49] Hence, her unrelenting efforts, during the civil struggle which ensued, to champion the Stuart cause—efforts effectively summarized by Michelle White:

> During the civil wars, Henrietta's involvement in state matters grew ever more pervasive. At Charles's request she sailed to Holland where she raised money, forged alliances, procured arms and ammunition, and summoned an army to send back to England. Additionally, whether from Holland (in 1642), or at Oxford (in 1643), or from France (from 1644-49), Henrietta continuously involved herself in military, diplomatic, political, and religious matters. . . . Diplomatically speaking, throughout the civil wars Henrietta was Charles's chief ambassador, negotiating for financial and military support with the French, the Dutch, the Danes, the Irish, and the Pope.

Whether in England or abroad, her advice to Charles was always the same: make no peace without her consent(!), or without first dissolving what she derisively referred to as "the 'perpetual' parliament."[50]

Indeed, anyone reviewing this queen's edited correspondence from those years will find her counseling and, at times, almost hectoring the king in ways that (for the historian) eerily foreshadow the language, in later upheavals, of Marie-Antoinette and Alexandra Feodorovna. Thus, in March 1642, Henrietta sternly informed Charles that "your want of perseverance in your designs hath ruined you." Two months later, she was reminding him: "remember your own maxims, that it is better to follow out a bad resolution, than to change it so often." In September of that year came this: "If you do not take care of those who suffer for you, you are lost." And when it came to Charles's handling of ever-thorny Irish issues, the notoriously Catholic Henrietta had this advice at hand: "if you do agree upon strictness against Catholics, it would discourage them to serve you. And if afterwords there should be no peace, you could never expect succour either from Ireland or any other Catholic prince, for they would believe you would abandon them after you had served yourself."[51] Even after the Stuart cause had been to all intents and purposes lost, the queen (in late 1646) would be warning Charles to "take care not to agree to the propositions" his adversaries might make, "before you are aware of what you are doing, and be well resolved thereupon, however they may promise you."[52]

The king's parliamentary foes, however, knew well before 1646 how important Henrietta Maria was to the royalist side in the Civil War. They acknowledged this in many ways: for instance, by trying to "order" Charles I (in 1642) "not to entertain any Advice or Mediation from the Queen, in Matters of Religion, or concerning the Government"; by actually impeaching her (May 1643) for her "treasonous" political and religious activities on the king's behalf; by sending representatives abroad to frustrate her efforts for the Stuart cause; and even, on one occasion, by chasing her ship all the way to France![53] In general society, too—as Michelle White has demonstrated—a myriad of anti-royalist tracts circulated painting a lurid picture of Henrietta as "a domineering, foreign, Catholic queen consort" lording it in an unholy fashion over an "acquiescent, weak, unreliable king." Because Charles I permitted this woman "to flourish at his court and interfere in state matters," White has concluded, "enemies of the regime discredited him by implication." The queen thus "inspired public hatred of Charles to a degree which irreparably undermined his credibility with his people. Largely because of Henrietta, Charles lost the aura . . . that normally would have engendered so much confidence in a monarch."[54] In light of what we know today, we would have to assign considerable weight to this judgment on Henrietta Maria.

In the end, we know, Charles I lost the "first" and "second" civil wars, and then (on January 30, 1649) lost his head as well. Henrietta Maria was in France at the time of Charles's execution; she would eventually die there (in September 1669) after having spent her last years unhappily drifting back and forth between England and France.[55] Unlike the ill-fated consorts in the revolutions-to-come, Henrietta Maria would thereby at least achieve the dignity of a "natural" demise. On the other hand, having so perfervidly supported her husband's disastrous policies from the late 1630s on, she would also assure herself an unflattering place in English history differing signally from that accorded by most latter-day scholars to Queen Elizabeth I. What remains to be discussed in the case of Henrietta Maria is the role that various *ideological/cultural* factors played in her misfortunes.

If English patriotism, because of its national security associations, overshadowed gender as a force making for Elizabeth's success in the sixteenth century, that same patriotism, refracted through the prisms of gender and resurgent Catholicism, complicated Henrietta Maria's work on behalf of her husband a half century later. To begin with, Diana Barnes has provocatively held that a "discourse of feminine friendship" inspired, in part, by Henrietta's fervent Catholicism, popularized a concept of the "sovereignty of the community of women" in English aristocratic and upper-class society that Puritans (and notably *men* of all faiths) found to be socially subversive. Barnes has elaborated on this:

> Many of the converts [i.e., to Catholicism] were women acting upon their own judgment with or without their husbands' approval. Contemporaries perceived this challenge to the patriarchal family to be the greatest threat to the nation. . . . At this time the dominant view was that women were subject to their husbands, whose authority was endorsed by God. In the 1620s and 1630s some women departed from this to follow God even if it meant disobeying their husbands to whom they were only conditionally contracted. This contravened . . . the religious justification for male superiority. Women took advantage of the political theories based upon the individual rather than upon family emerging at this time.

"In the pre-civil war climate," Barnes added, "traditional gender roles were contested as much as any other system of authority. [Catholic] Recusancy depended upon female sub-cultures which bypassed the authority of husbands and priests."[56] Yet for most contemporaries (we must suspect), gendered anxieties could not, in the end, be separated from more general concerns regarding threats not only to domestic social hierarchy but also to the country's *political* security in a dangerous world.

Indeed, other historians, while acknowledging the role of gender in all of this, have kept their eyes on the larger issue of state security—and on how it was so often perceived through the lenses of both gender *and* religion. "The more closely the king's critics looked at the royal family in the 1630s," Caroline Hibbard has observed, "the more popery they found. And the connection they drew between Catholicism and tyranny was no mere propaganda ploy. It rested on deeply rooted assumptions about the nature of government and the relations between church and state, on their interpretation of the king's secular policies in the light of . . . religious policies, and on their understanding of current European politics." For these affrighted individuals, the issue of "resurgent European Catholicism" could not be disassociated from the greater Habsburg/Bourbon power struggle on the Continent.[57] Much the same emphasis has emerged in Michelle White's biography of Charles I's queen. "While fears of Henrietta's sexual domination over Charles" were to "figure prominently" in much of the ferocious anti-royalist literature of the civil war years, White has allowed, gendered concerns such as these "never provoked the kind of hysterical fear which 'popery' had. In this case, *gender played a secondary role to religion.* The issue of religion remained at the forefront and—over and over again— anti-royalist propaganda targeted Henrietta as the standard-bearer of the

Catholic cause, even when her sexuality was not an issue."[58] Gender and religion were matters inextricably bound together in this crisis—but it was likely *religion* that most powerfully underscored the greatest *security* threats to England—above all, religion as feared in the person of Charles I's wife, Henrietta Maria.

In concluding this English section of Chapter 3, we can see that while both Queen Elizabeth I *and* Queen Consort Henrietta Maria had (in various ways) to contend with challenges related to their femininity, only Elizabeth can be seen in retrospect as successful in *state/security* terms. Elizabeth, if maddeningly inconsistent at times, usually managed to identify and prioritize her country's security needs in a perilous European environment, whereas Henrietta Maria (after some initial hesitation on the subject) eventually seconded her royal husband in pursuing foreign policies that were disastrously inconsistent with seventeenth-century English defensive needs. And if there was any *cultural factor* that was a key to one woman's success and the other's failure, it was a security-oriented patriotism—a sentiment sometimes mediated through *religion* even more powerfully than through gender.

Catherine De Medicis and the Suicidal Statecraft of Marie-Antoinette

Any comparison in French history between Cathérine de Médicis and Marie-Antoinette might seem at first glance a bit more problematic than that we have already drawn in English history between a Queen Regnant, Elizabeth I, and Queen Consort Henrietta Maria. After all, Cathérine, as noted earlier, exercised power largely by indirection—we might say *unofficially*—from the time of her royal husband's untimely death in July 1559 until her own death in January 1589. During that turbulent period, she was formally styled Queen Mother to three successive kings—Francis II, Charles IX, and Henri III—and also served *officially* as Regent during two cursory intervals.[59] This meant, of course, that (unlike Elizabeth I) Cathérine never fully ruled in her own right as Queen Regnant. Moreover, she could never claim to be "merely French" as her contemporary Elizabeth could vaunt her status as "merely English." Indeed, "in sixteenth-century France," R. J. Knecht has aptly commented, "Catherine offered the perfect target to a hate campaign fuelled by xenophobia, social snobbery and misogyny. As a Florentine, she was seen as deceitful by nature. . .; as scion of a family deemed . . . upstart (the Medici had risen socially through trade and banking), she was regarded as jealous of France's ancient nobility; and as a woman, she exemplified the 'monstrous regiment' denounced by John Knox and other male preachers and political theorists as unfit to rule."[60] Still, this last observation, by reinvoking the issue of gender, raises as well the possibility that a French Queen Mother, like an English Queen Regnant, could transcend the limitations of her sex to defend *national* interests that a later French consort queen (i.e., Marie-Antoinette) would betray.

To begin with, Cathérine confronted a strategic situation in Europe that was, if anything, even more discouragingly complicated than that faced by her contemporary Elizabeth I across the Channel. Like Elizabeth, Cathérine had perforce to function in a diplomatic world dominated by the great rivalry between the Austro-Spanish (especially *Spanish*) Habsburgs and France; but unlike Elizabeth, she also had to deal with a myriad of interrelated domestic and international problems imperiling the reigns of three successive (and largely impotent) sons. Even her biographer R. J. Knecht, never inclined to judge her too leniently, has written that Cathérine "certainly found herself in a particularly difficult situation when her husband was killed in July 1559. At the age of 40 and without any significant experience of government, she was left to defend the inheritance of her children." Even in state service (in 1560–63 and, briefly, in 1574) as Regent, Cathérine "lacked the authority of a king."[61] Furthermore, the widowed Queen Mother, while depending at least in theory on the support of the nobility, "had to maintain her independence in the face of the bitter aristocratic rivalries which flourished in the absence of a mature king." In addition, as every student of this period knows well, Cathérine's task was further complicated by the crown's near-insolvency, the lack of a centralized bureaucracy (only nascently developed under the later Bourbons), and—above all, perhaps—the virulent hatreds pitting Protestants (i.e. Huguenots) against resurgent, Trentine Catholics.[62] Finally, all of these issues were but the *domestic* ingredients in a veritable witches' brew of problems that bedeviled the Queen Mother's thirty years in power.

It is, perhaps, paradoxical but nonetheless true, as Nicola M. Sutherland has written, that the supreme challenge faced by "catholic France" in Cathérine de Médicis's time—that is, how to survive in a Europe dominated by the "catholic power of Spain"—forced successive Valois governments (as it would similarly compel the subsequent Bourbon ministries of Cardinals Richelieu and Mazarin) to look for Protestant as well as Catholic friends abroad. Sutherland has summarized the diplomatic situation as viewed from Paris in terms that allude to both home-grown and international challenges:

> France was never more effectively surrounded by the Habsburgs—whose system virtually embraced all catholic powers—than at the height of the ideological conflict of the sixteenth century. . . . This was the beginning of that embarrassing need for a policy of catholic at home and protestant abroad which necessity and shifting values in international affairs . . . . rendered acceptable. . . . Its inception might just be discerned in the

forbearance . . . between Catherine and Elizabeth, whose common fear of Spanish domination exceeded their mutual hostility.[63]

Indeed, the "forbearance" which developed in these years between the French Queen Mother and the English Queen Regnant reflected—at Paris—strategic *and* domestic pressures that were weighing upon a sorely weakened French government. If, on the one hand, Cathérine and her sons had increasingly to fear Philip II's Spain, they were (by the same token) increasingly incentivized to contest the influence of Spain's powerful Guise partisans *within* France. And obviously the same concerns that lay behind their overtures, from 1559 on, to England help to explain their openings to Protestants in the Netherlands, in Scandinavia, and even (at times) in the German principalities of the Holy Roman Empire.

But it was, perhaps, in her relations with Tudor England that Cathérine de Médicis most clearly demonstrated her acute grasp of issues. We touched earlier upon the grudging respect that developed between Cathérine and Elizabeth I. Susan Doran, poring over the English State Papers, found, we recall, that the Tudor Queen and her envoys "took Cathérine very seriously indeed as a major political player, especially during the reigns of her younger sons, Charles IX and Henri III."[64] In Cathérine's voluminous correspondence from those years one gains a similar impression of French attitudes toward England.[65] To be sure, there were major bones of contention between London and Paris from the very start. For instance, England long attributed to France a plan to press for a papal excommunication of (Protestant) Elizabeth— and then for her deposition and replacement by (Catholic) Mary Queen of Scots.[66] English reservations about Cathérine were only reinforced by her decision (after initial hesitation) to deputize French agents to the Council of Trent in the early 1560s—not to mention by her apparent involvement, a decade later, in the sanguinary massacre of Huguenots in Paris on St. Bartholomew's Day in 1572. For her part, Cathérine was (naturally enough) angered by Elizabeth's repeated efforts to abet Huguenots in provincial France; again, the Queen Mother was ever cognizant of the long-standing English ambition to recover Calais, lost to the French by Elizabeth's half-sister Mary.[67] All of this said, it remains true that, as Sutherland phrased it, the two women's "common fear of Spanish domination exceeded their mutual hostility." This could be seen, for instance, in their decision to find common ground on issues involving Mary Stuart—and, indirectly, her Guise and Spanish adherents. Doran sums up Cathérine's attitude:

Catherine was keen to collaborate with Elizabeth whenever problems arose over Scotland, since unlike Françis I and Henri II, she had no imperial dreams nor wish to compete with England for influence in that region. Distracted by the religious wars in France and determined to hold in check Guise ambitions, Catherine did not take advantage of civil unrest in Scotland to resurrect the 'auld alliance' or drive a wedge between the English and Scottish Queens.[68]

Indeed, over the years Cathérine gratified Elizabeth by thwarting Guise attempts to marry the widowed Scottish Queen (who after being deposed in 1567 lived in English captivity) to a candidate—a Valois or *Spanish* candidate—who might further Habsburg ambitions; and Elizabeth signified her appreciation of Cathérine's pragmatic attitude on Scottish issues by abandoning her own attempts to support Huguenot insurrectionists in France. In these and a variety of other connections, a realistic turn of mind displayed at Paris evoked an equally pragmatic response at London.

It is perfectly true that the kind of pragmatism so useful to Cathérine in great European affairs failed her miserably when it came to managing the explosive religious and other forces that tore at the French kingdom in the late sixteenth century. Most notoriously, of course, the Queen Mother and her son Charles IX failed to avert the massacres of Huguenots that engulfed Paris and much of provincial France in 1572, following on the murder, in the capital, of the Protestant Admiral Gaspard de Coligny. The exact extent and nature of Cathérine's involvement in this tragedy remain hotly debated among historians.[69] Yet what makes this unsavory event especially relevant to our evaluation of the Queen Mother is the *extent to which it dramatized the inextricable ties between domestic and state security matters* in this era. Although some scholars—most notably, perhaps, Ivan Cloulas and Marc Venard—have been especially harsh in their assessments of Cathérine,[70] N. M. Sutherland has argued strongly that the decision of the Queen Mother, Charles IX, and (so it seems) other members of the Council on August 23, 1572 to "eliminate" Huguenot leaders in the capital reflected their larger fear that a badly weakened France might be invaded either by the Huguenots' Dutch confederates or by the Catholics' Spanish champions—or, possibly, by both! And Sutherland went on to enumerate the many internal *and* external factors that fused dangerously together in this tragedy:

All the civil war elements—the weakness and indigence of the crown, the struggle for control of the council, the variegated, internecine rivalry of the nobility, subsequently engulfed into an international, ideological conflict, itself confused by a cynical struggle for power—all of these elements were present in the collapse of France in the massacre of St. Bartholomew in August 1572. The realistic validity of Catherine's reiterated fears and warnings could not have been more starkly apparent.[71]

We also know today that—ironically, perhaps—Catherine's "reiterated fears and warnings" about the situation in France reflected in part her awareness that Philip II of Spain was *himself* caught at this time between relentless Counter-Reformation pressures emanating from Vienna and, even more, from the Papacy at Rome, and Protestant pressures emanating from Elizabeth's most ardent acolytes in England and from Orangists combating Madrid in the Dutch Netherlands.

Yet, having discussed the interlocking of diplomatic and domestic affairs in this era, we would still do well to situate Cathérine's statecraft, if we desire to appreciate it fully, in the *longue durée* of French *administrative* history. True, the Queen Mother's career could most immediately be evaluated "in terms of her struggle against the breakdown of royal authority in the face of . . . the conflicts released by the Reformation." Nevertheless, while Sutherland has correctly commented to this effect, she has also—crucially—looked *beyond* the immediate and, at times, sordid politics of this period to point up Cathérine's greater *long-term impact* upon state formation in France. "The complexities of her career, and the confusion of the civil wars," Sutherland writes, "have tended to obscure the fact that she was also confronted—in circumstances of peculiar difficulty—by some of the underlying problems of the *ancien régime*. Without her . . . achievements the later monarchy would have had no foundations upon which to build." The Queen Mother thus anticipated later efforts "to promote a *national* policy."[72] Cathérine had not at her disposal the centralized bureaucracy, the *intendants* and *subdélegués* in the provinces, and the fiscal system on which the absolutism so characteristic of the late seventeenth and eighteenth centuries would be established. At the very least, however, by wrestling with complicated issues of foreign policy, even as she desperately sought to bank the fires of religious warfare at home, Cathérine de Médicis helped to prepare the way for stable Bourbon governance in France.

This foundational achievement was especially striking given the fact that (as we earlier noted) Cathérine "offered the perfect target to a hate campaign fuelled by xenophobia, social snobbery and misogyny."[73] Unlike her contemporary Elizabeth, this Florentine-born Queen Mother of France could *not* so easily bang the drums of patriotism—a patriotism infused (in England) with white-hot religious conviction. Nonetheless, for Cathérine, as for her great contemporary Elizabeth I, *gendered* concerns, if apparently a limiting factor in some ways, in other ways afforded opportunities that could be exploited. This was true, even though scholar Katherine Crawford rightly emphasizes the narrow parameters within which Cathérine, as a uniquely empowered *woman* in sixteenth-century France, had to operate:

Catherine de Médicis had to walk a very fine line. Whereas a good woman was obedient, deferential, and dependent, a good politician was commanding, aggressive, and independent. These are not precise antitheses, however, and their imprecision gave Catherine the slight room she had to maneuver. On a somewhat abstract level, Catherine . . . dampened the contradictory implication seemingly inherent in being a good woman and a politician by not pushing too hard on the particulars.

She more often claimed authority and implied that power necessarily followed instead of defining specific powers as flowing from her source of entitlement.[74]

In discharging her duties as Queen Mother and (at times) as Regent, in other words, Cathérine "not only demonstrated that she knew the expectations regarding her behavior as a woman, but also 'performed her conformity' with those expectations to carve out a political role for herself."[75]

To begin with, as Crawford and other Catherinian scholars have been quick to point out, Henri II's widow displayed a sensitivity to society's gendered expectations of her by the stately ways in which she mourned for the royal husband she had so suddenly lost at that disastrous tournament in July 1559. That (among other things) Cathérine insisted on wearing black *for the rest of her life*, and insisted (at least for a while) on a similar deportment by her household, testified to that sensitivity. But, as Sheila Ffolliott, Sharon Jansen and others have shown, the widowed Queen Mother also had other ways of satisfying gendered expectations—all the while marking out a unique role for herself in the unforgiving world of everyday geopolitics. She did so, for instance, by paying tribute, in murals and portraiture, to Artemisia, the widow-in-mourning of King Mausolus of ancient Caria. Here, again, we can see Cathérine striding that "fine line" between conflictual gendered roles in society. As Ffolliott has explained:

> Artemisia was an ideal prototype for a woman ruler because she possessed the virtues of a man while never losing the grace of a woman. . . . In . . . drawings Artemisia always appears tall, graceful, and beautiful, according to the contemporary canons of female beauty. She appears first as the ideal woman, but her actions show her to possess the masculine virtues of a ruler as well. She acted as was expected of a woman, spending the rest of her days mourning her deceased husband. But [even] in this marginalized position, she is shown to exercise great power.

As Ffolliott summed up matters: "Artemisia was the epitome of a nonthreatening prototype, providing the perfect imagery for Catherine de' Medici in her quest to maintain the French monarchy—against all odds—in a period of extreme conflict."[76] In resorting to this "prototype," we might also notice, Henri II's widow was anticipating its advantageous use by subsequent (and similarly ambitious) royal widows in France—specifically, Marie de Médicis and Anne of Austria.[77]

But if Cathérine skilfully utilized for political purposes the gendered "event" of her widowhood, she also carved out a path-blazing political role for herself by playing up her gendered—and persistently advertised—mission as *the mother to three consecutive French kings*. True, she was unable to exercise much power during the cursory (1559–60) reign of Henri II's first successor, Francis II—a reign ruthlessly controlled by the two Guise uncles of the young monarch's Scottish wife Mary Stuart. With the advent of Charles IX in 1560, however, and then with that of Henri III fourteen years later, Cathérine, playing upon her reputation as the devoted mother, was able to outmaneuver those institutions (including the Parlement of Paris, the Estates General, and the *prévoté* of Paris) that—partly for gendered reasons—tried to deny her any de facto acquisition of state power. "Throughout the reigns of both of her sons until her death in 1589," as Crawford stated, "Catherine continued to use her performance of typical female roles of wife, widow, and mother to claim access to political authority."[78] And having attained such gender-related authority, Catherine deployed it for specific *diplomatic* purposes—whether they entailed exchanges with Huguenots and Catholics at home or with friends and/or adversaries abroad. Furthermore, Denis Crouzet has gone so far as to maintain that "motherhood" for Cathérine extended (at times) not only to her royal sons but to all French subjects (Huguenot *and* Catholic) as well. By 1579, Crouzet found, Cathérine was portraying herself—in letters to Henri III—as driven in all statecraft by her "strong desire to be a mother to all your subjects." Crouzet's analysis of the Queen Mother's language here is extremely interesting, and directly germane to our discussion:

> An essentially gendered utterance thus emerges within a discourse that hitherto had revolved around . . . themes of "resolution" and "firmness." Catherine de Medici . . . was linking diplomatic practice with feminine identity, which derives not only from the natural "honor" of being the mother of the king of France, but more so from appropriating the role of a motherly figure who protects her son's subjects. Adopting this motherly persona enabled the queen mother to understand better. . . the Huguenot negotiators, as well as the more strident Catholic faction.[79]

Crouzet conceded that, in fact, Cathérine had already appropriated (from the Roman goddess Juno) the "persona of a maternal figure" as far back as the 1550s; but now, in 1579, she was attempting to find, in a *greatly expanded* gender role, the means to allay the destructive passions of the religious civil wars.

All such gender-related insights having been explored, we must yet conclude that, for Cathérine de Médicis as for her contemporary Elizabeth I, a hard-headed pragmatism remained essential for even a limited success in European affairs. It is useful to recall in this connection Susan Doran's cautionary comments about the Cathérine/Elizabeth relationship. "Their rapprochement," observes Doran, "owed nothing to their gender; neither queen laid down her sword because of a womanly disdain for war or chivalric values. Rather, pragmatic considerations and diplomatic practices kept them on a peaceful track."[80] Sadly enough, however, the resources of diplomacy in Cathérine's case could not realistically be expected to subdue the *internal* forces that were tearing away at her adopted country's unity.

At least Cathérine de Médicis's intelligent uses of the "resources of diplomacy" enabled her to transcend (at times) the xenophobia of French subjects who despised her Florentine origins: the issue of a "national identity" split between France and Italy, in other words, did not really defeat the Queen Mother's actions in the realm of high politics. Unfortunately, however, the same could not be said two centuries later for Louis XVI's Queen Consort, Marie-Antoinette. Born in Vienna in 1755, and daughter of Austrian Habsburg Empress Maria Theresa and Holy Roman Emperor (and erstwhile duc de Lorraine) Francis I, this ill-fated princess was espoused to the future Louis XVI at 14 and, upon his accession on May 10, 1774, became the queen of France.[81] Although John Hardman, one of Marie-Antoinette's recent and most authoritative biographers, has averred that Louis XVI's wife "lost" her Austrian identity fairly soon after her arrival in France and "became French" definitively in 1787, other specialists have not been so sure of this.[82] Thomas Kaiser, for instance, challenging Hardman's characterization of this queen, has instead stressed her *three* nationalities—Austrian, French, and Lorraine— nationalities that, persisting in a "complex and unstable" compound of identities, and politicized very dangerously in revolutionary times, would eventually help to send Marie-Antoinette to the guillotine.[83]

Of course, however latter-day specialists might disagree about the issue of national identity as it came to affect this Queen Consort's fortunes in France, there is little doubt about the "overwhelming popularity Marie-Antoinette enjoyed" at the start of her husband's reign in 1774. As Kaiser has lucidly explained, this popular favor stemmed from a multitude of factors.[84] For one thing, she profited from her association with the now-disgraced, but still influential, ex-foreign minister, Etienne-François, duc de Choiseul. Again, the young queen contrasted favorably in most subjects' eyes with the mistresses of Louis XV's now thoroughly discredited reign. As Kaiser has observed, Marie-Antoinette "projected an image of refreshing innocence particularly appreciated in a jaded age that was fast rediscovering the moral and sexual appeal of feminine modesty and virtue"—a gendered social reaction in itself! Also, popular expectations of the new Queen were enhanced by what appeared to be her genuine concern for the welfare of "ordinary" French subjects. And Kaiser has enlarged upon this point:

The crowds that followed her almost everywhere were convinced [that] she was a force to be reckoned with and would use her apparently immense influence to improve the lot of the French. Indeed, at the beginning of Louis XVI's reign they even expressed resentment at ministerial efforts to reduce the 'confidence' of the king in his adorable wife, a confidence Marie-Antoinette did in fact use to boost her popularity by lobbying Louis to lower the price of bread. . . . In the France of the 1770s . . .

anticipations of Marie-Antoinette's benign interventions in the new reign temporarily fed hopes for a national revival.[85]

Finally, as if to clinch her reputation in contemporary eyes—and in acknowledgment of the first duty of *any* Queen Consort—Louis XVI's wife was able in time to claim a maternal status with the birth of a daughter in December 1778 and (more significantly, given French "Salic" traditions) the birth of a son in October 1781.[86] Another son and daughter would subsequently be born to the royal couple.

Still, popular perceptions were one thing; the opinions held of Marie-Antoinette in the marbled corridors of power at Versailles were quite another. On this latter point, scholars have often disagreed. Munro Price, for instance, had no doubts initially about the queen's rapidly growing influence at court. "Although Louis governed with the aid of an informal first minister in the person of [J. F. P., comte de] Maurepas," argued Price, "the queen had a powerful political position that grew stronger as the reign progressed. . . . By 1781 she combined the emotional ascendancy of a mistress with the permanence of a queen: a formidable obstacle to any first minister who was not her creature." Indeed, Price went so far as to allege, "the emergence of the queen as a powerful political figure in her own right was the most significant development at Versailles in the reign of Louis XVI."[87] Yet Price's countryman Hardman, in his biography of Louis XVI, saw Marie-Antoinette's political influence—at least until the "prerevolution" of 1787–8, a presumably transitional event—as merely "tangential" and "fitful."[88] Admittedly, the two historians subsequently arrived at a more or less common view on this subject. Marie-Antoinette benefited, they came to agree, from the fact that Louis XVI took no mistress, from her ability (in 1778 and thereafter) to give him children, and from the occasional support of a clique of courtiers associated with, if (from 1770 on) no longer reliant upon, the now-cashiered foreign minister, Choiseul. In these circumstances, concluded Price and Hardman, the queen was able to wield a considerable and growing influence over the crown's patronage— including, most crucially, ministerial appointments.[89]

True, Price has since argued that any roseate expectations held of the new Queen, either by the public or by those in governing circles, were as unfounded in these late years of the ancien régime as they proved to be thereafter. "Unlike her mother," he has claimed, "Marie Antoinette did not have the stuff of a statesman, because she . . . lacked the patience . . . to see a policy through from beginning to end."[90] And, as if anticipating Price on this point, the comte (Florimund) de Mercy-Argenteau, Vienna's envoy to France, confided (in 1782) to Marie-Antoinette's brother, Emperor Joseph II:

> The queen is beginning to show some qualities of foresight . . . but . . . this august princess devotes neither the time nor the effort necessary to gain

the solid and preponderant influence that she could have if she displayed a firm and consistent will. . . . The need for constant amusement disturbs the ideas and methods that the queen should apply to serious matters; she does not accept this fact . . . great affairs need great preparation, without which activity displayed only at moments of crisis can only compromise her position.[91]

It is incontrovertible that a number of reputable modern historians have objected to such criticisms of the queen: Marie-Antoinette, they insist, was not necessarily a bit more "emotional" or shortsighted than the vast majority of her ministerial (and other) contemporaries, and she was attempting—at least until the "prerevolutionary" crisis and beyond—to do what she could to preserve the substance of the Franco-Austrian alliance. Yet the unflattering impressions of the queen, as, for instance, those recorded confidentially by Mercy-Argenteau, an Austrian diplomat who wanted, for reasons both diplomatic and personal, to "manage" Marie-Antoinette's lobbying activities on behalf of the authorities at Vienna, apparently did not surprise Joseph II in the least: like his mother Maria Theresa prior to her death in 1780, he advised his sister at Versailles, at least initially, to refrain from involving herself in the always tortuous ways of international politics.[92]

To be sure, there *were* times, during the late 1770s and 1780s, when first, Maria-Theresa, and then, after her death, Joseph II *did* ask France's Queen to intervene on Vienna's behalf—most notably, perhaps, during the Bavarian Exchange crisis of 1778 and the Scheldt imbroglio of 1784–5.[93] But such interventions by the queen, however eagerly seconded by her fellow-Austrian Mercy-Argenteau, were usually unavailing. She could never overcome Louis XVI's aversion to the (often pro-Austrian) Choiseul; she was consistently outmaneuvered by Maurepas and the foreign minister, Charles Gravier, comte de Vergennes, in the years prior to 1787; and she was unable (or perhaps, for private reasons, unwilling) to do much to secure an Austrian-favored replacement for Vergennes when he died in early 1787.[94] Still, what ultimately explained this Austrian-born Queen's frustrations in all of these affairs was the age-old Franco-Austrian competition in Europe—a rivalry encapsulated succinctly by Munro Price:

The French monarchy and the Habsburgs had been hereditary enemies since 1494, and all of the military and diplomatic glories of the reigns of Louis XIII and Louis XIV had been associated with an anti-Austrian foreign policy. This state of affairs had only changed in 1756 with the *renversement des alliances,* by which Louis XV, tiring of the unreliability of Frederick the Great as an ally . . . had substituted for the Prussian connection an alliance with the Habsburgs. Yet the new Franco-Austrian alliance was unpopular from the outset, and almost immediately damned by the disasters of the Seven Years War—the loss of French influence in India and the surrender of all her possessions in Canada—which it precipitated.[95]

From the very start, consequently, Marie-Antoinette had to stave off, in popular and in élitist quarters, attacks that, motivated most basically by Austrophobia—if also reflecting the defamatory misogyny of many of the Queen's critics—were destined to pursue her right into the revolutionary era.[96]

By common consent, that era began with the crown's increasingly desperate efforts, during the so-called "prerevolution" of 1787–8, to restore its solvency through systemic fiscal and administrative reforms.[97] Although the queen scored a long-coveted success with the dismissal, in April 1787, of the hated finance minister, Charles-Alexandre de Calonne, who had been unable to coerce needed reforms through the Assembly of Notables, she suffered a sharp defeat when his successor, Loménie de Brienne, whom she had long favored, was himself driven from power in August 1788. Marie-Antoinette, both of her primary British biographers write, was—reluctantly—forced into the political spotlight at this critical juncture by the king's profound depression and resultant withdrawal from statist politics. Munro Price has summarized a situation that offered little but increasing peril for the queen:

The queen did not act this way out of pure ambition and desire to grasp supreme political power . . . it is more likely that she only assumed the direction of public affairs because the king himself was unable to do so. The crisis of August 1788 offers further evidence that by now Louis XVI was periodically prostrated by a depression that left him incapable of conducting day-to-day policy. . . . August 1788 saw the ship of state rudderless with the king out of action and the key decisions in the hands of the queen and the Austrian ambassador.[98]

Unsurprisingly, too, this domestic crisis had dark foreign policy implications. "Efforts by the monarchy to solve the fiscal crisis," Kaiser has explained, "became indelibly tainted by fears that French finances were being drained to bankroll Austrian aggression and that France would be dragged into an avoidable catastrophic 'general war' on Austria's behalf." Popular suspicions that Marie-Antoinette (*"Madame Déficit"*) was involved in all of the rumored intriguing at Versailles to assist her brother Joseph II could only further damage her reputation as France now began to plunge into full-blown revolution.[99]

And, much like Henrietta Maria in the earlier English Revolution, Marie-Antoinette in the French upheaval found herself being pushed by relentless circumstantial pressures down a road leading to her husband's—and to her own—ruin. A first pivotal milestone along this dolorous road was the

Queen's involvement in the *séance royale* staged by the crown on June 23, 1789, in the self-proclaimed National Assembly. The new finance minister, Jacques Necker, had wanted Louis XVI to use this *séance* not only to restore the government's finances but also to satisfy many of the most salient demands in the Third Estate's *cahiers de doléances*. Thus, the king should admit qualified commoners to all key civilian and military employments, abolish the tax (*franc fief*) on plebeian owners of fiefs, and make it possible for peasants to redeem the feudal payments owed to their seigneurs. Additionally, Necker pressured the king to recognize the individual's rights to security and property, freedom of assembly and of the press, and indeed "all of the rights later appearing in the Charter of 1814."[100] But the advocates of reform in the ministries had reckoned without the queen's interference in this crisis. As Price has remarked:

> Despite her developing political maturity, Marie Antoinette had only been playing a significant political role for two years. Like her husband, she was prone to indecision, and she continued to view affairs of state in emotional and personal rather than political terms. . . . Added to this, she was herself under massive pressure from her *société*, especially Mme de Polignac and the latter's lover Vaudreuil, to harden her attitude to the third estate and come to the defense of the privileged orders.[101]

Perhaps even more crucially, the queen was lobbied on this last issue by Louis XVI's starkly reactionary youngest brother, the comte d'Artois. The end result of all of this was that the King, at the actual "royal session" of June 23, endorsed what amounted to Marie-Antoinette's "revised" stance on the sacrosanct nature of *privilège* and of the social hierarchy in France. "In all Louis's and Marie Antoinette's surviving correspondence after 1789," Price has argued, "the political programme they refer to most often is that contained in the declaration of 23 June."[102] Thus the queen's dramatic and ill-considered intervention in these early days of revolution in France adumbrated so much of what was eventually to come.

Viewed in retrospect, in fact, Marie-Antoinette's *confidential* reactions to French events are as incriminating as Henrietta Maria's earlier reactionary badgering of Charles I in England. On August 20, 1790, for example, she wrote Mercy-Argenteau that "matters are becoming more difficult and . . . painful with every passing day." Five days earlier, she had asked Mercy, rhetorically: "How could . . . any rational being think that we could ever . . .provoke civil war?" Yet just three days later she (and, likely, Louis XVI) drafted a position paper that addressed this lurking possibility equivocally: "One can never accept that civil war is necessary, but one can imagine the possibility that it becomes inevitable; [and] provided it comes about neither through the actions or the wishes of the king, he will prepare himself to accept it, without fear or remorse." By now, the royal couple was already scheming toward what would soon become the abortive "flight to Varennes."[103] Nor did the utter failure of that gambit (in June 1791) alter Marie-Antoinette's thinking. On August 26, 1791, she was reassuring Mercy-Argenteau that "Our only plan is to lull them [i.e. the revolutionaries] and inspire them with confidence, the better to confound them afterwords." To her Swedish admirer Axel von Fersen, the queen wrote these very provocative words on October 19, 1791: "Have no fear, I am not joining the wild men; if I see or have dealings with some of them, it is only in order to make use of them, and they fill me with too much horror to think of ever going over to them."[104] And finally—and most dangerously—by 1792 the royal couple's mounting desperation led them to what could only be viewed in revolutionary quarters as outright treason. "On 26 March 1792 in a letter to Mercy-Argenteau, and in notes to Fersen of 5 and 23 June and 11 July," we gather from Munro Price, "Marie-Antoinette passed on information about French war plans from what she had gleaned in the *conseil* [*du Roi*]." The "only remaining course of action" for king and queen at this juncture, so Price concluded, "was to remain in Paris and wait for the invading armies"—meaning, above all, presumably, the armies of the Queen's native Austria and Hohenzollern Prussia.[105] And so did yet another consort queen, throwing prudence to the winds in a revolutionary crisis, wager all upon the intervention of her adopted country's most dangerous adversaries!

It was a dangerous game to play; moreover, its exposure ensured that European high politics would dominate the trials, first of Louis XVI and then of his queen in 1793. As Antonia Fraser (along with many other authors) has pointed out, "it was . . . the direction of the war" that, with specific regard to Marie-Antoinette, turned out to be the most decisive—and thus, most damning—development:

> On 23 July the Austrian alliance recaptured Mainz . . . three days later they took Valenciennes, a victory that meant that Paris itself, too easily reached down the valley of the Oise, was in danger. On 1 August, [Bertrand] Barère, president of the Convention and a member of the Committee of Public Safety, deliberately established the lethal connection. Was it "our over- long forgetfulness of the Austrian woman's crimes . . . our strange indifference towards the Capet family" that had given the nation's enemies a mistaken impression of its weakness? If so, that could be remedied, and remedied immediately.[106]

The "lethal connection" between the queen's alleged crimes and deteriorating French military fortunes was, in the following days, posited as well by many another politician. At a secret, nocturnal meeting of revolutionary leaders on September 2–3, for instance, the death of Marie-Antoinette was demanded—in part, to reassure a Republic shaken by the news of the surrender of the French fleet at Toulon to the English.[107] Then, Bertrand Barère, returning to the charge at a turbulent session of the Convention on September 5, appeased the Parisians, aroused on this revolutionary *journée,* by promising, explicitly, "the blood of [J.-P.] Brissot and Marie-Antoinette."[108] At the queen's trial, staged on October 14–16, both A. M. Herman, presiding over the court, and the notorious public prosecutor, A. Q. Fouquier-Tinville, cited Marie-Antoinette's treasonous dealings with Austria (and other foreign powers) as justification for her execution. That sentence was pronounced and swiftly carried out (by guillotine) on the 16th.[109]

Can we also view *cultural* factors as playing, in this case as in the comparable case of Henrietta Maria, a significant role in determining how things turned out? Thomas Kaiser holds that the *national identity* question loomed large in this connection. Marie-Antoinette's "strategies for personal survival" were, he writes, "integrated into a larger political strategy built upon essentially the same dual national identity that she had developed before the Revolution." Yet Kaiser also concedes that the Revolution's radicalization along chauvinistic French lines meant that, in the end, the queen's desperate endeavor to maintain her old regime loyalties to both France *and her native Austria* proved to be "unsustainable," and ultimately led to her death in October 1793.[110] The queen could not, after all, cling indefinitely to multiple identities characteristic of a world the revolutionaries were determined to overthrow.

Then, again, there is the *gendered* question of misogyny, explored by feminist scholars. Joan Landes, Elizabeth Colwill, Lynn Hunt, Madelyn Gutwirth, and others, as we recall, have situated Marie-Antoinette in a context of growing male hostility toward powerful women in late-eighteenth-century/ revolutionary France.[111] Colwill, for instance, focusing on the queen's trial in October 1793, says: "By the end of 1793, a consensus had begun to emerge around a new, positive, and purportedly universal model of woman as moral mother that . . . severed them from political life. In this shift of mentality. . . . Marie-Antoinette's trial stands out as a watershed. Her execution on 16 October 1793 signaled the triumph of Rousseau's passive Sophie over the worldly models of aristocratic womanhood offered by the early modern court." Thus, for Colwill, "revolutionary antagonism toward the political prerogatives of queenship had evolved into a general proscription of female political action."[112] The way was open to a French future that would be marked by a male-dominated public "space" and a female-populated private "space." Lynn Hunt says generally the same thing (with Freudian overtones) in concluding that "When they executed Marie-Antoinette, republican men were not simply concerned to punish a leading counterrevolutionary. They wanted to separate mothers from any public activity, and yet give birth by themselves to a new political organism. In order to accomplish this, they first had to destroy the Old Regime link between the ruling family and the body politic. . . . In short, they had to kill the patriarchal father and the mother."[113] Again, in this view, the republican future would secure "fraternity between men" but, at the same time, ensure that women were "relegated to the realm of domesticity."

Still, however valuable this interpretation in challenging the specialist to move beyond narrow considerations of factional and court politicking and thus engage broader trends in political culture, it is problematic on several counts. To begin with, Colwill herself admitted that it was "political events" that "conspired to revive interest in the former queen by the summer of 1793"; she also referenced the key role played by Marie-Antoinette's trial "in the government's bid for the loyalty of the *sans-culottes*."[114] Here was at least an oblique acknowledgment of domestic *and strategic* politics driving this drama. At a more basic level, Dena Goodman has called for more subtle distinctions to be drawn between private and public spaces in gendered history.[115] Yet another scholar of unimpeccably feminist standing, Sarah Hanley, has queried the entire assumption about misogyny suddenly rearing its hideous head in the era of revolution; she suggests that, in fact, misogyny was prominent throughout the ancien régime, from, that is, the early sixteenth century onward, inspiring as it did the "Family-State compact" that (so she claims) lay at the heart of "monarchic state building."[116] Indeed, when we return to the matter of the queen's trial in 1793, we may find it hard to disagree with Kaiser's conclusion on the subject: "Marie-Antoinette's fate . . . was decided through a complex interaction of diplomatic and domestic political considerations, many of which bore upon matters of national security in the face of perceived Anglo-Austrian threats." That the prosecution and judges at the trial so frequently passed beyond the moral corruption charges gleefully circulated by the queen's enemies (and sometimes referring all the way back to the "Diamond Necklace Affair" of 1785–6) to press home embarrassing questions relating to her Austrian connections further valorizes this interpretation of her condemnation in court.[117]

In summarizing this French section of Chapter 3, we can compare the careers of Cathérine de Médicis and Marie-Antoinette in terms reminiscent of those we used earlier to compare Elizabeth I and Henrietta Maria. Once again, we are confronted with two powerful women, both of whom had, in one way or another, to deal with gendered and other cultural challenges, but only *one* of whom (at least for the most part) correctly identified and *prioritized* her adopted country's *most critical security concerns*. Insofar as cultural forces *were* indeed at play here, we can conclude that Cathérine knew how to turn them to her benefit in intriguing ways, whereas, for Marie-Antoinette, questions of *national identity*, just as much as the endlessly debated issue of revolutionary misogyny, proved to be her undoing.

Catherine II and the Disastrous
Statecraft of Alexandra Feodorovna

In the Russian case, as in the case of England, we compare a fully empowered queen (empress) regnant with a subsequent queen consort. That Catherine II came to power as a result of her husband's murder does not really modify the nature of our task—even though it may reflect the (somewhat) less civilized situation in this vast country on Europe's eastern flank. This Russian tsaritsa also resembled in some ways Cathérine de Médicis: like the Florentine Queen Mother/Regent, she acceded to power as a foreigner. Born in 1729 as Princess Sophie Auguste Friderike, the daughter of a minor German prince (of Anhalt-Zerbst) in service to Hohenzollern Prussia, the future Catherine the Great was sent to Russia in 1744, aged 14, to marry her 15-year-old second cousin, Peter of Holstein Gottorp, grandson of Peter the Great, and designated heir to the Russian throne.[118] The rule of succession in Romanov Russia had been contested ever since Peter I (the Great) had decreed in 1725 that the monarch could name his/her successor. That specific development, and tsar Peter III's subsequent inadequacies—most portentously in foreign policymaking—led to his murder (July 3, 1762) and to his replacement by his (renamed) widow Yekaterina Alekseyevna, already(!) proclaimed Empress Catherine II on June 28, 1762.[119] As we will see in some detail, this German-born empress would show all the pragmatism in state/security matters that Russia's final Consort Empress, Alexandra Feodorovna, would so disastrously lack.

Catherine's resounding successes in foreign policy, of course, presupposed her ability to master Russia's always treacherous *domestic* politics—politics that had engulfed her husband and would later engulf her son, Tsar Paul I. Catherinian scholars have pointed to the various elements in the Empress's "leadership style" that, in constant interaction, assured her ascendancy, from her accession in 1762 to her death in 1796. For one thing, David Ransel has noted, the "chief guarantee of life, honor, property, personal expression, or any other social value" in old regime Russia was "the power and cohesion of one's clientele group." Such groups were indispensable to rulers, "who needed disciplined hierarchies to implement policy. Rulers may have been ambivalent toward clientele groups and suspicious of their power, but monarchs had no more effective means of exerting their will." Thus, for Ransel, "the first interest of any statesman was to protect his patronage organization."[120] John P. LeDonne has pointed out that one of Catherine's strengths "was the ability to choose outstanding collaborators among the political families that sustained her power." Hence, for LeDonne, Ransel, and others, the influence, at various junctures in the empress's long reign, of such imperial favorites as Nikita Panin, the five Orlov brothers, and Grigory Potemkin.[121] Yet, seen from another angle, such individuals also belonged to a Russian nobility whose interests had to be championed, as, in fact, they were in legislation of 1775 and 1785. Such reforms, Paul Dukes has written, "put an official seal on the preponderance of the nobility over all the other classes." For Catherine II, in other words, managing patronage networks intersected with a defense of *dvorianstvo* (i.e., gentry) interests.[122] Finally, in governing day-to-day, the empress "encouraged competing viewpoints among her statesmen and tended to decide issues by giving the advocate of one policy the nod without permanently dashing the hopes of his rival." Such a style of decision-making not only benefited Catherine II by deflecting blame for policy failures from her own person; as Robert E. Jones has observed, it also enabled her—notably in the sphere of diplomacy and geopolitics—to change a policy "swiftly and relatively easily to meet changing circumstances."[123]

To discuss international affairs here is, in large part, to realize why posterity knows this tsaritsa as Catherine "the Great." True, the way had been eased for her by developments in prior decades. As early as the 1680s, in fact, the "Holy League" in central Europe had invited the Muscovite state to work with it in driving the Ottoman Turks out of the Balkans. From 1699 on, the tsars had labored to create "a network of diplomatic representatives abroad comparable in its extent and efficiency to that of any European State."[124] As a result of the Great Northern War (1700–21), waged concurrently with the Spanish Succession War to the west, Peter I's Russia had replaced Sweden on the eastern shores of the Baltic, thereby securing its permanent "window on the west." Even more important for Russia—and in fact for Europe as a whole—was the alliance struck with Austria in 1726. "Russia not only acquired an ally in its imperial movement west and south," E. V. Anisimov states, "but also entered, for the first time as a member, into the European community of great powers on an equal basis." The Romanov empire thereby "became an indispensable constituent of the political combinations and of the general balance of power in Europe."[125] Thus, for instance, St. Petersburg's intervention in 1733 in the Polish Succession struggle allowed it to impose on Warsaw its own candidate for the Polish throne; the French candidate (none other than Louis XV's father-in-law) was banished from Polish soil forever. Although Russia did not participate in the War of the Austrian Succession (1740–8), its renewed ties with Maria Theresa's Austria, dating from 1746, marked a further step in the process by which it involved itself in the affairs of neighboring states to the west.[126] Excluded from the negotiations terminating the Polish Succession and Austrian Succession wars, the Romanov state involved itself with a vengeance in the Seven Years' War of 1756–63. In that conflict, Isabel de Madariaga has correctly remarked, "Russian armies showed themselves able to stand up to the Prussian forces. Russian victories such as Gross Jägersdorf (1757) and Kunersdorf (1759), the occupation of East Prussia, the brief raid on Berlin in 1760, all served to increase Russian self-confidence. Russia had now become a fully integrated member of the European states system."[127] Only the sudden death of Tsarina Elisabeth in December 1761 and the *very* brief reign of Catherine's ill-starred Prussophile husband Peter III staved off—if but temporarily—an even deeper insertion of St. Petersburg's armies—and influence—into Central European affairs.

Catherine herself acceded to power largely as a result of a geopolitical impasse in Russia. "The failure of the Russian military leadership in 1758 to exploit to the full Russia's military victories over the Prussians," Madariaga has written, "led to a crisis at the Russian court." Pro-Prussian, pro-French, and pro-English factions jockeyed for power at St. Petersburg. The upshot was, in the short and unhappy reign of Peter III, a foreign policy which, by pulling Russia out of the struggle against Prussia, led to St. Petersburg abandoning its conquests, including East Prussia. By alienating powerful pro-war interests, not to mention religious and élitist interests at home, Peter sealed his own fate. His violent overthrow by an Orlov faction favorable to his German-born spouse meant that, for the next thirty-four years, Catherine II would steer an aggressive and, in the main, remarkably successful foreign policy.[128] Perhaps her most telling means to that end lay in her resolve (in LeDonne's words) "to establish Russia's leading role as a mediator between the two Germanic powers by a mixture of cajolery and threats." LeDonne unerringly identified here the critical geostrategic dynamic: the "dualistic" tensions between Berlin and Vienna:

> The rivalry of Prussia and Austria in their ambition to achieve similar objectives gave Catherine II the opportunity to balance one against the other and to make significant gains against both. The victims of their rivalry were the Polish and Ottoman empires and, to a lesser extent, the Holy Roman Empire, subjected for the first time to the conflicting destabilization policies of Russia and the Germanic powers.[129]

From the start, Robert E. Jones has held, this situation offered Catherine II a tempting choice between "an alliance with Prussia and the formation of a 'Northern System' of alliances to preserve the peace of Europe," advocated by Nikita Panin, and "an Austrian alliance that would permit expansion towards the Black Sea," as advocated warmly by [Count A. P.] Bestuzhev-Riumin and the Orlov brothers.[130]

As John LeDonne has rightly said, the implications of this situation were especially grim for the Poles, Ottoman Turkey, and Germany's Holy Roman Empire. Catherine, to begin with, wasted no time when it came to the Poles. Scarcely a year after her bloody elevation to power, she responded to the death of Polish King Augustus III by imposing her own ex-lover, Stanislaus Poniatowski, on Warsaw. A few years later, unrest among Stanislaus's subjects (related in part to the king's own campaign to resist Catherine's growing encroachments upon his Commonwealth) combined with Russia's crushing defeat of Turkey's land and maritime forces to cause deepening consternation in Prussia and Austria. From the start of 1771, Prussia, motivated chiefly by a desire to keep tensions in eastern Europe from boiling over into a conflagration involving all the Great Powers, invited Austria and Russia to join it in a partition of Polish territory. "The three eastern powers" consequently announced in August 1772 "that large areas of the Commonwealth would be partitioned between them." Russia acquired a large portion of eastern Poland; Vienna absorbed the province of Galicia; and Frederick II's state annexed "the much smaller but strategically crucial West Prussia linking East Prussia with . . . the Prussian heartland."[131] That Catherine's ambitions had been the primary force behind these events indelibly impressed the faraway Anglo-Irish legislator Edmund Burke: "Poland," he stated apprehensively, "was the natural barrier of Germany, as well as of the northern crowns, against the overwhelming power and ambition of Russia."[132] Further moves in that direction, he wrote prophetically, were to be expected. And, indeed, those moves came in the 1790s, when Catherine, taking advantage of central Europe's preoccupation with revolutionary France, forced through the Second Polish Partition (along with Prussia) and the Third Partition (along with the Hohenzollern and Habsburg states.) Poland thereupon disappeared from the map of Europe. These developments, Brendan Simms has so rightly observed, provided "a brutal illustration of the fate in store for those states which failed to find the inner cohesion to survive."[133]

Moreover, if Poland's lack of "inner cohesion" played outstandingly into Russian hands in this period, the same might be said of what was loosely referred to as "Germany." Austro-Prussian tensions also figured here in the equation. For instance, the dispute between Berlin and Vienna over the south German state of Bavaria, left temporarily without a ruler in 1777 by the decease of Holy Roman Empire Elector Maximilian Joseph, led to a brief Austro-Prussian war over the Bavarian Succession. The Treaty of Teschen (1779) ending that conflict not only thwarted Habsburg Emperor Joseph II's aspirations to acquire this duchy; more significantly, the Franco-Russian mediation that lay behind Teschen alerted all diplomatic observers to St. Petersburg's achievement "for the first time" of a "formal *locus standi* in German affairs." In December 1778, Anderson has noted, "the German representative to the Imperial Diet complained, with perfect truth, that Russia was now the dominant foreign influence in the politics of Germany, not, as for the last century and a half, France."[134] Unsurprisingly, the French envoy to the Diet protested similarly, at this time, about the growth of Russian influence (and diminution of French power) in central Europe.[135] Additionally, Catherine had other ways of signifying her growing interest in German affairs. Playing off her own Teutonic origins (in Anhalt-Zerbst), she set up a department in her foreign affairs ministry to deal with German politics; she increased Russia's diplomatic outreach to the Holy

Roman Empire; and in 1785 she pointedly had a Russian envoy, Count N. P. Romanzov, plead Austria's case for an arbitrated acquisition of Bavaria.[136] True, in this last case a Prussian-sponsored "League of German Princes" intervened to balk Joseph II once again in his designs on Bavaria. Still, it was symptomatic of the times that even the Habsburg emperor should have sought out Catherine II's support in what was ostensibly an internal German dispute.

It was of equal import that the Austro-Prussian rivalry in Central Europe should have facilitated Catherine's most stunning gains—those achieved at the expense of Ottoman Turkey. Granted, Russian designs on the Ottoman Empire dated back, in Hugh Ragsdale's words, "at least to the Azov campaigns of Peter I in 1695 and 1696."[137] But it was the opportunistic Catherine who, benefiting from Austro-Prussian tensions, translated those designs into reality. The process began with the Russo-Turkish War of 1768–74, when Britain allowed Russia to send three squadrons of men-of-war through the Channel and around Gibraltar to the eastern Mediterranean. In those waters, they annihilated the Turkish fleet. Great Russian victories on sea and land gained for St. Petersburg (1774) the Treaty of Kutchuk-Kainardji. As Simms has remarked, the Ottomans "surrendered the Crimean Khanate, which effectively became a Russian puppet. Catherine also forced the Porte to grant her the right to act as guarantor of the rights of Balkan Christians, just as Russia had long 'protected' Polish dissidents."[138] (We have already seen what dire implications these Russian triumphs against Constantinople had for the Poles, reverberating as they did in Prussia and Austria.) Soon thereafter, Catherine II pursued her long-anticipated "Greek Project" via Vienna. After concluding a defensive alliance with her Habsburg counterpart in 1781, the tsaritsa a year later proposed to Joseph II nothing less than an Austro-Russian partition of the Turkish Balkans—and quickly asserted Russian claims to the western Caucasus, the Crimean Peninsula, and the left back of the Dniester River. Catherine's breathtaking scheme envisioned the creation of a "restored Byzantine empire under a Romanov *basileus* or emperor"—to be ruled one day by her then-three-year-old grandson Constantine from a "liberated" Constantinople. Although Joseph, then and later, would have a host of reasons to distrust plans likely entailing major warfare in the Balkans, he *was* eventually inveigled into such a conflict—even as revolutions were starting to erupt in the West.[139]

It would be all too easy, in reviewing Catherine II's geopolitical triumphs during the years from 1762 to 1796, to overlook the reverses she occasionally sustained—and the parameters within which even this resourceful tsaritsa had to operate. Even in the matter of the "Greek Project," Ragsdale has noted: "the most authoritative Russian sources agree with Kaunitz that the Russians were not militarily prepared to implement the Greek Project in 1787." Nor did Austria's belated adherence to the "Project" late in 1787 alter the situation, as "the revolt in the Low Countries, the crisis in France, and the death of Joseph soon removed Austria entirely from the Turkish political theater." Even in Russia itself, Ragsdale contends, "two persons stood staunchly for the Greek Project, Catherine and Potemkin, and they stood virtually alone. When Catherine died, the Project disappeared."[140] Then, again, the empress's ability to pivot between the Northern System of Panin and the Balkan-oriented Greek Project did not spare her, late in life, from anti-Russian initiatives taken by the English/Prussian/Dutch "Triple Alliance." The old Anglo-Russian cooperation dating from the Russo-Turkish War of 1768–74 was simply a fading memory by 1780, when Catherine, reacting to British arrogance on the high seas, brought a group of states into a "League of Armed Neutrality" against London.[141] Still, whatever the weak points in her policies, the empress left a daunting legacy of Russian greatness to her tsarist successors. "When Emperor Paul I in 1800 asked the officials of the College of Foreign Affairs for an analysis of Russia's current standing and prospects in foreign-policy matters," Hans Bagger has concluded, "Count Fedor Rostopchin emphasized in his report that the Russian Empire, 'by virtue of its position and inexhaustible strength,' was—and ought to be—the world's leading power, the 'Hercules' of international politics."[142]

It is also noteworthy that Catherine II, like her adroit counterparts Elizabeth I and Cathérine de Médicis, found her femininity to be both a challenge *and* an asset. On the first point, the Empress had to put up with contemporaries such as British envoy Sir James Harris, whose misogynistic description of her has been recorded by scholars ranging from Isabel de Madariaga to Brenda Meehan-Waters:

> Her Majesty has a masculine force of mind, obstinacy in adhering to a plan, and intrepidity in the execution of it; but she wants the more manly virtues of deliberation, forbearance in prosperity and accuracy of judgment, while she possesses in a high degree the weaknesses vulgarly attributed to her sex—love of flattery, and its inseparable companion, vanity; an inattention to unpleasant but salutary advice; and a propensity to voluptuousness which leads to excesses that would debase a female character in any sphere of life.[143]

Nor were Harris's fatuous comments at all unusual at that time. A French officer in the Russian service, Charles F. Masson, saw Catherine's greatest weakness as vanity, "that unfortunate rock so fatal to every female." Her reign, so he predicted, "will ever bear this distinguishing characteristic of her sex."[144] The Chevalier de Corberon wrote in much the same vein, ascribing Catherine's flexibility and contradictions alike to the "whimsicality" so characteristic of all women. As Meehan-Waters has remarked, even those supposed avatars of enlightenment Voltaire and Diderot, long praised as the tsaritsa's "public relations agents" abroad, could not always get beyond the issue of Catherine's gender. Voltaire, in his extensive correspondence with her, was, we are informed, "always witty and flirtatious"; and Diderot in *his* letters to the Empress repeatedly differentiated between "the worn-out rags of your sex" and the "large views and masculine and patriotic designs, which are the proper concern of monarchs."[145] Furthermore, even latter-day Catherinian scholars, sensitive—as they should be—to the sexism inherent in such language, have acknowledged the problems the empress could generate for herself by her notorious liaisons with Orlov, Poniatowski, Potemkin, and (numerous) others. Madariaga, in this connection, has contended that the "example which the Empress so glaringly provided of total disregard for the rules of domestic morality . . . turned many of the Church hierarchy, such as Metropolitan Platon of Moscow, . . . the more strait-laced nobles . . . and the Moscow freemasons against her."[146] It was likely inevitable that, especially in her later years, the tsarina should also have frequently been accused of corrupting young people, and family life in general, by her sexual attachments at court.

Yet Catherine II, like her worldly-wise counterparts Elizabeth I and Cathérine de Médicis, could regard gendered issues—and for that matter easily utilized them—as an asset. Take, for example, the notorious matter of her paramours. Nicholas V. Riasanovsky and Mark D. Steinberg have a ready reply for readers who would see in those lovers little more than idle distractions for an insatiable tsarina:

> The empress allegedly had twenty-one known lovers, the last after she had turned sixty. The favorites included Grigorii Orlov, an officer of the guards who proved instrumental in elevating Catherine . . . to the throne and whose brother may have killed Peter III; Stansilaus Poniatowski, a Polish nobleman whom the empress made King of Poland; and, most important, Grigorii Potemkin. Potemkin came to occupy a unique position in the Russian government, to the extent that he can be considered the foremost statesman of the reign, and in the empress's private life; [and] he certainly continued to be influential after the rise of other favorites.[147]

Catherine, then, knew how to use her paramours—to her own (sometimes ruthless) purposes, and (she would always insist) to the greater glory of Russia. Again, like Elizabeth I and Cathérine de Médicis, the tsaritsa knew the value of gendered "mixed messages." As Richard Wortman has noted, a medal struck on the occasion of her accession painted her "as a formidable, bellicose Minerva . . . she exemplified male as well as female qualities, both prowess and graciousness." She enjoyed appearing at masquerades in guards uniform. "A man's dress is what suits her best," observed a British envoy, who continued: "she wears it always when she rides on horseback." Late in her reign, the tsarina continued the practice of wearing men's costumes (and, on occasion, playing at pursuing young ladies!).[148] Yet, as Gary Marker has stressed, the empress was equally quick to invoke the "chastity myth," imagery, and iconography associated in Russia with St. Catherine, so as "to establish her standing as an Orthodox ruler."[149] The tsarina, then, was as adept at harnessing to her own purposes feminized aspects of Russian Orthodoxy as she was at appropriating, simultaneously, female and male characterological traits. Yet what may most impress us is the extent to which Catherine won the plaudits even of those observers assuming the usual male/female dichotomy. French courtier Claude Carloman de Rulhière, for instance, agreed that the empress had "the air of a sovereign. All her features proclaim a superior character." George Macartney, British envoy to St. Petersburg in 1766, was even more emphatic on the subject. "I never saw in my life a person whose . . . manner and behavior answered so strongly to the idea I had formed to myself of her. . . . It is inconceivable . . . with what astonishing magic she inspires at once both respect and affection."[150] Catherine, in other words, like her predecessors in Tudor England and Valois France, knew how to transcend what might otherwise have been casually dismissed as the "limits of her sex."

Unhappily, however, we find nothing of Catherine II's statecraft (or of her social *savoir-vivre*) in Imperial Russia's last tsarina, Alexandra Feodorovna. Born as Princess Alix in the small, rather obscure German duchy of Hesse-Darmstadt on June 6, 1872, daughter of Grand Duke Louis and his wife Princess Alice of England (herself a daughter of Queen Victoria), Alix would eventually be engaged to Tsarevich Nicholas of Russia in April 1894, and on November 26 of that year married him as Princess Alexandra Feodorovna.[151] Within a short time, the premature death of Tsar Alexander III enthroned Nicholas and his 22-year-old wife in the enormous Romanov empire. If Charles I's Queen Consort, Henrietta Maria, had always struggled to reconcile her English duties with her French identity, and if Louis XVI's Queen Consort, Marie-Antoinette, had had to juggle Austrian, Lorraine, and French identities, Russia's final Empress Consort—if fated, ironically, to be ridiculed in wartime as "the German woman"—brought to Russia a pronounced dislike for the Germany that had forcibly absorbed her native Hesse-Darmstadt, and a lasting affection for her mother's and grandmother's Victorian England.[152]

Alexandra also brought to her adopted country an intense religiosity that, hitherto sustained in a German Lutheran tradition, now took on new dimensions in Russian Orthodox practices and beliefs. This turned out to be a tragic paradox for the young Empress Consort and her husband: the same faith that bound the two so closely together from the very start—thereby sparing them some of the marital difficulties that had afflicted Charles I and Henrietta Maria, and Louis XVI and Marie-Antoinette, early in *their* marriages—also tended to estrange Nicholas and Alexandra dangerously from even the most privileged elements of court society, let alone the millions of Russian subjects far removed from those *élitist* circles. Andrew Verner has analyzed this situation in an especially penetrating fashion:

> A sense of guilt born of deserting her deeply held Protestant faith, on the one hand, and of resisting Nicholas's entreaties for so long, on the other , . . cemented Alix's commitment. To the new faith and new relationship she brought the fanaticism and obsessive possessiveness of a religious convert. Her decision to marry Nicholas was the fruit of a religious experience, their marriage its continual reaffirmation. He as well as their children became the sole purpose of her earthly life. This preoccupation and the fact that she was a foreigner who was slow and hesitant to speak Russian contributed to her isolation at court.

"Nicholas, in turn" Verner continues on, "was totally absorbed with Alix. . . . The endless frustration of his fondest wish [i.e., for Alix] had intensified his private orientation and thus had accentuated his lack of identification with his public role."[153] Richard Wortman has drawn much the same picture of a marriage rock-solid from early on—and yet, by the same token, fated to isolate both tsaritsa and tsar from those around them. "No previous emperor and empress," Wortman goes so far as to allege, "were so similar in their personalities. . . . Nicholas and Alexandra . . . presented a common face to the outside world, one that was aloof and often both inscrutable and exasperating."[154]

We can retrospectively discern very early on signs of how Alexandra's intense religiosity would nurture a fatalistic outlook on life in general and, more specifically, on her husband's autocratic powers. In 1894, for example, even before being crowned, the erstwhile Alix was urging Nicholas *not* to permit anyone (including Alexander III's doctors) to intervene between himself and his dying father. "Be firm . . . see that you are the first always to know. . . . Don't let others be put first and you left out. You are Father dear's son and must be told all and must be asked about everything. Show your own mind and don't let others forget who you are."[155] When Alexandra's grandmother, Queen Victoria, wrote to exhort her to "retain and strengthen the love of [her] subjects," the newly crowned tsarina responded revealingly:

> You are mistaken, my dear grandmama; Russia is not England. Here we do not need to earn the love of the people. The Russian people revere their Tsars as divine beings, from whom all charity and fortune derive. As far as St. Petersburg society is concerned, that is something which one may wholly disregard. The opinions of those who make up this society and their mocking have no significance whatsoever.[156]

Again, Alexandra greeted the news, ten years later, of Russia's stunning loss of Port Arthur to Japan in the Russo-Japanese War by writing resignedly:

"But if it is God's will, we must bow our heads and bear this burden." "Don't lose your faith in God," she advised Nicholas. "A miracle *must* happen, pray for it, lovey, pray for it. . . . You, the Father of your people, have the right to *insist* in your prayers, and He must hear you."[157] In light of all this, tutor Pierre Gilliard's commentary on the tsarina's ill-advised *religious faith* in Grigory Rasputin's ability to heal her son Alexis's hemophilia rings true: "The Orthodox religion had fully responded to her mystical aspirations. . . . She had accepted it with all the ardor of the neophyte. In her eyes Rasputin had all the prestige and sanctity of a *staretz*."[158] Moreover, festering rumors about Rasputin's ascendancy over the empress, coinciding with Alexandra's anxiety not only over Alexis but also over her second daughter Tatiana's typhoid fever, further alienated her subjects at the time of the tercentenary jubilee celebrating the Romanov dynasty in 1913.[159] Here, surely, was a socially isolated empress utterly given over to faith, family, and autocracy on the eve of Russia's revolutionary chaos.

The historical backdrop to all of this was, we know, a growing Russian engagement in European politics that by 1914 was to draw the tsarist regime, along with the other great European powers, into an unprecedented war—and that, less than three years thereafter, would hurl Russia into revolution.[160] Soon, Nicholas II's regime would have a desperate need for transparency and ministerial accountability. Yet, with a total disregard for reality that can only remind us of Henrietta Maria during the English Civil War, and of Marie-Antoinette during the early Revolution in France, Alexandra Feodorovna repeatedly rebuffed and even sabotaged those laboring to salvage Russia's ancien régime. In November 1904, for instance, when the reformist Interior Minister P. D. Sviatopolk-Mirskii spoke to the tsaritsa of Russia's need for political representation, Alexandra retorted: "Yes, but that is very frightening; it must be done little by little."[161] ("Mirsky," as his admirers called him, was dismissed by the tsar soon after.) When, in 1911, the forceful, modernizing Prime Minister Peter Stolypin was murdered at Kiev, Alexandra reacted by remarking acidly to his successor, V. I. Kokovtsov: "You seem to do too much honor to his memory, and ascribe too much importance to his activities and to his personality . . . .you must not try to follow blindly the work of your predecessor. . . . Find your support in the confidence of the Tsar—the Lord will help you."[162] And the tsaritsa's follies only multiplied during the war years. In 1915, British diplomatic attaché Bernard Pares informs us, Alexandra (in league with Rasputin) persuaded Nicholas "to dismiss from the chief command the Grand Duke Nicholas, who was popular with the [parliamentary] Duma and the country. This both she and Rasputin regarded as the most essential victory of all. She then obtained the prorogation of the Duma."[163] But most catastrophic, perhaps, was the Empress's success in securing the dismissal of Russia's War Minister Aleksei A. Polivanov, who was performing miracles in staving off Russia's military collapse in 1915–16. He incurred Alexandra's wrath, it appears, by warning of the army's deteriorating morale, by collaborating with Duma politicians to finance urgently needed military upgrades, and (worst of all!) by criticizing Rasputin for his unwarranted meddling in the army's affairs. "Oh, how I wish you could get rid of Polivanov," the tsarina wrote angrily to Nicholas in January 1916. "He is simply a revolutionist."[164] Two months later, she got her wish: Polivanov went the way of so many other state servants who had (in effect) attempted to ward off the Romanov regime's eventual self-destruction. That British military attaché Alfred Knox had called Polivanov "undoubtedly the ablest military organizer in Russia" did not, it seems, impress the tsar. Thus, in a myriad of ways, the Empress (likening herself, reportedly, to Catherine the Great!) contributed to the "ministerial leapfrog" that, in Orlando Figes's words, "not only removed competent men from power, but also disorganized the work of government, since no one remained long enough in office to master their responsibilities."[165] Given this disastrous public behavior, we should probably not be astonished that, till the very end, Alexandra "regarded victory in the war as a foregone conclusion," nor that "her chief anxiety was that Russian influence might be overshadowed by British [influence] when the victorious peace was made."[166]

To follow Alexandra and her family to their sanguinary deaths in July 1918 in the Urals industrial town of Ekaterinburg, sixteen months after the tsar's abdication, is hardly necessary here. Torrents of scholarly ink have already been spilled on the question. Certainly, *circumstances* both international and domestic played the primary role in this tragedy.[167] But our task here is to show how *cultural factors*—above all, Germanophobia and gender—also contributed to Alexandra's demise. On the former point, we reckon with an ironic fact: Alexandra, and those of her subjects who loathed her, at least agreed in their hatred of the Germans. We noted earlier that Princess Alix—soon to become Empress Alexandra—brought to Russia a pronounced dislike for the Prussian state that, just before her birth, had swallowed up her native Hesse-Darmstadt. "That Alexandra long retained a self-conscious identity as Hessian and, with it, an enmity toward Prussia was especially evident during World War I," Steinberg and Khrustalev have written. Indeed, she traced the war's origins to the "idiotic pride and insatiable ambition" of the Hohenzollerns. As the conflict continued, the tsarina—no doubt thinking of Hesse-Darmstadt—viewed the small German states as among its victims, and blamed "Prussian troops" for outrages committed by combatants.[168] Unsurprisingly, therefore, Alexandra, even when in captivity in 1917–18, continued to vent her animus against the Germans. She railed against cousin Wilhelm II's "petty nature," exclaiming that she had "never thought he could sink down as far as coming to terms with the Bolsheviks." She was also heard to declare that she "would rather die in Russia than be saved by the Germans."[169]

But there was also that *other* point about wartime Germanophobia: it was being aimed at the Empress herself, and with deadly effect. Long before she and Nicholas were hurled from power in the early days of revolution, Alexandra was already widely execrated as the "German woman." There was, of course, historical context to this. For instance, Rex Wade has noted, "many Russian noble families and officers had German names, mostly dating from the eighteenth-century annexation of the Baltic region." Given their prominence in military, court, and governmental circles in the twentieth-century tsarist empire, such families and individuals could all too easily—if, in our eyes, questionably—be held responsible for Russia's humiliation at the hands of conspiratorial German (or pro-German) "forces."[170] That, unhappily, the German-born tsaritsa herself (like Henrietta Maria and Marie-Antoinette before her) was unavoidably tarred with the nationality of her adopted country's most hated wartime enemy only made the situation that much worse for the beleaguered authorities. Again, when Paul Miliukov, chief spokesman for the Kadet reformists in the Duma, declared in a celebrated speech in 1916 that if the Germans had indeed wanted to foment disorders in Russia, "they could not do better than to act as the Russian Government has acted," he was using the "German issue" to sap the authorities' (and, thus, the Imperial couple's) already waning legitimacy at St. Petersburg.[171] Perhaps most significant, though, was how Germanophobia—in a time of national humiliation administered by German arms—could so effectively *unify social, professional, economic, and ethnic groups in Russian society against the existing regime*. Hence, Orlando Figes and Boris Kolonitskii have argued, the danger of references to the tsarina as the "German woman," and of public discourse linking the Imperial family, the incompetent ministers (including the "German" Prime Minister Boris Stürmer), Rasputin's cronies, and others with unnamed (but presumably omnipresent) German "spies." If even a pillar of the establishment such as Grand Duke Nikolai Mikhailovich could castigate Germans and other "dark forces" in Russia, could it be long before the isolated Empress and her spouse were demonized and then deposed as "Germans" themselves?[172]

Yet if the national identity factor proved to be influential in Alexandra Feodorovna's downfall, it did so in combination with gendered prejudices. Take, for instance, the much-discussed question of the empress's religiosity. It was all very well if, in the safe confines of the old regime, she was (as Wortman would hold) "a devotee of the type of *feminized religion* that made maternal obligation and fulfillment principal Christian virtues."[173] But what if, in the chaos of total war, such religious devotion led her to embrace a profession—namely, nursing—that, in time, was mocked by the suffering Russian soldiery in such a manner as to undermine her husband's rule? If, for her friends, Alexandra was "motherly" and a "born nurse," reflecting in part her experience with a hemophiliac son, "the popular perception of the nurse in wartime," Figes and Kolonitskii remark, "was so transformed by the . . . war that photographs of the Empress and Grand Duchess in Red Cross uniforms became something of an embarrassment." The hardened front-line soldiers "either looked upon the nurses ('sisters of comfort') as sex objects . . . or else as useless women ('sisters without mercy') who rode in the staff cars . . . but had no medicine or other means of helping the soldiers." This, in turn, worked directly *against* Alexandra's effort to "gender" her role and that of her—supposedly masculine and, thereby, masterful—husband. As Figes and Kolonitskii correctly note: "Loss of manliness was the subtext of the question, 'Who rules Russia?'. . . It offended the patriarchal (not to say misogynistic) attitudes of the peasants and upholders of tradition to see the Tsar relinquish power to his wife. Tsarist power was growing weak because it was being feminized." Hence, we must ask: how could the *tsar' batiushka* (i.e., "little father") possibly be respected by his subjects in a time of supreme national testing?[174] Undoubtedly, then, issues of national identity and gender had a genuine role to play in undoing the Empress Alexandra (and, of course, her "feminized" husband).

As the reader can no doubt conclude from what we have all learned in Chapter 3, Elizabeth I of England, Cathérine de Médicis of France, and Catherine II of Russia can serve us usefully as foils for the woefully inadequate consort queens of genuinely revolutionary times—namely, Henrietta Maria, Marie-Antoinette, and Alexandra Feodorovna. Whatever the inclination among feminists and, more generally, *cultural* specialists to emphasize the roles played by gender, religion, and national identity in bringing the last-named "queens consort" to revolutionary disaster in their respective adopted countries, it was above all the factor of *strategic statecraft*—or, rather, the lack thereof—that differentiated them most clearly from their more pragmatic royal/imperial predecessors in *ancien régime* England, France, and Russia. This is yet another way of reaffirming the undiminished centrality of *politics*, and most notably *strategic politics*, in comparative revolutionary analysis, even as we dutifully acknowledge and carefully integrate into that analysis the most valuable insights to be gathered from gendered and other cultural inquiries. In the broadest theoretical/ historiographical terms as defined earlier in this study, we might conclude here that, by invoking such tried-and-true elements of "intersectionality" as statism, gender, religion, and national identity in connection with three very ill-omened consort queens of revolutionary times, we have rediscovered and reasserted the importance of structuralist as well as of postmodernist perspectives on revolution.

4

Women's Emancipatory Roles in England, France, and Russia

In his seminal study of feminism and Bolshevism in late Imperial, revolutionary, and early Soviet Russia, Richard Stites argued that winning the vote turned out to be a hollow victory for Russian as well as for other feminists. As Stites put the issue: "since the women's movement was divided sharply into a prominent bourgeois feminism and a weaker working-class women's movement, a division often further complicated by the presence of ethnic and confessional subgroups, the continuing efforts to secure the opening of public life to women on an equal basis were dissipated in wastefully repetitive and mutually hostile activities."[1] Yet this anticipation of what scholars now identify as the *intersectionality* of gender, class, race, and religion has not prevented some of them from heavily prioritizing either *class* or *gender* in discussing women's status in modern Russia. Barbara Clements, for one, emphasized that Bolshevik women (that is, *Bolshevichki*) disparaged feminism as a "bourgeois ideology that overrated the historical significance of gender inequality and ignored the obvious (to them) fact that all forms of social injustice sprang from the institution of private property."[2] More recently, Rochelle Ruthchild, endorsing here the conviction of many other women's scholars, has insisted that a "class analysis is not sufficient to explain the oppression of women, as women are in all classes, both inside the family and in the workplace." She has, accordingly, maintained that the early-twentieth-century struggle over "extending equal rights and especially voting rights to women clearly made gender a defining issue for many women."[3]

To her credit, Barbara Clements also astutely noted a larger *political irony* in Russia's situation—an irony that (as Chapter 4 will point out) applied to *all three* of our revolutions. "The *Bolshevichki*," she wrote, "believed that revolutionary upheaval would destroy the sources of injustice and thereby

make politics unnecessary. When instead their male comrades built a powerful
. . . autocracy, the Bolshevichki had to choose between defending their
earliest visions or adapting to the new realities."[4] This shrewd observation
is critical, for it highlights what is often the most salient element left out
of contemporary definitions of "intersectionality." In *Merriam-Webster's
Online Dictionary, intersectionality* is "used to refer to the complex and
cumulative way that the effects of different forms of discrimination (such
as racism, sexism, and classism) combine, overlap, and, yes, intersect—
especially in the experiences of marginalized people or groups."[5] Yet what is
lacking here is another, more comprehensive "form of discrimination"—that
is, *statism*. The *American College Dictionary* defines *statism*—in French,
étatisme and in Russian, *gosudarstvennost'*—as "the principle or policy of
concentrating extensive economic, political, and related controls in the state
at the cost of individual liberty."[6] In this situation, that is to say, *everyone*
excluded from power, regardless of gender, class, ethnicity, or religion, is
"marginalized." These considerations, then, indicate for us our major tasks
in Chapter 4, as we return to Europe's three sociopolitical revolutions. As
we move from England to France to Russia, we must first describe and try
to understand the various "emancipatory" roles that some women played in
their countries' unfolding revolutionary dramas. We should then discuss the
ways in which the *gender* dynamic intersected (but at times clashed) with
religion, secular ideology, and/or *class* in these upheavals. Finally, we must
show—in good *structuralist fashion*—how women's progressive causes
ultimately fared in the face not only of persisting patriarchy but also of
reinvigorated revolutionary/postrevolutionary *statist authority*.

England: Petitioning, Preaching, and Prophesying Women

In exploring the roles some Englishwomen played in their country's
revolution, we might begin by considering their subordinate legal status
(and, thus, rights) in the years leading up to the mid-century upheaval.
Against this inauspicious backdrop, these women's involvement in a wide
variety of civil war activities from 1642 to 1646 may strike us as surprising
and yet, at the same time, as rather predictable. Progressive behavior could
and did entangle some of them in genuinely perilous situations. More often,
perhaps, politicized Englishwomen petitioned for redress of their grievances,
frequently in concert with (or, at least, in support of) London-based
"Leveller" radicals of the late 1640s and early 1650s, published revolutionary
treatises, and, in sectarian gatherings, fulfilled pathbreaking religious roles
as preachers and prophetesses. Still, in the final analysis, we will need to
situate women's emancipatory activities in a greater historical context that

highlights the persistence, in revolutionary and postrevolutionary times, of patriarchy and of (now reconstituted) statist power.

The question of women's rights at law in seventeenth-century England has a long and somewhat contentious history of its own. "Within the vast majority of seventeenth-century families," Christopher Durston has assured us, "the father was an absolute ruler who exercised a largely unrestrained power over his wife and children." At most, Durston conceded, "during the 1640s and 1650s, some individuals began to suggest that the power of fathers should be limited in several important respects."[7] And in fact, scholars writing in the Whiggish tradition—such as Christopher Hill and Lawrence Stone—always tended to stress the benefits that middle-class Puritan women, at least, gained from the revolutionary era. What Hill termed the "new ethic" of the times was mirrored in "Puritan doctrines of the helpmeet, insistence on the wife's rights (in subordination) in the family partnership, on marriage for love and on freedom of choice for children (though not disregarding the parents' views)." True, Hill cautioned that "Puritanism was not a monolithic creed. Some old ideas died hard: the equation of adultery with theft, because the wife is the husband's property, can be found in many theologians popular with Puritans." Nonetheless, this historian of "The World Turned Upside Down" argued staunchly that the revolutionary decades witnessed a "significant acceleration" in the pace of middle-class women's emancipation, in the end attributing it largely to "a rise in economic importance of those middling-sized households, in town and country, in which the wife was a junior partner in the business."[8] For his part, Lawrence Stone, in like manner, associated the Puritans' celebration of individual conscience with an increased "respect for personal autonomy," and—intriguingly—also linked the parliamentary assault on Charles I's state with a weakening of patriarchy within the family.[9] For both Hill and Stone, the Puritans' basic respect for the wifely helpmate contrasted tellingly with the aristocracy's cynical contempt for women in this period.

Other specialists, however, have displayed scant sympathy for such a benign reading of at least some women's status in Stuart England. Indeed, as far back as 1958, Keith Thomas, in a classic *Past and Present* article, asserted unequivocally that "women's destiny was marriage, preferably at an early age, and then the hazards of continual childbearing. . . . As a married woman, she could own no property, at least not by common law . . . her sole duty [was] obedience to her husband under God." Admittedly, as if anticipating Hill and Stone in this regard, Thomas did allude to Puritans' "exalted conception of family life," their "protests against wife-beating and the double standard of sexual morality," and their timely dismissal of any "primitive view of women as shameful and unclean," and allowed that such an outlook "had done something to raise women's status"; still, it had not done very much. In fact, Thomas could not resist citation of the words of one contemporary and much-read moralist: "we would that the man when he loveth should remember his superiority." The patriarchal view of the family, then, on the eve of (and even during) the revolutionary decades in England was a "widely prevailing" view.[10] Scholars of later times have reaffirmed this interpretation. Margaret George, for one, as if rejecting Hill's efforts to associate *economic change* in town and country with elevation of women's status, wrote that if "a man needed a wife for companionship as well as for assistance in the "care and looking after" children, the care of household matters," and the maintenance and increase of "substance," he was also gratified that local preachers "were shaping the 'good woman' to . . . voluntary submissiveness."[11] Stevie Davies has described this state of affairs more bluntly: "women did not think, rule, advise, debate, except in a few atypical instances: they deferred. They deferred to an all-male establishment: God the Father and Son, male lords and male bishops, male electorate and MPs, all-male universities, preachers, judges, juries, army, patrilinear heirs." Despite some "exceptions" to this rule, concluded Davies, "common law did not acknowledge the existence of any woman not under the protection of a man."[12] Hence, predictably enough, Sir Robert Filmer's definition, in his *Patriarcha*, of the king as both "father over one family" and "father over many families." Constitutional and familial metaphors in England *were*, thus, conjoined.

But were there, then, as Stevie Davies seemed to suggest, some exceptions to such an otherwise joyless disposition of affairs for seventeenth-century Englishwomen? Specialists on the subject respond (at times) in the affirmative. Under the doctrine of *feme sole*, for instance, a widow, controlling her own property and entitled by custom to one third of her husband's estate, was—even Davies admits—"in an advantageous position." Antonia Fraser has enlarged upon this exception to the usual rules:

> The wealthy widow might or might not be racked with lust as the popular imagination believed. . . . Her position was nonetheless . . . in many ways enviable. City wives were particularly well treated: by the Custom of London a wife had the right to one third of her husband's property at death, and if there were no children, their one third share also. The potential strength in the position of the wealthy widow, if her settlement were unencumbered, her children free from restricting guardianship, may stand as one example of those possibilities which did exist for womankind in the real world, outside . . . her theoretical weakness.[13]

We cite, too, in this connection, Hill's earlier contention that, in London at least, it became "actionable to call a woman 'whore,' and wife-beating was also an offense." (The latter abuse was also frowned on, Hill insisted, in Yorkshire.[14]) Yet again, in the matter of *divorce,* women might conceivably win one (as *a vinculo matrimonii*) if an impediment to marriage such as male impotence could (somehow) be shown to have existed *prior to contract*. Legal separation (*a mensa et thoro*) could be obtained by a wife *after* marriage should "serious misconduct" be proven against the husband. Otherwise, Christopher Durston has intoned, the law, in this as in most other areas of female/male relations, was strongly biased against women's needs. "If . . . the absolute monarchy of husbands and fathers was seriously questioned, perhaps for the first time, during the period 1640-1660, these years saw only the tentative opening rounds of a long contest to establish greater rights and freedoms for wives."[15]

Interestingly, too, Durston speculated that any "discrediting of patriarchy" which may have set in during the revolutionary decades probably owed as much to wives' involuntary assumption of novel responsibilities, or at least sharing of civil war-related duties with spouses, as to any actual "ideological discord." Such an observation, recorded by one of England's finest historians of the family, can lead us on to review the myriad ways in which some of these women involved themselves in the day-to-day hurly-burly of civil conflict in the mid-century. In her absorbing "People's History" of the English Civil War, Diane Purkiss vividly describes some women's activities in this national drama:

> Women did do war work on occasion: in Coventry they filled in quarries "that they might not shelter the enemy". . . . Others nursed the wounded, or were camp-followers, cooking and washing for their men. Even more dramatically, women like Brilliana Harley commanded siege defenses. Still others acted as spies, intelligence-gatherers; a woman known only as "Mary the Scout" was rewarded by [Sir Thomas] Fairfax himself after the fall of Taunton. . . . Other women were involved in political intrigue: Ann Fanshawe, Anne Halkett, Henrietta Maria and Lucy Hay amongst them. . . . Women had to fight for pensions, for subsistence. They had to take on men's work in farms and businesses. Women [also] got involved in the print trade.

Of course, there was also a darker side to all of this. Some women, notes Purkiss, "had the experience of seeing their houses despoiled, their husbands and sons killed, their bedlinen burned, their children hungry. Some were stripped, others raped during sacks of towns." At best, Purkiss conjectures, such hair-raising experiences may have made women feel that "they had a stake in the Commonwealth just as the experience of the New Model Army and its victories gave confidence to its Leveller minority." In unheard-of numbers, Purkiss persuasively concludes, "women were active in wartime politics."[16]

Diane Purkiss's allusion to female involvement in the "print trade" also raises for us the salient issue of censorship (and the breakdown thereof) in prerevolutionary and revolutionary England—and this in turn introduces us to women's roles as publishers and polemicists during the 1640s and

1650s. Lawrence Stone had noted in 1972 how, even in the old regime, press censorship, if established in law, had been weakened "by aristocratic protection of puritan pamphleteers, the smuggling of books from abroad, and the operation of clandestine printing presses in England." Moreover, he had pointed out, the Long Parliament's initial session, by hobbling or abolishing most central governmental institutions, had all but destroyed press censorship in this revolutionary situation.[17] Given "mass illiteracy, meagre education and conditions of servitude," Stevie Davies has argued, it was natural that women should not have made too significant a contribution to the resultant flood of newspapers, broadsheets, treatises, books, and ballads that poured off the presses during the 1640s and 1650s. On the other hand, the fact that deceased male printers' rights transferred to their widows rather than descending to sons helped to ensure that no fewer than 34 Englishwomen during 1641–60 were (reportedly) able to operate as printers and booksellers. Furthermore, women writers often deliberately chose to publish with such female printers/booksellers rather than with men.[18] And what do we know about these adventurous authors' origins? "They came," so Patricia Crawford records, "from a range of social backgrounds." In their ranks we discover "daughters of ministers, wives of printers, comb-makers, poor tradesmen and soldiers, and servants." If most of them were obscure, some still figure prominently in historians' works today—activists such as Katherine Chidley, "probably the best known of the female controversialists for her arguments with Presbyterian minister Thomas Edwards," and (in time) famous for her advocacy of Independency and of pugnacious Leveller John Lilburne.[19] It is scarcely surprising, therefore, that in the early 1650s, when Quaker treatises, sermons and broadsheets began to roll off the presses, 82 out of 650 authors were (so it appears) women—authors, that is, of 220 out of 3853 publications.[20]

Well before the Quaker movement erupted in revolutionary England's rural counties, however, politicized women closer to London were gaining notoriety by bombarding Parliament with petitions on both private and (ever more, as time went on) *public* matters. As S. L. Arnoult has put it, such women, "well-positioned, geographically" and accustomed to running businesses, usually with their husbands, yet sometimes alone, were psychologically prepared to engage in petitioning activities that gradually took on political significance in the heated atmosphere of civil war England. Initially, such actions were motivated in part, to be sure, by religious reformist zeal but also by a desire for peace between the two warring sides in the early days of the civil war. Thus, on Tuesday, August 8, 1643, according to Arnoult, "a group of women showed up at the Houses of Parliament and began to clamor for peace. By now the war had been in progress for a year, and its economic effects were being seriously felt, especially by poorer women whose husbands were in the armies."[21] Such were the petitioners of that day; they, and those women who came after them in later stages of the

Revolution, have attracted the close attention of (among several specialists on the subject) Patricia Crawford:

> The demonstrators and petitioners may not have been the very "poorest shes." It is difficult to interpret the evidence about their social status. Sympathetic newsbooks described the women as the wives of prosperous citizens, while others attacked them as oyster wives, fish wives, women "of the inferior sort". . . . .Also disputed was the level of violence. Some reported that women came to parliament peaceably, with their children, but other newsbook writers depicted the women as aggressive. These differences arise partly from the different kinds of reportage. . . . But all male reporters were influenced by contemporary stereotypes of aggressive, disorderly women.

Aroused women demonstrating for peace in these early days of civil strife often wore *white* ribbons (for peace). Later, as female Londoners became radicalized, first by the deepening impasse between Charles I and his adversaries, and then by signs of growing tensions on the parliamentary side between the New Model Army generals and their critics on the Left, they would frequently arrive at Westminster wearing the Leveller movement's by now well-known "sea-green" colors.[22]

The revolutionary 1640s, then, apparently witnessed a radicalization—and, more specifically, a *secularization*—of the message some women brought to Parliament. They had progressed, it has been said, "from claiming an equality of sovereign souls with men, and public voice in defense of conscience and true religion, to claiming an equal share in the political sovereignty of the commonwealth and an equal voice in the polity. They had directly challenged the traditional 'compass' of women."[23] This portentous progression from *religious* sentiment to *political* sentiment appeared most startlingly in a petition presented in Westminster on May 5, 1649. The petition declared:

> that since we are assured of our creation in the image of God, and of an interest in Christ, equal unto men, as also of a proportional share in the freedoms of this commonwealth, we cannot but wonder and grieve that we should appear so despicable in your eyes, as to be thought unworthy to petition or represent our grievances to this honorable House. Have we not an equal interest with the men of this nation in those liberties and securities contained in the Petition of Right, and other good laws of the land? Are any of our lives, limbs, liberties, or goods to be taken from us more than from men, but by due process of law . . .? And can you imagine us to be sottish or stupid as not to perceive, or not to be sensible when daily those strong defenses of our peace and welfare are broken down and trod underfoot by force and arbitrary power?[24]

Nor did this mark the only occasion on which sentiments purportedly coming from outraged women of the capital (and, possibly, of the surrounding Home Counties as well) found a voice at Westminster—no doubt to the annoyance and, likely, the scandal of men debating public matters in the legislature. We also know that, two years later, a number of women addressed Oliver Cromwell demanding the reform of laws relating to debt. Their *Women's Petition* voiced disappointment over the fact that, contrary to popular expectations, the execution of Charles I had not banished "tyranny" from the land. Indeed, the petition went on, "the Norman laws of the Oppressors still bear dominion over us."[25]

Whether or not the celebrated petition of May 5, 1649—and other manifestoes written in the same period—in fact emanated from a female activist or activists will never be known for sure. Yet this would seem, in a sense, beside the point: such language must have reflected views of women affected by the recent unsettling and unprecedented political events in mid-seventeenth-century England. At the same time, however, historians as a rule have been careful *not* to accept such petitions too hastily (and too anachronistically) as smacking unambiguously of modern "feminism." Patricia Higgins, for instance, commenting specifically on the petition of May 1649, admittedly argued that, in it, women "reached the most extreme 'feminist' position of the period" by "challenging the very basis of the patriarchal society in which they lived." Yet, writing thereafter in a slightly different context, Higgins read these women's petitions, all taken together, as largely *deferring to men* in what she conceded was, in the final analysis, "a male-dominated society." Hence, we have her analysis of the rather ambivalent stance of politicized women at this crucial inflection-point in revolutionary England:

> There appears to be a contradiction between the female petitioners' admission of the inferiority of their sex and the intellectual case they made out for the equality of the sexes. . . . .However, it is not wholly surprising, for the society in which these women lived, and the air they breathed, was excessively patriarchal. The religious and political crisis caught up women, stimulated them into undertaking unconventional actions and into forming their own opinions on religion and politics. In such an atmosphere, strange speculations and new ideas flourished riotously. While not overtly challenging masculine superiority, women tentatively put forward justifications for the involvement of women in politics based on the equal rights of men and women.[26]

Other specialists have treated these questions with similar caution and nuance. Ann Hughes, for one, conceded that "many later discussions have . . . assumed that the . . . women's petitioning was a dramatic assertion of female political rights, and some contemporary sources agree." There is, furthermore, no doubt, Hughes agreed, that "many hundreds of women were involved in lobbying Parliament" in April and May 1649, and that "such mass action by women was clearly a dramatic and, to many, an alarming development." At the same time, she continued, "we should be cautious before accepting completely that this petitioning campaign was as outrageous as the women themselves insisted." After all, their campaign was chiefly aimed, argued Hughes, at "forcing home a sense of the enormity of the violation of Leveller households, and by extension, a realization of Parliament's betrayal of the early Civil War ideals."[27] Brian Manning, too, wrote about limits to the "feminism" of the female petitioners of 1649. In the face of misogynistic ridicule emanating from men assembled in the Commons, he noted, these women still "claimed the right as women to make their views known publicly on political and religious matters, but they did not call for votes for women, and they did not challenge directly the patriarchal organization of the family and society."[28] Perhaps Patricia Crawford has made the larger contextual point here most simply and bluntly: the female petitioners of revolutionary England "never, so far as I know, advanced claims to participate in politics as feminists concerned about the rights of women."[29]

The earlier reference to a "violation of Leveller households" requires naturally that we offer at this point some explanation of the connection between the radicalized female petitioners of the late 1640s and the Leveller movement of those momentous years. The Levellers, of course, have attracted an enormous amount of attention over the years; and the last decade or so has seen no diminution of scholarly interest in the subject.[30] By the time these London-based and army-aligned radicals achieved their maximum influence in the English politics of this era, they had developed (in G. E. Aylmer's words) "quite a comprehensive programme of reforms." Their demands included the absolute supremacy of the Commons, elections for future parliaments on a (somewhat) broadened basis, systemic reform of the law, abolition of corporate and other monopolies, comprehensive tax reform, and protection for all dissenting Protestant sects in the land.[31] This final point, involving religious freedom, could clearly be of special interest to women who were often themselves committed to free sectarian worship. Beyond this last consideration, there were also undeniable familial connections in the 1640s between leading Leveller agitators and the female activists we have already encountered. At least three of the latter, as S. L. Arnoult has notably emphasized, were "clearly tied to the Leveller movement." Elizabeth Lilburne was the (long-suffering) wife of the most celebrated Leveller, John Lilburne; Mary Overton was the wife of Lilburne's fellow-traveler Richard Overton; and Katherine Chidley, whose controversialist career has already attracted our notice (and who may possibly have authored the celebrated petition of May 1649) was mother to Leveller Samuel Chidley. It appears, in addition, that Elizabeth Lilburne's submission to Parliament as early as 1646 of a petition demanding immediate release of husband John, imprisoned for sundry seditious writings and actions, looked forward to the female Londoners' radical petitioning of the next few years, and may have also helped (along with other factors) to bring Leveller leaders and people like Katherine Chidley, Mary Overton, and Elizabeth Lilburne more closely together.[32]

What we may legitimately question in this connection, nevertheless, is the extent to which the Leveller campaign in these stressful times really *did* benefit women in any "modern" sense. It is all very well, for instance, to learn that John Lilburne, in *The Free Man's Freedom Vindicated,* grandly stated that "all and every . . . individual man and woman that ever breathed in the world, are by nature all equal and alike in their power, dignity, authority and majesty."[33] It is equally heart-warming to learn that, when imprisoned in the Tower of London by order of the House of Lords in 1646, Lilburne should have assured his captors that "I had rather you should immediately beat out my brains than deprive me of the society of my wife."[34] Still, rhetorical flourishes aside, when push came to shove, Lilburne (like most men of his times) gendered the term "Englishman's citizenship" to endow at least some men, but *not* women, with active political rights. In fact, one of Lilburne's most incisive biographers, Michael Braddick, has cited numerous instances of Lilburne's condescension toward his wife Elizabeth—sufficiently numerous, it must be said, to induce him to call this prominent Leveller out for "an apparent misogyny remarkable even for the seventeenth century."[35]

But the problem, we must admit, inhered in the very fabric of English society. In her unusually penetrating analysis of the issue, Ann Hughes contended that, in this era, "women's activity was firmly connected with the household, and their interventions were presented as . . . reaffirming family unity. Unity did not mean equality, of course. While a political rhetoric based upon the household validated activity by women . . . in certain circumstances, it also offered clear justification for the male head of household's monopoly of formal political rights." But Hughes delved even more deeply than this, in what we might describe today as a postmodernist rendering of the situation. Leveller literature, she suggested, contained "discordant writing on gender, indicating some of the instabilities and tensions surrounding early modern understandings of women."

> These incoherencies surely reflect some of the contradictions in households where women were seen as clearly subordinate, but also as capable, active partners whose co-operation was essential to the running of the whole enterprise. They are also a product of the discursive problems of establishing a picture of women who were both honest and active in a public world. In the end, for Lilburne at least, women's weaknesses and irrationality made them less dedicated to the public service, especially in a cause that was betrayed and embattled.

In the end, Hughes wrote, Lilburne, by emphasizing his wife's "active, but dutiful" role as his helpmate, was "also constructing himself as a good husband and a true man." He—and his masculine colleagues in the Leveller movement—appropriated their wives' opinions and actions "into a familial whole" *and* into a public political cause defined in the last analysis *by men*.[36]

It is hardly astonishing, then, that when Leveller and "Agitator" spokesmen famously debated, with Cromwell, Henry Ireton, and other Army Grandees at Putney Church in October 1647, the merits of the radical tract *The Agreement of the People*, they made no mention of *women's* right to the franchise in England when the question of voting came up.[37] Moreover, as Diane Purkiss has accurately noted, "no woman's voice was heard in the Putney Debates . . . [Colonel Thomas] Rainsborough spoke up for 'the poorest he,' but no one had a word to say for 'the poorest she.'" Henry Ireton said flatly at Putney that those who (like women) were economically dependent could never be expected to *vote* independently. People might believe that Englishwomen were "born free"; still, they lost their "liberty" upon marriage. Even if, as Purkiss has contended, women could be construed as "citizens" in the most minimal sense of being "inhabitants of the land," she no less added that "they could not defend the state in arms, so they were excluded from one of the most powerful—and most levelling—definitions of citizenship."[38] In the seventeenth-century English world, then, John Lilburne was scarcely the only "radical" for whom the notion of citizenship was essentially gendered *male*.

Yet however this may be, it is equally incontrovertible that—as we have already had occasion to note—Levellers held in common with many female activists a desire to protect free sectarian worship in England. Keith Thomas, in his foundational 1958 article on "Women and the Civil War Sects," expatiated upon this subject. He first introduced the issue by describing the Civil War sectarians in general as "the successors of the separatists who first appeared in Elizabethan England, who emigrated to Holland or to America to set up their independent congregations, or who continued to meet at furtive conventicles in this country, until they reappeared in great numbers in the early days of the Long Parliament, after which they enjoyed a large measure of practical toleration throughout the Interregnum." As Thomas explained, the sectarians were referred to variously as Brownists, Independents, Baptists, Millenarians, Familists, Seekers, Ranters, or (eventually, in the 1650s) Quakers; and they subscribed to a diversity of theological beliefs. Thomas attempted as best he could to distill the essence of those beliefs:

> they believed in a pure Church, they made spiritual regeneration a condition of membership and insisted upon separation from a national Church which contained ungodly elements. More often than not they believed in the complete self-government of individual congregations;

they usually thought in terms of direct inspiration by the Holy Spirit; and they tended to depreciate the role of a ministry, of "outward ordinances" and of human learning. Their assertion of the spiritual equality of all believers led to an exalted faith in private judgment, lay preaching, a cult of prophecies and revelations, and culminated in the Quaker doctrine of the spirit dwelling in all men.[39]

Most critically for us, and unlike in the arena of secular politics and "radical" citizenship, we can safely construe "all men" in the case of *sectarian* matters to include females as well as males. All scholars are explicit on this point, starting with Thomas, who insisted that "from the very beginning the separatists laid great emphasis upon the spiritual equality of the two sexes," and, beyond this, that "women were numerically extremely prominent among the separatists."[40]

Accomplished feminist historians of more recent years have not only "doubled down" on Keith Thomas's commentary, but also added a fascinating—if depressing—twist to the discussion by viewing women's prominence in revolutionary England's religious life through the telltale prism of male satire and misogyny. "Neither ministers nor members of Parliament," Patricia Crawford has noted, "could, or would have wished to, separate religion from its family and household meaning. They wanted women to obey, not to initiate reform." Hence, in part, the tendency of some resentful (and defensive?) males to deprecate female participation in the sectarian experiences of the times. Women often were said, in such circles, to join the sects "because they were weak and foolish and therefore easily seduced." Not too surprisingly, perhaps, some of the more hostile critics of the sects gave vent to their anger in crude satires. Such satires, as Crawford suggests, tell us more about male anxieties of the era than about the women being ridiculed themselves:

> Satire is a rhetorical device which works off normative values. Like jokes and laughter, it comes from a sense of the ridiculous in life, but in this case, behavior does not provoke mirth, but anger. For a woman to act in areas which men considered to be their own territory aroused men's fury. Consequently, men held women up to ridicule. Satire worked from known and accepted values which an author assumed that his readers shared.

It was assumed, in other words, that the actions being satirized "were ridiculous because they reversed the natural order." Associated with such a misogynistic perspective, unsurprisingly, was the suspicion—very frequently expressed in prurient terms—that women must be seeking experiences outside socially "respectable" spaces because they lusted after freedom—a freedom implying sexual licentiousness.[41]

It remains no less the case, nonetheless, that women figured prominently—at times, in fact, predominantly—in the sects of the Civil War era. We know, for instance, that at Norwich, in 1645, the eighty-three women of the local congregation palpably outnumbered the thirty-one men; while of the twelve founding members of the Baptist church at Bedford in 1650, no fewer than eight were women. (In the episcopal returns and indulgence records of Charles II's reign so soon thereafter, conventiclers were frequently described as "chiefly women," "more women than men," "most silly women," and so on.) Even more significant, perhaps, is the evidence regarding the *preaching* and *prophesying* roles that many women came to assume in the sects of the revolutionary era. In London, for instance, so Keith Thomas wrote, many of the Independent congregations went far beyond sectaries' so-called "gathered churches" on the Continent "by allowing all their members, women included, to debate, vote and, if not preach, then usually at least to prophesy, which often came to much the same thing." But women were prophesying as well (and, it may be, preaching, too?) in areas *beyond* the English capital, including Kent, Lincolnshire, Ely, Salisbury, and Hertfordshire—and indeed as far afield as Yorkshire and Somerset.[42]

It was, additionally, quite as hard as Thomas implied it was for contemporaries (many of them defensive and irritated men) to distinguish between women-as-preachers and women-as-prophetesses. Antonia Fraser, admittedly, has opined that the distinction between the two roles really could, in some situations, count for something. General prejudice, she has written, "could cause a woman preaching to be condemned first as a 'prater' or 'prattler,' so by implication as a scold, and lastly even as some kind of witch—remembering the connection in the popular mind between scolding and cursing." On the other hand, the prophetess had by tradition been treated, in Fraser's words, "with a certain nervous respect by society." Claiming "a direct inspiration from God, the prophetess might challenge accepted notions concerning religion and society, but she did not necessarily in her own person challenge the accepted order." What was remarkable about the prophetesses and "allied female seers" in the unprecedented circumstances of the late civil war period was the way their numbers grew—and, along with that, the way some of them, summoned to give witness before the most powerful English leaders in the country's revolutionary crisis, could momentarily acquire *political* significance of their own:

The point has been made that at least half a dozen times between 1647 and 1654 important deliberations were put aside, while some obscure prophetess (or prophet) delivered a message generally relayed by the Almighty via an apocalyptic vision. Nothing underlines more clearly the weird atmosphere of those times. . . . At the end of December 1648—the most crucial period for the Army Council as the King's future swayed in the balance—an unknown woman named Elizabeth Poole appeared in front of them to communicate her visions concerning "the presence of God with the Army."

God, so it seems, "instructed" Elizabeth to appear before the Grandees several more times during this decisive period; and although her advice to Cromwell *not* to execute Charles I was in the end unheeded, we remain struck by how this humble woman had "invoked the awesome role of the prophetess."[43] Yet in practice the distinction between preachers and prophetesses in these chiliastic times must have been blurred, and ignored altogether by other women who, like Elizabeth Poole, inserted themselves into the politics of prerevolutionary and revolutionary England. Katherine Chidley, for one, "had been involved in political and religious struggles on behalf of the Independent sects from as early as the late 1620s," and we already have seen that she was personally aligned with the Levellers in the 1640s. Sarah Wight, Anna Trapnel, and a radical sectary known to us only as "Mrs. Attaway" were among other activists who combined political and religious roles (and, probably, preaching and prophesying vocations) in ways that were uniquely characteristic of those topsy-turvy times.[44]

Did these female sectarians also achieve, through their multifarious activities in revolutionary England, a novel, emancipatory sense of themselves, or what Theresa Feroli has defined as "a sense of identity distinct from their roles as wives and mothers"? Although the women prophets were *not*, Feroli conceded, "feminists" in that they did not "intervene in the political sphere solely to improve the lives of women," she *does* contend, provocatively, that they *did* "represent an important moment in the history of feminism" insofar as they sought to "justify a role for women as political activists." Their statements included "denunciations of Charles I and Oliver Cromwell, predictions of the imminent apocalypse, and pleas for religious toleration," all of which "placed them in the forefront of political events." Feroli went on to praise women such as Eleanor Davies, Anna Trapnel, and Margaret Fell for attempting to envision a political order that might, in good time, "privilege individual agency over and against the dictates of a predetermined hierarchy" in society. Beyond this, Feroli eulogized long-imprisoned Quaker missionaries such as Katharine Evans and Sarah Chevers in even more incandescent terms:

Evans, for instance, does not speak of missing her family but instead agonizes over their spiritual well-being. . . . What matters is not her kinship with them but their relationships, as individual believers, with God. . . . For her part, Sarah Chevers opens her letter to her husband by stating her commitment to her faith. . . . Clearly, her loyalty to her God—who possesses her "love" and her "life"—far exceeds her allegiance to her own husband. Evans, too, implicitly derogates the significance of her marriage bond.

In all of this, Feroli was highlighting—in a unique, seventeenth-century revolutionary English context—the beginnings of what she took to be "feminist consciousness—namely, the recognition that women *as women* can effect political change."[45]

Yet Feroli's aggressively feminist interpretation of what the female sectarians were all about in mid-seventeenth-century England has to be seen as something of an "outlier" in this field of historical scholarship. Phyllis Mack, even before turning to the issue of Quakerism in her formidably researched study of visionary women and their "ecstatic prophesies" in revolutionary England, threw cold water on the argument that people such as (for instance) Anna Trapnel were instrumental in heralding a modern approach to "feminine consciousness" in their conventicles. "The Fifth Monarchist sect to which Mary Cary and Anna Trapnel belonged," Mack conceded, "respected women as prophets and may even have tolerated separate women's meetings, but the agenda of those meetings was set by men, and much of women's public activity as church members was in support of those male leaders." Indeed, according to Mack, "the potential of even collective behavior was limited for prophetic women, for all organized congregations, even radical congregations, excluded women from positions of real leadership." True, women spoke up at times in Baptist groups, but even in those forums, "their authority to preach or to lead meetings was contested." However eagerly some women may have turned to Quaker assemblies in the 1650s as they sought communities whose leaders would "dissolve *all* barriers to the equality of the saints," they remained disappointed. The most that Mack could conclude from her studies was that women's prophesying in the civil war period was "wide-ranging and utopian; yet it also entailed a denial of womanhood as a source of public power and expressiveness."[46] Regarding Quakerism specifically, Patricia Crawford, like Mack, has drawn careful distinctions. In *purely spiritual* matters, she has implied, Quaker women's dealings with "male leaders . . . differed from those of women in other radical religious movements." In this sect, at least, men and women were "more willing to challenge and transcend the constraints of sex and gender." But "men in the radical Quaker movement—one which truly horrified nearly all their contemporaries—shared . . . the conservative assumptions of their society." They were, in Crawford's words, "imbued with contemporary stereotypes," and this did much to guarantee that they would even oppose "a woman's attempt to exercise a spiritual authority which conflicted with the views of the majority."[47] And while Antonia Fraser was quick to note that in 1656 Quaker leader George Fox put out "the first defense in English of the spiritual equality of women since the Reformation," she also acknowledged that the occasional female "'quaking'" during minister's sermons which gave the Society of Friends its popular nickname confirmed many menfolk's darkest fears regarding women's "irrational" tendencies, and as such was "not calculated to win the respect of male authorities."[48] To some extent, then, even among Fifth Monarchists and Quakers, perhaps the most millenarian, most chiliastic of these revolutionary sects, men and women belonged in the end to separate spheres.

"After 1660," Fraser has somberly concluded, "the voices of the prophetesses died away except for a few lonely exclamations; the female clamor of the Commonwealth . . . gave way to the merry prattle of the ladies of King Charles II's England."[49] Along very similar lines we have Crawford's dampening but logical verdict: "It would be anachronistic to suggest that women found 'emancipation' in the sects." In society *at large*, furthermore, "there was no alteration in the basic connection between sexuality and reproduction; no change in the concept of women as the weaker vessel." Still, despite admitting that the sects failed to provide "a fundamentally different view of women from that of the Anglican church or of society at large," Crawford has endeavored to salvage some gain from the wreckage of millenarian female hopes in that era. At the very least, she has maintained, assumptions about the two sexes *did* on an ongoing basis "influence men's and women's behavior and spirituality"; hence, "there was a gender dimension in all the religious upheavals of the revolutionary decades."[50] This may indeed have been the case, even if, all too often, such a "gender dimension" in religious upheaval led to what another feminist scholar has called "snarling quarrels" breaking out in some of the "gathered churches." Fifth Monarchist John Rogers, experiencing such brouhahas in his own Dublin congregation, wrote disgustedly that "most men do arrogate a sovereignty to themselves which I see no warrant for"; yet Rogers, too, revealed an "excruciated dither" on issues of women's sectarian roles that has earned for him a less-than-flattering reputation among most modern feminists.[51] The consensual scholarly view seems in the end to be that, in Sharon L. Arnoult's words, "even the most radical women" of the 1640s and 1650s in England "never got completely away from the idea that their political identities were subsumed in men's."[52]

True, this last scholar, even in reaching such a cautionary conclusion, has attempted to reassess the female petitioners and sectarians of revolutionary England in as positive terms as possible. Arnoult has speculated that the Civil War *did* at least show that "the idea of the sovereignty of the soul carried a latent threat to the structures of the English religious, political, and social establishment."[53] Patricia Crawford, more imaginatively, has depicted women of this era as harboring a sense of what she terms "subterranean citizenship" consisting of female "involvement with community and public issues"—as manifesting, in other words, a nascent civic-mindedness that would produce in later generations female "citizens" not only active in Nonconformism but also actively instilling in their children English patriotic pride.[54] And, beyond even this, Katharine Gillespie has linked some of the sectarian writers of England's revolutionary decades with the fathers of eighteenth-century liberalism. Liberalism, if she is right, may have found its "fathers" in men like Shaftesbury and, especially, John Locke; but it just as certainly found its "mothers" in preachers and prophetesses like Katherine Chidley, Anna Trapnel, and Elizabeth Poole.[55] The harsh fact remains, nonetheless, that—as Chapter 5 will have occasion to reaffirm—even the most intrepid visionary women could not, in the final analysis, conjure away the patriarchal and misogynistic attitudes so prevalent in revolutionary (and, indeed, postrevolutionary) English society. Moreover, on a purely *political* level, female (and male) radicals of Leveller and other vintage were suppressed, first, by Cromwell and Company, as Commonwealth and "Barebones Parliament" gave way to Protectorate in late 1653, and—eventually, in 1660—by an even less responsive and sympathetic, because even more *conservative*, Stuart Restoration regime.

France: Activists, "Incomplete" *Citoyennes*—and the Jacobin Challenge

Any analysis of politicized Frenchwomen in revolutionary times should logically commence, as did our discussion of seventeenth-century Englishwomen, with a review of their prerevolutionary (and, predictably, subordinate) status at law. We will then need to confront a host of interrelated questions. First, what does the rich literature on women in the French Revolution tell us about their activist roles during the *grandes journées* of the upheaval in France—especially at Paris, of course, but also (where those roles are documented) in the provinces? What can we say about the sociological and vocational origins of these demonstrating Frenchwomen, and what kinds of anxieties and aspirations drove them out again and again into the dusty streets of their communities? Again, do we truly find their interests reflected, at the height of the Revolution, in seminal legislation such as that of September 1792 dealing with familial issues, and in clubs such as the Parisian Society of Revolutionary Republican Women? And how was the subsequent reaction *against* the phenomenon of female activism manifested in a general withdrawal from gendered patterns of "class inversion" to more traditional gendered class roles in late revolutionary France? We may discover, in this country's upheaval, less of an obsession with religious questions, more of a preoccupation with *secular* matters, than we did in revolutionary England. By the same token, however, we may also discover that, in France just as in England, even the most radicalized women were left in the end with little more than unrealized prospects for full secular citizenship.

To begin with, James F. Traer's research (building on that of earlier scholars) has left us with the same general impression of women's status in

French ancien régime law as we derive from similar work on women's legal status in prerevolutionary England.[56] Both customary and written French law prior to 1789, Traer has noted, "had been heavily influenced by Roman notions of *patria potestas*, the father's virtually unlimited power over his children and their property" until they were "emancipated" from that condition "by marriage, establishment of a separate household, or other formal act." Unsurprisingly, we gather, this legal disability in the old regime applied more strictly and consistently to daughters than to sons. "Women of any age," according to Traer, were, with only a few exceptions, "legally incapable of independent acts concerning property and hence they lived in a sort of permanent minority, under the authority of father, husband, or other male relative. Only as independent merchants or as widows did they acquire a measure of independent legal capacity." (Do we espy in this last connection a parallel to the *relatively* advantageous position enjoyed by the *"feme sole"* in seventeenth-century England?) The father was also entitled by law to punish a disobedient daughter (or the husband an adulterous wife) by imprisoning the offending woman through the notorious means of a royal *lettre de cachet*. Hence were the rights of individuals—most notably those of daughters and wives—subordinated to the patriarchal will and to the "honor or security of the family."[57]

Yet it is also true, in the French as in the English case, that experts have often differed over the extent to which women's status in revolutionary times was in fact superior to their status in the ancien régime. For instance, we saw earlier that Whiggish scholars such as Christopher Hill and Lawrence Stone identified Puritanism as one ideological force that arguably *did* ameliorate middle-class Englishwomen's status during the 1640s–50s—as we have seen, a hotly contested assertion. Do we discover a similar indecision in the way Frenchwomen's historians interpret the Enlightenment ideology of the eighteenth century? As a matter of fact, the scholarship seems as unresolved on this subject as does that dealing with Puritanism in Stuart England. James F. McMillan testifies eloquently to this fact in his conspectus on women in early modern France.[58] On the one hand, he assures us, *philosophes* such as Montesquieu (in the *Persian Letters* and the subsequent *Spirit of the Laws*) "denounced despotic rule in general and the exploitation of women in particular," while Diderot in some (though not all) of his writings "attacked the legal disabilities to which women were subjected by male legislators." On the other hand, McMillan cautions us, "it would be a mistake to exaggerate the degree to which Enlightenment thinkers devoted themselves to the issue of ending women's subordination." Along these lines, he reminds us that "in the vast *oeuvre* of Voltaire . . . there is only the odd reference to women." Indeed, McMillan reluctantly concedes that more than one of the *philosophes* were "overtly misogynous." At best, he concludes on this issue in a rather ambivalent fashion:

The legacy of the Enlightenment, then, was mixed. What is not in doubt, however, is that a vast amount of thought and discussion had gone into attempts to redefine the gender roles of men and women. An essentially new discourse had been elaborated, capable of appropriation by both feminists and antifeminists, as the nineteenth century would prove. At the end of the Old Regime, power remained unambiguously monarchical, personal and patriarchal. But . . . at least some women managed both to exercise political influence and, perhaps more importantly, to shape the language of politics. Such, indeed, was their influence that it generated a good deal of male anxiety.

"Enlightened" discourse, in McMillan's eyes, did not so much *discredit* an "ideology of separate spheres" identifying women largely as "wives and mothers whose destiny was domesticity and the reproduction of the species" as it *relegitimized* that ideology on the newer basis of "the authority of science and the best philosophical opinion of the day."[59] Women's "otherness" and critical inferiority were, as a result, redefined—but assuredly *not* renounced—in the eighteenth century's intellectual discourse.

James F. McMillan's discussion of the "mixed legacy" of the Enlightenment strikes us as largely predictable, given the spirited cut-and-thrust of the scholarly debate on the subject. On the one hand, numerous feminist historians have discerned in the Enlightenment a movement that, ironically, since it challenged the old regime's hierarchical world of noble *privilège*, undercut the influence of noble and bourgeois women at court and in the salons. By postulating a futurist society of rational autonomous individuals understood, at least implicitly, to be gendered *male*—with interests that the state would feel obligated to champion—the *philosophes*, publicists, and controversialists of eighteenth-century France were helping to prepare the way for a Brave New World in which female concerns might count for even less than they had counted for in the decades leading up to 1789.[60] Yet this reading of the past, however stimulating, has drawn increasing fire over the years in feminist circles. For instance (as we observed in Chapter 3), Sarah Hanley has queried the entire assumption of misogyny as having all of a sudden reared its hideous head in revolutionary times; she has accurately pointed out that this attitude was prominent throughout the old regime, from, in other words, the early sixteenth century onward.[61] Dena Goodman has, for her part, held historians such as Joan Landes to account for depicting the old regime's treatment of women in unduly optimistic colors, thereby contrasting it with the presumed misogyny of Frenchmen in the revolutionary period.[62] But perhaps it was Olwen Hufton who, writing here in the aftermath of the 1989 Bicentennial celebrations, most vigorously criticized some feminists' approach to this issue:

We have been asked to view the Revolution as a factor accelerating the banishment of women into the home [and] the private sphere, and quite extraordinary claims about the "freedom" and "public presence" of the "eighteenth-century woman" have been made in contrast to the domestic bondage of the 'nineteenth-century woman' on the flimsiest of evidence. . . . Such an exercise should not be confused with the actual experience of real women. We should, as historians, be conscious of the demarcation between theory and what actually happened.[63]

Hufton's acerbic commentary likely reflected in part her intensive research focus on provincial women. As such, it usefully reminds us that, later on, we will have to deal with conservative rural women as well as with their (presumably) more radicalized urban sisters. Still, the undoubted fact that feminists have often regarded the Parisian salon as a "quintessentially feminine institution" devoted to the diffusion of Enlightenment ideals will induce us first to revisit Frenchwomen's eighteenth-century and revolutionary experiences in Parisian and other urban settings.[64]

As James McMillan has relevantly pointed out, "women were no strangers to political protest in the years before 1789."[65] As far back as the winter of 1708–9, women at Paris—and elsewhere—were riotously demanding both lower bread prices and an abrupt end to the War of the Spanish Succession. At various times during the eighteenth century, women "in towns and cities, and notably in Paris . . . were regularly the prime movers behind disturbances at the marketplace." Such interventions often led to the imposition, by popular demand, of *taxation populaire*, the sale of commodities at a "fair" price "fixed by the rioters themselves." Fourteen women, McMillan has remarked, were among those arrested in the capital for their roles in the "flour war" (*guerre des farines*) in 1775; this was, for sure, a "classic case of protest against steep rises in the price of flour and bread."[66] Moreover, as McMillan and other women's historians have repeatedly stressed, many of these traditional features of female protest were destined to reemerge in women's demonstrations during the *grandes journées* that punctuated the history of the Parisian revolution in 1789 and subsequent years.

Although only one woman is known for sure to have taken part in the storming of the Parisian Bastille on 14 July 1789, women aplenty celebrated "*la prise de la Bastille*" in the days and weeks that followed. As the whole world knows, women played a much more decisive role in the equally storied October Days of that year: female Parisians, their ranks swollen to 6,000 or more, marched out on that occasion to Versailles and (with the crucial assistance of Lafayette and National Guardsmen) were able to coerce King, Queen, and family back to the capital. Perhaps even more revelatory, however, in the colorful details of social history, is the way a contemporary journalist, S.-P. Hardy, described a women's demonstration during the tense period that elapsed between the July and October Days:

> Toward . . . noon, a kind of procession of girls and women is seen once again passing along the rue St. Jacques, . . . accompanied by soldiers from the bourgeois militia and by musical instruments; these girls and these women returned from Ste. Geneviève to drumbeat with two consecrated breads, five large brioches, bouquets, and two branches of vines decorated with . . . bunches of grapes which they were going to offer to the Holy Virgin in the metropolitan church, having to go afterwards to the Hôtel de Ville. . . . These . . . *citoyennes* . . . appeared . . . to have no objective other than that of performing solemn thanksgiving to the Supreme Being for the visible protection he has just accorded to Parisians.

Just a few weeks after S.-P. Hardy recorded these impressions (on August 21, 1789), he would somewhat more apprehensively be reporting (on September 17) the following disturbing news:

> Toward the hour of noon, rioting women went out in large numbers to the Hôtel de Ville to complain about the bakers. They were sent for an audience at four in the afternoon and for some kind of answer from the mayor of the city and the representatives of the commune. These women said publicly "that men didn't understand anything about the matter and that they wanted to play a role in affairs."

Hardy, a (probably well-fed?) diarist might on this occasion grumble that "no one would experience the misfortune of lacking bread if each person limited himself to his usual consumption without committing the imprudence of hoarding surplus foodstuffs"; he had, nonetheless, unerringly pointed to the gnawing economic fears that, along with other concerns, drove Parisian market-women into the streets.[67] Such interventions, in 1789, heralded similar protests in the turbulent years to come. Women (and menfolk), having fetched "the baker, the baker's wife, and the baker's little boy" back to Paris in the October Days, were now prepared, psychologically, to interfere in their élitist compatriots' political disputes whenever necessary. They would show this, again and again—during the national panic precipitated by Louis XVI's abortive "flight to Varennes" in mid-summer 1791, during the food crises of early 1792 and early 1793, during the insurrection of May–June 1793, during the Commune-coordinated uprising of September 5, 1793, and up to (if, fatefully, *not* beyond) the "mass-mobilizing" Germinal/Prairial Days of 1795.[68]

Such was (in brief) the chronology of female protest during the revolutionary *journées* as they have been most thoroughly studied—in the French capital. Dominique Godineau, who probably knows these women better than almost any other scholar, informs us that "the majority were working women: seamstresses and laundresses, but also skilled artisans (publishers, book binders, etc.), merchants or domestics who enjoyed an extremely full social existence that was related to their political participation and which linked them with men within the popular movement."[69] Again, "it was taken for granted" by her contemporaries that "a woman of the people was a laborer." Thus, this "woman of the people" was necessarily regarded as an essential contributor to her family's economy:

> Although the collective *mentalité* assigned the task of supporting a family to the father, lower-class conditions of existence made the mother's work indispensable as well. In many house-holds her labor represented that critical difference between poverty and indigence. In the case of unemployment or an accident, families would have been unable to survive if women did not work. It was also absolutely necessary for women and young girls who lived alone to work for their livelihood. Thus, employed women were the norm in popular milieus and [they] played a constitutive role in the social and familial landscape.

And yet, according to Godineau, women's work "was not seen through a feminist perspective during the Revolution"; people in this era, in other words, did not *ideologically* link a woman's "right to work" with what some later researchers would term "women's emancipation." At the same time, however, the war that came in April 1792 undoubtedly *did* enhance women's "occupational mobility" and diversification; warfare may well have promoted these developments "by pushing women who had lived up to then by their spouses' work to seek employment to ensure their own and their children's subsistence." Hence, the hard-pressed authorities in time welcomed efforts to open the "mechanical" and artisanal trades to women, "even though these occupations were high in the hierarchy of professions."[70]

Social historians have at times disagreed rather strenuously about the precise *motivation* of female participants in the street politics of the Parisian revolution. Shirley E. Roessler, like some other unwavering feminists, has dismissed those studies that, even as they "focus on feminist issues," seem determined to "dwell on the idea that these women were motivated above all by economic concerns." Not for Roessler, the primacy of economic motives: "it is obvious," she insists, "that for the most part women's political awareness and understanding expanded as the Revolution progressed. They acted as citizens despite the fact that they were formally denied the rights of citizenship." The sustenance issue, Roessler grudgingly concedes, "may have been the one that brought women into the main arena of the Revolution, but once they were there, political interest triumphed."[71] Perhaps so; yet we recall all too vividly those hungry women so feared by "bourgeois" onlookers like S.-P. Hardy; we know, as well, that such women were scarcely limited to the earliest days of the Parisian upheaval. Other historians, more subtly, perhaps, have attempted to navigate between extremes on this question of the female activists' motivations. Dominique Godineau, whom we have already encountered, has acknowledged that "in all periods of food crisis, women of the people [have] passed into the front ranks, and many historians have concluded that women intervened in the Revolution only when this problem surfaced, leaving strictly political questions to their male companions." Still, even though "a special connection between women and subsistence does exist," Godineau affirms, "it must not blind us." Her treatment of the problem is more sophisticated: she identifies, in the crowds of the revolutionary era, "three overlapping groups of women participants: prominent militant women (*militantes marquantes*), militant women who formed the base of this group (*militantes de base*), and then the popular masses of women (*masses populaires féminines*)." For Godineau, *political* motivation was strongest for the "prominent militants," whereas sheer economic need most powerfully impelled the "popular masses" into action in the streets. Armed with such a typology, she could logically conclude (for example) that, in the Germinal/Prairial "Days" of 1795, "militant women" prioritized *political* needs, whereas "ordinary. . . rioters" prioritized "bread."[72]

If, for the sake of argument, we accept Dominique Godineau's categorization of ultra-militant, militant, and not-so-militant *Parisiennes* in the revolutionary period, it is the *political* motivation of the *militantes* that may especially draw our interest at this point. To what extent, we may inquire, does an analysis of *political* motives challenge us to pose larger questions about some Frenchwomen's desires for full-fledged *citizenship* in the Revolution? For an historian like Roessler, cited above, the answer to this query is obvious. "There is still a need," she maintains, "for a more general and scholarly study of the role of women during the French Revolution"— this, because so very many of these women "acted as citizens despite the fact that they were formally denied the rights of citizenship." Indeed, Roessler goes beyond even this, arguing that female involvement in politics was essential to "determining the directions taken by the Revolution in the years between 1789 and 1795."[73] Yet, once again, we find other specialists defining issues with more subtlety. If, for instance, Olwen Hufton is correct, evidence points to a woman of the working classes in revolutionary Paris as harboring, at best, political ambitions that "were ambiguous and may have varied enormously." This historian, hence, finds "no evidence to suggest that the overwhelming majority of women had any political pretensions on their own behalf on the issue of the vote." This was the case, even though wifely "endorsement of the representation of the household through the husband in local and national politics appears to have been total and strong." At the same time, Olwen Hufton goes on to explain in detail how these *Parisiennes did* make their presence known in France's capital city in the full tide of revolution:

Their own right to petition, denounce, fill the tribunes of the Assembly and later the Comités, and criticize politicians and address them as 'tu' to remind them of whose interests they were supposed to represent (emphatically, these women had no respect for a higher authority) was also . . . pressed. Spy, denouncer, critic, judge, and intense believer in the intrinsic rectitude of her assumption of these roles—*voilà la femme du sans-culotte.*

This archetypical *enragée Parisienne*, Hufton concludes, embraced a notion of "citizenship" which, in its own way, was decidedly *not* "passive," which exhorted her to be "vigilant in the elimination of the internal enemy" even as her husband, or (perhaps) her son, or her brother, or her lover, fought for the Revolution at the front.[74]

Olwen Hufton's characterization of a certain kind of feminine "citizenship" in the Revolution not officially certified, not officially acknowledged, comports well with Dominique Godineau's description of women's "incomplete citizenship" in the revolutionary decade. Such individuals, Godineau reminds us, were "legally excluded from the body politic and possessed none of the attributes of sovereignty (voting rights, the right to deliberate in the general assemblies of the sections, the right to organize in an armed body and sit on the Revolutionary Tribunal, etc.)." Their status was, so to speak, "ambiguous—that of *citoyennes* without citizenship." Still, in times of popular insurrection, women through their activities "constituted an integral portion of the Sovereign—although such insurrection was not included within the structure of *sans-culotte* organization." Moreover, if women were indeed excluded because of their gender from enjoying all the *official* "attributes of popular sovereignty," they attempted to compensate for this "exclusion" by developing what Godineau refers to as "certain behaviors and certain practices." In addition to the kinds of activities enumerated (as we have seen) by Hufton, Parisian and other urban women continually demanded, at least until the fall of 1793, the right to bear arms in organized fashion, the right to maintain "a strong presence . . . at the foot of the guillotine" in order to "ensure" that enemies of the *patrie* were capitally punished for their crimes, the right—at least indirectly—to "ratify" in local assemblages the Jacobin-inspired Constitution of 1793, and (paradoxically, perhaps) the right to be held accountable, as men certainly were, for political crimes against the Revolution.[75] In a final summation, Godineau tries to place this discussion of revolutionary women's "incomplete" citizenship in a broader historical context. In Rousseauistic terms, she concedes, the Republic of the 1790s, imperfectly formed as it was, separated female "subjects" who were "submissive to the law of the state" from male citizens who "participated in the sovereign authority." The "natural inalienable rights of each individual" were, ineluctably, gendered *male*. By the same (ideological) token, however,

Godineau also reassures us that "the universality of the revolutionary ideas asserted in the [1789] Declaration of Rights [of Man and the Citizen] opened the door to the future. Conformity to principles necessitated that one day the female citizen would acquire full political rights."[76]

The question of women's citizenship in the French Revolution also loomed behind the important family legislation and the female "political sociability" of this period. On the former issue, James F. Traer and other eighteenth-century historians have detailed for us the complicated precedents leading, finally, to the seminal legislation of 1792.[77] For instance, as Traer has observed, some of the leading figures of Enlightened persuasion—Turgot, Condorcet, Voltaire, Lafayette, Rulhière, Malesherbes, and so on—had joined reformists at the Bourbon court in advocating either the modification or the outright abrogation of Protestant legal disabilities in marital matters. Eventually, Louis XVI, apparently moved by arguments of social utility, statist needs, and principled tolerance, had signed legislation of November 1787 which, if not altogether guaranteeing Protestants freedom of worship, did at least establish the legality, in the kingdom, of Protestant marriage. The 1787 Edict, Traer has argued, was significant for the later history of legal reform for French subjects/citizens at large: it was, he reminds us, "the first instance of a purely secular law governing the marriages of a large number of French citizens and, as such, it foreshadowed the introduction of civil marriage for all Frenchmen during the revolution."[78] As the ancien régime in France gave way to the revolutionary years, reformists desiring specifically to ameliorate women's and children's fates within the household often adopted the telling tactic of likening the "despotism" of old regime monarchs and ministers, theoretically and rhetorically, to that of abusive heads of household. Some significant results followed. For instance, the Constituent Assembly early on abolished *lettres de cachet*, replacing them with family "tribunals" and thereby limiting the father's control over his family. The Assembly then abolished primogeniture (in 1790) and decreed in the following year that intestate legacies had to be divided equally among children regardless of gender or birth order. The Constitution of 1791, very crucially, made marriage in France a civil, rather than a religious, contract. The Legislative Assembly of 1791-92 innovated further in this area of law (as, for instance, on the matter of adoption); but the major break-through of these years came in late September 1792, with legislation modernizing both marriage and divorce procedures.

As James Traer has explained in considerable detail, the legislation of 20 September 1792 dealt with the so-called *état civil* (the registration, by local authorities throughout France, of births, marriages, and deaths); with the requirements for valid (and now *civil*) marriage; and with the procedures relating to divorce.[79] For one thing, the registers of "civil status" were to be maintained by officials appointed by the municipal governments of the communes, who were also obligated to submit annual statistical records of such matters to the authorities at Paris. (Unfortunately, the enforcement of these provisions was fated at times to be sabotaged by hostile "non-juring" clergy; at other times, it was hampered by what Traer has called "the pitfalls of ignorance and incompetence of public officials.") Then, again, the 1792 statute fixed fifteen and thirteen as the minimum age for marriages of males and females, respectively—this, with the requirement of a father's consent, or that of a mother, should the father be deceased or otherwise "unable to act." The age of majority was set at twenty-one for both men and women; at such age, in other words, the individuals concerned were deemed to be free from requirements of parental consent. The revolutionary lawmakers palpably desired to end such abuses as clerical impediments unnecessarily set to these "companionate marriages"; to promote society's assumed goals of "good public morals and population growth" as well as to satisfy the individuals' natural desire for happiness; and, in general, "to enhance citizenship by emphasizing the duties of the married couple to the *patrie.*" Finally, the 1792 legislation provided for three basic kinds of divorce. First, the parties might resolve to end a marriage "by mutual consent" before a family "council" or "court" composed of relatives or friends. Second, a spouse could ask for a divorce on the grounds of alleged "incompatibility of temperament or character," again airing all pertinent issues before a family court. Third, divorce might be granted on more drastic grounds, such as mental illness, cruelty or serious injury, "notorious disorder of morals," two years of abandonment, emigration, and so forth. During the most advanced phase of the Revolution (1793–4), additional measures would be proposed by radical deputies to expedite divorce procedures, as well as to continue the process of democratizing inheritance practices in the French Republic.[80]

But what, we may query, were the *gendered* implications of all this? Feminist historians such as Suzanne Desan have quite understandably focused on this question in their work. Desan largely concurs with scholars like James Traer that the revolutionaries genuinely wanted to "cultivate emotional bonds between husband and wife, parent and child." Nevertheless, she has also held that Traer's discussion of the 1792 legislation failed adequately to deal with its potential (and more specific) implications for the status of married Frenchwomen. For instance, according to Suzanne Desan:

[Traer] pays little attention to how power dynamics might operate within the "companionate marriage," nor does he ask how the revolutionaries imagined that gender differences would sustain intimacy. Although various male and female club members, pamphleteers, deputies, clergymen, and family members did not agree on the ideal characteristics of male and female nature, they all shared the assumption that men and women had different but complementary roles to play in forging conjugal affection as well as political unity. . . . These assumptions often demanded that women dedicate themselves to converting men and children [to patriotism?] and to expressing their own patriotism primarily through [traditional] familial roles.[81]

The reference to "patriotism" is also significant, for, as Desan and a myriad of other specialists on this subject have observed, the larger issue of *citizenship* also emerged here; it could not be disassociated, that is, from considerations of each woman's role within the Revolution's newly legislated schema of "companionate marriage"—and possible divorce. Again, we have Desan's words on the subject:

> For marriage to be truly regenerative and central to citizenship, it had to be happy, freely chosen, mutually contracted and fulfilling to each individual: the freedom to sever that bond was fundamental to the very essence of republican marriage. But at the same time, the revolutionaries counted on marriage to stand as the quintessential unit that naturally, morally, and legally underpinned the social unity of the Republic and citizenship. For this reason, divorce seemed simultaneously necessary and deeply threatening.[82]

Hence, treatments of the "marriage question" in revolutionary France must unavoidably point, not only to the huge stakes that Frenchwomen of every persuasion and every region held in this domain of law, but also to the deeper paradox rooted here in the irreducible tensions between the need for freedom and individuality, on the one hand, and the need for greater (and *state-related*) social cohesion, on the other. It is hardly surprising that virtually all scholars working in this field, from James F. Traer (in the 1980s) to Jennifer Heuer (in 2005), and those experts writing since, have in similar fashion underscored the need to situate the questions dealt with in the legislation of 1792 in this larger context involving the obligations of citizenship and the advent of the modernized French state.[83]

We find similar issues implicit in Frenchwomen's "political sociability" during the revolutionary era. Here, the outstanding example has always been the clubs and societies of militant *citoyennes* that sprang into existence— both at Paris and in the provinces—in the early 1790s.[84] The most celebrated of these clubs was the Parisian Society of Revolutionary Republican Women, founded in May 1793 by women's advocates Pauline Léon and Claire Lacombe. The principles of radical female citizenship were encoded formally—and defiantly—in the Society's regulations of July 9, 1793. They were summarized forthrightly in what we might call the Preamble to those regulations:

> Convinced that there is no liberty without customs and principles, and that one must recognize one's social duties in order to fulfill one's domestic duties adequately, the Revolutionary Republican *citoyennes* have formed

a Society to instruct themselves, to learn well the Constitution and laws of the Republic, to attend to public affairs, to succor suffering humanity, and to defend all human beings who become victims of any arbitrary acts whatever. They want to banish all selfishness, jealousies, rivalry, and envy and to make good their [Society's] name.[85]

Expanding upon these regulations, Darline Levy and Harriet Applewhite have noted how the Parisiennes in this organization inextricably linked women's right to bear arms with their civic responsibility "to live for the Republic or to die for it," and have emphasized how such a linkage in this conception of militant citizenship was deliberately "placed at the center of women's political self-definition." They have also cogently remarked that, by the summer of 1793, such *militantes Parisiennes* were insistently identifying the performance of "patriotic duties" as a critical "precondition" for fulfilling one's domestic duty as a "wife and mother."[86] And who, specifically, *were* these women? Dominique Godineau's meticulous research suggests that, since most of them were "rather young (25 to 30 years old)" or "aged (60 to 70 years old)," they must largely have been "relatively free from family responsibilities, with either one or no children, or no longer responsible for their children." The professions they represented included "commerce, clothing, crafts, domestic service, and even acting!" (Secondarily, we find chocolate and cake merchants, haberdashers, washerwomen, linenworkers, dressmakers, cooks, menders, printers, and gold polishers[!] appearing in Godineau's lists.) The officers of the Société, Godineau informs us, belonged to what she calls the "petite bourgeoisie," and they recruited women of a somewhat "lower class" for the regular membership. At most, so it would seem, the Parisian Society could boast about 170 members; perhaps 100 or so could be counted upon to attend meetings regularly in 1793.[87]

Thus for the members of the Society of Revolutionary Republicans, mobilized (if only briefly) in Paris at the height of the popular revolution. And what about their counterparts in the provinces? Are we talking here about a truly *national* phenomenon? The answer would seem to be, unqualifiedly, yes—even if, in outlying reaches of the country as at Paris, the experience was not a lasting one. Women's clubs "flowered in about 60 towns throughout France," comments Suzanne Desan, who has analyzed them in meaningful detail. The cities of Bordeaux, Dijon, Lyon, and Besançon may have hosted the most active clubs outside the capital, although they were also found in some smaller communities, "especially in the southwest." They ranged in size, according to Desan, "from the tiny society of 22 girls at Civray in Poitou to the largest Jacobin women's organization of Bordeaux, which claimed "seven hundred to eight hundred *citoyennes*" as members in 1793." As was the case in Paris, so in provincial venues, a handful of especially dedicated members could usually be counted upon to organize "clubbist" activities. As we might expect, members came "primarily from bourgeois backgrounds, although women of shopkeeping or artisanal classes also participated." The usual patterns of recruitment held at Dijon, Grenoble, and Besançon, where leaders, often the "bourgeois" spouses of active members of men's clubs, would try to attract to their founding ceremonies and revolutionary festivals women of somewhat less well educated and less affluent status. As Desan has observed, these provincial women's clubs "provide a window into a little-explored aspect of the French Revolution—the developing political consciousness and actions of ordinary provincial women far from Paris and the national legislature." At best, they contributed "over the long term to the political education of French women."[88] In provincial France as well as at Paris, consequently, we can see, in women's activities, what another social historian has called the merging of two traditions, "the relatively new one of structured political organization through a women's club and the age-old one of direct female action which had produced the October Days."[89]

But here again, as in matters relating to marriage and divorce in the Revolution, we discern both gendered and civic/constitutional questions lurking in the background. It was, to begin with, only to be expected that the main run of (male) politicians—even many supposedly "radical" ones—would in time riposte violently against the kind of *class inversion* practiced by some market-women in connection with the October Days and subsequent *journées révolutionnaires*. Here were those women in October 1789, as vividly described on the pages of social history:

> women seated astride cannon—the world turned upside down, a *tableau vivant* of feminine empowerment; women marching with swords in hand, women waving the branches of trees, women threatening the captured royal bodyguards and fraternizing with the National Guardsmen who carried loaves of bread on the tips of their pikes; women shouting and chanting as they marched [and causing] demotion of the king from sacrosanct absolute authority, [from] patriarchal provider and protector, to a mere provisioner, a fundamentally untrustworthy baker who . . . must be subjected to continual popular surveillance, backed by armed force.

Hence the celebrated *boutade* about "the baker, the baker's wife, and the baker's little boy"—patently responding to the chronic hunger of Parisians (and French people in general). Observers were as quick to cite the "carnivalesque behavior" of these market-women on the night of October 5 as they besieged the National Assembly at Versailles, enacting class reversals—"sitting in the president's chair, voting on motions; impromptu farce—shouting, singing, declaiming; and . . . chiding the deputy [J.-J.] Mounier for his support of *Monsieur le Véto, ce vilain véto,*" and so on.[90] Such scenes, we all know so well, would repeat themselves throughout the most agitated years of the Revolution, and would go largely unchallenged—

as long as the politicians struggling for state power needed the muscle-power of the popular masses.

But what would happen once the revolutionary state in France had begun to consolidate power? Would the leading revolutionaries continue to "indulge" the masses—and, most notably, the politicized women in their midst? Or would greater domestic (and geopolitical) security allow the country's latest ruling politicians—now, Robespierrist Jacobins—to return to a more traditional discourse on gender issues? The answer came, in the National Convention and in the more intimate setting of the Parisian Jacobin Club, in the fall of 1793. Here was André Amar, expatiating on the "true" nature of women at the Convention on 9 Brumaire, Year II—this, as part of an effort to discredit *militantes féminines*:

> What character is suitable for woman? Morals and even nature have assigned her functions to her. To begin educating men, to prepare children's minds and hearts for public virtues, to direct them early in life towards the good, to elevate their souls, to educate them in the political cult of liberty: such are their functions, after household cares. . . . Doubtless they must educate themselves in the principles of liberty . . . but as they are made for softening the morals of man, should they take an active part in discussions the passion of which is incompatible with the softness and moderation which are the charm of their sex?

How unlike *man*, Amar ran on, who is "strong, robust, born with great energy, audacity, and courage," and, hence, fit for all kinds of actions, civilian and military, in the public realm.[91] One of his colleagues, Fabre d'Églantine, addressed the issue more crudely at the Jacobins, attacking members of women's societies as a "species of adventurous women, errant cavaliers, emancipated girls, female grenadiers," fit only to be contrasted with gentle mothers of families, young girls at home, sisters caring solicitously for younger brothers and sisters, and so forth.[92] Is it any wonder, then, that the Convention went on to decree the abolition of women's clubs and popular societies in Paris on 9 Brumaire, or that, eighteen days later, it even prohibited women's deputations to the Paris Commune?

And what was true in the capital city held as well for towns and villages in provincial France. As Suzanne Desan writes, "even the most docile women's provincial clubs, which got along quite well with their male Jacobin compatriots," increasingly encountered in 1793 a "marked [male] ambivalence, more than occasional satire, and the . . . suggestions of possible impropriety." To account for this ambivalence, and (at times) outright hostility, Desan resorts to an analysis that pivots upon (if in some respects it also complicates) the distinction between a male-dominated "public space" and a female-managed "private space." Essentially, she argues, male politicians like André Amar and Fabre d'Églantine perceived in the Revolution's female militancy a phenomenon that, by challenging the conventional distinctions between what was properly "male" and what was properly "female," made it well-nigh impossible for men—that is, "strong, robust, courageous" men—to dominate not only the public *but also* the domestic sphere in the recently proclaimed French Republic. As Desan presents the issue:

> In sum, republicans such as Amar suppressed woman's clubs because they sought not only to undermine the public role of women, but also to curtail their traditional moral dominion over the private as well. In the context of a revolution that demanded virtually total subordination of the private, or at least the invasion of the public into the private sphere, to reiterate the lines of sexual difference, emphasize the domestic role of women as republican mothers, and delineate the limits . . . of female *sensibilité* was to reconstitute the social order and to clarify the muddled relationship of the public to the private as well.[93]

To be fair to Desan, she does in part broaden out her analysis with a reference to the extensively studied "political and economic dynamics of the fall of 1793" in France; nonetheless, like some other prominent feminists, she regards the (male-sponsored) crackdown on women's political organizations (and, indeed, the Revolution *in toto*) as crucial "events" foreshadowing an historically unprecedented domestication of women in postrevolutionary France.

Yet, as useful as gendered considerations may be in explaining the closure of women's clubs and the overall reaction against female militancy in France in 1793, do we not have to review these matters ultimately in a broader constitutional and structuralist framework? To begin with, we unavoidably recall that some scholars with impeccable feminist credentials—Sarah Hanley and Dena Goodman come most readily to mind—have found contrasts between an ancien régime allegedly tolerating feminine influence in the public sphere and a revolutionary/postrevolutionary France supposedly ever more disfigured by male misogyny in the public domain to be simplistic and, therefore, overdrawn.[94] Then, again, we note how other authorities on women's affairs in revolutionary France such as Olwen Hufton and Dominique Godineau have grasped at larger civic issues in interpreting the demise of militant female sociability in 1793. Hufton, admittedly, has acknowledged that "many of the recent histories of women during the Revolution seize upon latent Jacobin antifeminism" as the "overriding reason" for the closure in 1793 of the Society of Revolutionary Republican Women. Still, she has insisted that "there was no widespread protest at the disbanding of the Républicaines révolutionnaires or expressed protest at the elimination of women from a separate club life, which in any case had never attracted women on a large scale." In addition, Hufton has pointed out, the Société appears to have been "divided amongst itself," as well as engaged in continual strife with other women—notably, hard-pressed market-women and consumers in the capital. For Hufton, the more basic question is really whether, in the end, the revolutionaries could have "[given] female citizenship a positive role" by "placing the war on hoarders and the crusade against the internal enemy" in women's hands. In retrospect, she writes, such a concession was highly unlikely, since it would surely have put Parisian *citoyennes* "in competition with the Jacobins for control over the engendered crowd."[95] Godineau, for her part, has placed Olwen Hufton's argument in an even broader context, pointing to the "fundamental . . . retreat" in late 1793 "from the entire sans-culottes movement, and . . . from the women who were a part of this group." By deriding militants in clubs such as the Society of Revolutionary Republican Women, Godineau is saying, leading politicians like André Amar and Fabre d'Églantine were not only targeting women as such but were also condemning more generally "political groups to which the club of Parisian women was or had been linked, such as the *enragés*, the Cordeliers, and the militant [male?] members of the sections."[96]

This in turn reminds us of a long-standing commonplace in French Revolutionary historiography: namely, that much as had happened in the English Revolution (and would transpire again in the Russian Revolution), the process of change in France led inexorably toward a greater and greater consolidation of state power at the expense of popular initiative and spontaneity. In Albert Soboul's famous gloss on the subject: "democracy, as practiced by the sans-culottes, tended spontaneously toward a direct form of government, which appeared incompatible with the exigencies of wartime conditions." The popular militants, Soboul long ago reminded us, "had called for a strong government which would eradicate the aristocracy; they were not prepared for the fact that in order to win, this government would be obliged to force them to toe the line."[97] Can we be astonished, then, if, as a result of all of this, the spontaneity and militancy of the Parisian (and other urban) masses atrophied, as the energy and enthusiasm of the sections and streets were transferred to the bureaucracy and armies of the securely ensconced Jacobin government? And should we be at all surprised that the waning of female activists' revolutionary fervor factored into this key development? As a matter of fact, by the time the Robespierrists fell from power on 9 Thermidor, Year II (i.e., in late July 1794), women's sympathy for the Jacobins—much like that of their male counterparts—had largely evaporated. True, as one feminist scholar has asserted, "the most conscious female militants clearly and immediately perceived the stakes of 9 Thermidor and . . . took the side of the Robespierrists." Nonetheless, she has also admitted, "most women of the people, who were essentially preoccupied by the cost of living, perceived 9 Thermidor only as a distant event that did not really affect them." But if Dominique Godineau reached this balanced conclusion, she has also retained her concern for the implications of all of this for the question of *women's citizenship* in France. After all, she argues, "the experience of 9 Thermidor once again raised the fundamental question of the place of women within the revolutionary movement. Women were members of the people but excluded from sovereignty, female citizens who did not have access to the whole of their citizenship."[98] Again, we are left with this notion of women's "incomplete citizenship" in a country whose revolution, having largely reconsolidated the state, could afford in most respects to dispense with "popular spontaneity" (female most notably but also, to a large extent, male). Such had also been the situation—if in a less massively bureaucratic, *statist* fashion—in revolutionary England; and, as we will discover in the pages that follow, such would also be the case, but now even more emphatically, in revolutionary Russia.

Russia: Feminists, Women Workers— and the Bolshevik Challenge

As we turn, accordingly, to the issue of women's roles in the 1917 Russian Revolution, we might want at the start to recall Richard Stites's observation that "almost everywhere" in modern Europe "the women's movement was divided sharply into a prominent bourgeois feminism and a weaker working-class women's movement." In fact, nowhere was this more decidedly the case than in Russia, a realm in which a veritable chasm yawned between a tiny social elite ("census" or "privilege" Russia) and the rural (and, increasingly, urban) masses.[99] Hence, we will find that, in this case, *class*, rather than *religion* or *secular ideology*, was the factor that most notably complicated *gender* dynamics as women, along with men in Romanov Russia, were eventually swept up into the revolutionary maelstrom. We should begin here, as we did in discussing England and France, with women's markedly inferior legal status in the old regime—and note how arguments over that status were increasingly caught up in the larger controversy over *sosloviia* (estates), *class*, and the relative merits of traditional and modern values in Imperial Russia. We can then trace the troubled history of élitist/middle-class feminism in Russia from tsarist times down to women's acquisition of the vote in July 1917, as well as study working-class women's activities as they extended from the abortive 1905 "revolution" to the eventual full-fledged upheaval of 1917. Finally, we will see how women's élitist *and* proletarian roles, like those of men, were gradually appropriated by the reconsolidated postrevolutionary state—in this case, the ever more autocratic Bolshevik state.

There can be no doubt that, in William Wagner's words, "Imperial civil law gave Russian women good grounds for lament."[100] Russian women, whether married or single, had virtually everything stacked against them under the last tsars. "Everything" included Orthodoxy as well as patriarchal authority, the patrilineal kin-group, and tradition in general. A wife, obligated (as in old regime England and France) to dwell with and obey her husband, "needed her husband's consent to enter employment, to undertake higher education, to execute a bill of exchange, or to receive a separate passport, which was necessary for residence and often for employment." A husband, admonished (at least in theory) to "love, respect, and defend his wife," had only one "substantive" obligation—namely, to "support his wife in a fashion commensurate with his means." Married women could, it is true, bring criminal actions against severely abusive husbands, but, as Wagner has noted, few of them did—not least because the law obliged them, even in cases of successful prosecution, to live with their supposedly chastened mates after their release from prison! Women's options for divorce in Imperial times varied; each faith officially recognized by St. Petersburg provided its own standards in this area, and those set by the Orthodox Church "were among the most stringent." Most of the women who concern us here, raised as Orthodox, could file for divorce only in rare cases of "adultery, sexual incapacity arising before marriage, exile to Siberia due to criminal conviction, or disappearance." As for unmarried daughters, they, too, "felt the strictures of patriarchal authority." Parents could not, literally, have recourse to the *lettres de cachet* consigned to oblivion by the earliest revolutionaries in France; still, they "enjoyed extensive power to punish their daughters, and could have them confined for disobedience." Daughters, enjoined by Church and patrilineal kin-group to honor and respect their parents, were specifically barred from bringing any legal action against them. Women, in addition, whatever their marital status, fared little better in inheritance law and litigation, in which sons and brothers or their direct heirs were usually favored.[101]

Was there at least some parallel, in late Imperial Russia, to the rights enjoyed by English widows under the doctrine of *feme sole*, or to the independent legal capacity that was claimed by Frenchwomen as independent merchants or as widows in the *ancien régime*? In one respect, at least, William Wagner replies, there was—even if, in this case, the parallel most commonly applied to married women. Since marriage created no "community of property" under Imperial law, females of age "enjoyed unlimited power to use and dispose of their own property, including their dowries." This right, an outgrowth of both the clan social structure and the system of state service tenure inherited from earlier times, "was unusually extensive compared with the property rights of other European women." Yet in practice even this prerogative ran up against the custom, still widespread in the Russian Empire, of giving the wife's dowry to her husband to use for whatever he designated as "family needs."[102] Hence, in most respects, the legal position of women in Romanov Russia, regardless of marital and confessional status, was (to employ William Wagner's blunt but accurate term) "dismal."

Nonetheless, Russian forces of change were beginning to stir in the realms of family, property, and inheritance law during (and after) Tsar Alexander II's reformist reign (1855–81), and all of this held potential implications for women's legal status. "Beginning in the 1860s," Wagner has written, "jurists first of all harshly criticized these legal arrangements as unjust and as socially dysfunctional, and then scathingly condemned them as the remnants of an outdated social order." The family's proper function, these jurists declared, was "to enable the fullest possible development of each individual, and to foster civic-spirited, patriotic, and productive citizens." Existing legal arrangements in Russia, by emphasizing patriarchy, obedience, and unequal status, prevented the attainment of the family's "social objectives." A number of would-be reformers took these arguments into the government, especially its Ministry of Justice, from the 1860s all the way down to 1917.[103] Crucially, too, the "turn" to debate family, property, and inheritance issues (and their implications for women) was part and parcel of the broader tendency in Romanov Russia—at least in reformist circles—to criticize the old society of juridical estates (*sosloviia*) and associated mentality (*soslovnost'*) and to think in more "modern" terms of *class* and of the aspiring *individual*. As Orlando Figes has effectively sized up the situation:

> The old hierarchy of social estates (*sosloviia*), which the autocracy had created to organize society around its own needs, was breaking down as a new and much more mobile social system began to take shape. Men born as peasants, even as serfs, rose to establish themselves as merchants and landowners, teachers, doctors, engineers, writers, publishers and patrons of the arts. The sons and daughters of noblemen entered the liberal professions. Merchants became noblemen. Marriages between the estates became commonplace. Overall, people neither could nor wanted any longer to define themselves in the old and rigid terms.[104]

And yet—as the research of Gregory Freeze, Leopold Haimson, Sheila Fitzpatrick, and others has equally shown—the desire of men *and women* in late Imperial Russia for a society more accommodative of their needs was continually thwarted by "the strong hereditary patterns, the persisting legal distinctions, the segregation of groups in administration and law, the deeply rooted cultural differences among various groups, and the conscious effort of the state to preserve the *soslovie* separation."[105] Moreover, the last two tsars' unyielding opposition to major social change in Russia after 1881 was, down to the very end, seconded by reactionaries in the Orthodox Church and the provincial gentry (*dvorianstvo*). It remained no less the case that, against the backdrop of this struggle between the advocates of social change and the avatars of resistance to that change, women's "legal status became both the measure of . . . society's development and a means for promoting further change."[106]

The promotion of further change for Russian women in this era also became the raison d'être of an increasingly active feminist movement. The roots of Russian feminism, Linda Edmondson has opined, went back to Alexander II's reign. Its ultimate objective, as first articulated in the promising 1860s, was "to establish a woman's right to independence and freedom and ensure her equal status as a citizen; its immediate objectives were to open the universities to women, greatly extend the range of employment opportunities and set up charities to aid women in need and save them from prostitution."[107] For a host of reasons, however, the achievements of the movement over the next half century, if "remarkable" in some respects, were no less "limited." This was due, at least in part, to national political developments: the untimely assassination of Tsar Alexander II in 1881 marked a critical watershed between the reforms of the 1855-81 period and oppressive governmental reactionism under the last two Romanov emperors, Alexander III (1881–94) and Nicholas II (1894–1917). But, upon closer examination, we find that Russian feminists had eventually almost as much to fear from their supposed "liberal" confederates in the leftist political parties that agitated for change during the stillborn 1905 Revolution as they had to fear from misogynistic hard-liners in the government's most conservative ministries. Again, Linda Edmondson has underscored the irony of this situation for those championing women's issues in Russia:

> [Women] had themselves created a political discourse in which concepts of equality, freedom, citizenship and rights predominated. The civil rights rhetoric of 1905 spoke of "equality before the law of all citizens," "inviolability of the person," "freedom of conscience, speech, movement, assembly and association." Liberals of all persuasions . . . adhered to this rhetoric. . . . But as soon as feminists began to use the discourse for their own interests, they encountered gentle mockery, outright hostility, uncomfortable silences and shifting glances from individuals many of whom they had believed to be their allies.[108]

Feminists most frequently encountered male ambivalence on the problematic issue of *suffrage*. Indeed, a future Foreign Minister, Paul Miliukov, openly quarreled with his wife, Anna Miliukova, at the first and second Kadet Party Congresses (in 1905 and 1906) over whether or not to include female suffrage in the Party platform. Anna Miliukova prevailed over her husband on this question, and Paul Miliukov—along with most other (male) Kadets and other liberals—eventually came around to the feminist position.[109]

More significant, as an ominous augury of the future, was the emergence at this time of *class* as a dividing line within Russia's women's movement. Both the All-Russian Union for Women's Equality, a feminist advocacy group founded in 1905, and the All-Russian Women's Congress, staged in December 1908 to preserve the momentum of earlier women's achievements, divided along class lines. In 1905 and beyond, Stites has written, Social Democrats like Aleksandra Kollontai "campaigned fiercely against any effort, however well-intended, to entice female workers into an all-women's movement and away from their 'natural' place in the S. D. trade unions and parties." Indeed, "from the very beginning of the suffrage movement in 1905," it would seem, "Social Democratic women agitators appeared at feminist meetings to harass the leaders."[110] For this and other reasons, the overall situation for feminists in Russia remained bleak in the years of reaction leading up to the outbreak of the First World War. On the one hand, women remained divided along ideological lines. "While liberals sought to expand women's rights in the public sphere, radicals, the Marxist parties foremost among them, believed that nothing short of a thoroughgoing revolution could achieve women's equality."[111] For Russians on the far Right, on the other hand, "proposals to change women's status represented the ultimate front in the battle to preserve the traditional family. Allowing women to gain political rights would undermine patriarchal authority in the family, and by extension threaten the foundations of autocratic rule." As a result, the "intersectionality" of *gender* and *class* in Russia discloses to us once again— here, in a uniquely Russian fashion—the *statist* implications ever lurking behind the "woman question," as liberals and conservatives polarized over the "commitment to transforming Russia into a modern state."[112]

War breaking out in Europe on an unheard-of scale in 1914 put that commitment to a hard test. The *gendered* irony here was that Russian involvement in the Great War, "viewed by the government as a means of preserving and enhancing the masculine authority of the autocrat, became a vehicle for the mobilization of the female masses."[113] Substantial research now exists on the impact of the First World War on Russian women's lives.[114] Most women, like their male counterparts, were swept along initially in a gust of patriotic support for the regime's war effort. Some of them, not satisfied to remain at home knitting scarves and sewing bandages for the wounded, or aiding refugees from the German-occupied western borderlands, or teaching (for the first time) in secondary schools, or taking jobs in the industrial sector previously held by men now at the front, deliberately came to much closer grips with the war effort as nurses and (both before and after the outbreak of revolution in 1917) as active combatants.[115] The First Petrograd Women's "Battalion of Death," formed in May 1917 at the behest of Mariia Bochkareva, was only the most famed of the female units that sprang up in defense of the Motherland at this time.[116] In preparing themselves for potentially lethal conflict, Russia's female warriors may have helped to erode existing boundaries of class, gender, and political loyalty, and hence facilitated the transition of Russian women in general from old regime to revolution. Melissa Stockdale has elaborated on this process:

> [The women's] self-mobilization for combat was not solely or even primarily a "bourgeois" or intelligentsia outpouring . . . . The movement's transcendence of class and social status reminds us that class conflict and class identity, as important as they became, existed alongside and sometimes yielded to other . . .loyalties. The patriotism of women soldiers also cut across political boundaries. Most were democratically inclined, but monarchists as well as republicans, liberals, socialists, and the politically undefined were prepared to shoulder a rifle and swear an oath that proclaimed, "my death for the Motherland and for the freedom of Russia is happiness."[117]

Laurie Stoff, too, has emphasized that "Russia's female soldiers of the Great War . . . demonstrated that women could . . . successfully participate in the public sphere and could endure the most challenging and difficult conditions. They . . . showed men that they possessed a strong sense of civic responsibility and dedication to the state."[118] True, both Stockdale and Stoff have prudently acknowledged that Russia's wartime authorities wanted less to "expand the boundaries of gender" than to shame reluctant men into combat roles; they have also conceded that "even some of the most radical feminists" were made "uncomfortable" by the spectacle of patriotic women engaged in warfare.[119] Russia's female warriors were, nonetheless, significant protagonists in the early-twentieth-century women's movement.

The revolution that broke out in Russia in February 1917 powerfully reinforced what one scholar has called the "mobilizing, transformative effects of the war." Indeed, by investing traditional concepts of gender, patriotism and citizenship with new meaning, warfare and revolution together created new opportunities for Russian women not only to become citizen-soldiers, as we have seen, but also to play many other roles as well. Acknowledging in addition the *class* factor here, we can follow the "woman question" along two tracks, one of them involving the—finally successful—effort of élitist/ middle-class feminists in revolutionary Russia to achieve female suffrage and other political reforms, and the other involving the experiences of laboring women in 1917 and immediately thereafter.

Admittedly the conferral of voting rights on Russian women in the summer of 1917 was not, in the narrowest sense, a "class affair." When the Provisional Government, in its initial Kadet-dominated iteration, failed to include "sexual equality" in its political program, Barbara Engel has written, "feminists mobilized. They held conferences and meetings that sometimes proved so popular that people had to be turned away." In March, an enormous procession "numbering up to 40,000 people" marched upon the government, in session at the Tauride Palace, "to lobby it on behalf of women's suffrage." Female advocates like Vera Figner and Poliksena Shishkina-Iavein demanded that women be invested with the full citizenship that brought with it voting for the projected Constituent Assembly.[120] Rochelle Ruthchild has pointed out that the Provisional Government had a variety of reasons to endorse this call for female suffrage. To begin with, élitist Kadets like Paul Miliukov had long since abandoned their opposition to this reform. Even government conservatives like Mikhail Rodzianko "recognized that women's suffrage was part of what defined the modern state." Dogmatic Marxists (e.g., Lenin, Kollontai) who might have used the occasion to retail their usual suspicions of "bourgeois feminists" were still in exile. Again, the Provisional Government, seeking to maintain popular support for continuation of Russia's involvement in the war, may have regarded concessions to women as "enhancing the war effort."[121] For these and other reasons, the electoral law of July 20 formally ratified the right of Russian women to vote (as well as to run for office) in the upcoming Constituent Assembly elections. Women had already won the right to vote in municipal elections; a number of them were soon serving on city and *zemstvo* councils. They were eventually allowed as well to be jurors and were fully admitted to legal practice and to civil service employment on an equal footing with men. The government also attempted to restrict female and child labor in industry. In summarizing this sudden outpouring of reforms, even Richard Stites has grudgingly conceded that "the Provisional Government, had it retained power longer, would have . . . established at least the mechanics of the emancipation as conceived by feminists everywhere."[122]

Yet we know, with all the wisdom of hindsight, that the Provisional Government's writ was *not* fated to run for very long. Historians still differ over the degree to which *class* considerations from very early on jeopardized this "honeymoon phase" of revolution in Russia. Rochelle Ruthchild, for one, has admitted quite recently that "questions of the intersection of class and gender complicate the matter for women"; still, she questions whether it is even accurate to utilize the term "bourgeois feminism" in writing about this period in Russian history. Ruthchild points, for instance, to abundant indications of class-transcending patriotic solidarity in 1917—not only in metropoles like Petrograd and Moscow, but also in the vast rural hinterland of the newly proclaimed Russian republic:

Women's suffrage appealed to a broad range of activists throughout 1917 . . . the newsreel of the March 19 women's suffrage demonstration shows the intersectionality of the feminist appeal, with women from the working and middle classes marching [together]. . . . Among the masses, suffrage as an issue resonated among both women and men, and all over . . . Russia. Meetings demanding women's suffrage were so popular that at some places the halls had to be emptied three times to accommodate all those who wished to hear the speakers. Women workers in Kostroma and Iaroslavl, in the Russian heartland, joined equal rights organizations. In Siberia, an Irkutsk meeting of 3,000 women and men sent a telegram to the Provisional Government demanding full electoral rights for women in the Constituent Assembly.

And so on. Furthermore, Ruthchild informs us that Russian women in the chaotic conditions of 1917 actually went to the polls at higher rates than their US counterparts would in 1920 and subsequently.[123] This transcendence of *class*, we should also recall, seems to have extended to female soldiers as well as to women demonstrators and voters in 1917. When American journalists Louise Bryant and Bessie Beatty interviewed some of Mariia L. Bochkareva's recruits in the First Petrograd Women's Battalion at that time, they conceived the impression that "the majority of women . . . were not from the privileged classes." Yet another American war correspondent wrote that the women she had encountered in the "Battalion of Death" included "six nurses and a female doctor, . . . ten women who had fought in men's regiments, clerks and office workers, domestic servants, and girls from factories and farms, as well as middle-class and aristocratic women who had never worked for wages."[124] There are, then, some signs of solidarities of gender and patriotism trumping class-consciousness in the women's movement in Russia—at least in these earliest days of patriotic war complicated by mass-mobilizing social revolution.

Still, with all due respect to scholars like Rochelle Ruthchild, Melissa Stockdale, and Laurie Stoff, there was always that other side to this story—a side of (apparently intensifying) class-consciousness in the "new" Russia. Indeed, from the very inception of the February revolution, working-class women had been as insistent upon denouncing high prices of bread and other necessities, and the general economic crisis in metropoles such as Petrograd and Moscow, as upon decrying their lack of full citizenship rights. Soldiers' long-suffering wives—that is, the *soldatki*—were a case in point. "Linking their demands with the interests of the nation," Barbara Engel has commented, "*soldatki* sought economic rather than political rights and identified themselves as wives and mothers, rather than as autonomous citizens."[125] In the course of 1917, massive strikes by (for example) laundresses and dye-workers disclosed the primacy of economic interests for many Russian women. An even more symbolically revealing indication of how divisive *class* could be for the feminist cause, even quite early in the revolution, was the reaction of some working-class women to the news, in July, of the government's ratification of female suffrage:

[Feminist] Ariadna Tyrkova, with some irony, tells us how this news of the long-awaited feminist victory was received by the woman on the street. After Prince Lvov made the announcement, one of the feminists, in a flurry of enthusiasm, approached a crowd of women queued up at a bakery. "I congratulate you, citizenesses," she announced. "We Russian women are going to receive our rights." The women, tired of waiting in line, looked at the lady with indifference and lack of comprehension. Then a nearby soldier smirked and said: "Does that mean that I can't hit my wife?"[126]

There were other ways, as well, in which Russian women prominent in the revolutionary politics of 1917 experienced the limitations of a gendered [female] identity and the growing strength of class sentiment. For instance, throughout the critical February-to-October period, Ekaterina Kuskova, ex-Populist, Kadet, now part "nonparty Marxist" and part "democrat," discovered that "in a political culture that mirrored patriarchal society in assigning women a nurturing and supportive role," she had "only so much room to manoeuvre without violating the conditions of female political participation." Her efforts to cooperate politically with male leaders of the liberal and radical intelligentsia, Barbara Norton has written, even if laudable, must still appear to us "naïve in the circumstances of intense class conflict and sharp political polarization that characterized Russian life throughout most of the year."[127] Moreover, the conflictual dynamics of *class* and of social polarization only further intensified in the course of 1917. As the labors of William G. Rosenberg and Diane Koenker (among others) demonstrate, initially promising auguries of political and social reconciliation were steadily undone by the ever-growing assertion of class interests on *both* sides of the industrialist/proletarian divide in urban Russia.[128]

Significantly, in this connection, even an unqualifiedly feminist historian like Rochelle Ruthchild remains keenly aware of the limitations as well as the achievements of women's progressive legislation in 1917. Reforms may have "placed Russia ahead of most other countries in its laws about women," she writes, "but much remained to be done. No sweeping equal rights code emerged, laws on marriage and the family remained unchanged, and the registration of prostitutes continued."[129] All of this reminds us that we need to pursue the woman question in revolutionary Russia along that promised "second track" as well—a track that takes us away from the polite élitist and "bourgeois" *monde* of Western-oriented feminism and into the unpretentious and roughly hewn *mir* of Russia's working women. And whereas, in the realm of feminism, we have seen *class* as complicating *gender*, in the proletarian realm we might say just the opposite—namely, that *gender* (coded female *or* male) in some ways complicated *class*.

To begin with, we should note that 1905 served as prologue or "dress rehearsal" to 1917 when it came to women's workplace issues, class, and gender as it did in so many other respects. "Women industrial workers, clerical workers, pharmacists, professionals, even domestic servants," Barbara Engel has recounted, "joined unions and walked off their jobs to attend mass meetings and demonstrations that called for an end to autocracy and a representative form of government." Additionally, as political strikes increasingly became the means through which workers verbalized their grievances during 1905, women took up their male counterparts' activism. "In factories where women predominated, the textile industry in particular, strike demands clearly reflected their presence. Factory after factory demanded day care, maternity leave, nursing breaks, and protection of women workers, reflecting not only the preponderance of women but also the influence of the Marxist S. D. L. P. and liberals, both of which had long supported maternity-related benefits."[130] Yet, as we also know from Rose Glickman's foundational research, the *gender differential* complicated what might otherwise have been *class solidarity* on these work-related questions— and, in so doing, foreshadowed what was to come twelve years later:

> virtually all the demands that applied to women touched on their role as mother, not on their actual working conditions, and only in a few known instances did workers claim that a woman should be paid the same as a man for performing identical work. Most commonly, existing wage differentials and women's unequal status were reinscribed in strike demands that called for wages that would have maintained women's earnings at a fraction of men's. In a few cases, in an effort to assert a solidarity based on gender, male workers went even further and sought to exclude women workers altogether from "men's" trades.[131]

Thus, even in the abortive upheaval of 1905, considerations that were gendered in large part *male* could be seen as complicating what might otherwise have been *class solidarity* among working Russians, male and female. Still, class solidarity was not, in spite of such tactics, dead: in December 1905, for instance, women joined together with men in a last-ditch attempt to erect street barricades against a now rapidly regrouping tsarist autocracy in its gilded capital city, St. Petersburg.

The story would be different, of course, after several years of crippling Russian involvement in the First World War. By 1916, Anna Hillyar and Jane McDermid have written in their group biography of female revolutionaries in Russia, "an increased number of demonstrations" were sweeping the country, "and women had become not simply a constant presence in them but were playing a more proactive and militant role. Women's protests were centered on economic demands as well as reflecting a growing anti-war mood among the rest of the Russian population." Even before the onset of all-out revolution in February 1917, women workers from the Vyborg district of Petrograd had organized a huge anti-war protest in the center of the capital, which had to be forcibly suppressed by mounted police.[132] As the whole world now knows, the February Revolution appropriately(?) began on February 23 [i.e., March 8], International Women's Day, when thousands of furious housewives and female workers, ignoring pleas from labor leaders to remain quiescent, stormed into the streets. As a worker at the Nobel engineering complex in the Vyborg district vividly recalled:

We could hear women's loud voices in the lane overlooked by the windows of our department: "Down with high prices!" "Down with hunger!" "Bread for the workers!" I and several comrades rushed for the windows. The gates of [the] mill were flung open. Masses of women workers in a militant frame of mind filled the lane. Those who caught sight of us began to wave their arms, shouting: "Come out!" "Stop work!" Snowballs flew through the windows. We decided to join the demonstration.

By the next day, according to Steve A. Smith, "200,000 workers were on strike in Petrograd. By February 25, armies of demonstrators were clashing with troops, and the revolution had commenced."[133] There can be little doubt, too, that a growing concentration of women workers in industrial employment in the embattled Russian Empire contributed significantly to this dramatic turn of events. Indeed, Hillyar and McDermid have found, "while in 1914 the proportion of women in industry as a whole was 26.6%, after three years of war it had risen to 43.4%. In 1917 over a million women were employed in factory work. Even in the metal industry they were on the increase." This last tendency involving female employment only accelerated as the old regime in Russia approached its demise.[134]

Crucial, too, was the revolutionary role played in 1917 by peasant women—customarily soldiers' wives (*soldatki*) increasingly frustrated by the war, by their husbands' prolonged absence, and by the (at times irregular) pace of land partitioning in the Russian countryside. One contemporary, I. Rusanov, in a brochure tellingly entitled *The Revolution and the Woman Question*, described a riot—apparently quite typical—led by such aggrieved individuals in the early summer of 1917 in Voronezh guberniia:

It started when a request by 30 of them for a postponement to the partitioning of village land, until the return of their husbands from the front, went unheeded. Later 200 soldiers' wives gathered in the main . . . town. First, they scattered boundary posts, then they raided farmsteads of landowning peasants, "destroying their kitchen gardens, taking out window frames, doors, and in some cases, having entered houses, they broke stoves, demolished or stole furniture, house implements and other property. Groups of women [then] burst into properties, initially encouraged by cries from the men following them. . ."

In a neighboring village, according to this source, a delay in the payment of war benefits to the *soldatki* touched off a riot that lasted, on and off, for three weeks.[135] As the summer stretched on into the fall, and with no relief in sight from the monstrous tribulations of the war, peasant women—often assisted now by detachments of returned soldiers—rioted throughout the central "black soil" provinces—that is to say, provinces such as Tambov, Saratov, Penza, Kazan, Orel, Tula, and Riazin'. "With the approach of the autumn ploughing," Orlando Figes has written, "the time seemed ripe for a final reckoning with the old agrarian order."[136] Incontrovertibly, then, women of the laboring classes participated in the "final reckoning" with the Russian *ancien régime* in countryside as well as in city.

But it was above all in the industrial complexes of urban Russia where women most vociferously articulated grievances—grievances whose *class* appeal increasingly supplanted *gendered* concerns as Russia sank ever more deeply into revolution. For instance, an unreckoned number of Russian women, speaking on behalf of the "Smolensk Initiative Group of Women and Mothers" on May 5, 1917, added their voices to what they assumed to be a nationwide "protest of working people against the war":

> Enough of sacrificing our sons to the capitalists' inflamed greed. We don't need . . . annexations or indemnities. Instead, let us safeguard our sons for the good of all the working people the world over. Let them apply all their efforts not to a fratricidal war but to the cause of peace and the brotherhood (*sic*) of all peoples. And let us, Russian women and mothers, be proud knowing that we were the first to extend our brotherly hand (*sic*) to all the mothers the world over.[137]

Insofar as gender was invoked here at all, it was as much male as female. But patently, it was an appeal to *class solidarity* rather than to *gender* as such that really carried the day. We find a similar emphasis in this letter from a woman (Maria Kutsko) at the Petrograd Munitions Works, dated June 25, 1917:

> Comrade women workers! Not long ago we won higher wages for women at the Munitions Works, and this ought to show us how great is the strength and significance of organization. What would we have achieved if we had acted alone, by ourselves? Absolutely nothing! So we got together a general meeting of all the women workers at the plant and, after considering our situation, decided to turn to our factory committee and ask these comrade workingmen to raise our rates like those at other factories. . . . It is understandable that the . . . committee agreed, for . . . this is a comradely organization, not an owners' one, and they understand our situation.[138]

Once again, we are struck by the preponderance, here, of an appeal to *class interests* over any specific conjuring up of gender—especially, *female* gender. It light of all this, Barbara Engel's general conclusion on the subject seems entirely reasonable: "Among workers, the language of class rather than of gender exerted the greatest rhetorical force in 1917."[139]

However, this emphatically does *not* mean that, in 1917 as earlier in 1905, gender construed in terms of *male agency* did not play a cardinal role in reinforcing male workers' self-identity. Historians reconsidering this issue have generally agreed on this point, noting how, in so many concrete situations in revolutionary Russia, female workers "ceded the limelight" to their male counterparts. When Diane Koenker (for example) homed in on workplace dynamics in the historic capital, Moscow, she was struck on one level by "the diversity of the working class there and the potential for antagonisms and conflicts *within* the class"; on another level, however, she was equally impressed by the conflicts "between the sexes." Women workers, she noted, "were generally much more passive than men politically." Not only did women "work long hours, but they bore the brunt of standing in line for scarce food and keeping a household together while men served in the army." In addition, Koenker found, a "sense of competition between men and women workers" tended further to radicalize male laborers, whose wages could be threatened by the lower pay ordinarily given by industrialists and other employers to women.[140] These impressions concerning male workers' identity—and their radicalization—in 1917 have been confirmed, and even more revealingly discussed, by Orlando Figes and his Russian colleague Boris Kolonitskii:

> male workers set themselves apart from female workers either on the grounds of their role and status in the factory (women workers did less heavy work with machinery, were lower paid and on the whole less skilled) or on the grounds that women tended more often to return to the village for seasonal employment and retained more elements of the old . . . culture (attachment to the Church and rural superstitions, folks songs and expressions, peasant ways of dress), all of which could be deemed marks of lower status by the type of factory laborer yearning to escape the peasant way of life and acquire the . . . urban manners and attitudes, central to their new self-identity as "conscious" workers.

Paradoxically, then, women as "marginal" workers (and whatever their *rural* pursuits) may have actually radicalized male laborers along *masculinist lines* as 1917 unfolded.[141] But whether such a paradox also radicalized the majority of *women* workers along *feminist lines* in this upheaval seems debatable: Anna Hillyar and Jane McDermid, for instance, have held that in 1917 "the gulf between feminists and women workers deepened because of the continuing support of the former for the war and tendency to dismiss the workers' preoccupation with bread as base materialism." Even the "Bolshevik feminist" Aleksandra Kollontai, they suggest, "did not fundamentally challenge the sexual division of labor, either within the family or in society as a whole."[142] This said, we conclude here that, in spite of the growing stridency of class rhetoric among Russia's male *and* female workers in 1917, it could still be complicated at times by gendered appeals, whether those appeals were coded male or female—or, for that matter, *both*.

Finally, there was in Russia (as, earlier, in England and France) the *structuralist* phenomenon of statist cooptation—in one way or another—of women. Hillyar and McDermid have noted that efforts to attract female workers into Party ranks were made "not only by Social Democrats but also by Socialist Revolutionaries, especially in those factories where women were in the majority."[143] Women's causes, in time, were increasingly subordinated to statist or "official" needs. Leveller women, prophetesses, and preachers in England, only grudgingly tolerated by the Cromwellians, had been suppressed later by the Stuarts; activist *citoyennes* in France had been, eventually, silenced by Robespierrist Jacobins and their Napoleonic successors; and, in revolutionary Russia, feminists and working-class women *alike* would find themselves "absorbed" after October 1917 into an increasingly autocratic Bolshevik "new regime."

This is certainly *not* to say that substantial numbers of Russian women failed to benefit from the new polity, now to be known as "Soviet Russia." Outstanding in this regard were the family reforms of 1917–18, reminiscent of but far exceeding in some respects the September 1792 legislation promulgated in revolutionary France. "In two brief decrees, published in December 1917," so Wendy Z. Goldman has commented, "the Bolsheviks accomplished far more than the Ministry of Justice, progressive journalists, feminists, the Duma, and the Council of State had ever even attempted." Civil marriage was substituted for religious marriage, and divorce was made available to either spouse. A complete "Code on Marriage, the Family, and Guardianship" was then ratified by the regime's Central Executive Committee (*VTsIK*) a year later, in October 1918. Among other things, the 1918 Family Code (as it is customarily known) set up local statistical bureaux (*ZAGS*) for registration of marriages, divorces, births, and deaths. Again, the Code abrogated illegitimacy and (at least theoretically) entitled all children in Russia to parental support. Most interestingly, perhaps, from a historical point of view, the Family Code reaffirmed the old Imperial ban against any community of property within marriage; consequently, "a woman retained full control of her earnings after marriage and neither spouse had any claim on the property of the other."[144]

Unremarkably, the 1918 Family Code was controversial at the time, and it has remained so ever since. Contemporaries immediately clashed over its provisions and possible ramifications: if, on the one hand, N. A. Roslavets, a female deputy from Ukraine to the VTsIK, condemned the Code as a reactionary token of "bourgeois survivalism," Bolshevik jurist Alexander Goikhbarg unenthusiastically but staunchly defended it as a "temporary necessity."[145] In more recent times, a feminist like Beatrice Farnsworth has seen the 1918 legislation as debatably "modern and Western," but without being truly "socialist," while her colleague Wendy Z. Goldman has maintained more positively that, "from a comparative perspective, the 1918 Code was remarkably ahead of its time." A balanced reassessment of the

Code has come from Lewis H. Siegelbaum, whose well-researched synthesis of sociocultural developments in Soviet Russia of the 1918–29 period has been generally praised:

> The 1918 Code did not aim to abolish the rite of marriage, but to detach it from the Orthodox Church's clutches; it did not seek to destroy the nuclear family, but to remove its exploitative character; and it did not provide for the public maintenance of children, but rather sought to inculcate a sense of civic obligation among parents for their upbringing. In this sense, then, Farnsworth is right. But it is difficult to accept her characterization of the Code as "socially conservative" without radically altering the conventional meaning of that term.

As Siegelbaum added here, "it was not so much the . . . bourgeois family that stood in the way of women's emancipation" in Russia as it was the "traditional patriarchal peasant household"—not to mention (and likely of paramount importance) the "dislocating and disorienting effects" of world war, of subsequent civil war, and of the eventual recourse to market economics under the NEP (New Economic Policy).[146]

It is only fair to add at this point that, in other ways as well, the new Soviet regime in Russia did endeavor to address what we would today still term "women's issues." Most outstandingly, perhaps, the triumphant Bolsheviks (now officially and defiantly calling themselves "Communists") allowed two leading exponents of "feminism," Bolshevik-style—namely, Aleksandra Kollontai and Inessa Armand—to organize and oversee the first All-Russian Conference of Working Women. At this conference, convened in November 1918 and attended by well over one thousand women, Kollontai, Armand, and other Party members argued incessantly and passionately for women's emancipation as an essential component of the new socialism in new, postrevolutionary Russia. Inessa Armand, for instance, lectured the attendees "about the need to establish state-sponsored nurseries, laundries, and kitchens in order to free women to participate in public life." In August of the following year, the ruling Central Committee of the Russian Communist Party approved the establishment of a so-called Women's Bureau (*Zhenotdel*) to assist in the coordination of Party work among Soviet women, hence (presumably) carrying on the work initiated the year before at the Conference of Working Women by Kollontai, Armand, and others. Armand, regarded by Lenin and his associates as less militant than Aleksandra Kollontai, was chosen to be the first director of *Zhenotdel*.[147] As it turned out, *Zhenotdel* would survive as a "women's section" in the Party only until 1930, at which time other, more urgent, nongendered imperatives would be driving policies in Russia.

Long before 1930, however, the all-male Communist leadership would face *practical* difficulties in managing the "woman question" in Russia that, prior to the Bolsheviks' seizure of power, had barely existed even in *theoretical* terms. For one thing, since classical Marxism had never seriously addressed issues that might confront state revolutionaries attempting social reconstruction in an overwhelmingly *agrarian* society, the Bolsheviks, once empowered in Russia, naturally focused their attention on urban workers rather than on peasant women, whom they regarded as "the residue of earlier stages of social development." As Gail Lapidus has observed, V. I. Lenin *et al.* "never fully addressed the fundamental problems of the vast majority of Russian women, the rural peasants, to whom such notions as female economic independence, communal child-care, and the destruction of the family would have seemed incomprehensible and even threatening."[148] But problems in the Bolshevik stance toward *proletarian* women cut even more deeply, involving as they did the *class/gender* divide. Again, Gail Lapidus:

> Bolshevism accepted the right of women to full civil and political rights in a democratic republic, while maintaining at the same time that political equality was not the ultimate goal but merely a stepping stone to full liberation. It rejected classical feminism by subordinating the woman question to the larger reconstruction of society and by insisting that class and not sex was the fundamental social division. The legitimacy of an appeal to women *as women* remained in question [in] the Party, accepted as a tactical necessity but viewed with enormous suspicion.

Hence, the old issue of "class versus gender" was reappearing now in new socialist garb in Soviet Russia. But—as Lapidus and other women's historians have explained—there were also concrete organizational implications to all of this. If Lenin accepted (in 1920) that the Party "must have organs— working groups, commissions, committees, sections, or whatever else they may be called," he also insisted, crucially, that they be entrusted "*with the specific purpose of rousing the broad masses of women, bringing them into contact with the Party and keeping them under its influence.*" This was not "bourgeois feminism," Lenin declared; it was "practical revolutionary expediency."[149] But, as Elizabeth Wood has noted, this meant, for *Zhenotdel* and for so many female activists, an ever more imperative need "to struggle with what it meant to be female, and how "femaleness" might mesh with citizenship in the workers' state and with *partiinost'* (identification with the party)." And so the woman question took on the official trappings of so-called "state feminism" or "feminism from above" in a country rapidly trending towards a revivified, but now one-party, modernized version of statist autocracy.[150] And for women like Aleksandra Kollontai, Inessa Armand, E. D. Kuskova, and others, the difficult question would be: whether or not—and, if so, on what specific terms—to make peace *as women* with this imposing postrevolutionary autocracy.

It is not that, for *Bolshevichki* (i.e., female Bolsheviks) in particular, there were no major rewards to be reaped by conforming to the new Party expectations in the new Russia. "The liberation that young women felt on becoming Bolsheviks should not be underestimated," Barbara Clements has observed; "it was extraordinary in a society as traditional as Russia's, and in fact few other political organizations of the time anywhere were so open to female participation." Still, she somberly reminds us, "there was a price to be paid" for this "liberation," Bolshevik-style:

> Bolshevichki had to prove themselves worthy of inclusion by adapting to an ethos that was strongly masculinist. They were to be "hard," like men. They were to suppress their identifications with other women and not to think critically about the gender discrimination that occurred within the Party. . . . As the party evolved from an egalitarian underground movement into a governing power, the pressures for conformity only increased. By the 1930s, being a communist meant suppressing one's own criticism of the party completely.

The ultimate dilemma of the *Bolshevichki*, then, was "one often debated by feminists—how to oppose gender discrimination from a position of weakness within a patriarchal society."[151] Yet, beyond even this obvious "gender dilemma," we can appreciate that, for women *and* men, adjusting to postrevolutionary realities must have come at an exceedingly high cost— possibly even at the cost of abandoning much of their idealism, by now a sad relic from earlier days. For some, the choice must have been a cruel one.

In concluding Chapter 4, we are led unavoidably to reemphasize three essential points. First, we have seen how, in each of these classic European upheavals, women unwilling to accept their traditional relegation to passive roles in society capitalized upon politically fluid situations to voice their grievances and to express their aspirations in public and novel forums. In England, to begin with, women delivered petitions to [male] policymakers, published treatises, and played unprecedented roles as prophetesses and preachers. In France, women descended "into the streets" again and again to articulate economic concerns and created at times unheard-of patterns of sociability in political societies and clubs. Finally, in Russia, élitist and middle-class women embraced suffrage and other feminist causes and (sometimes) interacted with proletarian sisters who were frequently motivated more urgently by bedrock economic issues than they were by traditional feminist concerns. In these revolutionary situations, then, *female advocacy* (and, thus, *agency*) took on genuinely new dimensions of meaning.

Second, in advancing from one revolution to the next, we have seen *gender* (coded female and, sometimes, male) as interacting—and often as clashing—with other historical factors, most prominently religion in England, a mixture of religion, secular ideology and (increasingly) *class* in France, and—above all, yet not exclusively—class interests in Russia. Indeed, by the time we arrive at Russia, we find *female gender* in particular to be invested with a plethora of novel meanings: feminists in the erstwhile Russian Empire, for instance, had now to respond to *international* forces of feminism emanating from markedly more advanced Western societies even as they were simultaneously dealing with *domestic* extremes of power and powerlessness, wealth and poverty, and ultra-privileged and underprivileged existence. (This last, enormous challenge for some women could constitute the central theme of yet another book!)

Third, and likely most significantly, we have witnessed ways in which women in these upheavals started to wrestle with *civic questions* that, in the end, proved (ironically) to be less and less *immediately* relevant in authoritarian revolutionary and postrevolutionary regimes. *Intersectionality*, at least in these situations, turned out to include structuralist *statism* after all. This was even true, it bears repeating, in England, where Cromwell suppressed Leveller men *and women* and where his Stuart successors largely silenced the Interregnum's outspoken prophetesses and preachers. But it was especially in the mass-mobilizing, continental upheavals where female political and economic activism provoked authoritarian responses. We will have to return to this final development in Chapter 5, where we will *also* find that Cromwellian, Napoleonic, and Stalinist settlements, by rolling back some of women's most historic gains achieved during the heydays of revolution in England, France, and Russia, respectively, catered, at least in part, to the desires of these countries' less visionary, more traditionally inclined women.

5

Disillusioned and Traditionalist Women Confronting Revolution

The reader will recall that, at an earlier point in this book, we challenged Valentine Moghadam's jarringly simplistic distinction between a "patriarchal" French Revolution and an "emancipatory" Russian Revolution. We held then, and indeed still do, that Moghadam (like, possibly, some other accomplished sociologists in this field) had "failed to differentiate adequately between *conservative* and *radicalized* women in *both* revolutionized polities."[1] Hence, our determination, in this study, to discuss (in separate chapters) the reactionary as well as the more radical roles of women in the English, French, and Russian Revolutions. At the same time, with an eye to the state's role in revolution, we recall historian Barbara Clements' ironic conclusion regarding Bolshevik women (*Bolshevichki*) in the Russian Revolution: "The *Bolshevichki* believed that revolutionary upheaval would destroy the sources of injustice and thereby make politics unnecessary. When, instead, their male comrades built a powerful new autocracy, the Bolshevichki had to choose between defending their earliest visions or adapting to the new realities."[2] In a sense, Clements was only echoing here, for Russia, what historian-and-sociologist Charles Tilly had already conceded for France in the revised edition of his groundbreaking study of the *Vendée*—namely, that scholars like himself must never again understate "the daring expansion of the central government the French revolutionaries sought to accomplish from 1791 to 1793."[3] Statist tendencies, we conclude, held significant implications for traditionalist as well as for radicalized women in revolutionary times.

Such scholarly observations provide the requisite grist for our mills as we attempt to move from Chapter 4, with its discussion of élitist, bourgeois, and working-class women committed to revolutionary activism in England, France, and Russia, to a chapter taking up the different roles played by disillusioned female revolutionaries and traditionalist women caught up in the same three revolutions. In Chapter 5, to be more specific, we shall be encountering Englishwomen of various religious faiths and women of France and Russia either forced to question their own revolutionary premises or naturally predisposed to defend settled ways of faith and tradition. We will, moreover, explore how *gendered* considerations affecting these women interacted and at times clashed with other elements of intersectionality such as religion and class. Finally, much as in Chapter 4, we will reconsider in Chapter 5 the *statist* component in intersectionality, as we see how women reappraising their own initially revolutionary aspirations or trying to survive in ways of life long consecrated by faith and tradition, but now threatened by radical change, responded to (and may at times have even identified with) structuralist (i.e., statist) forces looming behind these periods of political and sociocultural change.

England: Conservative Religionists and the Idealized Stuart State

Comparative analysis, when applied (as in this specific case) to the sociopolitical revolutions that buffeted mid-seventeenth-century England, late-eighteenth-century France, and early-twentieth-century Russia, must obviously acknowledge significant differences as well as telling similarities. The scholar, for instance, who desires to follow the fortunes of conservative women defiantly displaying female agency in the English case can most easily group and study such individuals by their religious identities—that is to say, as Catholics, Anglicans, Presbyterians, or "Puritans"—rather than by laboriously (and, most likely, unsuccessfully) searching, as she or he might do in the cases of France and Russia, for stories of humble townswomen and peasants. What we will find equally arresting with respect to the English Revolution is the degree to which at least two lettered and articulate Englishwomen *justified in theoretical/historical terms* the seventeenth-century absolutist state of the Stuarts.

In discussing Catholic (or "recusant") Englishwomen in this period, we need first to review very briefly the important *political* aspects of Roman Catholicism in Stuart England.[4] As we saw in Chapter 3, Charles I's Catholic consort, Henrietta Maria, arrived in England from her native France at a time (in the mid-1620s) when her adopted kingdom was witnessing the great continental power struggle pitting the Austro-Spanish Habsburgs against Bourbon France—and at a time when England itself was precariously divided between warring "conspiracy theories" tying together threads of constitutional, religious, and geostrategic issues.[5] The "popular" conspiracy theory, destined in the 1640s to motivate the country's Puritan revolutionaries, explained political conflict (Ann Hughes has noted) "in terms of an authoritarian popish plot to undermine English laws and liberties as well as true religion, a plot which had alarming support from evil counselors at court." On the other, traditionalist (and soon counterrevolutionary) side, Charles I and his aides naturally regarded such views as a "subversive attempt to undermine his God-given authority: 'popularity,' not popery, was the great threat to the stability of English (and British) subjects." Such all-encompassing theories were, as Ann Hughes has concluded, "mutually reinforcing."[6] Given, in addition, the fact that "popery" conjured up for most English subjects such traumatic events as the Marian persecutions of the 1550s, the treason of Mary Stuart and the Spanish Armada of the 1580s, the Gunpowder Plot under James I, and the sanguinary Catholic assassinations martyring Protestants on the Continent, it would be difficult to overestimate the early-seventeenth-century tendency in *all* ranks of English society to detect priests and other "papists" under every bed, and to detest and fear Ireland (and even, to some extent, Scotland) as avenues for Catholic infiltration of evangelical England. Could, then, the presence of a notoriously Catholic and French queen at London after 1625 have possibly failed to aggravate the religious/political tensions already so pronounced in English society?

This was especially predictable in that Henrietta Maria, once ensconced in England as Charles I's consort, reigned informally over an ever-growing society of converted recusant courtiers of both sexes—a situation which extended well into the revolutionary 1640s. The prominent role played in all of this by *aristocratic women*—some of whom became counterrevolutionary advocates of the Stuart cause—has long been highlighted by scholars. "Burgeoning Catholicism at court," Michelle Anne White has written, was "evidenced in the number of conversions taking place there." While a number of these conversions resulted from the aggressive proselytizing in the late 1630s of papal agents such as George Con, others owed much, White informs us, to the agency of Olive Porter, niece of the late Duke of Buckingham:

> An enthusiastic Roman Catholic, and quite popular with Henrietta, Porter successfully converted her father and brother-in-law on their deathbeds. More conversions followed in considerable numbers, and of these the most controversial, perhaps, was that of Lady Anne Weston, the Countess of Newport. Her conversion brought the queen into direct collision with William Laud, now Archbishop of Canterbury. Laud . . . urged Charles I to re-enforce the laws against Catholics and proposed that the queen's chapel at Somerset House, as well as [those] of . . . ambassadors, be closed to English subjects.

Although an anti-Catholic proclamation was eventually published at Laud's urging, White has noted, the queen and many of her co-religionists "made a point of deliberately flouting it."[7] Indeed, one dismayed contemporary alleged that, on Sundays and special religious holidays, "no less than 6,000 people" heard Mass in the queen's chapel. What was more, Catholic worship was widespread all over London in these prerevolutionary years. According to Anzolo Correr, the Venetian legate to England, not only were the "chapels of the queen and of the ambassadors . . . frequented with freedom, but anyone who wishe[d] a celebration [of Mass] in his own house [could] avoid . . . danger . . . with very slight circumspection."[8]

Thus, a courtly Catholicism which would figure (at least marginally) in the royalist politics of the early revolutionary years was already flourishing in England in the severely polarized 1630s. Of course, we have long known that the king and queen—ruinously for themselves—helped associate the crown's cause with the Catholic menace in the civil war by recruiting Catholic soldiers not only from Ireland, the Papacy, and continental theaters of the Thirty Years' War but also—perhaps even more damagingly—from Catholic ranks of English society itself![9] Yet what must especially intrigue us here are the ways in which *religious* and *political* issues were *gendered* in the England of the late 1630s and early 1640s. This was manifestly to be seen, for instance, in the interactions between Rome and Papal envoy George Con on the eve of the English Revolution. Con quite bluntly informed the Vatican that he would promote Catholicism at London "by means of women." The truth was, he wryly admitted, that "when I go to visit [court ladies] I never ask for their husbands, so as not to arouse suspicions." Pope Urban VIII would later assess matters with equal (gendered) bluntness, lauding Englishwomen enjoying the queen's protection as true "amazons . . . who do day and night employ their utmost endeavors for the dignity of the apostolic see."[10] But, as we have already had occasion to note, Henrietta Maria's "courtier Catholicism" was also construed by English men *in society in general* as subversive of national security "by corrupting the state from within, beginning with the family." Catholic Recusancy, Diana Barnes has argued, like oppositional sectarianism on the Left, was "particularly attractive to women" because it was not subject to the same institutional controls as prevailed in established continental worship. Many of the women converting to Catholicism, Barnes has concomitantly remarked, "were women acting upon their own judgment with or without their husbands' approval." Since at this time "the dominant view was that women were subject to their husbands, whose authority was endorsed by God," any effort by Englishwomen to "follow God" in their own fashion clearly "contravened . . . the religious justification for male superiority" and, as such, could be adjudged by (male) contemporaries as being a "challenge to the patriarchal family" and, hence, to England's geopolitical security in an always dangerous world.[11] Indeed, it seems quite safe to argue in retrospect that gender, (courtly) class, religion, and politics were tightly fastened together in England's brewing revolutionary crisis *and* that the gender/

recusancy/security connection could jeopardize Stuart rule at *both ends*—that is, Catholic *and* sectarian—of the religious spectrum.

Moreover, the association between gender and Catholic recusancy so palpable at the Caroline court in the prerevolutionary and early revolutionary years manifested itself in well-bred country society as well. Feminist historian Marie B. Rowlands recounts, as a telling example of this, the tribulations of Jane Vaughan of Gloucestershire. This resourceful lady was imprisoned during the "no popery" panic of 1641 in Gloucester Castle for having sheltered on her manor at Ruarden for several years a Benedictine monk named John Broughton. Broughton was arrested in 1641 and tried in the English capital for his priestly activities; his Catholic patroness, summoned to the assizes at Gloucester, was imprisoned and expected, like her *protégé*, to be put on trial. In the event, as we learn from Rowlands, "the matter was not put to the question." Jane's son John petitioned Charles I, who, moved by this high-born (and likely pro-royalist) lady's dilemma, arranged to have the warrant for her arrest "recalled under the royal seal" on July 26, 1641. But more was probably involved here than the advantages of genteel class, religion, and pro-royalist sentiment. As Rowlands has observed, *gender*, too, likely factored in such situations:

> During the [wars] a considerable number of [Catholic] women had shown themselves articulate, obstinate in resistance and resourceful in expedients. The state [was] hampered in controlling them by the countervailing need to maintain the co-operation of the gentry and burgesses who were not prepared to allow the state to invade the integrity . . . of the family, or to override their rights as husbands and fathers. To make a wife . . . responsible for her conscientious resistance was to go beyond the bounds of acceptable public policy.[12]

True, in this specific case the recusant involved was rescued by a son rather than by a father or husband. All the same, it was a *male* relation who made the essential difference here. But Rowlands tells us that the "no popery" panics in Stuart England could equally motivate "matriarchal households" of high-born Catholics, households led, that is, by *women* rather than by *men*, to act in defense of the imperiled faith. Gentlewomen in such circumstances, "precisely because they had no public role and were protected to some extent by public opinion, were able to engage in resistance."[13] Cases like these characteristically seem, therefore, to have tied together considerations of class, gender, religion, and statist politics.

As we would anticipate, however, we find traditionalist female agency during the revolutionary 1640s on a much larger scale in the ranks of "established" Anglican royalists than among recusants who remained faithful to Rome. This should hardly surprise us, since, as Patricia Crawford, who studied this subject as assiduously as anyone, assured us in her standard conspectus on the subject, "the majority of [Englishwomen] were probably content with the Anglican church" throughout the era. Indeed, if we are to believe this specialist, matters were even more propitious in this regard in the troublous mid-century than they had been in earlier times. "By the 1620s and 1630s," Crawford contended, women, like men, were "attending church more regularly, and participating more usually in annual communion, than they had been during the Elizabethan period."[14] Other indications of increasing feminine commitment to the Anglican Church may have included women's attitudes toward the ceremony of "churching" after giving birth and their endorsement of *religious* rites of marriage. The former ritual was recognized during the 1630s by fully 93 percent of the mothers in at least one London parish, while during the Interregnum female attachment to *traditional religious* (as opposed to secular) rites of marriage seemingly remained strong all over the country.[15] "All of this suggests," Patricia Crawford concluded, that established Anglicanism "had secured a measure of popular acceptance" among Englishwomen and—most significantly for our purposes—that "its survival during the Civil Wars owed much to the devotion of the [female] laity."[16]

As we will proceed now to see, the devotion of Anglican women to church, crown, and—most poignantly, perhaps—*husbands* dramatically revealed itself during the revolutionary period. In delving into this matter, we can most effectively divide Anglican/Royalist Englishwomen into three categories: (1) those women who actively participated in Civil War sieges and battles; (2) those women acting on behalf of their imprisoned or exiled husbands in cases involving the "sequestration" of family estates; and (3) those women who personally pleaded—sometimes successfully, more often in vain—for their husbands' lives. In all these situations, the evidence points to a *conservative* female activism every bit as authentic as the activism documented on the better-known radical side in the 1640s and 1650s.

If, to begin with, Diane Purkiss (among others) has described for us the military and intelligence activities of Englishwomen identifying with Parliament, Puritanism, and—in season—Levelling radicals in the Civil War, other specialists have expatiated upon other women's counterrevolutionary actions.[17] Often, too, such countervailing heroics (inevitably?) drew the gendered commentaries of contemporary writers. There was, for instance, the Countess of Portland, who, at Carisbrooke Castle, "behaved like a Roman matron" and, rather than surrendering to Roundhead troops, "declared that she herself would fire the first cannon." Then there was the "lioness" Lady Mary Winter, wife of Royalist commander Sir John Winter, who, by declining to yield Lidney House, near Gloucester, to the Parliamentary commander Colonel Massey, ensured that the humiliated Massey's hopes would be "disappointed by the resolution of a female." Equally arresting was the case of Lady Bankes, wife of former Attorney-General and one-time Common Pleas Justice Sir John Bankes, who (in the absence of her exiled husband) defended Corfe Castle for two years, from 1643 to 1645, against the repeated assaults of Roundhead forces. "She had the honor," wrote another memoirist, "to have borne, with a constancy and courage far above her sex, a noble proportion of the late calamities." (Her husband had died in exile the year before.[18]) But perhaps most memorable of these "Great Heroics of the theoretically weaker sex" in revolutionary times— and, simultaneously, most revealing of 1640s misogyny—was the saga of Elizabeth Twysden, Lady Cholmly, who "stayed resolutely at her husband's side" throughout the hopeless royalist defense of Scarborough Castle in the wake of Cromwell's victory at Marston Moor (1644). Sir Hugh Cholmly afterward lauded his wife's gallantry in terms typical of the century: "My dear wife endured much hardship. . .; though by nature, according to her sex, timorous, yet in greatest danger [she] would not be daunted, but showed a courage even above her sex."[19]

Similar dynamics played out when it came to the sequestration of defeated Royalists' estates and rents.[20] Parliament, ever straitened financially, decreed in 1643 that the lands and rents of Royalist "delinquents" be administered by "sequestration committees" in the counties where such properties were located; derivative rents might serve as security for parliamentary loans. Wives of such Royalists, as legal dependents whose rights at law were "swallowed up" in those of their husbands, were allowed up to a fifth of sequestered incomes, if they pleaded personally at Goldsmiths' Hall in the City of London. It also fell often to Royalist/Anglican wives (after January 1644), notably if their husbands were in exile or imprisoned, to "compound" on their behalf (i.e., to reclaim family estates) by paying an assessed sum toward public relief. Although Margaret Cavendish, Duchess of Newcastle, observed that gentlewomen were "running about with their several causes," acting unnaturally as "pleaders, attornies, petitioners and the like," Antonia Fraser has since conceded "women's peculiar fitness to play the suppliant role" in such cases. This was assuredly what the incarcerated Royalist Thomas Knight assumed when writing to his wife in 1644: "I think it will be fit for thee to come up [i.e. to London] and appear in the business, for women solicitors are observed to have better audience than masculine malignants."[21] Dr. Denton, the exiled Royalist Sir Ralph Verney's neighbor, wrote reassuringly to Verney in a similar manner in August 1646: "Women have never been as useful as now . . . I am confident, if you were here, you would do as our sages do, instruct your wife and leave her to act . . . with the committees; their sex entitles them to many privileges and we find the comfort of them more now than ever."[22] We should also acknowledge in this connection the grinding physical hardships endured by some Royalist women seeking to rescue familial dwellings from the clutches of Parliamentary sequestration. Typical in this regard were the tribulations of Lady Cholmly (whom we have already encountered.) To safeguard her home at Whitby, this resolute lady "in the depths of winter . . . went on foot 'over the bleak and snowy moorland' of North Yorkshire, a distance of some twenty miles 'as the crow flies,' and rising to nearly a thousand feet. Attended by only one manservant and one maid, she took possession of her house again." Then, again, Isabella Twysden, wife of a Kentish gentleman, saved the family estate by submitting at one point to the "loathsomeness" of prison and by repeatedly undertaking, while heavily pregnant, "great journeys in Kent." Her death in 1657 would elicit from her husband this self-congratulatory tribute: "never man had a better wife, never children a better mother."[23]

Finally, we have the even more stirring cases of pro-Stuart gentlewomen reduced to begging for their defeated husbands' lives. Sometimes their efforts were successful. When, for instance, Sir Richard Fanshawe was incarcerated following upon Charles II's utter defeat at Worcester in 1651, his wife, Lady Anne Fanshawe, appealed to Oliver Cromwell for her husband's release on bail, pleading his ill health. The appeal was, apparently, granted. Again, we have the example of Elizabeth Mordaunt. When her husband, John, Viscount Mordaunt, was imprisoned and eventually tried (in 1658) for plotting against the Lord Protector, Elizabeth sagely counseled the Viscount "not to antagonize his captors by disputing their authority," somehow managed to arrange for the escape of a critical witness for the prosecution, and "as a result was largely responsible" for Mordaunt's eventual acquittal.[24] Still, there were times when appeals for Cromwellian mercy (probably inevitably) fell upon deaf ears. Such was the case with Sir John Penruddock, whose leadership of the fabled, but failed, Western Rising against the Protectorate in early 1655 cost him his life. We sense heartbreak and deep despair in the words that his wife, Lady Arundell Penruddock, penned to him after they had exchanged their final farewells:

My sad parting was so far from making me forget you that I have scarce thought upon myself since, but wholly upon you. Those dear embraces which I yet feel and shall never lose . . . have charmed my soul to such a reverence of your remembrances that, were it possible, I would with my own blood cement your dead limbs to life again, and, with reverence, think it no sin to rob heaven a little longer of a martyr.[25]

Such language, stilted as it may appear to the reader in "modern" times, nonetheless speaks eloquently of this titled lady's devotion to her Royalist husband—a devotion which, as we have seen, was common to those high-born women who presumably loathed the new political situation in England.

Do we find a similar "counterrevolutionary" or at least conservative sentiment agitating women of Presbyterian faith in revolutionary England? There is, exemplary of this, the prominent (if notorious) case of Lucy Hay, Countess of Carlisle (1599–1660). An English courtier of Percy family origins (i.e., from Northumberland) long famed for her beauty and wit,

Lucy was involved in many political intrigues (and likely turned coat more than once) in the early Civil War years.[26] Although scandalmongers portrayed her as (incongruously) sharing the affections of the Royalist Earl of Strafford and parliamentarian leader John Pym in 1640–1, and though at one point Lucy held the confidence of Queen Henrietta Maria, she seems soon to have found (Diane Purkiss has written) "a pathway to a sterner, fiercer kind of love, the love of God. . . . She became, and ardently remained, a Presbyterian, an adherent of the Scottish Kirk, one of those who longed to see the achievements of the Scots repeated in the English Church." If this was indeed the case, it made her "counterrevolutionary" up to a point, for, although disliking Laudian High Anglicanism, the Countess found Strafford's execution (in May 1641) reaffirming in her "an ideology of monarchy limited [only] by strong Protestantism and aristocratic counsel, an ideology she was to adhere to throughout the Civil War years."[27] Lucy managed to combine— at least to her own satisfaction—a Presbyterian faith with adherence to the Stuart cause in years to come: she was, for instance, pent up in the Tower of London for eighteen months because of her pro-royalist machinations during the "Second" Civil War (1648), and was later involved in Stuart plotting against the Protectorate during its final chaotic months following upon Oliver Cromwell's death in September 1658. If we can accept, with Purkiss, that the Countess of Carlisle "arguably pursued a consistent set of political goals, in her own stylish manner," we can imagine that there were also other Presbyterian women, who, whatever their reservations about the Stuarts' Anglicanism (not to mention their flirtations with Catholicism), were sufficiently alienated by the excesses of radical sectarian religion to endorse the general cause of a Stuart Restoration. We may also discern in Lucy Hay a harbinger of later female revolutionaries (such as Olympe de Gouges in France and E. D. Kuskova in Russia) whose paths, like that of the Countess of Carlisle, would eventually diverge from those of ruthlessly committed (and almost invariably *male*) state revolutionists.

Yet if Presbyterian Royalism in one sense inspired the exploits of some women in revolutionary England, it also (indirectly) played a role in *reaffirming* the inferior legal status of *all* women in English society at the time. This was due to the way *religious* and *political* calculations came together during 1650–1 in the recently established Commonwealth. As specialists have long known, the new regime in England had to confront at this time a major Royalist-Presbyterian conspiracy against its rule, and would not rest secure until Cromwell had decisively vanquished both factions in the conspiracy at the battle of Worcester (September 3, 1651).[28] Well before this came to pass, however, the government sought (as Keith Thomas has written) to "woo the Presbyterians in order to avert their threatened alliance with the royalists." The Rump Parliament's statute of May 10, 1650 "for suppressing the detestable sins of incest, adultery, and fornication," passed at a time "when men and women were pleading conscience to justify adultery, divorce, and bigamy," was undoubtedly, at least in part, a mainstream Puritan reaction against radical sectarian justifications of rumored sexual license. But when viewed in *political* terms, the statute also reflected the Commonwealth's eagerness to conciliate the Presbyterians (both those in England and those in Scotland) and, by doing so, sever their political cause from that of the Stuarts.[29] To "conciliate the Presbyterians," however, meant (among other things) to reaffirm *women's* subjection to *men*. As Fraser pointed out: "The harsh new Act of 1650 made adultery a capital crime; however, the man could escape execution by pleading that he did not realize the woman was married (a convenient loophole)! The woman on the other hand could in theory only avoid execution if her husband had been absent for more than three years." Whether "theory" here was matched by reality, the fact remained that, even in this age of supposed revolution, "the principle of the greater guilt of the female was explicitly stated."[30] Keith Thomas might insist stoutly that the Act of 1650 "did not necessarily imply an unequal conception of the marriage relationship." Still, he conceded that a wife's *legal* status as *property* made adultery *as such* "a threat to the whole system of property relations." Thomas thereby acknowledged in so many words that historians must view the 1650 legislation as embodying an "iniquitous double standard."[31]

Nevertheless, if the Act of 1650 (as stated earlier) was in part "a mainstream Puritan reaction" against the scarifying extremes of radical sectarianism in seventeenth-century England, it probably also mirrored traditionalist concerns held by Englishwomen of *all* religious persuasions in this era. That this was true, for instance, where the *political* rights of women and men were concerned is something that Sharon Arnoult stressed when analyzing in gendered terms the doctrine of the "sovereignty of the soul." Since the accepted wisdom held that "the authority embodied in the order of society and government was either divinely instituted, or at least divinely sanctioned," Arnoult remarked, "Anglican women and most Puritan women did not believe that the sovereignty of women's souls meant women could claim an equal share of *political* sovereignty and the right to a voice in the public arena of *political* debate." Consequently, their share in the commonwealth was, at best, "derivative." Such a philosophy was likely accepted by most Catholic (and, of course, Presbyterian) Englishwomen at this time as well.[32]

But there was also another way in which most Englishwomen rallied to what Arnoult referred to as "the defenses of the traditional order." This involved the decision of the "Barebones Parliament," on August 24, 1653, to abrogate the traditional *religious* wedding ritual and replace it with a *civil* ceremony before a justice of the peace. While we must note that this statute, passed by an unrepresentative and (as it turned out) merely temporary assemblage of religious and legal reformists, hardly anticipated the radical acts on marriage and divorce approved later on in France and Russia, it still managed to alienate most Englishwomen at the time.[33] Throughout the Interregnum, Christopher Durston observed, "many couples did, of course, marry in accordance with some or all of the requirements of the Barebones Act, but many others continued to wed in church." The issue even generated a split within Oliver Cromwell's own family: his daughter Frances wed in a "lavish civil ceremony," but Frances's sister Mary insisted on an old-fashioned "Royalist/Anglican procedure!"[34] Less anecdotal and more impressively *demographic* information on the question comes to us from E. A. Wrigley and R. S. Schofield, whose research suggests that more marriages were hurriedly contracted in England during September 1653— just *before* the new statute could actually take effect—than during any other month in the entire period.[35] More moderate legislators (in 1657 and then again in 1661) would reinstate the traditional religious marriage rites. "The reforming zeal of a minority of Puritan politicians and soldiers," Durston has aptly concluded, was in this matter no match at all for what was demonstrably "a widespread attachment to custom and tradition" in purportedly "revolutionary" England.[36]

Finally, in discussing traditionalist Englishwomen in the seventeenth century we are intrigued by the fact that some of them translated their "attachment to custom and tradition" into *constitutional* and *political* terms by theorizing and indeed celebrating Stuart absolutism. We need only cite in this regard two unusually articulate women—Mary Pope, who briefly flourished during the Puritan revolution in the late 1640s, and Mary Astell, who forged her more substantial reputation largely in the aftermath of the "Glorious Revolution" (1688–9). Neither of these individuals was a true feminist in the "modern" sense of the term, yet both women—in different ways—proved eager to address certain issues of relevance to members of their sex in their contemporary world.

We know relatively little about the first of these two formidable Marys. We can at least say that Mary Pope was one of three "prophetesses"—the others being Katherine Chidley and Elizabeth Poole—who addressed the State Council and Parliament prior to Charles I's execution in January 1649.[37] But she is better known, at least to some students of English political theory, for her *Treatise of Magistracy*, written in the form of a petition and two letters to Parliament two years earlier, that is, at some point in 1647.[38] In this lengthy and rather complex essay, the author came down repeatedly and unreservedly on the side of absolute monarchy in mid-seventeenth-century England. We quote here cursorily from this uncompromising work on constitutional arrangements in England:

> Sovereignty lies in Rule and Dominion. . . . Subjection lies in duty and obedience; Rule is that which makes a King: Obedience is that which constitutes a Subject. Rule and Dominion . . . is that which ties a King to his subjects. . . . The Parliament . . . and Army . . . have acted their parts

much worse (and that the whole Kingdom can witness) than our King did before He went away. . . . And this I am sure, our King was born our natural King; and seeing we have good laws and righteous Statutes by which he was constituted, why may not the same lawful, warrantable, and legal way be renewed again?[39]

Sharon Arnoult, one of the scholars who seems to have most painstakingly studied this 1647 tract, and who singled its author out as "the only Anglican/ Royalist woman to publish a defense of her religious/ political position during the [civil] war," was admittedly ready to evaluate the *Treatise of Magistracy* in *gendered* as well as in political terms. Thus, she correctly noted that Mary Pope saw a conceivable link "between the sovereignty of the [female] soul and *political* sovereignty, and [she] condemned it." Pope, added Arnoult, went out of her way to denounce "teachers, that have taught our women to follow their new-found-out truths, *without their husbands*." Hence, in Arnoult's reading of the case, Mary Pope was at this inflection point in the English Revolution associating a *gendered* hierarchy in the country with a *social* and *political* hierarchy.[40] Nevertheless, what we are chiefly left with in pondering Pope's message to her contemporaries is an almost Filmerian insistence, in these unprecedentedly topsy-turvy times, upon divinely ordained and *absolutist* governance for all subjects. That she so stridently consigned to infamy "what the radicals say, that there is a rational reason in man, to direct for the ordering of civil affairs" might, indeed, have even taken her— beyond Sir Robert Filmer—in a Hobbesian direction, had she not adhered so faithfully to a more conventional Royalist and Scriptural inspiration.

We know considerably more about the second of these two Marys, that is, Mary Astell (1666–1731), whose controversial career and prolific writings have both fascinated and (at times) perplexed a host of feminists and other scholars over the years.[41] Born in Newcastle upon Tyne into an upper- and middle-class (and primarily Royalist) family of gentry, lawyers, clergymen, and merchants, Mary Astell moved to London in her twenties soon after her mother's death, lived there—in unmarried state—from then on, and was active in prominent literary and Anglican circles until her death in 1731. Astell became a noted polemicist engaged in both writing against and personally debating Dissenter clerics of the era, advocating for the cause of Englishwomen's religious and secular education, and authoring many works. Among the best-known of those screeds were: *A Serious Proposal to the Ladies for the Advancement of Their True and Greatest Interest* (1694); *Some Reflections Upon Marriage* (1700); and, likely of greatest constitutional and political significance, *An Impartial Enquiry into the Causes of Rebellion and Civil War in this Kingdom* (1704). Because she so strongly rejected contemporary patriarchal assumptions about women's *intellectual* (if not *civic*) inferiority to men, Astell spent much of her time discoursing about and working toward the establishment of female educational institutions in and near London.

We retrospectively find in Mary Astell an uneasy but no less intriguing mixture of feminism—at least, *intellectual* feminism as refracted through the prism of Stuart social expectations—and forthright (if, in Astell's case, somewhat dated) defense of Stuart governance *at its most absolute*. On the former issue, Joan Kinnaird has noted that while "feminism proper, associated with the late nineteenth century, is the doctrine of the complete equality of the sexes," such "protofeminists" as Astell, Hannah Woolley, and also Lady Mary Chudleigh "preached only equality of 'souls' and hence, according to the philosophic understanding of the time, equality of the rational faculties God had given to men and women alike." In Kinnaird's words, Mary Astell was convinced that "God had . . . allotted to each sex its proper sphere . . . men were made for public life, women for private life." The way was consequently prepared, at least in Mary Astell's philosophy, for a world in which she (and other like-minded women) could with total consistency advocate for women's *intellectual* development, even while accepting society's patriarchal arrangements within marriage, and even while accepting the "separate spheres" argument that insisted upon a *public* and *political* life dominated by menfolk.[42]

It is scarcely surprising, then, that "there is a notable tension in the broader body of scholarship when it comes to categorizing [Astell] as the unequivocal 'first English feminist'."[43] No such "tension" exists in learned circles, however, when it comes to Mary Astell's *political* theorizing in her 1704 essay entitled *An Impartial Enquiry into the Causes of Rebellion and Civil War in this Kingdom*. As all those chronicling Astell's life and analyzing her thought have stressed, this Englishwoman revealed, even at the dawn of a new century, an unaltered allegiance (in general) to Stuart absolutism and (in particular) to the long-dead Charles I. Perhaps Joan Kinnaird has most effectively summarized a turn of mind that brought Astell even more closely than we have already intimated to the civil war–era Mary Pope:

> As [Astell] saw it, the Civil War was not an uprising by liberty-loving Englishmen against a Stuart despot but an "unnatural Rebellion" against one of the "most Virtuous and most Religious of our English Princes." Factious sectarians, abetted by Jonn Milton, Buchanon, and those "Mercenary Scribblers whom all sober Men condemn," had seduced the "Good Natured English people." Under the banner of popular rights and liberties, these sectarians had set out to destroy the government in church and state. . . . The lesson Mrs. Astell drew from the Civil War was that the established order should be preserved inviolate to protect religion, civil rights, and property.

Interestingly, Kinnaird notes that Mary Astell's relatively cursory treatment of James II and the uprising against him in 1688 yielded references that were only, at best, "oblique and ambiguous."[44] But another feminist scholar,

Ruth Perry, as if taking up the story at this point from Kinnaird, has since informed us that "after 1714, Astell's sympathies were with the Jacobites, that remnant which, after the arrival of Hanoverian George, swore loyalty to the true Stuart succession and schemed to put the Pretender [i.e., "James III"] on the throne."[45] It appears obvious, then, that for Mary Astell, the loyalty of women (if married, that is) to their husbands and the loyalty of subjects to the "legitimate" Stuart monarchs were ideally of one piece. Gendered and political/constitutional realities were thereby, in the best of worlds as theorized by Mary Astell as by Mary Pope, destined to dwell together and to be mutually reinforcing.

What emerges in the end from this story of traditionalist Englishwomen who could not accept the revolutionary legacy of the 1640s and 1650s is the fact that, just like their more radicalized sisters, they had, willy-nilly, to deal not only with what scholars today call the intersectionality of gender, class, and religion, but also with inescapable questions concerning politics and the state. But while the wives, sisters, daughters, and mothers of the Levellers were rudely dispersed by the Cromwellian regime, and while the Interregnum's prophetesses and female preachers were silenced or casually ignored by Oliver Cromwell's Stuart successors, Royalist women of all religious persuasions were understandably eager to oppose the revolutionary forces that had been unleashed in their country. In fact, as we have just seen, two of the most educated and articulate among them praised in Filmerian if not quite Hobbesian terms the *traditionalist* state power manifested in the Stuart monarchy. When Mary Pope anathematized the radical notion that "there is a rational reason in man, to direct for the ordering . . . of civil affairs," she was, we might argue, only anticipating Mary Astell's subsequent argument that "it is better . . . some innocents should suffer, than [that] the majesty of government . . . should be violated."[46] Englishwomen of this type were, Melinda Zook has rightly written, bound in the end to be "disturbed by what they saw as the slow demise of traditional England, with the monarchy as its sacred center, and the increasing acceptance of religious pluralism, social mobility, and parliamentary government."[47] What such individuals could *not* have foreseen, of course, was that in two major revolutions to come, women as staunchly traditionalist as *they* were—not to mention certain other women disabused of initially progressive hopes by the harsh realities of revolutionary politics—would also find themselves opposing ultra-radical governments.

France: Disillusioned *Citoyennes*, Peasant Women, and the Jacobin/Napoloenic State

When Lucy Hay, Countess of Carlisle, turned her coat in revolutionary England, thus transferring her bruited affections from John Pym to "a sterner, fiercer kind of love, namely the love of God," and so from an early parliamentarian orientation to a Presbyterian-associated Cavalier and Stuart royalism, she could not have imagined that she would be anticipating such future disillusioned women as Olympe de Gouges and Madame Roland in revolutionary France—to go no farther at this time. Olympe de Gouges and Roland were "disillusioned," that is, in that they, too, came in the end to repudiate a revolutionary cause with which they had initially identified, and revolutionary leaders with whom they had originally consorted. At the same time, it is also true (and *every bit as significant*) that, as revolutionary changes came to Louis XVI's antiquated kingdom, Frenchwomen of the laboring classes (most notably, for these purposes, in provincial walks of life) showed themselves determined to defend settled ways of faith and tradition. In doing so, they would have to confront not only interrelated issues of gender, religion, and class but also the regenerated state authority that appeared (in France, as, emphatically, later in Russia) to loom behind the course and processes of revolutionary change.

Gendered interpretations of Olympe de Gouges (as, for that matter, of Mme. Roland) have had to compete increasingly with political explanations. Born Marie Gouze at Montauban (in what would later be Tarne-et-Garonne) in 1748, Gouges earned renown as a playwright in the Paris of the 1780s.[48] Her passionate advocacy of human rights embraced not only matters such as marriage and divorce, and women's and children's roles in French society, but also the question of slavery. Ineluctably, Olympe de Gouges welcomed the outbreak of revolution in France in 1789; yet she soon became disillusioned by the revolutionaries' failure to extend "equal rights" to women. In 1791, responding to the ballyhooed 1789 "Declaration of the Rights of Man and the Citizen," Gouges published what is probably her most celebrated pronunciamento, the "Declaration of the Rights of Woman and of the Female Citizen," in which she duly "challenged the practice of male authority and advocated for equal rights for women."[49] Because of her ties with the (by then, moderate) Girondist faction in 1792–3, her opposition to the execution of Louis XVI, and, above all, her writings stridently criticizing Robespierre, the Montagnards, and the revolutionary government during 1792–3, Olympe de Gouges was eventually imprisoned and (on November 3, 1793) guillotined—less than three weeks after the execution of Marie-Antoinette.

Unsurprisingly, this talented playwright, publicist, and humanitarian, struck down at the apogee of revolution in France, has attracted the sympathy of numerous feminist historians. Two of them, Janie Vanpée and Gabrielle Verdier, contributing to a 1994 anthology of articles, have been especially vocal in portraying Olympe de Gouges in gendered terms.[50] For Vanpée, the "real issue" condemning de Gouges was *not* "one of holding opinions from the wrong side of the political spectrum, but rather of articulating political opinions at all." It was exactly because de Gouges "insisted on maintaining her political identity [i.e. *as a woman*] that [she] had to be executed."[51] Verdier, for her part, has contextualized Olympe de Gouges' written *oeuvres* even more sweepingly. Her plays, in Verdier's words, "denounce social abuses, but her preoccupation with issues that raise ... the problem of woman's place within family, society, and state give them a dimension that is at the same time gendered and ... universal." Indeed, for Verdier, de Gouges, "anticipating later feminisms, ... saw the similarities among various forms of oppression based on race, class, and sex."[52] Yet it is striking that, while both of these scholars have also invoked in their work the name of Joan Wallach Scott, Scott herself, while indeed providing her own advanced feminist "take" on Olympe de Gouges, has fallen back in the end upon a more conventional *political* explanation for the tragic fate of this celebrated Frenchwoman at the height of the Terror in France. Granted, Scott, like so many other feminists, argued that "Jacobin centralization" in the Terror "was accompanied by ruthlessly masculine political assertions and by the expulsion of prominent women from the Jacobin club." Still, in the final analysis, she conceded, de Gouges "was sent to the guillotine in 1793 not for her feminism, but for plastering the walls of Paris with posters urging that a federalist system replace Jacobin centralized rule."[53] *Politics*, in other words, even more than *gender,* spelled disaster for Olympe de Gouges.

Joan Scott's judgment in this matter, like that of all scholars accentuating the *political* nature of Olympe de Gouges' downfall, finds dramatic vindication in many of the posters with which de Gouges was—to cite Scott once again–"plastering the walls of Paris." Here, for instance, were selections from a posted assault (of November 5, 1792) on the "Incorruptible" himself, Maximilien Robespierre:

> What is it that you want? What is it that you claim? Upon whom do you seek revenge? . . . whose blood are you still thirsty for? . . . You would have the last of the Louis assassinated in order to avoid his being judged legally? You would have Pétion, Roland, Vergniaud, Condorcet, Louvet, Brissot, Lasource, Guadet, Gensonné [all of them Girondists] . . . assassinated, basically all of our Republic's shining patriots? . . . Such a coarse and vile plotter!

And, a month later, in December 1792, we have this posted defense of the already dethroned Louis XVI:

> I believe that as King, Louis is in the wrong, but, shorn of that banned title, he ceases to be guilty in the eyes of the Republic. . . . The greatest of Louis Capet's crimes, . . . is to have been born King at a time when philosophy was silently preparing the Republic's foundations. . . . Let us be good enough to leave him his life. . . . In dethroning him, we have shattered the world's sceptres: the people's sovereignty has taken back

its rights, and we shouldn't punish him for our ancestors' ignorance and [for] the crimes perpetrated by *his* ancestors.[54]

In fact, de Gouges had already shown her complete lack of political realism (if not of abiding idealism) by dedicating her 1791 "Declaration of the Rights of Women" to—of all people—Marie-Antoinette, and by subsequently lashing out at "Philippe Égalité" for *failing to defend* Louis XVI.[55] There is one feminist historian who, following up on the earlier commentaries of scholars such as Vanpée, Verdier, and Scott, has since endorsed Scott's interpretation of Olympe de Gouges—but in a manner challenging the "public/private dichotomy" that undergirds so much recent historiography. In refuting the tedious and misogynistic Jacobin descriptions of de Gouges as guilty, above all, of "invading the space" reserved—even, it seems, in revolutions!—for *male* politicians, Annie K. Smart has portrayed this woman, and indeed all her contemporary *citoyennes*, as advocating a citizenship transcending the frequently posited boundary between the "public sphere" and the "private sphere." As Smart put it, in a short but telling analysis of de Gouges' most famous feminist pronunciamento:

> Gouges' *Déclaration* clearly intertwines the social and sexual contracts: civic equality in the public sphere and sexual equality within the marriage are *interdependent*. The home is thus an important site for citizenship. Gouges does not . . . assert that revolutionary work is done in one sphere and private work in the other. Women belong in both spaces, and Olympe de Gouges grants equal importance to both spheres.

In other words, according to Smart, de Gouges' *citoyennes* ideally "promote the Constitution, support the Revolution, and sacrifice their own interests for the common good—and they ensure that the home generates the ideals of the new Republic."[56] Hence, for this historian, Olympe de Gouges, even though (ironically) she was marched to the scaffold in November 1793 largely for *political,* rather than *gendered,* reasons, was nonetheless still far ahead of her time in advocating a kind of citizenship that, at its best, would be able to accommodate civic-minded women as well as civic-minded men.[57]

If Mme. Roland shared Olympe de Gouges' sanguinary fate on the guillotine at Paris in 1793, she likely did so for reasons even less gender-related than was the case for her contemporary de Gouges.[58] Born Marie-Jeanne Phlipon at Paris in 1754, this future victim of the Terror initially led a relatively quiet provincial life with her "economist" husband, Jean-Marie Roland de la Platière. The Roland couple, after spending the early days of the 1789 upheaval at Lyon, eventually came to reside in Paris in 1791. There, Madame Roland soon became prominent in the "Girondist" group of politicians, playing a host of roles: that is, as lobbyist, "influencer," and hostess of a salon that she assembled several times weekly for leading personalities at this stage of the Revolution. Her public influence only grew when her husband became Minister of the Interior in 1792. Mme. Roland appears to have been involved, for instance, in decisions about political appointments, and was even in charge of a bureau set up to influence political opinion in France. Inevitably, she was caught up, along with her husband and his cohorts, in the Girondist/Jacobin power struggle of 1792–3. Marie-Jeanne Roland, in June 1793, was the first Girondist to be arrested by the triumphant Jacobins; she was guillotined in early November—five days after Olympe de Gouges.

Madame Roland, like her renowned contemporary Olympe de Gouges, has drawn considerable feminist interest—and sympathy. Mary Trouille, for example, contributing to the same anthology as did Janie Vanpée and Gabrielle Verdier, argued (on the basis of the misogynistic rantings of revolutionaries like P.-G. Chaumette and J.-B.-A. Amar) that Mme. Roland's execution, "like that of Olympe de Gouges and other 'public' women, was being used as a warning to women activists: If they did not give up their political activities and conform to the passive domestic role prescribed for them by the revolutionary government, they, too, would risk imprisonment and death." In addition, Trouille, citing from Roland's eleventh-hour memoirs and correspondence, spoke admiringly of her "desire to develop her talents to the fullest, her secret pleasure at manipulating power relations behind the scenes, and above all her deep satisfaction at fulfilling her adolescent dream to escape the confines of her sex and class in order to help shape the future of the new French Republic." Here, insisted Trouille, were feelings revelatory of "the woman behind the mask who consciously subverted the limited gender role imposed on her by society."[59] No wonder, then—we might certainly conclude from all this—Marie-Jeanne Roland suffered the same poignant fate as did Olympe de Gouges!

Yet *was* Roland's "adolescent dream" really that anticipatory of modern-day feminism? There are, according to Gita May and other scholars, reasons for doubting it. Back in 1783, in the relatively staid and safe world of the ancien régime, Mme. Roland had written to a (male) acquaintance, L.-A.-G. Bosc, in quite a different vein:

Do not imagine, therefore, that I delude myself about what we [women] can demand or expect. . . . Govern the world, change the surface of the globe, be proud, terrible, clever, and learned. You [men] are all that without our help, and through all that you are bound to be our masters. But without us you would not be virtuous, loving, loved, or happy. . . . As for us, we have and wish no other supremacy than that over your morals, no other rule than that over your hearts. I shall claim nothing beyond that.[60]

Rousseau himself, it would seem, could hardly have found fault with such language. But did the onset of revolution in France a few years later materially alter her views? It may possibly have "pushed her some way towards different conclusions," Siân Reynolds has written. For example, Mme. Roland commented approvingly upon female participation in street demonstrations in the faubourg St. Antoine in 1791, and she often expressed impatience with women who "thought about nothing but their appearance, or who made household duties their entire existence." Still, on April 5, 1791, she could also confide to another male acquaintance, J.-H. Bancal des Issarts, thoughts reminiscent of her 1783 remarks to L.-A.-G. Bosc:

> I don't believe that our social habits yet allow women to show themselves; they should inspire the good and nourish and kindle all the sentiments useful to the *patrie* but should not appear to contribute to political matters. They will not be able to act *openly* until all the French have deserved the name of free men.[61]

At best, Reynolds has tentatively concluded, Mme. Roland remains "a difficult woman to pigeonhole in the 'women in the French Revolution' debates." She seems to have been (in today's colloquial parlance) somewhat "conflicted" about such gendered issues.

What seems beyond any reasonable doubt, nonetheless, is that Mme. Roland, like all the other Girondists, was above all caught up fatally, in 1792–3, in circumstances which were now dominated by *international war* and its multifarious ramifications. Here, Gita May was particularly perceptive, zeroing in on the connection, in wartime France, between *Parisian* and *provincial* politics. She pointed out that Roland, as a native Parisian, had originally viewed the capital as the natural champion of the revolution's cause, and had repeatedly decried the reactionary inclinations of Lyon and its surroundings. But under the influence of her Girondist colleagues, her attitude "underwent a significant change," leading her (by 1792–3) to denounce what she now regarded as the *sans-culotte* "dictatorship" of Paris. In a time of national emergency, however, this was to be, for her, a fatal change in attitude:

> Frantically, she urged her friends to rally the provincial deputies behind their [Girondist] cause and to oppose a common front to the increasing threat of Parisian domination. In her agitated state of mind, it did not occur to her that such action, instead of saving the Revolution, could well wreck it irremediably. Most of the Montagnards, too, came from bourgeois origins, and Robespierre shared Mme. Roland's dislike for vulgarity and slovenliness. . . . But . . . it was Roland's fatal mistake to believe that the Jacobins represented only the ragged mobs of Paris while the Girondists were the spokesmen of the whole people of France.

As Gita May rightly concluded, in a time of "national crisis" the cause of the Girondists was "doomed to failure. . . . Even moderate republicans who bore a grudge against the overwhelming power of Paris . . . now rallied behind the existing government for the sake of national survival."[62] In a word, the waging of war *abroad* required governmental centralization *at home*—something that the Robespierrist Jacobins fully realized, but that, to their ruin, Marie-Jeanne Roland and her associates failed to appreciate.

It seems clear, then, that if (in the terms of our larger study) both Olympe de Gouges and Mme. Roland, like Lucy Hay in the English Revolution, turned "counterrevolutionary"—in factional terms—at a perilous juncture in revolutionary times, they did so with *differing degrees* of commitment to what we know today as "feminism." Their tragedies were, chiefly, *political* in nature; insofar as gender played a role in all of this, Susan Dalton has shrewdly suggested, it highlighted the "activist feminism" of women like Gouges and the somewhat less assertive "indirect feminism" of women like Marie-Jeanne Roland.[63] Or, preferably, we should be satisfied, in the end, with Siân Reynolds' judgment on the latter individual: "We certainly do not find her making claims for women's public role, like Olympe de Gouges."[64]

If Parisian publicists and *salonnières* such as Olympe de Gouges and Mme. Roland only soured on the revolutionary process when—late in the game—it turned terroristic and violent, many laboring women in provincial France had begun to show counterrevolutionary inclinations even earlier on after 1789. As, accordingly, we shift over from a Parisian to a provincial perspective on revolutionary issues, we can analyze the actions of provincial Frenchwomen by posing three central questions. First, how did these individuals react to and (in time) resist the revolutionary legislatures on socioeconomic and (most notably) religious matters in the early and "radicalizing" days of revolution in France? Second, how did provincial women continue to oppose many governmental policies in the post-Terrorist (Directory) era? Finally, how (very briefly) did Napoleonic legal and religious reforms affecting these women foreshadow certain gender-related developments over the *longue durée* of the French nineteenth century?

To begin with, archival research has uncovered myriad examples of women in rural communities resisting the fiat of Paris on *economic* issues during the early 1790s. In much of what Olwen Hufton calls "producer France"—away from Paris—the "first *citoyennes* to boycott the Revolutionary paper currency and to trigger inflation were peasant women at the markets who refused to hand over basic foodstuffs like milk and vegetables for anything but coin." Hufton goes on to explain how the economic changes incidental to the Revolution reinforced feminine discontents in provincial France:

> The slump in luxury industries, the deliberate destruction of the old
> agencies of poor relief in small towns and villages without organizing

replacements, price fixing which was very clearly opposed to the interests of producing France and also to those [interests] of towns which were not a priority in the government's provisioning schemes. . . . [All these factors] created a huge pool of dissidence by late 1792.[65]

So (apparently) did legislators' efforts to sell off common and waste lands, so useful in the "off season" to peasants for traditional rights of gleaning and harvesting. Moreover, regional studies disclose in more granular detail how fiscal and economic policies typifying the new era stoked resentment among female rural populations. Thus, Harvey Mitchell, reading from a women's manifesto, or complaint, of January 2, 1792, in the West (Vendée region), found that "so determined was the resentment against the new taxes that the women of Ile-D'Yeu demanded their abolition, and the restoration of 'the old ways, that is to say . . . the former administration,' which meant exemption from taxes."[66] Then, again, in the far South—in the Département of the Gard—Gwynne Lewis has cited "the inadequacy of relief programs, coupled with the rise in the price of essential food-supplies," as accounting for what he termed the "explosive situation confronting the authorities during the winter of 1791-92." Here, once again, it was infuriated women who took the lead in coordinating local action—action which culminated in major bread riots at Nîmes on January 31, 1792. The harried Nîmois authorities could do little but vaguely promise an end to escalating bread prices and the accompanying suffering "which manifested itself on every street-corner in Nîmes."[67] And so it went, all over France, in these early years of the Revolution: women who were obsessed, as always, with securing the wherewithal to feed their families could find in the upheaval of the early 1790s scant "liberation" from daily, grinding economic need.

Nevertheless, it is through the lens of *religious protest* that we can most effectively comprehend the *mentalité* of these provincial Frenchwomen. Timothy Tackett has gone so far as to hypothesize that "it was perhaps these humble women of provincial and rural France, protesting with their whole beings the "change in religion" thrust upon them by the men in Paris, who delivered the single most influential political statement by any women of the revolutionary decade."[68] The "change in religion" alluded to here was brought about by the Civil Constitution of the Clergy, decreed by the Constituent Assembly in July 1790. If humble parish priests might have had good reason to applaud the Constitution's abolition of chapters and benefices "without cure of souls," its reduction of the scandalous inequalities between episcopal and priestly incomes, and some of its other measures, the most principled among them often saw the Civil Constitution as imposing such changes without prior consultation of the Church in France and, ultimately, of the First Shepard at Rome.[69] But, as we know from the careful research of Tackett and others, it was especially the oath of allegiance to the new religious regime, imposed in late 1790 on local clergy throughout France, that ignited the opposition not only of "Tridentine priests," wedded still to a vision of ecclesiastical institutions resisting the secular state's supremacist claims, but also of local Frenchwomen loyal to such clergymen. Most notably in "fringe areas" of the country—that is, the West, northeastern provinces, the far South—such female opposition could flare up into the kinds of religious violence in some ways almost reminiscent of the sixteenth century's ugly "civil wars of religion."[70]

What were they like, these devout *provinçiales*, living so far away— often in both geographical *and* psychic terms—from their radicalized Parisian sisters? Perhaps Olwen Hufton has most arrestingly portrayed these individuals, who, from the early 1790s, "moved into the defense of traditional religion and its priesthood" and were, as a result, "transformed little by little into [counter-revolutionaries] with a distinctive role to play" in their embattled country's political drama:

> Women who boycotted the mass of the constitutional priest, who in the hard years of 1793-94 organized clandestine masses, who continued to slap a cross on the forehead of the new-born, who placed a Marian girdle on the stomach of the parturient, and who also gathered to say the rosary and taught their children their prayers, were . . . committing counter-revolutionary offenses. . . . They resented the *décadis* which destroyed traditional sociability patterns. They buried their relatives secretly in the dead of night. They probably encouraged their sons to defect [i.e. from the army] and they certainly did not send their children to state schools.

Unlike the revolutionary woman, the *femme contre-révolutionnaire* evolved slowly. "She surfaced in the countryside, in some areas sooner than in others, or in the small town which *knew* it was not a priority in the government's provisioning schemes." Furthermore—Hufton adds, and as we, too, shall discover later—this woman "began to win after 1795, though the victory was far from absolute or clear cut."[71]

We also have, from existing sources, a plethora of pungent descriptions of the actions taken by provincial Frenchwomen in defiant defense of their beloved priests and religious ways. In the West, in northeastern reaches of the country, and in much of the South, "where threats or actual violence were involved, a distinct majority of Frenchwomen would seem to have rejected the oath and supported the [non-juring] refractories." This is surely what Tackett has found, as we gather from even this very brief selection of riotous religious incidents culled from his extensive research:

> In Les Moûtiers parish [in the West], women threatened to hang the municipal officers if they attempted to administer the oath; in St.-Pierre-sur-Dives they ripped down notices of the oath decree, cheered the refractories, and made "scornful faces" at the officials. In Balleroy they

shouted and screamed in the church for half an hour when the curé's [non-juring] oath was rejected. In Vendes . . . nearly all of the women of the parish rose and swarmed into the choir, bringing a halt to the ceremony and escorting the clergymen out of the church. In a number of towns of Rouergue and Languedoc, women were said to have opposed the publication of the oath decree and to have mishandled the town criers in charge of proclaiming it. Women and girls in Craponne (Haute-Loire) would refuse to permit the vicaire and four other priests to fulfill the National Assembly's requirements.[72]

And so on. The incident involving women's "scornful faces" made at the luckless municipal *officiers* at St.-Pierre-sur-Dives resembles in an almost burlesque fashion what happened at a church in the Haute-Loire region during the Terror. Here, "at a sign from an old woman, the entire female audience arose, turned their backs on the 'altar of liberty,' and raised their skirts to expose their bare buttocks . . . so as to express their feelings to the new deity." The unfortunate "patriotic" priest in this situation, who was all too obviously checkmated by this "spectacle of serried rows of naked female backsides," was reportedly "reduced to gibberish!"[73]

Yet, for all of this, we should remember that in the regions of France centering on the Parisian Basin, much as in a very broad sweep of provinces cutting diagonally across the country's interior from the border of the Austrian Netherlands to the mouth of the Gironde River, clerical (and, likely, female) acceptance of the oath to the Civil Constitution was common. At the very most, there was not, in such areas, *that* certain a progression from women's presumed unhappiness with the new religious oath to any extensive counterrevolutionary violence. "Although some Catholics in these regions opposed the Revolution," Suzanne Desan has observed, "many others welcomed its political and social reforms and simply objected to dechristianization and the existence of rival revolutionary cults." Beyond this, Desan has also noted, women desiring to retain their Catholicism knew how to turn the Revolution's ideology to their own purposes. In the Yonne, for instance, "women . . . were keenly aware that the revolutionary concepts of "liberty" and "popular sovereignty" provided an ideological backing for their demands for religious freedom and their right to take autonomous action." Or, as the women of the community of Vaux guilelessly put it: "Since everyone [now] had the freedom of opinion, we desired our religion, and thought we were authorized to demand it."[74] For such *citoyennes* as these, clearly, ideology intended for *secular* purposes at Paris could easily enough be turned to (age-old) *religious* ends.

This having been said, there remains the undoubted fact that, in the peripheral reaches of the country less amenable to revolutionary indoctrination, provincial women implicated in religious rioting had in mind what Olwen Hufton has termed "the restoration of community solidarity as expressed in communal worship." For such individuals, defending the traditional faith meant rejecting new patterns of sociability in favor of the old and (to them) proven ways of doing things *in common*:

> The women wanted a warm, comforting, personal and familial religion with its own sociability patterns. . . . .The state cults, with their emphasis on reason and liberty, were not only a religious travesty but an irrelevance to the peasant world. Liberty may have been a goddess to replace the old patriarchal God, but she offered nothing in the way of solace. . . . There is nothing rational about the vagaries of life and individual pain, and a religion that did not hold out hope to the despairing through prayer and the possibility of change had little to attract them.[75]

In the Maine-et-Loire *Département* in western France, Harvey Mitchell has found, the predisposition to oppose the "new" religion, *curés*, and *officiers* associated with the godless writ of Paris frequently went hand in hand with a tendency—on the part of young and pregnant peasant women—to trust the older, native midwives over possibly more qualified "foreign" midwives when birthing services were required. Here, as in many other outlying regions of France, the "violent struggle to maintain the present meant keeping the external world out"—an unwanted "external world" that, in peasant eyes, extended from faraway, "secularized" Paris to the nearest significant provincial communities.[76]

We should also consider how such factors as *class* and (most pertinently) *gender* figured in the phenomenon of female religious protest in these years of radical change in France. With respect to the former issue, there appear to be conflicting indications not lending themselves to easy generalizations. For instance, we know that in Strasbourg (in far eastern France) "a peaceful procession of 250 women presented a petition to the departmental directory" in 1791 "announcing their fears for the Catholic religion if the [Constitutional] oath were enforced." The petitioners represented "a wide range of social backgrounds, from women of the aristocracy . . . to relatively humble members of the common people." Religious sentiment in this case, then, may have been a unifying force in society.[77] Again, in the Yonne valley in north-central France, pro-Catholic activists "came from diverse backgrounds within towns and villages," and even later rioters from this area "seemed to represent a cross-section of the Third Estate in Old Regime rural society."[78] On the other hand, Tackett's meticulous study of the religious troubles of 1791 in Sommières, located in the South near Nîmes and Montpellier, suggests a potential for, if not "class-consciousness" in a modern sense, at least a kind of socioeconomic solidarity among rioters:

> these rioters were anything but a typical cross-section of the women of Sommières. . . . Clearly, virtually all of them came from relatively humble

social milieus. They were the wives or sisters or daughters of peasants, of wool workers, of gravediggers, of soldiers, and, above all, of an assortment of men following the traditional crafts (shoemakers, tailors, locksmiths, etc.). . . . The overwhelming majority of the rioting women seem to have been illiterate, and a substantial number were somewhat older, lower-class women without husbands . . . [who were] inclined to orthodox religious piety.

Such women, very possibly socializing *in addition* in common crafts and trades as well as related through familial/marital connections, were also frequently linked as members of local Rosary and other religious confraternities.[79] In general: *class*, at this level, as analyzed in various regions of revolutionary France, may not have been as universally *divisive* a force—meaning, in part, as universally threatening a force to landed gentry and other *notables*—as it was to be later in revolutionary Russia.

As for *gender*, it operated in Frenchwomen's religious protests in ways somewhat reminiscent of situations that had once confronted women in revolutionary England. Timothy Tackett, for instance, tells us of the anger with which Jacobins and other "patriots" in religiously polarized towns and villages taunted and insulted local women as they attended "refractory" masses during the years of deepening revolution in France. We discern a mixture of revolutionary idealism and more primitive *male* anxieties in such patriotic reactions at the local level:

Some patriots were convinced of the existence of a kind of conspiracy between the priests and their own wives which threatened not only the Revolution but their very authority as family patriarchs as well. The women of Ardèche were said to be "tormenting their husbands, children and servants like so many devils." In the district of Brioude, dévote wives, supposedly won over by the clergy in the confessional, were acting like "Trojan horses" to corrupt whole households. In Chartres and Loire-et-Cher there were bitter [male?] complaints of the oath crisis destroying domestic tranquility and bringing several women to abandon their husbands altogether.

The historian, Tackett goes on, cannot help but sense here, at least at times, a revival of husbands' fears, in the old regime, of "the sexual power and attraction of the clergy over their women."[80] But, as Tackett himself points out in this context, such heated reactions betrayed as well something that was even more fundamental: "the common assumption of [women's] inferior nature and irresponsible character"—an assumption that conveniently allowed revolutionary leaders to dismiss local opposition to their religious policies as the "overheated effusions of hysterical women manipulated by fanatical priests."[81]

And since, of course—whatever their "natural" weaknesses—female rioters of provincial France (like the élitist ladies we earlier encountered in revolutionary England) were deemed to be necessary to their husbands, the latter were customarily quick to intervene on their behalf. At Avallon, for instance, male petitioners argued successfully that, when townswomen occupied the village bell tower for several days, this amounted to "just a few hysterical cries and the agitations of women out of control." At Vaux, rioting women were released since, after all, "they were mothers of families and it was useful to return them to their households." Furthermore, we are told, these presumably contrite women of Vaux (in the words of a local judge) "promised to abjure their fanatic ideas and to replace them with the principles of reason." Indeed, as Suzanne Desan has added in discussing these incidents, "the immunity and leniency toward women before the law was so great that some men dressed as women to avoid arrest."[82] Thus, whatever the *class* differential between Royalist gentlewomen pleading for their husbands' estates—or lives—in revolutionary England and rural Frenchwomen of a lower station embroiled in religious troubles in revolutionary France, certain *gendered* attitudes seem to have been common to both situations.

Such gendered attitudes in France, as we would expect, lived on in the 1795–9 period under the constitutional system known as the Directory. The Thermidorian/Directorial leaders have garnered scholarly plaudits for trying to inculcate a new "civil religion" in the minds and hearts of the citizenry.[83] Yet there is scant evidence to suggest that the new faith, with its transparently political overtones, ever caught on significantly among the traditionally Catholic masses.[84] What is more, the authorities, even in the relatively tolerant times preceding the leftist Fructidor *coup* (of September 1797), only grudgingly allowed Catholics liberties. Sundays were ordinary working days under the revolutionary calendar, and sacred holidays similarly fell victim to the new temporal schema. In addition, local officials exercised an intrusive role of surveillance over religious services: priests were often dismayed to find *agents de police* attending their sermons. Again, *curés* and *vicaires* were subjected to civic tests reminiscent of the Civil Constitution of 1790, and were answerable, under penalty of arbitrary deportation, for violations of the myriad rules concerning the opening of church buildings, the ringing of bells, and other exterior signs of worship. Yet again, those courageous enough to open Catholic schools could incur official wrath if they failed in any respect to observe the Republican calendar. Predictably, the regime's treatment of Catholic clergy and communicants only hardened in the wake of Fructidor. It imposed a tough loyalty oath on all priests resolved still to minister to their flocks and arrogated to itself the power to incarcerate or deport "refractory" priests by simple administrative fiat.

In the light of all of this, we would be amazed were we not able to document many incidents—and, indeed, many kinds—of women's religious protest in provincial, post-Terror France. Some of these reactions, in their gendered symbolism, went far beyond any remonstrances about the Civil Constitution and its accompanying loyalty oath. Olwen Hufton, for instance, has told us about what transpired in the village of Saint Germain de Laval (in the Mâconnais, in southeastern Burgundy) in 1795:

> local Jacobins took a classical nude from a local château and painted a tricolor on her. Having felled as a symbol of obsolete papistry the crucifix which had stood in the village square, they stood the statue in the vacant spot and proclaimed her the goddess of liberty. Days later it began to rain and, as the paint started to wash off and to run down her legs, the young guard proclaimed the "miracle of the menstruating goddess." The village women, outraged by these tasteless remarks, seized the statue, carried her several miles to the river, washed her, and laid her on her side, a purification ceremony which restored her dignity as a female symbol. The next day they broke into the church and reclaimed it for Catholic worship.

"A striking response," Hufton has commented, "to mockery of female dignity and to change imposed in such a way as to slight the women of the community."[85]

Moreover, the incensed *citoyennes* of Saint Germain de Laval (Mâconnais) were hardly unique in their determination to resist (among other things) the Directory's ideas about church openings and the Sunday ringing of bells. Incident after incident illustrated the state of affairs in provincial France.[86] At Mende (in the Cévennes), two women (Rose Bros and a "Citoyenne Randon," spouse of a former district official of the Terror), fought for the honor of reopening their erstwhile cathedral as a parish church. At Vouneuil-sur-Vienne (Vienne), women, brandishing sticks, forced the local church open. Chancing upon vestigial records of the defunct *société populaire*, they tore up the *Declaration of the Rights of Man*, the Laws and Constitution [of 1793?], and smashed and burned the president's chair. In one of the urban parishes of Bayeux (in Normandy), Madame Le Morgue, braving the hostility of her fishmonger husband who had sacrilegiously opened a fish-market in one of the churches, forced it open and led in a team of cleaning women to "scour it out." At Ribérac (in Dordogne), women devised a persuasive "battle plan" for regaining control of the Sunday church bells: "Pregnant and old women were lined up . . . to swell the ranks of forefront protesters, while the young and able-bodied [women?] of the parish brought up the rear with aprons full of stones and ashes to blind any assailants." In Franche Comté, to the East, many women turned to bells not only to summon the faithful to Mass but also—it seems—to celebrate local victories over insufficiently devout (and, naturally, male) officialdom. And so it went, all over France.

Escalating efforts by the Directorial authorities after the Fructidor *coup* to harass local *curés* and *vicaires* only provoked escalating reactions on the other, disproportionately *female* side: women, we are informed, not only "wrested chalices and sacred vessels from . . . authorities" wherever possible but also "rescued dissident priests from prison."[87] And such resistance was not limited to peripheral redoubts of "counter-revolution" in France. "Local documents are full of examples of strife and resistance over the religious issue," Clive Church has affirmed. Indeed, in the ordinarily "quiet department of the Haute Marne this was practically the only cause of public disorder, leading on one occasion to a whole village rioting when two luckless gendarmes tried to arrest a refractory priest." Whereas we may assume that most villages aroused at times from political quiescence in this period were not exercised solely about religious questions, we can certainly concur with Church that the government's increasingly draconian treatment of priests and their (women-led) flocks was "a major cause of the alienation of public opinion during the later stages of the Directory's existence."[88] And to *religious* causes of that alienation were added *economic* causes. "In famine times of the 1790s," Suzanne Desan has noted, "the theological link between bread and salvation took on added poignancy in the demands of rioters who sought both grain and religion." Yet, Desan furthermore maintains, female protest under the Directory had the additional benefit for provincial Frenchwomen of reaffirming a kind of *gendered solidarity and worth*. "Women's creation of both personal and collective forms of piety" became, in her phrasing, "an expression of their autonomy and self-worth within the patriarchal structures of the community."[89]

But if what Olwen Hufton has described as a "female-engineered religious revival" swept many provincial communities in Directorial France, it was paralleled to some extent *nationally* by a revelatory debate in the legislature over the historic statute of September 20, 1792 reforming (among other things) marriage and divorce procedures. "Conservative opponents of divorce for incompatibility," as Suzanne Desan has observed, "played upon anxiety over gender roles, emphasizing both the weak, susceptible character of the flighty female and the dangerous quality of feminine sexuality."[90] Many a deputy, likely reflecting regretfully upon the path-blazing legislation of September 1792, now argued that abrogating divorce—at least on the grounds of incompatibility—would "guarantee" male fidelity within marriage and protect "vulnerable" women from being seduced or somehow tricked out of their dowries. What was more, some Catholic deputies accused women of "forgetting the natural shyness of their sex," and of abusing the 1792 statute to shirk their responsibilities to husbands and children. Inevitably, *gender* and *religion* became fused together in this debate. As one legislator put it: "The sweetness, obscurity, retreat, silence, interior care of the family, prayer, and reading of the Holy Scriptures are the lot and the happiness of the woman who wants to fulfill her duties."

"Women," he went on, "need religion to make them strong, to assure their virtue and happiness." After analyzing all this rodomontade, Desan has, in sum, divined in it the "shared concern of both opponents *and* proponents of divorce with strengthening the [divides] between the public and private spheres and with creating a strong domestic sphere as the basis of the social and political order—whether republican or royalist."[91]

Although the legislative debate over divorce in the Directory had no immediate statutory effect, it does prompt several observations on our part. For one thing, we cannot help but notice, throughout the revolutionary decade, a persistent leitmotif of "nonpartisan misogyny" in the attitudes of the men governing France. This was true from the antifeminist rantings of Jacobins like J.-B.-A. Amar and Fabre d'Églantine during the 1793–4 Terror to the sexual tirades of prominent Directorians in the late 1790s. Second, we are also struck at this point by the parallel between the waxing strength of the "masculinist reaction" in the English Revolution—as witnessed, for example, in the 1647 Putney Debates, the 1650 Adultery Act, and the eventual silencing of prophetesses, preachers, and petitioners—and the gathering strength of a similar reaction in revolutionary France—as seen, at both national and provincial levels, in the late Terror and subsequent Directory. Finally, we note that, for more than one historian of France, the revolutionaries of the eighteenth century, forging as they did linkage "between feminine *sensibilité*, religion, and domesticity," can help us to understand now why religion became "increasingly *feminized*" in the nineteenth and even, perhaps, twentieth centuries.[92]

This last contention takes us, clearly, beyond the French revolutionary era altogether, positing as it does what one scholar has termed an increasingly stark "sexual dichotomy in religious practice," or—what amounts *for us* to the same thing—a "feminization of religion" in the nineteenth and twentieth centuries in France. Yet the precedents for this phenomenon emerged very early on, with Napoleon's Civil Code and religious Concordat of 1801.[93] If the 1804–7 Code (in Jennifer Heuer's words) "reversed many of the dramatic changes in family law introduced during the Revolution," hence spelling defeat for some of the most audacious reformists of the 1790s, the Concordat of 1801, hammered out with Rome, catered to the conservative religious perspectives of countless provincial Frenchwomen by securing for them their beloved Catholicism and (in many cases) restoring their non-juring clergy as well.[94] As Heuer and other feminist historians have accurately pointed out, the Bourbon Restoration would preserve and, in fact, further institutionalize the reaction *against* gender-related reforms promulgated in revolutionary times and at the same time reaffirm a traditional faith associated above all with provincial France. But these same specialists, casting their eyes over the nineteenth century as a whole, have also stressed the "staying power" of what Suzanne Desan has called the "conflicting legacies regarding women's position within households and their relationship to the state and politics."[95] Annie K. Smart and Jennifer Popiel have in effect addressed the same issue by stressing that (in Smart's words) "the borderlines between domestic and public spheres" were to remain doggedly "porous."[96] Such comments suggest to us how unresolved, over the *longue durée* of the nineteenth century, would be questions about Frenchwomen's "domestic" and "civic" roles in this polity. Still, it may well be that, lurking behind all this admittedly significant sociocultural commentary is, arguably, the greatest of all consequences stemming from the 1789 Revolution—namely, the revitalization of the French state. We will undoubtedly have more to say about this issue (and about how it may have affected women) in the concluding pages of Chapter 5.

Russia: Disillusioned Socialists, Peasant Women, and Bolshevik Autocracy

If the Countess of Carlisle, by turning her coat in the English Civil War, anticipated disillusioned *citoyennes* in the French Revolution such as Olympe de Gouges and Marie-Jeanne Roland, she must also be viewed as prefiguring, in the Russian Revolution, such disillusioned socialists as Ekaterina D. Kuskova and Alexandra Kollontai. Both E. D. Kuskova and Kollontai, as we will presently see, motivated in part by feminist concerns but just as much by other considerations, played distinctive roles in the lead-up to the upheaval that overthrew Russia's tsars in 1917 before eventually—at different points and for different reasons—souring on this country's progression toward a revitalized autocracy under Bolshevik auspices. At the same time, the laboring woman in Russia—most notably, at least for our purposes, the peasant woman (*krest'ianka* or *baba*) in the endless reaches of the countryside—had to confront after 1917 the escalating statist demands of her new Communist rulers. In doing so, she, like her rural predecessors in revolutionary France, would find herself grappling with interrelated issues of gender, religion, class, and revamped statism as she decided when to accept (and when, on the other hand, to resist) the enormous changes unleashed in revolutionary and postrevolutionary Russia.

Ekaterina Dimitrievna Kuskova, born at Ufa, west of the southern Urals in Russia in November 1869, was a prominent economist, journalist, and politician involved in many of the events that led to the collapse of tsarism, Russia's brief flirtation with Western-style democracy, and, finally, the Bolshevik "coup" late in 1917.[97] That Kuskova contributed, at one time or another, to the foundation of both the Russian Social Democratic Labor Party (RSDLP) and the liberal—and, hence, non-Marxist—Constitutional Democratic (Kadet) Party serves immediately to suggest to us that here, once again, we are dealing with someone destined at some point to abandon the cause of genuinely extreme revolution. Kuskova was briefly aligned with Father Gapon, charismatic leader of the "Bloody Sunday" uprising at St. Petersburg (January 1905), and then—having already parted ways with the RSDLP—helped, in the course of 1905, to establish the Kadet Party. After 1905, E. D. Kuskova, lacking any close party affiliation, channeled her energies into Russia's Masonic organization, playing a salient role in efforts to unite all elements of the oppositional intelligentsia in the country. Kuskova would later adopt a moderate "Defensist" stance on Russia's engagement in the First World War. She fell out irrevocably with Lenin by denouncing the Bolsheviks' anti-war agitation, their seizure of state power in October 1917, and their subsequent suppression of the Constituent Assembly. Expelled in 1922 from what was now Soviet Russia, along with her husband Sergei Prokopovich and assorted other liberals and moderate socialists, Kuskova settled first in Berlin (1922–4), then in Prague, and later, fleeing from the Nazis, in Geneva (1939). Ekaterina Kuskova died in Switzerland, largely forgotten by her contemporary world, on December 22, 1958.

Kuskova was, in her own way, almost as much a feminist as Olympe de Gouges had been in the French Revolution. As early as 1908, according to Barbara Norton, Kuskova strongly promoted Russian women's interests at the First All-Russian Congress of Women. Four years later, her continuing focus on women's issues moved her to participate actively in an historic congress on Russian women's education. In the year of revolution, 1917, Kuskova argued vociferously for women's suffrage in two major forums: the League of Women's Equality (convening in March) and the April meeting of the All-Russian Congress of Women.[98] Furthermore, as we gather from a plethora of scholarly accounts, E. D. Kuskova was one of those Russian feminists who, dissatisfied with all "unofficial" pleas for women's liberation, personally harangued the newly formed Provisional Government's prime minister, Prince Georgii Lvov, on Russian women's right, not only to vote, but to run for office as well. Undeniably, the landmark legislation of July 20, 1917, conferring electoral and office-holding rights on women in the new Russia owed something to the warm and sustained advocacy of Ekaterina Kuskova.[99]

True, even Kuskova's principal biographer has granted that, however authentic her support for women's suffrage and other rights in Russia, "her politics during 1917 were not the politics of feminism. This was due in part to her conviction that genuine equality for women would come only with Russia's fundamental socio-economic transformation."[100] Yet Kuskova's long-standing *gradualist* approach to the much-debated issue of Russia's transformation led her to dissent from Lenin's uncompromisingly "hard" position on this question—and, thus, to oppose subsequently Bolshevik plans for post-Romanov Russia. In fact, this had all been foreshadowed years before, during Lenin's 1897–1901 European exile, when Kuskova and other "revisionist" Marxists, influenced by theorists like Eduard Bernstein, had contended that capitalism, far from automatically worsening Russian workers' conditions, could in fact "coexist" with socialism under democratic political auspices. Nadezhda Krupskaya, Lenin's wife, recalled in her memoirs the fury with which her husband had reacted to this gradualist philosophy:

> The exiled Lenin was thrown into a rage by the "heresy." Krupskaya recalled that during 1899, after reading the works of Kuskova and [Karl] Kautsky, Lenin became depressed and lost weight and sleep. . . . He had embraced Marxism as the surest way to revolution. . . . Yet here was Marxism being stripped of all its revolutionary meaning and transformed into little more than the wishy-washy type of social liberalism of which no doubt his own father would have approved. Lenin led the attack on Economism with the sort of violence that would later become the trademark of his rhetoric.[101]

Clearly, we can retrospectively see in this *contretemps* pitting Lenin against Kuskova, Kautsky, and other semi-Westernized theorists the early signs of a fissure in Russian Marxist ranks that, before long, would help to alienate Ekaterina Kuskova irreversibly from the Bolshevik revolutionary cause.

Upon the advent of revolution in 1917, we are thus unsurprised to learn, E. D. Kuskova, deeming herself still to be a "critical socialist" if no longer a strict Marxist partisan, was generally content with the political agenda of the Provisional Government. While holding on to her basic conviction that the quest for women's rights in Russia must, in the end, advance hand in hand with the education of the masses, Kuskova concerned herself more immediately with the country's war-related emergency in 1917. It is of interest that this concern translated into two emphases in her writings at this time: (1) a preoccupation with the government's *geopolitical* position; and (2) an equally pronounced preoccupation with the idea of *pre-emptive statism* as such. On the former point, we have Barbara Norton's apt summary:

> Although Kuskova was deeply sympathetic to the suffering of the working classes . . . the limited economic measures she sought were . . . intended chiefly to take the pressure off the Provisional Government so that it might continue the struggle against Russia's external enemies. Only the successful conclusion of the international conflict could provide the security and stability she considered necessary to address the country's . . . socio-economic problems. . . . Like [Alexander] Kerensky, she sought a peace without annexations or indemnities. . . . Until such a plan could be fully elaborated, however, the successful conduct of the war remained a priority.[102]

On the latter point, we have Kuskova's own remarks as 1917 progressed. The Provisional Government, she wrote in July, needed the services of "people who believe in the principle of the state and who act decisively." The Revolution, she added on 30 August, must promote "the creative forces," or, again, the "able forces" of "state organization . . . in the spirit of the national (and not its *class*) interests." That in her writings Kuskova drew repeatedly upon derivatives of the Russian term *gosudarstvo*—that is, *the state*—revealed her obsession (at least in the crisis of the moment) with the absolute need to prioritize *national unity* over Lenin's more narrowly conceived *class* or *workers' interests*.[103]

In the end, of course, Lenin's emphasis upon *class* over *state* and *national unity* (and, it must be said, over *gender* as well) won out—at least in the short term. Precisely *because* we agree with Norton's argument that Kuskova's "commitment to above-party, above-class cooperation" appears "naïve in the circumstances of intense class conflict and sharp political polarization" in revolutionary Russia, we must regard her follow-up speculation that a course of gradualism and compromise *might* have afforded "an acceptable way out of [Russia's] political impasse" as much less persuasive.[104] It is true that Kuskova and her husband Sergei Prokopovich lingered on in Russia for some time to come; indeed, having refrained (wisely) from supporting counterrevolutionary partisans during the Civil War, they could help in famine relief efforts at its conclusion. They were, nonetheless, expelled from Soviet Russia, as we have already seen, in 1922. Ekaterina D. Kuskova, however intellectually engaged in discussions over Russia's future both before and during the 1917 cataclysm, would never see her native country again.

If, in the case of Kuskova, a prescription for *evolutionary* change in modern Russia fell victim to the irreconcilable demands of *class* and *nation* (with the requirements of *gender* lurking furtively in the background), what can we say about Alexandra Kollontai? Born Aleksandra Mikhailovna Domontovich at St. Petersburg on March 30, 1872, the future Bolshevik feminist, daughter of an Imperial Army general and—for a time—wife of another officer, V. L. Kollontai, had by the late 1890s abandoned both familial and societal identities in "privilege Russia."[105] Having joined the Marxist RSDLP in 1899, Kollontai, whose political activism led to her exile in the West (1908–17), broke with her earliest Menshevik associates in 1915 to align herself more closely with V. I. Lenin's Bolshevik faction of the RSDLP. In Soviet Russia, Kollontai, first as People's Commissar for Public Welfare and then as co-founder of the Bolshevik Party's Women's Bureau (*Zhenotdel*), advocated insistently for the reform of marriage and divorce procedures, for the toleration of "free love" among Party comrades, for the destigmatization of illegitimate children, and for general improvements in women's and children's status in society. Her participation (along with Alexander Shliapnikov and S. P. Medvedev) in the so-called "Workers'

Opposition" movement of 1920, which called for greater workers' influence and "democracy" in Party ranks, placed in doubt for a time her Bolshevik membership. From 1922 on, Kollontai, sidelined in the Commissariat for Foreign Affairs, held a series of diplomatic assignments: Norway (1923–5), Mexico (1926–7), Norway again (1927–30), and, finally, Sweden (1930–45). She, died, "honored" but largely ignored, on March 9, 1952 at Moscow.

If it was advisable, earlier, to document E. D. Kuskova's commitment to women's causes, such an exercise hardly seems necessary in the much more widely known case of Alexandra Kollontai. What we need to do, instead, is to show how, for at least three reasons, Kollontai's emphasis on Russian women's liberation ultimately fell short (if not failing altogether) in Soviet Russia's "Thermidorian" period. First, there was the long-standing conflict between *class* and *gender* in the Marxian tradition. Second, there was the uncomfortable, yet undeniable, issue of misogyny in Marxist leaders' attitudes. Finally—and this is a factor that is too frequently underplayed by feminist scholars themselves—there was the *domestic* and even more the *international* environment in which, during the 1920s, Lenin and his eventual successors had to struggle to secure Soviet rule in postrevolutionary Russia.

On the first of these points, Beatrice Farnsworth has designated as a "myth" the notion that, in prerevolutionary times and thereafter, "Russian socialists were actively committed to . . . the liberation of women." Indeed, she has written, "the opposite was true." It was all very well and good to panegyrize, in Western European fashion, the cause of women's equality and of their hoped-for incorporation into the mainstream of public life; but how, in specifically *socialist* (and *Russian*) terms, was one to reconcile such eulogistic language with the concept—and the daily, unadorned realities—of *class*?

> With the development of Marxism as a political movement, [late] in the nineteenth century, the term "feminism" became suspect in European socialist parties. It implied not simply equality for women but a union of women as a separate group, linked by bonds *that transcended those of class*. This was, of course, deviant thinking, the mere suggestion of which made Marxists uneasy. Specific clauses concerning women and separate institutions held for them the threat of dividing the working class. Therefore the [RSDLP] preferred that the liberation of women be treated not as a specific, revolutionary goal but rather as an eventual result of the class struggle.[106]

There was, of course, a subtle irony in all of this for Alexandra Kollontai. As we noted earlier, during and after 1905 this prominent Social Democrat had herself derided "bourgeois feminism" and fought against any élitist attempts to entice female workers away from their "predestined" roles in SD trade unions and other groups.[107] In prerevolutionary times, that is to say, *class*, for

Kollontai, had at the very least held a parity with *gender*, however significant the latter category might be. But come Soviet ascendancy in the new Russia, Kollontai, advocating militantly for Russian working women, would find herself, to a certain degree, hoist on her own petard—trumpeting, now, the "rediscovery" of *gender* against predominantly male Party comrades only too happy to prioritize (as in fact they always had) *class* over *gender.*

On the second point, Kollontai's need to celebrate the continuing importance of *gender* in Party circles reflected prevalent attitudes toward women that, albeit unsurprising in the Russia of the 1920s, would be labeled as sexist by most scholars today. Lenin himself reportedly conceded (before his death in 1924) that many of his associates were still "Philistine" in their mentality regarding women's issues. But, beyond this, historians have often divined a continuity on such matters that extended from Marx and Engels themselves, writing in mid-nineteenth-century Europe, down to their ideological acolytes in early-twentieth-century Russia. Beatrice Farnsworth has elaborated on this point in connection with the Bolsheviks' preparation of a Family Code intended (in 1925–6) to supplement the 1918 Code:

> Trotsky shared a view of women that caused him to praise as socialist the legislation Kollontai condemned as petty bourgeois. Nor was his perception "un-Marxist." Once, in a lighthearted moment, Karl Marx . . . wrote that the virtue he admired most in men was "strength." The virtue he admired most in women? "Weakness." Both Marx and Engels believed that the weak must be protected from the strong. Men must protect women. This theme ran through the debates over the new family code. . . . The Bolsheviks believed in equality for women, of course, but few understood that phrase with Kollontai's sensitivity.

As Farnsworth and other biographers of Kollontai have remarked, this Bolshevik feminist's effort to have the alimony payments discussed in the projected new legislation replaced by a general fund based on a graduated tax struck her male comrades—as, for that matter, did some of her other observations on the projected Code—as being "simply further evidence of her Left deviation."[108]

Finally, there was the question of domestic and diplomatic challenges confronting the Bolshevik (Communist) leadership in "Thermidorian" Russia. It was one thing for Kollontai, in her *Zhenotdel* role, to rhapsodize about a future world in which "everyone would live in communes" and "women would be free to choose whatever sorts of romantic relationships met their needs."[109] On a later occasion, as Mark Steinberg has emphasized, Kollontai would return to this utopian theme by insisting that "criticism and struggle" were *in themselves* more important than any specific accomplishment, inspiring as they would be to cohorts of female reformists yet to come.[110] But, unavoidably, such an ardent advocacy of Russian women's interests "set other party members' teeth on edge."[111] And no wonder: the men—and it *was,* after all, primarily men—who had to secure and defend Soviet Russia in the 1920s and beyond had less visionary concerns to deal with. At home, such matters included (among other things) finding some way to bridge the fearful chasm, psychological *and* developmental, yawning between urban and (crushingly peasant) rural Russia.[112] Abroad, there were traditional *and* novel geostrategic challenges that required Moscow's concentrated attention.[113] In a world of such unsparing realities, the idealism of feminists like Alexandra Kollontai, however praiseworthy in itself, was destined to be relegated to second place. *Class* and *state,* in our customary terms of analysis, would necessarily contend for primacy over *gender.*

In view of the foregoing discussion, we can easily point to significant differences between these two imposing women of old regime and revolutionary Russia. Whereas E. D. Kuskova, as a Legal Marxist or "critical socialist" at most, diverged early on from hardened revolutionaries like V. I. Lenin, Alexandra Kollontai remained a Bolshevik (at least in formal partisan terms) until the end. The former woman was an "evolutionist," while the latter woman entertained radical, even utopian dreams for a revolutionized Russia. Nevertheless, Kuskova and Kollontai shared certain things in common. They were both, in their own unique ways, *feminists.* They both found ways to oppose specific tendencies in Bolshevik thinking and policy. Finally, hailing as they did from "privilege Russia," they both failed adequately to appreciate (as, for that matter, did even Lenin's most discerning followers) the huge gap separating the fast-paced, (relatively) modernist world of Moscow and other metropoles from the traditionalist world of peasants in the countryside—peasants who, after all, constituted the vast majority of people in this land.

It is in connection with this last point that we turn now to examining peasant women's attitudes and behavior in the vast expanses of rural Russia during the decade or so after 1917. We can best do so by asking three fundamental questions. First, how did the Russian peasant woman (formally *krest'ianka,* but rather pejoratively, *baba*) react to political, economic, religious, and gendered issues during the Civil War and the early 1920s? Second, how did she react to the controversy attending the new Family Code of the Russian Soviet Federative Socialist Republic (RSFSR) in 1925–6? Finally, how did she respond to Stalin's campaign of compulsory collectivization as it gathered steam in the countryside after 1928, and what does this response tell us about her future in the world of Russia's "second revolution?"

With respect to the first of these queries, Sarah Badcock, Aaron B. Retish and other historians of provincial Russia would first stress the general *withdrawal* of provincial women from positions of public responsibility they had often occupied during the war years. Badcock, for instance, provides us with this telltale passage from a report issued by a State Duma committee in April 1917:

> There is opposition from workers and peasant [men] to the participation of women in elections. Nothing is said to women, and in places they not only do not participate in the building of public life, but also often don't know about their rights that they [have] received in the course of the revolution. When delegates tried to clarify the situation . . . the [male] peasants with resentment observed that "You stir up our women, then they will not go into the shafts" [i.e. back to work]. And there are almost no cases of women being elected in the village.

"The realities of Russian political life in 1917," Badcock herself adds, "showed that the electorate largely speaking wanted to vote for local working men, and not women, to be their political representatives in 1917." Men "dominated political decision making in village life," and in factories, too, "men dominated the political scene." In years to come, provincial women would continue to be "relegated to backroom possibilities by the needs of mass democratic politics."[114] This was, Badcock says, the story in Kazan and Nizhegorod provinces in the south Volga region. Aaron B. Retish has found a similar situation prevailing farther north, in Viatka province. There, he has discovered, women who had dominated the electorate in all the 1917 village elections played only a minor role in elections two years later. "Because women viewed themselves in local politics" as being essentially "surrogates of their menfolk," Retish explains, they failed, in large part, to resist men's resumption of village assembly roles. Hence, by attempting to "bring the rural poor to power and quickly build a reliable state apparatus in the countryside," Retish concludes generally, "the Bolsheviks reinforced traditional gender divisions, placing class considerations above gender."[115] Soviet (that is to say, *state*) political culture was, from the start, "classed," and firmly gendered *male*. Donald G. Raleigh's research has uncovered similar class, gender, and political realities in Saratov province (in the Volga region) during the turbulent years from 1917 to 1922.[116]

To emphasize this point unduly might be seen as begging the legitimate question: were women in rural Russia *that* commonly opposed to embracing civic activism in early Soviet times? As the above discussion suggests, the answer to that query appears to be: often, *yes*. Much of this had to do with the chaos of the times, which, if anything, reinforced female peasants' innate conservatism. Russia's *baba* may have been willing at times to revolt against her in-laws, and against village patriarchs' domination of traditional *extended* families; but she was far less willing to challenge a husband or a father. Barbara Clements has summarized such attitudes against the backdrop of a Russian society still trying to recover from the traumata of world war, social revolution, and civil warfare:

Most women were probably frightened by the war and by the unrest all around them. Social upheaval, especially if it destroys families, imperils the weak in society, and women had always been far weaker than men in Russia. . . . Far from weakening the loyalty of the great majority of peasant women to a traditional marriage, which granted the husband great power over the wife, the Civil War may even have strengthened their beliefs by demonstrating forcefully how crucial marriage was to their survival. It was a family in transition to which they clung, but they defended it as unchanged and unchanging.[117]

These realities asserted themselves dramatically when agents of *Zhenotdel* visited villages and tried to preach "women's liberation" to the female population. Women's reactions "ranged from avoidance to sullen silence to outright attacks." *Zhenotdel* workers were waylaid and beaten, meetings were broken up by cursing men, groups of older women set on younger ones accused of having attended Bolshevik- sponsored gatherings, and "women who criticized the commune were ostracized by other women."[118] In Saratov province, an activist from Atkarsk found "few women truly sympathetic to Communism," and most of them all too prepared to anathematize the Bolsheviks for their "awful economic conditions."[119] In Nolinsk district in Viatka province, one newspaper quoted a peasant woman as saying: "It is true that many women among us are against organizing. Women say to those who have joined [*Zhenotdel*] that the *baba* needs to be in the home, and not wander off to public meetings."[120] Kollontai's image of the peasant woman (*krest'ianka*) as pining to be liberated from the shackles of tradition seems to have had little in common with the reality of the conservative village *baba* in Russia's endless countryside.

This is not, for sure, to contend that Russia's rural women would have absolutely nothing to do with Bolshevik-appointed activists in these years: as Retish, for instance, has discovered, those living in Viatka province at times cooperated with *Zhenotdel* in "maternal" roles such as establishing children's cafeterias and helping to direct programs in schools. Moreover, the female peasantry in this region, if shunning official Party organs, was not above using land courts and petitions to governmental agencies in Moscow to deal with matters such as famine relief.[121] Still, a cursory review of religious, educational, and, above all, *economic/developmental* affairs in provincial Russia in the early 1920s cannot help but underscore for us the chasm between Bolshevik and rural female perspectives—and, in doing so, point up the oppositional mentality of the traditionalist *baba* in the country's countless villages.

On the first of these matters, Lenin's Bolsheviks moved soon after seizing power to "replace the worship of God with veneration of the state, to substitute revolutionary icons for religious ones."[122] The Decree on the Separation of Church and State (January 1918) sought to subordinate

Orthodox clergy in the localities to the general population by abrogating clerical ownership of property, denying all charges for religious services, and outlawing religious instruction in schools. The assault on Russian Orthodoxy only intensified with the conclusion of the civil war: provincial Soviets were enjoined to remove from the churches all precious items—icons and crosses, chalices and mitres, and so on—and to continue to vilify the clergy as "fat parasites living off the backs of the peasantry and plotting for the return of the Tsar." Orlando Figes has written that "in many places angry crowds took up arms to defend their local church. In some places they were led by their priests, in others they fought spontaneously." In such impromptu confrontations, "troops with machine-guns fought against old men and women armed with pitch forks and rusty rifles." Numbers of the dead and wounded only multiplied during 1922–3.[123] Characterizing peasant women's reactions to all of this in the villages of central Russia, Beatrice Farnsworth enables us to grasp something of their confusion and apprehension:

> Atheism and the new iconography—Karl Marx flanked by Lenin and Trotsky on the wall of the village Soviet in the place of St. Nicholas— were a graver threat. Women, traditionally close to Christianity, saw their old faith attacked and slipping away, and . . . feared that their husbands who ate meat on fast days and ceased going to church were damned. Icons hanging in the corner of the hut, frequently side by side with lurid atheistic posters, testified to the clash of cultures.[124]

Yet this "clash of cultures" in revolutionary Russia (much as, earlier, in revolutionary France) seems not to have done that much to undermine peasant women's religious convictions. "Octobered babies and Red Weddings," as Orlando Figes has put it, "failed to supplant their religious equivalents." Moreover, mothers and widows in mourning "continued to bury their dead rather than cremate them, despite the shortages of coffins and graves and the free state provision of cremations." State-authorized morgue officials predictably threw up their hands at what they dismissed as "superstitious" attitudes.[125]

If the Russian *baba* in the early 1920s proved stubbornly conservative on religious matters, she manifested a comparable resistance to change when it came to education.[126] *Zhenotdel*, as a cultural mediator on this subject between the new Soviet state and its female citizens, bore the brunt of their hostility. This was true whether it was the peasants' children or the adult peasants themselves whose education was taken in hand by proselytizing urban females in *Zhenotdel*'s ranks. When, for instance, rumors circulated among village women in Penza province (central Russia) that their children were to be instructed in "communism" in a summer nursery, the following resolution was adopted by mothers: "The woman's meeting . . . under the chairmanship of Evgeniia Romanovka, unanimously refuses to open and organize a kindergarten and nursery since, in our community, we don't have mothers who would refuse to bring up their children."[127] Then, again, in Tver province (northwest of Moscow) we know of female villagers reacting against *Zhenotdel* agents by protesting that their teenaged daughters had no legitimate reason to be going to school—which, in any case, their straitened families could ill afford.[128] As for the adult villagers themselves, they were likely to strive to impose their own cultural values upon well-wishing urban educators by (for example) demanding some *tangible* form of compensation for the time they were allegedly losing from their work activities due to their literacy classes.[129] Significantly, too, the village *baba* who, in all these ways, at all levels of education, doggedly resisted state efforts to create a more literate female population could count on the support of her husband and her Orthodox priest, both of whom had fairly obvious ideological reasons to oppose such a state policy.[130]

But it was in the domain of *economic/developmental* affairs that the traditionalist mentality of Russia's female peasantry clashed most resoundingly with the Bolsheviks' modernizing outlook in the early 1920s. True, Lenin before his death cautioned his comrades that the "socialization of agriculture" in rural Russia must be achieved "patiently, as a series of gradual steps, awakening the consciousness of the laboring sections of the peasantry and moving forward only as their consciousness is awakened."[131] Such caution was certainly well advised—all the more in light of what we know today about the village *baba's* attitude toward agricultural property and labor at this time. As Farnsworth has written:

> Women certainly did not live as socialists. They were not members of the . . . village assembly and their earnings were considered private property. . . . A woman's dowry, frequently including some livestock . . . remained under her own control, to be passed on to her daughters. Consequently, a woman's sense of private property was more developed than that of her husband. Unlike men who worked communally, many women lived, at least part of each day, by the capitalist ethic.

Hence, it was hardly surprising that the Bolsheviks found it all but impossible to convince such women to "act collectively for the general good"—let alone begin to comprehend the need for "mutuality between city and village" in a polity on the eve of forced industrialization.[132] Female ire (even in the early 1920s) over being dragooned into communal labor is reflected in this report from Simbirsk (Volga region):

> All the field work, including the ploughing, and all the pastoral duties, fall exclusively upon the women and the youths. The woman in the *kommuny* [i.e. commune] works even harder than she does in the village;

she never has a rest-day; in the autumn she no longer has the time to spin or weave, so that she and her children walk around in rags. The women curse Communism when they see that in all the huts in the village the peasants are scutching their tow (*sic*) and [already] preparing their looms.

Moreover, lacking even a *crèche*, women in the *kommuny* had to carry their infants around with them while laboring in the fields![133] This was likely *not* what "revolution" had meant to such individuals in 1917, and they found myriad ways to signify their disillusionment to the state as the years went by.

In the mid-1920s, female peasants' discontent was reflected as well in the ways they reacted to the 1926 RSFSR "Code on Marriage, Family, and Guardianship."[134] This legislation, following up on the Family Code ratified in 1918 by the Soviet regime's Central Executive Committee (*VTsIK*), recognized de facto marriage as juridically equal to registered marriage, thus extending property and alimony rights to women in non-registered unions; established joint ownership of marriage property and its equal division in the event of divorce; and greatly simplified divorce procedures by (among other things) providing for notification of divorce *via postcard*. It may well be true that, as Lewis H. Siegelbaum has held, the 1926 Family Code was rooted in part in Lenin's sincere "condemnation of household bondage" and Kollontai's similarly well-intended "dissection of the shackles of the marriage tie"; yet Siegelbaum has in the same breath granted that "sexual freedom"—notably in backward 1920s Russia—was an "avant-garde rather than vanguardist ideal."[135] Given what we have already seen about the country's chaotic condition in the wake of over a decade of world war, revolution, and civil war, we can scarcely register surprise that the submission of the drafted Family Code to the *VTsIK* should have occasioned so much acrimonious debate among its 434 assembled delegates. In the event, the government decided to delay any decision about the Code, agreeing that it first be submitted to local soviets and other forums.

Urban female workers freely criticized the proposed Code in meetings called by *Zhenotdel* and on the pages of *Working Woman* (*Rabotnitsa*).[136] But it is peasant women's opinions in the more than 6,000 village meetings called to discuss the new statute that especially engage our interest—and those opinions, represented nationally in the *VTsIK* debates, bristled with suspicion and even, at times, with outright sarcasm regarding the "new sexual freedom" popularly associated with the proposed statute. Gnipova, born into a family of needy peasants in Kursk province, argued angrily: "I can't forgive a man who lives with a woman for 20 years, has five kids, and then he decides his wife no longer pleases him. Why did she please him before, but now she doesn't? Shame on you, comrade men." Pasynkova, a delegate from Viatka province, spoke in similar fashion: "Men always say that women are guilty; they swear they have nothing in common with their wives. This is completely ridiculous: is it really possible to marry so many times and never to have anything in common?"[137] Another villager put it this way: "Yes, it's all very well to talk about divorce, but how could I feed my children? Two is better than one when it comes to that. [Alimony?] Yes, I know about that—but what good would it do to me when I know my husband has nothing in his pocket to pay me? And if my husband goes away, or if I get land somewhere else, how can I work the land alone? Together we can manage somehow."[138] Volkhova, a Communist *baba* from the provinces, summed matters up in a manner reflecting not only suspicions about the prospective Family Code, but also age-old *rural* resentments toward *urban* Russia:

> The majority of our rural population wish to preserve a system described as *domostroy* [that is, patriarchal family relations], according to many of our speakers here. . . . It is true that the villages do not wish to attract to the rural areas the marriage instability that exists in the towns. Who is responsible for the neglected children? The villages? The towns, begging your pardon! What will happen if 85 per cent of the population of our country, formed of the peasantry, did as the towns do? We should all flounder in disintegration.[139]

Whereas the new Code was (in Wendy Goldman's words) "premised on the socialist vision of marriage as a freely chosen, freely dissolved companionate bond between two equal individuals," working-class women in the villages (as well as in urban Russia) knew marriage to be "a working partnership, a joint commitment to the . . . survival of the family." Or, to put it in macro-economic terms: "painful problems ensued from applying a vision of legal freedom to an economic structure ill designed to support it."[140] It is true that the Soviet regime went ahead at this time with the new Code, but, ten years later, it would enact new statutes discouraging divorce, facilitating alimony payments, and outlawing abortion.

That it did so in the 1930s was likely inevitable, due (in part) to the perdurable conservatism of urban and rural women on familial issues, but due even more, perhaps, to the Soviet state's shift—as of the late 1920s— from the NEP toward a more accelerated program of industrialization and agricultural collectivization. Siegelbaum has summed up much in this regard, writing that the Stalin "revolution" of those years stemmed from "the deep-seated mutual suspicion and antipathy between the party and the peasantry, the commitment of the communists to industrialization which derived from both ideological and national security considerations, the growing consumption needs of an expanding urban population, and the social and political tensions arising out of the NEP system itself."[141] Ironically, the mild economic recovery achieved under NEP, altering as it did the balance of power between cities and countryside in favor of the former, made it easier for Communists already weaned on simplistic notions about "kulaks," "middle peasants," and "poor peasants" to continue to think in such primitive sociological terms and to objectify kulaks (much as in civil war days) as "class enemies" of poor rural *muzhiki* as well as of workers in the expanding urban sector. So the potentially perilous gap in Russian life (and cultural perceptions) between citified Communists and ruralized peasantry (of both genders) remained: as Helmut Altrichter has emphasized, "many peasant actions and practices, institutions and customs, had their own internal, compelling logic and functionality . . . with the family as the basic unit of production and consumption, and with the village, the *mir*, as a world in itself."[142] It was probably a foregone conclusion that the intrusive presence of Soviet agents of collectivization in the Russian countryside after 1928 would evoke a strong response in particular from a female peasantry whose social conservatism might have been, but was not adequately, accommodated in advance by harried Soviet economic planners.

Katerina Clark has written of two "utopian" phases in city/countryside relations in early Soviet Russia—the first corresponding roughly "to the years of revolution and War Communism, 1917-21," and the second corresponding "to the years of the First Five-Year Plan, 1928-31."[143] Something of this may be reflected, as she has indicated, in the peasant literature of those years; yet behind such "utopianism" lurked the undeniable and increasingly brutal reality of Communist efforts—first ad hoc, and later more permanent— to collectivize agriculture in rural Russia. Barbara Engel has graphically described female peasants' roles in the resultant rioting that tore across the rural landscape in the latter period:

> Enormous numbers of women engaged in acts of collective resistance, the so-called *bab'i bunty* (that is, rural women's riots). Women would stand at the forefront of hostile crowds resisting collectivization; they would shriek at the top of their voices and block the path of activists who attempted to confiscate livestock. Sometimes, women set fire to collective stables, barns and haystacks; they destroyed tractors and attacked local officials. . . . When the official refused to leave the house in which he had taken refuge, the women threatened to remove him by force, or pour kerosene over the house and set it alight. Women often arrived at protests armed with pitchforks, staves, knives, and other farm implements, which they were . . . prepared to employ.

That such peasants "also demonstrated against the closing of churches and continued to baptize their children despite prohibitions against the practice" must, in addition, remind us of their predecessors in revolutionary France.[144] Lynne Viola, who has sedulously studied the *bab'i bunty*, has granted that "the general scale of peasant resistance to the state during collectivization should not be exaggerated," even while emphasizing that Stalin *himself* acknowledged the need for a "retreat" in 1930 in this unrelenting campaign in the countryside. Still, the thrust toward collectivization of agriculture in Russia continued—as, to some extent, did the assault on religion. As Viola somberly reminds us, "the state always retained the ability to respond to peasant unrest in an organized fashion with a show of force."[145]

As we prepare to take our leave of the female peasants of Russia in the early 1930s, we remain impressed by the ways in which forces of gender, religion, class, and *state initiative* interacted to shape their destinies. On the one hand, we find behind the *bab'i bunty*—as we detected behind genteel ladies' actions during the English Civil War, and behind peasant women's riots during the French Revolution—a *male deference* to the "weaker sex" that (in reality) testified to women's *subordination* in the customary scheme of things. Lynne Viola's commentary on the *bab'i bunty* underscores this reality:

> Women tended to lead the village riots because they were less vulnerable to repression than peasant men. There were even reports of *bab'i bunty* in 1929 when the women brought their children with them into battle or lay down in front of tractors to block collectivization. In the *bab'i bunty*, the men stood to the side. In non-violent protest, the situation was similar . . . the men did not go to the meetings on collectivization but sent the women instead . . . at least some peasant men recognized both their own vulnerability and the far greater leverage that peasant women had in speaking out against state policies.

"It is likely," Viola pointedly adds, "that peasant women who rebelled against . . . collectivization clearly understood *how* they were perceived and appreciated the power of their "irrational behavior."[146] At the same time, we have Barbara Clements's picture of the "new Soviet woman" in early Stalinist Russia—and see in it a portrayal that is all too reconcilable with Viola's gendered commentary:

> The new Soviet woman was always a servant of the regime. A central question for the Bolshevik government . . . was *order*, how to restore order to a ruptured society, and the means chosen in all areas of Soviet life became increasingly authoritarian as the twenties gave way to the thirties. The resurgence within the Party of traditional values regarding woman's responsibilities to the family was part of the growth of this authoritarianism. Seeking to establish control over Russia, the Bolsheviks shored up the two institutions—the state and the family—once condemned by them to extinction.

"This is why," Clements concludes here reluctantly but realistically, "the daughters of October, born in the freedom of the civil war years, did not survive the twenties."[147] In the end, gender, religion, class, and state requirements converged in postrevolutionary Russia—though probably in a more violent way than they had in postrevolutionary England and France.

In attempting now to arrive at general conclusions for Chapter 5, we find ourselves making three essential points. First, we reaffirm our earlier contention that "comparative analysis," if it is to be at all convincing, "must . . . acknowledge significant differences as well as telling similarities." In the case of our three European revolutions, this cautionary note applies especially in the domain of *class analysis*. Most English specialists would agree with Lawrence Stone that one of the English Revolution's "most striking features" was the almost total quiescence of its *rural masses*.[148] This sharply differentiated the English Revolution from the later upheavals in France and Russia, where, as we have seen, peasants, both male *and female*, were profoundly agitated over religious, economic, and other public issues. Thus, we have found it easiest to follow the fortunes of traditionalist (and, ordinarily, genteel) women demonstrating agency in the English Revolution by categorizing and studying them under *religious* headings—that is, as Catholics, Anglicans, Presbyterians, and Puritans—rather than by categorizing and studying them (as we generally have their nearest French and Russian counterparts) under rubrics of *class*.

Second, having just made this reservation regarding *class analysis*, we must still underscore the unifying factor of *gender* in the case of women in all these revolutions. Here, what especially excites our interest is the fact that, whether we are looking at genteel Englishwomen speaking for the Stuart cause, fighting revolutionaries, and striving to save sequestered properties and defeated husbands' lives, or at female peasants in provincial France objecting to economic and religious policies hammered out at Paris, or at the village *baba* in Soviet Russia opposing ever more draconian economic plans handed down from Moscow, we *always* seem to discover a male "deference" reflecting women's ever disadvantaged status in society. This is assuredly one way in which the student of even the most thoroughgoing revolution is forced to acknowledge the *limits* of revolutionary change. It is also one way in which, as we might word it, class was being "gendered" rather than gender being "classed."

Finally, we must deal with the *statist* element in intersectionality as we conclude our review of women who either "fell off the bandwagon" of revolution at some advanced point or fiercely opposed revolutionary policies from early on. It appears safe to conclude that, as we move forward in time, we find such women *increasingly confronting the "statist phenomenon" in revolutionary trappings*. In the case of England, Royalist gentlewomen came up against the unprecedented authoritarianism of Oliver Cromwell even as (at the same time) conservative authors like Mary Pope and Mary Astell idealized the Stuarts' absolutist—if somewhat more *traditionally* authoritarian—monarchy.[149] In the case of France, disillusioned revolutionary *citoyennes* like Olympe de Gouges and Marie-Jeanne Roland were in the end destroyed by centralized proto-bureaucratic Robespierrist Jacobinism, while the female peasantry found its priests and its Catholic rituals hedged in by Jacobin and Directorial politicians alike and its provincial autonomy—although *not*, assuredly, its Catholicism—curbed by Napoleonic and Bourbon governments. Finally, feminists in Russia like Ekaterina Kuskova and Alexandra Kollontai were disillusioned, sooner or later, by the powerful, revitalized autocracy of Lenin's Bolsheviks, while the rural *baba*, if sharing some common ground with the country's new "tsars" in marital and other familial matters, forfeited most of her economic and religious autonomy under Lenin's and, even more, Stalin's auspices. Indeed, from the perspective of the peasant *baba* in particular, Orlando Figes has not altogether wrongly concluded, the tumultuous events of 1917 and thereafter "were in many ways a revolution lost."[150] Perhaps, then, the ultimate irony for *all* of the disillusioned and traditionalist women of revolutionary times studied in this chapter, just as for their more radical, more "emancipated" sisters studied earlier, was that the advent of fundamental sociopolitical change portended, to one extent or another, the triumph of the modern administrative state.

Conclusion

Race/Ethnicity and Statism as Women's Revolutionary Problematics

In *Women in the Great European Revolutions,* I have tried to provide a sympathetic yet balanced reappraisal of the *mentalités* and roles of women, both ordinary and not-so-ordinary, in the three major sociopolitical cataclysms of early modern/modern Europe—that is, in mid-seventeenth-century England, late eighteenth-century France, and early twentieth-century Russia. As I freely confessed at the start of this study, I wanted thereby to make up for the most significant deficiency left over from my 2014 book *The Anatomy of Revolution Revisited*—that is to say, the failure to concentrate adequately upon *women* in the "legions of disillusioned citizens" who acted so dauntlessly "on both the left *and* right sides of the political spectrum" through the storms of the English, French, and Russian upheavals. In Chapters 1 and 2, I set out to furnish for the reader a framework for the in-depth discussion to follow—first, by showing how feminist historians and other social scientists over the years have theorized the concepts of gender, sexuality, and patriarchy against the backdrop of European as well as "extra-European" revolutions, and second, by sketching out the successive phases of revolutionary developments in (specifically) England, France, and Russia. In Chapter 3, I reevaluated the relative significance ascribable to *gendered/cultural* and to *geostrategic/statist* factors in the disastrous revolutionary careers of Henrietta Maria of England, Marie-Antoinette of France, and Alexandra Feodorovna of Russia, and did this especially by contrasting their political ineptitude with the astute leadership displayed earlier in those countries by, respectively, Elizabeth I, Cathérine de Médicis, and Catherine II. Finally, in Chapters 4 and 5, I reinvestigated the two sides of the historically postulated "woman question" in these three upheavals. Chapter 4 detailed the ways in which some women, no longer willing to accept their traditional relegation to powerless roles in society, took advantage of unprecedentedly dynamic circumstance to voice grievances and to articulate novel aspirations in public venues. Chapter 5, on the other hand, recounted some of the equally stirring histories of women who, in these same dynamic situations, either modified their initial hopes for radical sociopolitical change or—*almost from the very start*—defended *on principle* their deeply felt allegiances to religious faith and social tradition.

Meanwhile, running like Wagnerian *leitmotifs* throughout these pages have been the tensions between postmodernism and structuralism and the concept, robustly debated by feminists and others ever since its formulation, of intersectionality. Partly in response to the challenges posed by this latter controversy, our inquiry has gone out of its way to underscore the multiple ways in which *gender/sex* interacted dynamically with other "analytical factors" or "systems of discrimination" such as religion, class, national identity, and statism during the turmoil of the English, French, and Russian revolutions. At the same time, the factor of *race/ethnicity*, so obviously uppermost in mind for Kimberlé Crenshaw when she introduced the notion of intersectionality into legal and civil rights discourse more than four decades ago, has since then played less of a role in *European* revolutionary scholarship than have the other analytical factors mentioned above. In the remaining pages of this Conclusion, we need, first, to expand somewhat our discussion of racial/ethnic matters in connection with Europe's revolutions, and then, to return to the ever-contentious question of "the postrevolutionary state as historical problem."[1]

Regarding the former question, we will need to insist on something of a separation between the English and French Revolutions, on the one hand, and the subsequent Russian Revolution, on the other. There is no question that, in the case of the two earlier upheavals, some recent scholarship, adhering to the postmodernist tendency to "decenter" traditional fields of historical inquiry, has played up themes of "colonialism/postcolonialism." Thus, for example, Carla Pestana and John Donoghue have held that a transatlantic "English world" arose in the revolutionary 1640s; as a result, they would argue, events of that period on both sides of the Atlantic became caught up in a grand dialectic affecting not only those Englishmen (and Englishwomen?) remaining "behind" in England but also male (and female?) colonists (and, palpably, indigenous men *and women*) in the New World.[2] Yet, however stimulating we may find this "Atlanticist" scholarship to be, enriching as it does our knowledge about interactions between the English and Atlantic colonial worlds in Stuart and revolutionary times, it does *not* conceptually displace what we still refer to as the "English Revolution" beyond English (or, at most, British) shores.[3] Hence, we feel fairly secure in preserving, in this study, our analytical focus upon *Englishwomen* in revolutionary England itself. By the same token, we acknowledge analogous colonialist/post-colonialist tendencies in recent decentering accounts of the French revolutionary era by historians such as David Armitage, Wim Klooster, Laurent Dubois, Paul Cheney, and Pierre Serna.[4] Dubois, notably, has reconceived the French and Haitian Revolutions as basically two localized episodes in a much larger and fully integrated process of "macro-historical transformation" agitating the wider Atlantic world of the times.[5] Yet Jeremy Popkin, like many another specialist on Haitian revolutionary affairs, has felt it best to pursue as *separate* (if, at times, as *interacting*) the trajectories of French and Haitian history.[6] We therefore conclude from such judgments that here, as in the case of revolutionary England, Atlanticist emphases in history, however provocative and enlightening, do *not* conceptually displace what was an essentially *European* revolution beyond European shores. We consequently feel justified in retaining, in this study, our analytical focus upon *Frenchwomen* in revolutionary France, much as we feel entitled to preserve a primary focus upon the élitist and (at times) not-so-élitist women of revolutionary England.

But if the issue of race/ethnicity is not likely to loom that large in the case of women involved in revolution in England and France (with all due respect to the slaves of color occasionally encountered in both of those colonizing countries), this question may be somewhat more complicated where Russia is concerned. We recall Melissa Stockdale's distinction between *rossiiskie zhenshchiny* (that is, *all* women in *ancien régime* Russia) and *russkie zhenshchiny* (ethnic Russian women) and the fact that non-Russians constituted nearly 50 percent of the Empire's population.[7] We note as well that the new Constitution of 1924 established the Union of Soviet Socialist Republics (USSR) as "a pseudofederal state that both eliminated political sovereignty for . . . nationalities and guaranteed them territorial identity, educational and cultural institutions in their own language, and the promotion of native cadres into positions of power."[8] As Gregory J. Massell has amply documented in his fascinating study *The Surrogate Proletariat*, patriarchal arrangements moderated in the RSFSR under the auspices of the 1926 "Code on Marriage, Family, and Guardianship"—resulting, for instance, in *Russian* equality between de facto and registered marriages— were less drastically affected in the peasant-dominated, more conservative Muslim/Turkic republics that extended from Azerbaijan, in the Caucasus, eastward to Soviet Central Asia.[9] Significantly, however, we note that Russia's new Communist rulers on at least one occasion in the 1920s *did* attempt to "intervene directly in the family to weaken the power of traditional elites" in the largely Muslim Turkic republics.[10]

Specifically, the Soviet regime during 1926–9 aggressively promoted, in that region, a militant campaign (*khudzhum*, in Turkic) against all forms of female seclusion and oppression. Logically enough, it was the Central Asian *Zhenotdel*, the Bolshevik "Women's Bureau" with which we are already familiar, that took the lead in this movement. The issue which became the symbolic rallying point for *khudzhum* (most notably, if not exclusively, in Uzbekistan and Tajikistan) was the *Zhenotdel-sponsored* unveiling of traditionally veiled Muslim women. Gregory Massell has enlarged upon the nature—and the potentially explosive ramifications—of such a campaign in one of Soviet Russia's most custom-bound regions:

> The veil could be seen not only as the most tangible, publicly perceived embodiment of physical and symbolic apartheid, but as the very linchpin of seclusion itself. If women could be moved to unveil massively and in public, their act would, in and of itself, constitute a challenge to all other manifestations of seclusion. If the former [action] would succeed, the latter could not possibly endure for long. The black veil was clearly the most dramatic public indication of female status; conversely, unveiling could be expected to be the most dramatic . . . act in violation of traditional taboos and of the entire primordial status-structure.

Such a publicly symbolic act, in Massell's interpretation of this matter, "would revolutionize women's imagination as well as the attitudes of the world around them, would open up for women an entirely new world of social contacts, roles, and functions, and would . . . directly undermine the entire traditional pattern of human relationships and ties."[11]

Yet how likely was it that this issue, combining as it did questions of gender, religion, ethnicity, custom, and (ultimately) statism, would permanently revolutionize the status of women in the severely traditionalist world of the Soviet Turkic republics? Although, to be sure, Gregory Massell's research has uncovered numerous striking examples of Muslim/Turkic women—in "especially engineered emotional situations," in urbanized locales, and under *Zhenotdel* leadership—who were willing and, indeed, eager to "exercise their rights and challenge the traditional *status quo* through massive, public, and dramatic violation of traditional taboos," his archival labors also reveal a campaign of women's liberation that by the spring of 1929 had largely, if not entirely, run its course.

For this setback there seem to have been three main reasons. First—and this was entirely to be expected—the unveiling mobilization and associated activities evoked an increasingly virulent male and traditionalist tribal backlash in many towns of Uzbekistan and neighboring republics.[12] Second— and this fact will inevitably recall for us similar realities in rural Russia— many Muslim/Turkic women themselves betrayed a growing uneasiness about reforms that appeared suddenly to be wresting them violently out of their traditional cultural/religious milieux and ways of living. Even some of the local indigenous Party (and female) operatives expressed increasing qualms about all of this. As one Tajik Bolshevik organizer, a woman named Khoziat Markulanova, put the matter:

> It is generally the adventurous, daring, and, naturally enough, rather good-looking woman who flings aside her *parandzha* [veil]. . . . As a reaction to her previously enforced meekness, she now tends to become more self-assertive and unrestrained than is good for her . . . [for] in her relations with the opposite sex she is helpless. Not having been trained since childhood to meet men, she has not built up the particular defenses which a woman needs if she is to meet men freely, on an equal basis. . . . The woman here needs a good deal of discipline and balance. . . . A compliment or an embrace was [i.e. for this specific individual] a grand experience. I lost my head.[13]

If these were indeed the words of a typical female Party stalwart, we can well imagine the hesitation of non-Party women before such an unprecedented militant campaign in Turkic Central Asia. Finally, there was, likely, the ultimate—and unconquerable—obstacle to the success of *khudzhum*: i.e., the ever more imperative demands of Stalin's *statist* campaign of industrialization (and of rural collectivization) in 1929 and beyond. As Lewis Siegelbaum has duly reminded us, the curtailment of *khudzhum* in Turkic regions of the USSR mirrored "the uneasiness within the upper echelons of the party about female mobilization in particular and, more generally, any social activism that could not be controlled; and the subordination of sexual emancipation to the imperatives of the Stalin revolution."[14]

But any consideration of the *racial/ethnic* component of intersectionality (at least in connection with revolutionary Russia) would appear to bring us naturally back to the factor of *gosudarstvennost'*, or what we earlier referred to as statism prioritized over individual liberty. Here, we have recourse, as we did in Chapter 1, to Max Weber, who in his seminal writings defined the *state* as "a compulsory political organization with continuous operations" that would qualify as a state "insofar as it successfully upholds the claim to the *monopoly* of the *legitimate* use of physical force in the enforcement of its order."[15] Our final thoughts upon this element of intersectionality, in the context of our present inquiry, should briefly address *three* issues: (1) the finest "informed wisdom" on the *nature* of the state; (2) the implications of revitalized state power for women, whether of radical or traditionalist inclination, in the English, French, and Russian Revolutions; and (3) the *globalist* implications of ongoing statist developments for women's status in the present and in the foreseeable future.

On the first of these matters, scholars of the great European revolutions have inevitably had to reckon with Theda Skocpol's endeavor, from the late 1970s on, to restate Weberian conceptions of the state. For Skocpol, the "state properly conceived" is "no mere arena in which socioeconomic struggles are fought out," but is, rather, "a set of administrative, policing, and military organizations headed, and more or less well coordinated by, an executive authority."[16] But specialists on the English, French, and

Russian upheavals have frequently come to qualify such unabashedly structuralist language. In the case of England, for instance, Jack Goldstone has cautiously held that late Tudor and early Stuart states may have boasted modern attributes of "centralized national rule making and rule-enforcing authority," but, he has insisted, they also shared "political space with other actors and authorities."[17] Likewise, Michael J. Braddick has conceded that there *was* a state in the seventeenth century characterized by "a network of offices wielding political power derived from a coordinating center by formal means"; yet at the very same time, he has also argued, this "early modern state" was only "a partially differentiated and weakly coordinated state."[18] In the domain of French revolutionary studies, however, such judgments have at times given way to even more explicitly deconstructionist objections to reifying the state as an historical "actor" that is able, somehow, to impose its will on society. Feminist historian Suzanne Desan, regarding the state as—arguably—"both a discursive and institutional entity," has exemplified this tendency:

> Scholars across a range of disciplines have theorized the state … flexibly, as a site of structured negotiations over power, resources, and relationships, rather than simply as a coercive entity separate from society. Although it is made up of organizations wielding coercive power and of laws meant to structure all power relations and social interactions in a uniform way, the state takes shape only in a set of local practices in which power is repeatedly contested, sometimes reinforced and sometimes redistributed.[19]

Desan's opinions would certainly find favor with Russian revolutionary scholars such as Steve Smith and William Rosenberg. Smith, for instance, has held that historians need to extend their "concept of power beyond that of simple coercion," and should "understand" power "as capacity, as something implicated in all social activity."[20] Rosenberg, for his part, has favored much the same culturally oriented approach to conceptions of the state and to Russian revolutionary politics in general in his writings.[21]

Nonetheless, we may suspect that even "culturally oriented" specialists, as inclined as they may be to deconstruct the state as an analytical category in their research on England, France, or Russia, will in the end find it difficult to get away altogether from Weberian/Skocpolian notions on the subject. It is, perhaps, telling in this connection that Suzanne Desan's assurance to her readers (in the pages of *French Historical Studies*) that she "is not calling here for 'bringing the state back in' as a policy-making entity independent from society" refers (manifestly) to one of Theda Skocpol's coedited anthologies on statist and revolutionary issues.[22] Such an allusion suggests to us that the shadow of Skocpolian structuralism—whatever its palpable shortcomings— continues to fall across even the fashionably sculpted landscape of French cultural studies. Nor is that shadow very likely to be entirely dissipated by Keith Baker's more recent insistence that, especially when it comes to revolutionary politics, "scripts [rather than, possibly, statist initiatives?] generate events."[23] It is also worth citing, in this connection, political scientist Noel S. Parker's dampening reaction against all theories that claim to consign the bureaucratic state to what we might regard as postmodernist oblivion:

> We should hesitate . . . before jumping to conclusions about the priority of a new "post-national" and discursive arena in place of the collective agent [i.e. the state] embodied in the European revolutionary narrative over more than two centuries. . . . Even a thinker acutely aware of how vulnerable are the nation-state's claims to spatio-temporal identity acknowledges that states are "exceptionally dense political practices" which have not . . . disappeared.[24]

For Noel Parker, resultantly, and for many of us as well, his theoretically defined "nation-state as a place of collective autonomy" is likely to remain, in the final analysis, the durable and even formidable entity it has *especially* become in more recent times.

This insight in turn leads us to reconsider briefly the implications of *revitalized statist power* for women in the English, French, and Russian Revolutions. After all, as Max Weber has been freely taken as warning in 1918, "revolutionary change always results in the development of larger, more pervasive . . . institutions to replace the ones the revolutionaries have toppled."[25] What we discover in applying this maxim to the women we have studied in this book is that (1) *they found themselves ever more affected by, and—consequently—vulnerable to, reconsolidated statism in all three of these European upheavals;* and (2) *this was the case regardless of whether they were playing "emancipatory" or traditionalist roles in these situations.* Thus, in revolutionary England, aristocratic women had to deal with a Cromwellian dictatorship that Mary Pope and (in time) Mary Astell rejected in favor of a restored Stuart absolutism, even as the Levellers' female followers, aspiring women publicists, women preachers, and prophetesses found progressively less support from that same Cromwellian dictatorship to which they had pledged a millenarian allegiance. In revolutionary France, disillusioned liberal bourgeois publicists and *salonnières* like Olympe de Gouges and Marie-Jeanne Roland and radical Jacobin and clubbist *citoyennes* alike were crushed by the same proto-bureaucratic Robespierrist regime whose anticlerical and economic policies, imposed with increasing ruthlessness on towns and lesser rural communities, antagonized traditionalist peasant women. Finally, in revolutionary Russia, disheartened feminists and socialists such as Ekaterina Kuskova and Alexandra Kollontai sooner or later fell out with the revitalized autocracy (under Bolshevik auspices) that, in the country's vast rural spaces, temporized with the peasant *baba* on *family* questions even while increasingly alienating her on *religious* and *economic* issues. In sum, to follow the destinies of women in these revolutionary situations is both to marvel at the diversity of their concerns and roles *and*, at the same time, to acknowledge the durability of revolutionary/postrevolutionary statism.

What is still left for us to do, at this juncture, is to ponder the implications of continuing statist developments *in general* (and *not* solely in postrevolutionary situations) for women in the world of the present and future. It is clear, to begin with, that the nation-state, however challenged at times *locally*, has no more been "deconstructed away" by discursive analysis than rationalized by Marxian dialectics. When we look back (for a wider context) at political events in Europe of the 1920s and 1930s, and then compare them to developments in the early years of the twenty-first century, we are instantly struck by their common *authoritarian* and *populist* characteristics. In the earlier situation, the European state was often seized by unscrupulous politicians, usually (if not invariably) for warlike purposes. Such individuals could then continue to channel into their causes popular resentments and fears generated by economic depression, by irredentist nationalism, and by a presumed Bolshevik threat emanating from the (Soviet) East. In the Europe (and, increasingly, the extra-European world) of today, demagogic individuals have once again been able, frequently, to seize state power, tailoring to their purposes popular resentments and anxieties. This time, the *popular* element in such authoritarianism has involved insecurities bred by globalization and by pandemic-related problems and campaigns against racial and gendered "others" as well as against migrants from outside Europe, North America, and Australia/New Zealand. If statist and cultural tendencies merged a century ago in much of Europe to create totalitarian states that menaced the world's democracies, something uncomfortably like this appears once again to be happening today—but now, seemingly, on an ever more globalized scale. The "state as postrevolutionary problem" has, in other words, morphed into what we might call the "state as generic international problem." Whether or not this latter formulation leaves theoretical space for what some specialists have called the "color" or "people power" revolutions of the past three or four decades—and hence, it must follow, for *women* involved in these upheavals—is something that only the future will fully resolve.[26]

What, then, does all of this portend for women? We can only hope that when Shamiran Mako and Valentine Moghadam, in a volume on recent events in the Middle East and North Africa referenced earlier, speculated that democracy in today's world is "unlikely to arise without women's rights being part of its foundation," they were foretelling something of a progressive future involving women as well as men. Clearly, at the very least, continuing statist developments will present perils *and* opportunities for women of whatever countries, conditions, and perspectives.[27]

NOTES

Introduction

1 Bailey Stone, *The Anatomy of Revolution Revisited: A Comparative Analysis of England, France, and Russia* (New York: Cambridge University Press, 2014). As its title suggests, the principal inspiration for this study was Crane Brinton's very durable classic *The Anatomy of Revolution*, rev. ed. (New York: Vintage Books, 1965).

2 Stone, *The Anatomy of Revolution Revisited*, 319.

3 Patricia Higgins, "The Reactions of Women, with Special Reference to Women Petitioners," in *Politics, Religion, and the English Civil War*, ed. Brian Manning (London: E. J. Arnold, 1973), 222.

4 Ann Hughes, "Gender and Politics in Leveller Literature," in *Political Culture and Cultural Politics in Early Modern Europe*, ed. Susan D. Amussen and Mark A. Kishlansky (Manchester: University of Manchester Press, 1995). Citation here is from 181–2.

5 Olwen Hufton, *Women and the Limits of Citizenship in the French Revolution* (Toronto: University of Toronto Press, 1992), esp. 94–7.

6 Refer, in this connection, to the following studies: Anne Borbroff, "The Bolsheviks and Working Women, 1905-1920," *Soviet Studies* 26 (1974): 540–67; Barbara E. Clements, *Bolshevik Women* (Cambridge: Cambridge University Press, 1997); and Elizabeth Wood, *The Baba and the Comrade: Gender and Politics in Revolutionary Russia* (Bloomington, IN: Indiana University Press, 1997).

7 A somewhat dated, but still very useful, anthology of leading sociologists' contributions to this realm of studies is that of John Foran, ed., *Theorizing Revolutions* (London: Routledge, 1997). Most recently, we can benefit from a valuable review essay by Jack A. Goldstone, "The Generations of Revolutionary Theory Revisited: New Works and the Evolution of Theory," *Critical Sociology* 50 (2024): 1–17. Profound thanks go (as always) to Professor Goldstone for apprising me of some of the latest developments in this always fascinating field of research.

8 Refer, in this connection, to: Stone, *Rethinking Revolutionary Change in Europe: A Neostructuralist Approach* (Lanham, MD and London: Rowman & Littlefield, 2020), esp. the Introduction.

9   See Valentine Moghadam, "Gender and Revolutions," in Foran, ed., *Theorizing Revolutions*, 161–2.

10   Shamiran Mako and Valentine M. Moghadam, *After the Arab Uprisings: Progress and Stagnation in the Middle East and North Africa* (Cambridge: Cambridge University Press, 2021).

11   Beverley Southgate, *Postmodernism in History: Fear or Freedom?* (London, Routledge, 2003), 48–9. He elaborated upon this postmodernist rendering of history in a subsequent book: *What Is History For?* (London: Routledge, 2005).

12   The definition of intersectionality offered here comes from: https://en .wikipedia.org/wiki/Intersectionality. The reader may wish to review Kimberlé Crenshaw's writings, which include: "Demarginalizing the Intersection of Race and Sex: A Black Feminist Critique of Antidiscrimination Doctrine, Feminist Theory, and Antiracist Politics," archived at the *Wayback Machine* (1989); and, also, "Mapping the Margins: Intersectionality, Identity Politics, and Violence Against Women of Color," *Stanford Law Review* 43 (1991): 1241–99.

13   See, for instance, Lisa Downing, "The Body Politic: Gender, the Right Wing, and Identity Category Violations," *French Cultural Studies* 29 (2018): 367–77; and Barbara Tomlinson, "To Tell the Truth and Not Get Trapped: Desire, Distance, and Intersectionality at the Scene of Argument," *Signs: Journal of Women in Culture and Society* 38 (2013): 993–1017.

14   Moghadam, "Gender and Revolutions," 161–2.

Chapter 1

1   Quoted from Karen Offen, *The Woman Question in France, 1400-1870* (Cambridge: Cambridge University Press, 2017), 14.

2   Valentine Moghadam, "Gender and Revolutions," in *Theorizing Revolutions*, ed. John Foran (London: Routledge, 1997), 161–2. Moghadam had already had ample opportunities to articulate this viewpoint, as in: Moghadam, *Modernizing Women: Gender and Social Change in the Middle East* (Boulder, CO: Lynne Rienner, 1993); and the essays anthologized in Moghadam, ed., *Identity Politics and Women: Cultural Reassertions and Feminisms in International Perspective* (Boulder, CO: Westview Press, 1994).

3   The reader might want to approach this question first of all by consulting the following anthology: *The Woman Question: Selections from the Writings of Karl Marx, Frederick Engels, V. I. Lenin, Clara Zetkin, Joseph Stalin* (New York: International Publishers, 1977).

4   For examples of men's history and masculinity studied in revolutionary contexts, see: Michael Roper and John Tosh, *Manful Assertions: Masculinities in Britain since 1800* (London: Routledge, 1991); Jeffrey Merrick and Bryant Ragan, *Homosexuality in Modern France* (New York: Oxford University

Press, 1996); Anne Verjus, *Le Bon mari: Une histoire politique des hommes et des femmes à l'époque révolutionnaire* (Paris: Fayard, 2010); and Jeffrey Merrick, "Gender in Pre-Revolutionary Political Culture," Ch. 6 in *From Deficit to Deluge: The Origins of the French Revolution*, ed. Thomas E. Kaiser and Dale K. Van Kley (Stanford, CA: Stanford University Press, 2011), 198–219. The growing literature on LGBT/queer issues has been fairly recently surveyed in: Regina Kunzel, "The Power of Queer History," *American Historical Review* 123 (2018): 1560–82.This latter issue (i.e. LGBT/queer studies) is addressed in detail below.

5   These comments are from Joan Acker, *Class Questions: Feminist Answers* (Lanham, MD: Rowman and Littlefield, 2006), ix–x; they are provided by the editors for Joan Acker's book, Judith A. Howard, Barbara Risman, and Joey Sprague.For the earlier work from which they cited, see: Beth Hess and Myra M. Ferree, eds., *Analyzing Gender: A Handbook of Social Science Research* (Newbury Park, CA: Sage Publications, 1987).

6   See Joan Wallach Scott, *Gender and the Politics of History*, rev. ed. (New York: Columbia University Press, 1999).Cited from the Preface to the Revised Edition.Scott—and a number of her like-minded colleagues in the field—have had further observations to make on this issue in: Scott, ed., *Feminism and History* (Oxford: Oxford University Press, 1997); Scott, ed., *Women's Studies on the Edge* (Durham, NC: Duke University Press, 2008); and Judith Butler and Elizabeth Weed, eds., *The Question of Gender: Joan W. Scott's Critical Feminism* (Bloomington, IN: Indiana University Press, 2011).

7   Citations here are from Merry Wiesner-Hanks, *Gender in History* (Oxford: Blackwell, 2001), 1–5.

8   For this interesting discussion of the factors making for "analytical ambiguity" in recent scholarly treatments of long-posited distinctions between sexuality and gender, refer to ibid., 1–5 and 208–11.

9   The term is quoted by Agarwal from trans scholar Susan Stryker.See Kritika Agarwal, "What Is Trans History? From Activist and Academic Roots, a Field Takes Shape," *Perspectives on History* 56 (May 2018): 17–20. The many foundational works in this genre include: Joanne Meyerowitz, *How Sex Changed: A History of Transsexuality in the United States* (Cambridge, MA: Harvard University Press, 2002); Elizabeth Reis, *Bodies in Doubt: An American History of Intersex* (Baltimore, MD: Johns Hopkins University Press, 2009); Emily Skidmore, *True Sex: The Lives of Trans Men at the Turn of the Twentieth Century* (New York: New York University Press, 2017); and Susan Stryker's general survey on the subject, *Transgender History: The Roots of Today's Revolution*, 2nd ed. (Berkeley, CA: Seal Press, 2017).

10   Cited from Agarwal, "What is Trans History?," esp. 19.

11   See Regina Kunzel, "The Power of Queer History," *American Historical Review* 123 (2018): 1560–82.This citation is from 1565. Some of the foundational work on sexuality in its various historical manifestations was, of course, done by Michel Foucault in earlier decades. Consult, in this connection: Michel Foucault, *The Archaeology of Knowledge*, trans. A. M. Sheridan Smith (New York: Harper & Row, 1972), and *The History of*

Sexuality, trans. Robert Hurley (New York: Vintage Books, 1980). In her review essay in the *AHR*, Kunzel provides numerous examples of more recent articles, books, and anthologies devoted to queer and other subfields of LGBT/queer studies. They are far too numerous to inventory here!

12   Consult, in this connection, Maria Mies, *Patriarchy and Accumulation on a World Scale* (London: Zed Books, 1986), esp. 22–3. Similar Marxian and feminist views would be forcefully articulated several years later by Margaret Randall in *Gathering Rage: The Failure of Twentieth-Century Revolutions to Develop a Feminist Agenda* (New York: Monthly Review Press, 1993).

13   Cited in Mies, *Patriarchy and Accumulation on a World Scale*, 23.

14   See Anne Verjus, "Gender, Sexuality, and Political Culture," in *A Companion to the French Revolution*, ed. Peter McPhee (Oxford: Wiley-Blackwell, 2013), esp. 196–7.

15   Refer again to Offen, *The Woman Question in France*, 15–6.

16   Refer here to Sylvia Walby, *Theorizing Patriarchy* (Oxford: Blackwell, 1990). This work followed by just four years the equally influential monograph by Gerda Lerna, *The Creation of Patriarchy* (New York: Oxford University Press, 1986). Lerna had also accommodated in her arguments the connections between patriarchy and gender.

17   Walby enlarged upon this, not in her 1990 book, but rather in a subsequent article: "The 'Declining Significance' or the 'Changing Forms' of Patriarchy?" found in Valentine Moghadam, ed., *Patriarchy and Development: Women's Positions at the End of the Twentieth Century* (Oxford: Clarendon, 1996), 19–33.

18   Refer again to Wiesner-Hanks, *Gender in History*, 12–13. For a stimulating sampling of feminist sociological inquiries into the subject, inquiries focusing on countries all over the modern world, consult the many articles in Moghadam, ed., *Patriarchy and Development: Women's Positions at the End of the Twentieth Century*.

19   See again Scott, *Gender and the Politics of History*, 2nd ed., 33–4. Sheila Rowbotham, Sally Alexander, and Barbara Taylor had earlier debated the meanings to be assigned to the term "patriarchy." See Raphael Samuel, ed., *People's History and Socialist Theory* (London: Routledge and Kegan Paul, 1981), 363–73. So had many another feminist scholar, especially since the late 1960s. Refer to Carole Pateman, *The Sexual Contract* (Stanford, CA: Stanford University Press, 1988), 19–38. Pateman, on the other hand, deemphasized (p. 225) *gender* in feminist analysis.

20   See, in this connection: Tristan Bridges and James W. Messerschmidt, "Joan Acker and the Shift from Patriarchy to Gender," in *Feminist Reflections*. (See https://thesocietypages.org/feminist/2016/07/06.)Online article of July 6, 2016.

21   This, from Joan Acker, in "The Problem with Patriarchy," *Sociology* 23 (1989): 239–40. See also, by Acker, the following: "Hierarchies, Jobs, Bodies: A Theory of Gendered Organizations," *Gender and Society* 4 (1990): 139–58; and *Class Questions: Feminist Answers*, passim. Yet Acker also came in

for some pointed criticism regarding her post-modernist (more, perhaps, than her Marxian) leanings from her fellow-sociologist Charles Tilly. See, by Tilly, *Roads From Past to Future* (Lanham, MD: Rowman and Littlefield, 1997), esp. 27–8.

22 Cited in Moghadam, ed., *Patriarchy and Development*, 4.

23 The classic work to consult in this connection is: Friedrich Engels, *The Origin of the Family, Private Property, and the State* (London: Penguin Classics, 2010). But follow up his thoughts, accessible also in *The Woman Question: Selections from the Writings of Karl Marx, Frederick Engels, V. I. Lenin, Clara Zetkin, Joseph Stalin*, passim.

24 Once again, consult Lerner's standard monograph: *The Creation of Patriarchy* (New York: Oxford University Press, 1986).

25 Wiesner-Hanks, *Gender in History*, 12–13.

26 As cited in Mies, *Patriarchy and Accumulation on a World Scale*, esp. 175–204.

27 Consult again Walby, "The 'Declining Significance' or the 'Changing Forms' of Patriarchy," in Moghadam, ed., *Patriarchy and Development*, esp. 22–3. Walby also faults Mies for *not* regarding the "nuclear family" (and other social institutions) as predating, in ancient times, the "rise of capitalism."

28 Ibid., esp. 23–5, for a full exposition of her ideas on this subject.

29 See, on this issue, Beverly Guy-Sheftall and Evelyn M. Hammonds, "Whither Black Women's Studies: Interview," in *Women's Studies on the Edge*, ed. Joan Wallach Scott (Durham, NC: Duke University Press, 2008), 155–67.

30 See, for examples of their work: Beverly Guy-Sheftall, *Words of Fire: An Anthology of African American Feminist Thought* (New York: New Press, 1995); bell hooks, *Feminist Theory: From Margin to the Center*, 3rd ed. (New York: Routledge, 1984); and Leslie McCall, "The Complexity of Intersectionality," *Signs: Journal of Women in Culture and Society* 30 (2005): 1771–800. For a much more detailed discussion of both patriarchy *and* intersectionality, refer again to the online article on intersectionality cited earlier, in the Introduction to this book.

31 Refer again to Acker, *Class Questions: Feminist Answers*, esp. 21–3, 35–7, and 39–40. For similar thoughts on white and middle-class biases on these issues, see: Catherine Hall, *White, Male, and Middle-Class: Explorations in Feminism and History* (New York: Routledge, 1992).

32 Laura Lee Downs, *Writing Gender History*, 2nd ed. (London: Bloomsbury Academic, 2010), 110–1 and 137.

As we will see subsequently, Downs has been one of those feminists who has most sharply challenged the kind of "cultural" postmodernism (or "post-structuralism") associated with (for instance) Joan Wallach Scott.

33 See Mihály Simai's "Preface" to Moghadam, ed., *Patriarchy and Development: Women's Positions at the End of the Twentieth Century*.

34 Refer again to Walby, "The 'Declining Significance' or the 'Changing Forms' of Patriarchy?" in ibid., 29–31. Also, see again Walby's 1990 monograph cited earlier: *Theorizing Patriarchy*, passim.

35 Moghadam, in the "Introduction" to *Patriarchy and Development*, 4.

36 For this analysis, see, in ibid., Moghadam, "Patriarchy and Post-communism: Eastern Europe and the Former Soviet Union," 349–50.

37 See (in the same anthology) Tuovi Allén, "The Nordic Model of Gender Equality: The Welfare State, Patriarchy, and Unfinished Emancipation," 303–26. In these countries, Allén found, "private patriarchy" was constantly undermined by "modernization" while—paradoxically—"public patriarchy" was actually *reinforced* by the same phenomenon.

38 Refer, here, in ibid., to John Lie, "From Agrarian Patriarchy to Patriarchal Capitalism: Gendered Capitalist Industrialization in Korea," 34–55. For radically differing appraisals of the "female marginalization thesis," see once again Scott, *Gender and the Politics of History*, 33–4; and Randall, *Gathering Rage*, passim.

39 Cited from the "Preface" of Scott, *Gender and the Politics of History*.

40 Refer to the "Preface" of Moghadam, ed., *Patriarchy and Economic Development*, where Miháli Simai warmly recommends these research articles to "all those who are interested in gender issues embedded in the overall human aspects of the development process."

41 Cited in Downs, *Writing Gender History*, 192.

42 Refer again to the online article authored by Bridges and Messerschmidt in July 6, 2016, in *Feminist Reflections:* referenced in https://thesocietypages.org /feminist/2016/07/06.

43 For these quotations, consult again Moghadam, "Gender and Revolutions," in Foran, ed., *Theorizing Revolutions*, 167n. and 161–2. She, and a number of like-minded colleagues, have elaborated—in postmodernist fashion—on the importance of national identity formation in revolutionary situations. Consult their pertinent articles in Moghadam, ed., *Identity Politics and Women: Cultural Reassertions and Feminisms in International Perspective* (Boulder, CO: Westview Press, 1994).

44 For some provocative reflections on the tensions between structuralist and postmodernist analysis in historical writing in general, see Richard J. Evans, *In Defense of History* (New York: W. W. Norton, 1997). On how these kinds of tensions play out, specifically, in *European revolutionary* analysis, see: Noel S. Parker, *Revolutions and History: An Essay in Interpretation* (Cambridge: Polity Press, 1999); and Bailey Stone, *The Anatomy of Revolution Revisited: A Comparative Analysis of England, France, and Russia* (New York: Cambridge University Press, 2014).

45 The literature on this subject is (of course) vast. For some useful and still current commentary on the causes of the three classic European upheavals, see: Keith Thomas, "When the Lid Came Off England," *The New York Review of Books*, May 27, 2004; John Adamson, "Introduction: High Roads

and Blind Alleys—The English Civil War and Its Historiography," 1–35, in *The English Civil War: Conflict and Contexts, 1640–49* , ed. John Adamson (New York: Palgrave Macmillan, 2009); Stone, *The Anatomy of Revolution Revisited,* esp. the Introduction; and Ronald Grigor Suny, *The Soviet Experiment: Russia, the USSR, and the Successor States,* 2nd ed. (New York: Oxford University Press, 2011), esp. 1–68.

46 Examples of this classic revisionism include Alfred Cobban, *The Social Interpretation of the French Revolution* (Cambridge: Cambridge University Press, 1964); George V. Taylor, "Noncapitalist Wealth and the Origins of the French Revolution," *American Historical Review* 72 (1967): 469–96; and Conrad Russell, *Unrevolutionary England, 1603–1642* (London: The Hambledon Press, 1990).

47 Refer, in this connection, to: Chalmers Johnson, *Revolution and the Social System* (Stanford, CA: Hoover Institution Studies, 1964); *Autopsy on People's War* (Berkeley, CA: University of California Press, 1973); and *Revolutionary Change,* 2nd ed. (Stanford, CA: Stanford University Press, 1982).

48 Works exemplifying this tendency in the social-scientific literature on revolutionary causation include: Ted. R. Gurr, *Why Men Rebel* (Princeton, NJ: Princeton University Press, 1971), and *Rogues, Rebels, and Reformers* (Beverly Hills, CA: SAGE, 1976); and James C. Davies, *When Men Revolt and Why* (New York: Free Press, 1979).See also the commentary in: Michael S. Kimmel, *Revolution: A Sociological Interpretation* (Philadelphia, PA: Temple University Press, 1990), esp. on 47. Kimmel reviews all of these "pre-structural" theories of revolution in ibid., 46–82.

49 Citations taken from ibid., 25, 86–7, and 145–6.

50 Ibid., 151–2.

51 Consult, among his chief works, the following: *The Modern World-System: Capitalist Agriculture and the Origins of the European World-Economy in the Sixteenth Century* (New York: Academic Press, 1974); *The Capitalist World Economy* (New York: Cambridge University Press, 1979); and *The Politics of the World Economy* (New York: Cambridge University Press, 1984).

52 Other studies in "capitalism-centered structuralism" include Karl Polanyi, *The Great Transformation* (Boston, MA: Beacon Press, 1957); and Ellen Kay Trimberger, *Revolution from Above: Military Bureaucrats and Development in Japan, Turkey, Egypt, and Peru* (New Brunswick, NJ: Transaction Books, 1978).

53 See, in this connection, Kimmel, *Revolution: A Sociological Interpretation,* 147. Additionally, for subsequent scholarly comments on state formation as it unfolded specifically in early modern Europe, see: Jack Goldstone, *Revolution and Rebellion in the Early Modern World* (Berkeley, CA: University of California Press, 1991), 5n; and (in much greater detail) Michael J. Braddick, *State Formation in Early Modern England* (Cambridge: Cambridge University Press, 2000), 19–20.

54 As quoted in Kimmel, *Revolution: A Sociological Interpretation,* 147.

55 As cited in ibid., 149.

56 Theda Skocpol, *States and Social Revolutions: A Comparative Analysis of France, Russia, and China* (Cambridge: Cambridge University Press, 1979). Additional structuralist insights on modern revolution from Skocpol (and other theorists) were to come in: Peter B. Evans, Dietrich Rueschemeyer, and Theda Skocpol, eds., *Bringing the State Back In* (New York: Cambridge University Press, 1985); and Skocpol, ed., *Social Revolutions in the Modern World* (Cambridge: Cambridge University Press, 1994).

57 For these (and related) reflections, see Charles Tilly, *From Mobilization to Revolution* (London: Addison-Wesley, 1978), passim.; and "War making and state making as organized crime," in Evans, Rueschemeyer, and Skocpol, eds., *Bringing the State Back In*, passim.

58 Quoted in Tilly, *European Revolutions, 1492–1992* (Oxford: Blackwell, 1993), 10.

59 Consult Eric Selbin, "Revolutions in the Real World: Bringing Agency Back In," in *Theorizing Revolutions*, ed. John Foran (London: Routledge, 1997), esp. 133.

60 Goldstone, *Revolution and Rebellion in the Early Modern World*, 37–8 and 61–2.

61 Refer, in this connection, to Goldstone, "The Social Origins of the French Revolution Revisited," in *From Deficit to Deluge: The Origins of the French Revolution*, ed. Thomas E. Kaiser and Dale K. Van Kley (Stanford, CA: Stanford University Press, 2011), 67–103.

62 For this carefully reasoned critique of statist structuralism, see: Jeff Goodwin, "State-Centered Approaches to Social Revolutions: Strengths and Limitations of a Theoretical Tradition," in Foran, ed., *Theorizing Revolutions*, esp. 24 and 26. Goodwin would subsequently enlarge on this issue in *No Other Way Out: States and Revolutionary Movements, 1945-1991* (Cambridge: Cambridge University Press, 2001)—although he also utilized this forum to criticize in detail the post-structuralist ideas of Foucault, Derrida, and others.

63 See Timothy P. Wickham-Crowley, "Structural Theories of Revolution," in Foran, ed., *Theorizing Revolutions*, esp. 43–4.

64 As cited in Misagh Parsa, *States, Ideologies, and Social Revolutions: A Comparative Analysis of Iran, Nicaragua, and the Philippines* (Cambridge: Cambridge University Press, 2000), esp. 7–9 and 21.

65 Refer to Foran, "Discourses and Social Forces: The Role of Culture and Cultural Studies in Understanding Revolutions," in Foran, *Theorizing Revolutions*, 219. Foran, incidentally, would have more to say on this subject later on in *Taking Power: On the Origins of Third World Revolutions* (Cambridge: Cambridge University Press, 2005).

66 Sarah Hanley, "Engendering the State: Family Formation and State Building in Early Modern France," *French Historical Studies* 16 (1989): 4–27.See esp. 26–7 for these ruminations by Hanley.

67 Julia Adams, *The Familial State: Ruling Families and Merchant Capitalism in Early Modern Europe* (Ithaca, NY: Cornell University Press, 2005), esp. 29–33 and 202.

68 Tilly, *European Revolutions, 1492-1992*, 5–6.

69 See, in this connection: Michael Foucault, *The Archaeology of Knowledge*, trans. A. M. Sheridan Smith (New York: Harper & Row, 1972), and *The History of Sexuality*, trans. Robert Hurley (New York: Vintage Books, 1980). Jacques Derrida's ideas are intelligibly discussed in (among other works): Jonathan Culler, *On Deconstruction: Theory and Criticism after Structuralism* (Ithaca, NY: Cornell University Press, 1982).

70 Evans, "Postmodernism in History," 1–2. A contribution to the "Great Debate on History and Postmodernism" hosted at the University of Sydney, Australia, in July 2002. Evans had already dealt with these issues extensively in a thought-provoking book: *In Defense of History* (New York: W. W. Norton, 1997). For one anthropologist's highly critical reassessment of postmodernism in general, see: Ernest Gellner, *Postmodernism, Reason and Religion* (London: Routledge, 1992).

71 Evans, "Postmodernism in History," 1.

72 Beverley Southgate, *Postmodernism in History: Fear or Freedom?* (London: Routledge, 2003), 51. Southgate here was reacting to Evans's 1997 book *In Defense of History* rather than to his later article; yet his response, we sense, would have been essentially the same in either case.

73 Pauline Marie Rosenau, *Post-Modernism and the Social Sciences: Insights, Inroads, and Intrusions* (Princeton, NJ: Princeton University Press, 1992), 3n. Rosenau even plunges into the debate over whether these terms should be hyphenated or left non-hyphenated in ordinary usage; but we will not go there!

74 Southgate, *Postmodernism in History: Fear or Freedom?*, 58.

75 Ibid., 47.

76 See, for instance, Southgate's subsequent work *What Is History For?* (London: Routledge, 2005).Other efforts in this genre include: Keith Jenkins, *Rethinking History* (London: Routledge, 1991); Alun Munslow, *Deconstructing History* (London: Routledge, 1997); and Frank Ankersmit, *Historical Representation* (Stanford, CA: Stanford University Press, 2001).

77 Refer again, in this connection, to Scott, *Gender and the Politics of History*, 206–7 and 200.

78 As cited in Southgate, *Postmodernism in History*, 48–9.

79 Keith Michael Baker, "A Script for a French Revolution: The Political Consciousness of the Abbé Mably," in his study *Inventing the French Revolution: Essays on French Political Culture in the Eighteenth Century* (Cambridge: Cambridge University Press, 1990).

80 Cited in Keith M. Baker and Dan Edelstein, eds., *Scripting Revolution: A Historical Approach to the Comparative Study of Revolutions* (Stanford, CA: Stanford University Press, 2015), 3.

81 Scott, *Gender and the Politics of History*, cited from the Preface, xiii.

82 Citations here are from Tilly, *Roads From Past to Future*, 25–32. Here, Tilly was specifically responding to (among other post-structuralist polemics) Joan Scott's critique of sociologist Cynthia Fuchs Epstein's, *Deceptive Distinctions: Sex, Gender, and the Social Order* (New Haven, CT: Yale University Press, 1988).

83 On the first of these questions, see, for example, Roger Chartier, *The Cultural Origins of the French Revolution*, trans. Lydia G. Cochrane (Durham, NC: Duke University Press, 1991).

84 Roger Chartier, *On the Edge of the Cliff: History, Language, and Practices* (Baltimore, MD: Johns Hopkins University Press, 1997), 77. In this instance, Chartier was commenting on the radical postmodernist (or post-structuralist) writings of intellectual historian Keith M. Baker.

85 Ibid., 23–5.

86 Refer again, in this connection, to Evans, *In Defense of History*, 185–86. For the quarrel between Scott and Downs, consult: Downs, "If 'Woman' Is Just an Empty Category, Then Why Am I Afraid to Walk Alone at Night? Identity Politics Meets the Postmodern Subject," *Comparative Studies in Society and History* 35 (1993): 414–37; and (in the same issue), Scott, "'The Tip of the Volcano'," 438–43. In this exchange, Scott angrily dismissed the notion that she had moved too far from an "identity-based" analysis of women's affairs to a purely *discursive* analysis.

87 For a good example of such reservations, see the comments of Gary Wilder in "AHR Forum: Historiographic "Turns" in Critical Perspective," *American Historical Review* 117 (2012): 743–4.

88 See, in this connection, Denise Riley, *"Am I That Name?" Feminism and the Category of 'Women' in History* (Basingstoke: Macmillan, 1989), 1–2.

89 Citation from Catherine Hall, *White, Male, and Middle-Class: Explorations in Feminism and History* (New York: Routledge, 1992), 24. It should be added, however, that Hall had also (mildly) criticized some aspects of Scott's post-structuralism. Refer to her article "Politics, Post-Structuralism and Feminist History," *Gender and History* 3 (1991): 204–10.

90 Refer to Parpart's article "Gender, Patriarchy, and Development in Africa: The Zimbabwean Case," esp. 149, in Moghadam, ed., *Patriarchy and Economic Development*. See also, along these lines, the essays in Marianne Marchand and Jane Parpart, eds., *Feminism/Postmodernism/Development* (London: Routledge, 1995), and the germane essays in Michèle Barrett and Anne Phillips, eds., *Destabilizing Theory: Contemporary Feminist Debates* (Cambridge: Polity Press, 1992).

91 Refer again, on this point, to the essays in Judith Butler and Elizabeth Weed, eds., *The Question of Gender: Joan W. Scott's Critical Feminism* (Bloomington, IN: University of Indiana Press, 2011).

92 See, in this connection, Dore, "Patriarchy and Private Property in Nicaragua, 1860-1920," esp. 56–8, in Moghadam, ed., *Patriarchy and Economic Development*.

93 As quoted in Victoria Bonnell and Lynn Hunt, *Beyond the Cultural Turn: New Directions in the Study of Society and Culture* (Berkeley, CA: University of California Press, 1999), 11. Valentine Moghadam had already said much the same thing, denying the exclusive role of "culture" in explaining "both stability and change" in modern societies: see Moghadam, ed., *Identity Politics and Women*, 6.

94 Cited in Wiesner-Hanks, *Gender in History*, 6. See also, here, the thoughts of Michael Roper, "Slipping Out of View: Subjectivity and Emotion in Gender History," *History Workshop Journal* 59 (2005): passim.

95 For this commentary on the literature, consult Robyn Wiegman, "Feminism, Institutionalism, and the Idiom of Failure," in Scott, ed., *Women's Studies on the Edge* (Durham, NC: Duke University Press, 2008), esp. 39–40. An especially polemical critique of post-structuralist feminism's supposed "hip quietism" on all matters political is: Martha Nussbaum, "The Professor of Parody," in *The New Republic* of 22 February 1999, 37–45. In her own reflections on the controversy, Wiegman clearly regarded the charge of "hip quietism" brought against radical feminists like Judith Butler and Joan Scott as being somewhat unfair.

96 Cited in Downs, *Writing Gender History*, 100. As Laura Downs put it elsewhere: "If Scott's discursive notion of gender . . . has anchored gender history solidly within the discipline, this conceptualisation has nonetheless left historians . . . faced with a new challenge: that of finding ways to write about bodily and emotional experiences that do not treat such experiences as wholly composed by and through ideological formations." Ibid., 193–4.

97 Refer to Sheila Rowbotham, *Women, Resistance, and Revolution: A History of Women and Revolution in the Modern World* (New York: Pantheon Books, 1972), 23. Readers may also want to consult, along these lines, the essays in: Siân Reynolds, ed., *Women, State, and Revolution: Essays on Power and Gender in Europe Since 1789* (Amherst, MA: University of Massachusetts Press, 1987); and Guida West and Rhoda Blumberg, eds., *Women and Social Protest* (New York: Oxford University Press, 1990).

98 Rowbotham, *Women, Resistance, and Revolution*, 25–6.

99 Ibid., 37–8 and 45. The literature on Jean-Jacques Rousseau and feminism is, of course, vast, and cannot possibly be dealt with here. Still, the interested reader should consult the essays in: Lynda Lange, ed., *Feminist Interpretations of Jean-Jacques Rousseau* (University Park, PA: Penn State University Press, 2002). Also relevant here would be: Sylvana Tomaselli, "The Enlightenment Debate on Women," *History Workshop Journal* 20 (1985): 101–24; and Dorinda Outram, *The Enlightenment*, 3rd ed. (Cambridge: Cambridge University Press, 2013), esp. Ch. 7, "Enlightenment Thinking About Gender."

100 Rowbotham, *Women, Resistance, and Revolution*, 25–6.

101 Citations here are from ibid., 246.

102 Ibid., 246–7.

103 Refer again, in this connection, to the Introduction and to 22–3 and 37–8 in Maria Mies, *Patriarchy and Accumulation on a World Scale* (London: Zed, 1986).

104 See again Sylvia Walby, "The 'Declining Significance' or the 'Changing Forms' of Patriarchy?," in Moghadam, ed., *Patriarchy and Development*, esp. 22–3, for her critique of Maria Mies and of other "dual systems" feminists.

105 See, in this regard, Margaret Randall, *Gathering Rage: The Failure of Twentieth-Century Revolutions to Develop a Feminist Agenda* (New York: Monthly Review Press, 1993), 159–60.

106 Ibid., 162.

107 Cited in Maxine Molyneux, "Mobilization without Emancipation? Women's Interests, State, and Revolution," in *Transition and Development: Problems of Third World Socialism*, ed. Richard Fagen, Carmen Deere, and José Luis Corragio (New York: Monthly Review Press, 1986), 280–302. Citation here is from p. 281. See also, for related insights, the essays in Carol R. Berkin and Clara M. Lovett, eds., *Women, War, and Revolution* (New York: Holmes and Meier, 1980), and the essays appearing in Sîan Reynolds, ed., *Women, State, and Revolution*, passim.

108 Refer again, for this analysis, to Molyneux, "Mobilization without Emancipation?," esp. 281–3. Some of the studies in which Molyneux was subsequently to pursue this distinction between "women's interests" and "gender interests" are: *Women's Movements in International Perspective* (New York: Palgrave Macmillan, 2002); and *Change and Continuity in Social Protection in Latin America* (New York: UNRISD, 2007).

109 See Molyneux, "Mobilization without Emancipation?," 283–5. Molyneux's arguments here were taken up a decade later in Moghadam, "Gender and Revolutions," in Foran, ed., *Theorizing Revolutions*, 137–67.

110 Molyneux, "Mobilization without Emancipation?," esp. 285–86.

111 Ibid., 286.

112 Cited in Mary Ann Tétrault, ed., *Women and Revolution in Africa, Asia, and the New World* (Columbia, SC: University of South Carolina Press, 1994), 427.

113 Ibid., 434.

114 Ibid., 438–40. Italics here were provided by the author herself.

115 Moghadam offered this very intriguing classification of revolutionary outcomes in her 1997 article "Gender and Revolutions," esp. 142–4 and 152–4, in Foran, ed., *Theorizing Revolutions*. One of her subsequent attempts to reinterpret feminism in *global* terms is: *Globalizing Women: Transnational Feminist Networks* (Baltimore, MD: Johns Hopkins University Press, 2005).

116 Refer again, for all of this, to Moghadam, "Gender and Revolutions," esp. 152.

117 The reader may wish, in this connection, to revisit Molyneux, "Mobilization without Emancipation?"

118 Moghadam, "Gender and Revolutions," 143–4 and 152.

119 Thus Jeffrey Merrick, "Gender in Pre-Revolutionary Political Culture," 198 in Kaiser and Van Kley, eds., *From Deficit to Deluge*. Merrick has maintained that "masculinity . . . has been studied less extensively and creatively than femininity." But for other works in this genre, refer again to n. 4 above. And, once again, for updated and cogent assessments of the growing literature on LGBT/queer issues in general, the reader should be sure again to consult Kritika Agarwal, "What is Trans History? From Activist and Academic Roots, a Field Takes Shape," *Perspectives on History* 56 (2018), esp. 17–20; and Regina Kunzel, "The Power of Queer History," *American Historical Review* 123 (2018): 1560–82.

Chapter 2

1 See my discussion of this issue in *The Anatomy of Revolution Revisited*, esp. 10–11. For Hunt's initial critique of Theda Skocpol in this regard, see: Lynn Hunt, *Politics, Culture and Class in the French Revolution* (Berkeley, CA: University of California Press, 1984), esp. 221–4.

2 See Johnson, *Revolutionary Change*, 174–8.

3 Citation from Kimmel, *Revolution: A Sociological Interpretation*, 185.

4 Consult again Valentine Moghadam, "Gender and Revolutions," in *Theorizing Revolutions*, ed. John Foran (London: Routledge, 1997), 161–62.

5 Kevin Sharpe, *The Personal Rule of Charles I* (New Haven, CT: Yale University Press, 1992), 794.

6 G. E. Aylmer, *The King's Servants: the Civil Service of Charles I, 1625–1642* (New York: Columbia University Press, 1961), 420–1. For corroboration of this bleak assessment, consult: Conrad Russell, *The Causes of the English Civil War* (Oxford: Clarendon, 1990), 163–4.

7 On all of these issues, see the following: Russell, *The Fall of the British Monarchies, 1637–1642* (Oxford: Oxford University Press, 1991), 7; Kenneth R. Andrews, *Ships, Money, and Politics: Seafaring and Naval Enterprise in the Reign of Charles I* (New York: Cambridge University Press, 1991); and Andrew Thrush's article in Mark C. Fissel, ed., *War and Government in Britain, 1598–1650* (New York: Manchester University Press, 1991).

8 Mark C. Fissel, *The Bishops' Wars: Charles I's Campaigns Against Scotland, 1638–1640* (Cambridge: Cambridge University Press, 1994), 292–3.

9 Conrad Russell discusses these radical reform proposals in *The Fall of the British Monarchies*, 121–3.

10 A point made by Valerie L. Pearl, *London and the Outbreak of the Puritan Revolution: City Government and National Politics, 1625–43* (London: Oxford University Press, 1961), 91–105. See also, on this subject, Robert Ashton, *The City and the Court, 1603–43* (Cambridge: Cambridge University Press, 1979), who largely endorses Pearl's analysis.

11 See, for this analysis, Lawrence Stone, *The Causes of the English Revolution 1529–1642* (London: Routledge, 1972), 135–6. A study that places these statistics in a broader context is: Mark Kishlansky, *Parliamentary Selection: Social and Political Choice in Early Modern England* (Cambridge: Cambridge University Press, 1986).

12 Fissel, *The Bishops' Wars*, 287–9.

13 A point also stressed by Peter Donald, *An Uncounselled King: Charles I and the Scottish Troubles, 1637–1641* (Cambridge: Cambridge University Press, 1990), esp. 134–5; and by Allan MacInness, *Charles I and the Making of the Covenanting Movement* (Edinburgh: University of Edinburgh Press, 1991), 191–2.

14 On all of these issues, see: Caroline Hibbard, *Charles I and the Popish Plot* (Chapel Hill, NC: University of North Carolina Press, 1983), 83–9, 147–9, and 150–2; and Jonathan Scott, *England's Troubles: Seventeenth-Century English Instability in European Context* (Cambridge: Cambridge University Press, 2000), 136–42.

15 Hibbard, *Charles I and the Popish Plot*, 94–5.

16 On this crisis, see: George V. Taylor, "The Paris Bourse on the Eve of the Revolution, 1781–1789," *American Historical Review* 67 (1962): 951–77; John F. Bosher, *French Finances, 1770–1795: From Business to Bureaucracy* (Cambridge: Cambridge University Press, 1970); and Robert D. Harris, *Necker and the Revolution of 1789* (Lanham, MD: University Press of America, 1986).

17 The classic source here is: Ernst Labrousse, *La Crise de l'Economie française à la fin de l' Ancien Régime et au début de la Révolution* (Paris: Presses Universitaires de France, 1942). Labrousse's work has, to be sure, been conceptually challenged subsequently by historians such as Rondo Cameron, Charles Freedman, David Weir, Philip T. Hoffman, and Jean-Laurent Rosenthal (among others).

18 See, in this connection: Gail Bossenga, "Financial Origins of the French Revolution," in Kaiser and Van Kley, eds., *From Deficit to Deluge*, Chapter 1. Also very useful here: Eugene N. White, "Was There a Solution to the Ancien Régime's Financial Dilemma?," *Journal of Economic History* 49 (1989): 545–68; and David Weir, "Tontines, Public Finance, and Revolution in France and England, 1688–1789," *Journal of Economic History* 49 (1989): 95–124.

19 The classic source on the French "pre-revolution" of 1787–88 remains: Jean Egret, *The French Prerevolution, 1787–1788*, trans. Wesley D. Camp (Chicago, IL: The University of Chicago Press, 1977). But consult also Vivian Gruder, *The Notables and the Nation: The Political Schooling of the French, 1787–1788* (Cambridge, MA: Harvard University Press, 2007).

20 Egret, *The French Prerevolution*, 103.

21 See ibid., 183–5, for all of this.

22 On these reforms, refer to: Samuel F. Scott, *The Response of the Royal Army to the French Revolution* (Oxford: Oxford University Press, 1978), esp. 27–33; and Egret, *The French Prerevolution*, 47–54.

23 See John Hardman, *Louis XVI* (New Haven, CT: Yale University Press, 1993); Munro Price, *Preserving the Monarchy: The Comte de Vergennes, 1774–1787* (Cambridge: Cambridge University Press, 1995); and Thomas Kaiser, "Who's Afraid of Marie-Antoinette? Diplomacy, Austrophobia, and the Queen," *French History* 14 (2000): 241–71.

24 Citations here drawn from ibid., 263–4, and from Kaiser, "From Fiscal Crisis to Revolution: The Court and French Foreign Policy, 1787–1789," in Kaiser and Van Kley, eds., *From Deficit to Deluge*, 141.

25 Commentary by the duc de Montmorency-Luxembourg, cited in Egret, *The French Prerevolution*, 40–2. On the Dutch uprising in the 1780s, see also: Simon Schama, *Patriots and Liberators: Revolution in the Netherlands, 1780–1813* (New York: Vintage Books, 1992).

26 Norman Stone, *The Eastern Front 1914–1917* (London: Scribner, 1975), 288. See, also, on these issues: Hans Rogger, *Russia in the Age of Modernisation and Revolution 1881–1917* (London: Longman, 1983).

27 W. Bruce Lincoln, *Passage Through Armageddon: The Russians in War and Revolution, 1914–1918* (New York: Simon and Schuster, 1986), esp. 296–7.

28 Orlando Figes, *A People's Tragedy: The Russian Revolution, 1891–1924* (New York: Penguin Books, 1996), 278. On this "ministerial leapfrog," see also the first-hand recollections of British observer Bernard Pares, in *The Fall of the Russian Monarchy* (New York: Vintage Books, 1961).

29 For vivid testimony to this effect, see Lincoln, *Passage Through Armageddon*, 296–7.

30 Ibid., 309–10.

31 See, for instance: Mark D. Steinberg and V. M. Khrustalev, *The Fall of the Romanovs: Political Dreams and Personal Struggles in a Time of Revolution* (New Haven, CT: Yale University Press, 1995), 5.

32 Allan K. Wildman, *The End of the Russian Imperial Army: The Old Army and the Soldiers' Revolt* (Princeton, NJ: Princeton University Press, 1980), 105–15 and 119–20.

33 On this last point, see: R. K. Massie, *Nicholas and Alexandra* (New York: Atheneum, 1967); and George Katkov, *Russia, 1917: The February Revolution* (London: Longman, 1967), esp. 157–60.

34 Orlando Figes and Boris Kolonitskii, *Interpreting the Russian Revolution: The Language and Symbols of 1917* (New Haven, CT: Yale University Press, 1999), 158–64.

35 Wildman, *The End of the Russian Imperial Army*, 114–5.

36 Cited in Lawrence Stone, *Causes of the English Revolution 1529–1642* (New York: Routledge, 1972), 51–2.

37 As quoted in Jacques Godechot, *The Taking of the Bastille*, trans. Jean Stewart (New York: Charles Scribner's Sons, 1970), 261–2.

38 Citations are drawn from Figes, *A People's Tragedy*, 351–3.

39 For this discussion, see: Russell, *The Fall of the British Monarchies*, 285–9; Hibbard, *Charles I and the Popish Plot*, 197–8; and Anthony Fletcher, *The Outbreak of the English Civil War* (London: Edward Arnold, 1981), 35–6.

40 Sharpe, *The Personal Rule of Charles I*, 938–9.

41 Fletcher, *The Outbreak of the English Civil War*, 44.

42 Stone, *Causes of the English Revolution*, 138.

43 For a succinct discussion of the essential events here, see: G. E. Aylmer, *A Short History of Seventeenth-Century England: 1603–1689* (New York: Mentor Books, 1963), 120–3.

44 On the revolution in London, see: Valerie Pearl, *London and the Outbreak of the Puritan Revolution* (London: Oxford University Press, 1961), esp. Chapter 4; and Keith Lindley, *Popular Politics and Religion in Civil War London* (Aldershot: Scolar Press, 1997), passim.

45 Cited in Georges Lefebvre, *The Coming of the French Revolution*, trans. Robert R. Palmer (Princeton, NJ: Princeton University Press, 1947), 185.

46 This clandestine—and very revealing—manifesto is cited in a number of sources, including: Jean Egret, *Necker: Ministre de Louis XVI, 1776–1790* (Paris: Champion, 1975), 372; and Hardman, *Louis XVI*, 174.

47 As was convincingly demonstrated by Thomas E. Kaiser in "Meddling Abroad: Austrian Intervention in French Politics and the Construction of the 'Austrian Committee,' 1787-1790," a paper presented (in April 2008) at the 54th Annual Meeting of the Society for French Historical Studies.

48 On this subject, see: Norman Hampson, *The Constituent Assembly and the Failure of Consensus, 1789–1791* (New York: Blackwell, 1988); Harriet B. Applewhite, *Political Alignment in the French National Assembly, 1789–1791* (Baton Rouge, LA: LSU Press, 1993); and Timothy Tackett, *Becoming a Revolutionary: The Deputies of the French National Assembly and the Emergence of a Revolutionary Culture* (Princeton, NJ: Princeton University Press, 1996).

49 This story is engagingly retold (with ample documentation) by Timothy Tackett, *When the King Took Flight* (Cambridge, MA: Harvard University Press, 2003).

50 On this discussion of *dvoevlastie* and *mnogovlastie* in revolutionary Russia, consult Figes, *A People's Tragedy*, esp. 359–60.

51 On Miliukov's dilemma, see: Melissa K. Stockdale, *Paul Miliukov and the Quest for a Liberal Russia, 1880–1918* (Ithaca, NY: Cornell University Press, 1993).

52 These conflicting dynamics, in both the national government and in the provinces and villages of rural Russia, are best analyzed by Rex Wade, *The Russian Revolution, 1917* (Cambridge: Cambridge University Press, 2000).

53 On Irakli Tsereteli in particular, see: W. H. Roobol, *Tsereteli: A Democrat in the Russian Revolution: A Political Biography*, trans. Philip Hyams and Lynne Richards (The Hague: Nijhoff, 1976). Nikolai N. Sukhanov reviewed the agonies of the short-lived Miliukov-dominated Provisional Government from a contemporary standpoint in: *The Russian Revolution, 1917* (New York: Harper & Brothers, 1962).

54 On this "April Crisis," see: Wade, *Russian Revolution*, 80–6; and Sheila Fitzpatrick, *The Russian Revolution*, 3rd ed. (Oxford: Oxford University Press, 2008), 48–9.

55 See, on these issues, the sobering commentary of Orlando Figes in *A People's Tragedy*, 384. For Figes, the "April Crisis" only "accelerated . . . political and social polarization" in Russia rather than stabilizing the situation.

56 See, in this connection: Rochelle G. Ruthchild, *Equality and Revolution: Women's Rights in the Russian Empire, 1905–1917* (Pittsburgh, PA: University of Pittsburgh Press, 2010).

57 Fletcher, *The Outbreak of the English Civil War*, 334.

58 On all of this, consult: Hibbard, *Charles I and the Popish Plot*, esp. 225–6; and Fletcher, *The Outbreak of the English Civil War*, passim.

59 On the political dynamics of all this, see: Lawrence Kaplan, *Politics and Religion during the English Revolution: The Scots and the Long Parliament, 1643–1645* (New York: NYU Press, 1976); and Robert Ashton, *The English Civil War: Conservatism and Revolution* (London: Weidenfeld and Nicholson, 1978).

60 On the evolution of politics within Parliament during 1645–48, see ibid., esp. 194–249; and David Underdown, *Pride's Purge: Politics in the Puritan Revolution* (Oxford: Clarendon, 1971).

61 On the "second" civil war, see: Ashton, *Counter-Revolution: The Second Civil War and Its Origins, 1646–48* (New Haven, CT: Yale University Press, 1994). On the decision to execute Charles I, see the essays in: Jason Peacey, ed., *The Regicides and the Execution of Charles I* (New York: Palgrave Macmillan, 2001).

62 Refer, in this connection, to Underdown, *Pride's Purge*, 58–9.

63 See, on the New Model: Mark Kishlansky, *The Rise of the New Model Army* (Cambridge: Cambridge University Press, 1979); and Ian Gentles, "The New Model Officer Corps in 1647: A Collective Portrait," *Social History* 22 (1997): 127–44.

64 There is, of course, a huge literature on the Levellers. See, among more recent works tying them in with the Cromwellians: Austin Woolrych, "Putney Revisited: Political Debate in the New Model Army in 1647," in *Politics and People in Revolutionary England*, ed. Colin Jones, Malyn Newitt, and Stephen Roberts (Oxford: Basil Blackwell, 1986), 95–116; and Gentles, "The

Politics of Fairfax's Army, 1645–49," in Adamson, ed., *The English Civil War*, esp. 176 and 187–8.

65 G. E. Aylmer, ed., *The Levellers in the English Revolution* (Ithaca, NY: Cornell University Press, 1975), 50.

66 On Lafayette, and the overall Feuillant dilemma, see: T. C. W. Blanning, *The Origins of the French Revolutionary Wars* (London: Longman, 1986), esp. 97; and Kaiser, "La Fin du Renversement des Alliances: la France, l'Autriche et la déclaration de guerre du 20 avril 1792," *Annales historiques de la Révolution française* 351 (2008): 77–98.

67 Consult here, in addition to Blanning and Kaiser: C. J. Mitchell, *The French Legislative Assembly of 1791* (Leiden: E. J. Brill, 1988).

68 See, on all of this: Alison Patrick, "Political Divisions in the French National Convention, 1792–93," *Journal of Modern History* 41 (1969): 421–74; Gary Kates, *The Cercle Social, the Girondins, and the French Revolution* (Princeton, NJ: Princeton University Press, 1985); and Susan Dunn, *The Deaths of Louis XVI: Regicide and the French Political Imagination* (Princeton, NJ: Princeton University Press, 1994).

69 See, in these connections: John A. Lynn, *The Bayonets of the Republic: Motivations and Tactics in the Army of Revolutionary France, 1791–1794* (Urbana, IL: University of Illinois Press, 1984); Samuel F. Scott, *The Response of the Royal Army to the French Revolution* (Oxford: Oxford University Press, 1978); and Jean-Paul Bertaud, *The Army of the French Revolution*, trans. Robert R. Palmer (Princeton, NJ: Princeton University Press, 1988).

70 See, on this: Malcolm Crook, *Elections in the French Revolution* (Cambridge: Cambridge University Press, 1996); John Markoff, *The Abolition of Feudalism: Peasants, Lords, and Legislators in the French Revolution* (University Park, PA: Pennsylvania State University Press, 1996); and Suzanne Desan, *The Family on Trial in Revolutionary France* (Berkeley, CA: University of California Press, 1994).

71 The best sources here are still, after all these years: Robert D. Warth, *The Allies and the Russian Revolution: From the Fall of the Monarchy to the Peace of Brest-Litovsk* (Durham, NC: Duke University Press, 1954); and Rex Wade, *The Russian Search for Peace, February-October 1917* (Stanford, CA: Stanford University Press, 1969).

72 On these events, see: Louise Heenan, *Russian Democracy's Fateful Blunder: The Summer Offensive of 1917* (New York: Praeger, 1987); George Katkov, *Russia 1917: The Kornilov Affair* (London: Longman, 1980); and Alexander Rabinowitch, *The Bolsheviks Come to Power: The Revolution of 1917 in Petrograd* (New York: W. W. Norton, 1978).

73 See Figes, *A People's Tragedy*, 480.

74 On developments in the army, refer again to Wildman, *The End of the Russian Imperial Army*, 404–5. On the situation in the navy, see: David A. Longley, "Officers and Men: A Study of the Development of Political Attitudes among the Sailors of the Baltic Fleet in 1917," *Soviet Studies* 25 (1973): 28–50.

75 A landmark study of *labor radicalization* tendencies in urban Russia is that of John Keep, *The Russian Revolution: A Study in Mass Mobilization* (New York: Norton, 1976). But see also Stephen A. Smith, *Red Petrograd: Revolution in the Factories, 1917–1918* (Cambridge: Cambridge University Press, 1983); and also Michael Melancon, "Soldiers, Peasant-Soldiers, Peasant-Workers and their Organizations in Petrograd," *Soviet and Post-Soviet Review* 23 (1996): 161–90.

76 On all of this, see again Keep, *The Russian Revolution*, 68–9, 172, and 185; and the essays of Orlando Figes and others in Esther K. Mann and Timothy Mixter, eds., *Peasant Economy, Culture, and Politics of European Russia, 1800–1921* (Princeton, NJ: Princeton University Press, 1991).

77 Crane Brinton, *The Anatomy of Revolution* (New York: Prentice-Hall, 1938), esp. 198, 203.

78 For recent discussions of the relative merits of circumstantial and ideological interpretations of terror in the European revolutions, see: Arno J. Mayer, *The Furies: Violence and Terror in the French and Russian Revolutions* (Princeton, NJ: Princeton University Press, 2000), esp. 96–9; and Bailey Stone, *Rethinking Revolutionary Change in Europe: A Neostructuralist Approach* (Lanham, MD: Rowman & Littlefield Publishers, 2020), esp. Chapter 3.

79 Ronald Hutton, *The British Republic 1649–1660* (New York: St. Martin's Press, 1990), 15.

80 The standard work on this subject, after all these years, remains David Underdown, *Royalist Conspiracy in England, 1649–1660* (New Haven, CT: Yale University Press, 1960). It largely supersedes Paul Hardacre, *The Royalists during the Puritan Revolution* (The Hague: Nijhoff, 1956).

81 The connections here between the government's military campaign and indiscipline within the army are most carefully sketched out in Norah Carlin, "The Levellers and the Conquest of Ireland in 1649," *Historical Journal* 30 (1987): 269–88.

82 See, on this issue, the works of Ian Gentles: for instance, *The English Revolution and the Wars in the Three Kingdoms, 1638–1652* (London: Pearson, 2007).

83 Discussion of sporadic terrorism in the English Revolution is covered in works ranging from Underdown, *Royalist Conspiracy in England*, passim., to Bailey Stone, *The Anatomy of Revolution Revisited: A Comparative Analysis of England, France, and Russia* (New York: Cambridge University Press, 2014), esp. 342–46.

84 Ian Gentles, *The New Model Army in England, Scotland and Ireland 1645–1653* (Oxford: Blackwell, 1991), 319. See also, on all of this, Mark Kishlansky, *The Rise of the New Model Army* (Cambridge: Cambridge University Press, 1979), passim.

85 Gentles, *The New Model Army*, 318.

86 See ibid., 324. See also the germane discussion provided by Patricia Higgins, "The Reaction of Women," in *Politics, Religion, and the English Civil War*, ed. Brian Manning (London: E. J. Arnold, 1973), 200–5.

87 On the so-called Barebones Parliament of July–December 1653, see in particular the commentary of Austin Woolrych, *Commonwealth to Protectorate* (Oxford: Clarendon Press, 1982), esp. 165–93 and 232–3.

88 Consult, in this connection: Bernard Capp, *The Fifth Monarchy Men: A Study in Seventeenth-Century English Millenarianism* (London: Faber and Faber, 1972); and the essays in J. F. McGregor and Barry Reay, eds., *Radical Religion in the English Revolution* (Oxford: Oxford University Press, 1984).

89 See Karl A. Roider, Jr., *Baron Thugut and Austria's Response to the French Revolution* (Princeton, NJ: Princeton University Press, 1987), esp. 131–5. For Roider, too, Austria was then "closer to defeating revolutionary France than it would ever be again during Thugut's tenure as foreign minister."

90 On the conflation of *ideological* and *strategic/territorial* threats as perceived by statesmen at London, refer, in particular, to: Jeremy Black, *British Foreign Policy in an Age of Revolutions, 1783–1793* (New York: Cambridge University Press, 1994), 470.

91 On federalism, for instance, see: Bill Edmonds, "Federalism and Urban Revolt in France in 1793," *Journal of Modern History* 55 (1983): 22–53; and Paul Hanson, *The Jacobin Republic Under Fire: The Federalist Revolt in the French Revolution* (University Park, PA: Pennsylvania State University Press, 2003).

92 P. M. Jones, *The Peasantry in the French Revolution* (Cambridge: Cambridge University Press, 1988), esp. 207, 223–4. Arno Mayer reached the same conclusion for, specifically, the Vendée, in *The Furies*, 329.

93 Cited from Richard T. Bienvenu's article on "Terror" in Samuel F. Scott and Barry Rothaus, eds., *Historical Dictionary of the French Revolution, 1789–1799* (Westwood, CT: Greenwood Press, 1985), 942–6. The best statistical analysis of the Terror still remains Donald Greer, *The Incidence of the Terror during the French Revolution* (Cambridge, MA: Harvard University Press, 1935).

94 See R. B. Rose, *The Enragés: Socialists of the French Revolution?* (Sydney: Sydney University Press, 1965), 73. An updated anthology of *enragé* writings by Roux, Leclerc, and Varlet is provided in Marc Allan Goldstein, ed., *Social and Political Thought of the French Revolution, 1788–1797* (New York: Peter Lang, 1997), 362–70, 456–69, and 474–88.

95 A number of their manifestoes are highlighted in: Darline Gay Levy, Harriet Branson Applewhite, and Mary Durham Johnson, eds., *Women in Revolutionary Paris 1789–1795* (Urbana, IL: University of Illinois Press, 1979).

96 This characterization of the Hébertist movement of early 1794 is provided by R. R. Palmer, *Twelve Who Ruled: The Year of the Terror in the French Revolution* (Princeton, NJ: Princeton University Press, 1941), 294.

97 Review especially, in this connection, the verdict of Albert Soboul, *The Sans-Culottes: The Popular Movement and Revolutionary Government, 1793–1974,* trans. Rémy Inglis Hall (Princeton, NJ: Princeton University Press, 1980), esp. 252. George Rudé had already reached similar conclusions in: *The Crowd in the French Revolution* (Oxford: Clarendon Press, 1959), esp. 128–41.

98 Palmer, *Twelve Who Ruled,* 312.

99 David S. Foglesong, "Foreign Intervention," in *Critical Companion to the Russian Revolution 1914–1921,* ed. Edward Acton, Vladimir Cherniaev, and William G. Rosenberg (Bloomington, IN: Indiana University Press, 1997), 106–7). Consult also, on this concept, Evan Mawdsley, *The Russian Civil War* (Boston, MA: Allen and Unwin, 1987); and G. A. Brinkley, *The Volunteer Army and Allied Intervention in Southern Russia, 1917–1921* (Notre Dame, IN: University of Notre Dame Press, 1966).

100 After all these years, the best study of the Treaty of Brest-Litovsk is still John Wheeler-Bennett, *The Forgotten Peace: Brest-Litovsk, March 1918* (New York: William Morrow, 1939).

101 Refer again to Foglesong, "Foreign Intervention," passim., and to Richard K. Debo, *Revolution and Survival: The Foreign Policy of Soviet Russia, 1917–1918* (Toronto: University of Toronto Press, 1979), esp. 356–7.

102 The most recent assessment of the Left SRs as a (possibly?) cohesive political force in 1918 and thereafter is: Scott B. Smith, *Captives of Revolution: The Socialist Revolutionaries and the Bolshevik Dictatorship, 1918–1923* (Pittsburgh, PA: University of Pittsburgh Press, 2011).

103 Refer once again, for comparisons between France's Jacobin Terror and Russia's Red Terror, to Mayer, *The Furies,* passim. Consult also Alter Litvin's succinct history of the *Cheka* in "The Cheka," in Acton, Cherniaev, and Rosenberg, eds., *Critical Companion to the Russian Revolution,* 317–20.

104 On Kronstadt in March 1921, see: Paul H. Avrich, *Kronstadt 1921* (New York: Norton, 1971); and Israel Getzler, *Kronstadt, 1917–1921: The Fate of a Soviet Democracy* (Cambridge: Cambridge University Press, 1983).

105 On those domestic questions, involving workers, peasants, and the general bureaucratization of government under the Leninists, see: Oliver H. Radkey, *The Sickle Under the Hammer: The Russian Socialist Revolutionaries in the Early Months of Soviet Rule* (New York: Columbia University Press, 1963); and Michael Melancon, "The Left Socialist Revolutionaries, 1917–1918," in Acton, Cherniaev, and Rosenberg, eds., *Critical Companion to the Russian Revolution,* 291–9.

106 See, in this connection: Barbara E. Clements, *Bolshevik Feminist: The Life of Aleksandra Kollontai* (Bloomington, IN: Indiana University Press, 1979); Beatrice Farnsworth, *Alexandra Kollontai: Socialism, Feminism, and the Russian Revolution* (Stanford, CA: Stanford University Press, 1980); and Richard Stites, *The Women's Liberation Movement in Russia,* 2nd ed. (Princeton, NJ: Princeton University Press, 1991).

107   Workers' issues in the Russia of 1918–21 are insightfully analyzed in Oskar Anweiler, *The Soviets: The Russian Workers', Peasants', and Soldiers' Councils, 1905–1921*, trans. Ruth Hein (New York: Pantheon, 1974); as well as T. F. Remington, *Building Socialism in Soviet Russia: Ideology and Industrial Organization 1917–1921* (Pittsburgh, PA: University of Pittsburgh Press, 1984).

108   Figes, *A People's Tragedy*, 753. See also, on this question: Vladimir Brovkin, *Behind the Front Lines of the Civil War: Political Parties and Social Movements in Russia, 1918–1922* (Princeton, NJ: Princeton University Press, 1994); and Donald J. Raleigh, *Experiencing Russia's Civil War: Politics, Society, and Revolutionary Culture in Saratov, 1917–1922* (Princeton, NJ: Princeton University Press, 2002).

109   The unsavory details of this crackdown—carried out with the full support of the Leninist rulers at Petrograd—are extensively described in Avrich, *Kronstadt 1921*, passim., and Getzler, *Kronstadt, 1917–1921*, passim.

110   For Daniels's commentary on this issue, see: Robert V. Daniels, "Does the Present Change the Past?," *Journal of Modern History* 70 (1998): 431–5. For Fitzpatrick's ideas about Thermidor, see *The Russian Revolution*, 2–4.

111   On the *political* aspects of this reaction in France, see: Denis Woronoff, *The Thermidorean Regime and the Directory, 1794–1799*, trans. Julian Jackson (Cambridge: Cambridge University Press, 1994); and Bronislaw Baczko, *Ending the Terror: The French Revolution After Robespierre*, trans. Michael Petheram (New York: Cambridge University Press, 1994).

112   On the *economic* aspects of all this, see again Woronoff, *The Thermidorean Regime*, esp. 8–13; and William Doyle, *Oxford History of the French Revolution*, 2nd ed. (Oxford: Oxford University Press, 2002), esp. 285–90.

113   On women's issues here in particular, consult such sources as: Marcel Garaud and Romuald Szramkiewicz, *La Révolution française et la famille* (Paris: Presses Universitaires de France, 1978), esp. 167–76; and Suzanne Desan, *The Family on Trial in Revolutionary France* (Berkeley, CA: University of California Press, 2004).

114   See, on this question: François Gendron, *La Jeunesse Dorée* (Québec: Presses de l'Université de Québec, 1979).

115   Olwen Hufton, *The Prospect Before Her: A History of Women in Western Europe, 1500–1800* (London: Harper-Collins, 1995), 481–6.

116   See, for instance, the comments in Colin Lucas, "The First Directory and the Rule of Law," *French Historical Studies* 10 (1977): 258; and Isser Woloch, *Jacobin Legacy: The Democratic Movement Under the Directory* (Princeton, NJ: Princeton University Press, 1970), esp. 92–3, 95–6, and 112.

117   Isser Woloch has written on all of this somewhat more recently in *Napoleon and His Collaborators: The Making of a Dictatorship* (New York: W. W. Norton, 2001).

118   Woolrych, *Britain in Revolution*, 580.

119 Ibid., 582. Ronald Hutton has also pointed out that, in this final phase of the upheaval, four notoriously antiroyalist judges were removed from the bench, and nearly thirty incarcerated royalists were set at liberty. Hutton, *The British Republic*, 62–4.

120 Refer to Coward, *Oliver Cromwell*, 99–102. On Court ceremonial under the Protectorate, see Roy Sherwood, *The Court of Oliver Cromwell* (Cambridge: Cambridge University Press, 1999).

121 Christopher Hill, *God's Englishman: Oliver Cromwell and the English Revolution* (New York: Harper Torchbooks, 1970), 150–1.

122 Roger Howell, "Cromwell and His Parliaments: The Trevor-Roper Thesis Revisited," in *Images of Oliver Cromwell*, ed. R. C. Richardson (Manchester: Manchester University Press, 1993), esp. 134.

123 Peter Gaunt, *Oliver Cromwell* (Oxford: Blackwell, 1996), 205.

124 Refer, here, to: David L. Smith and Patrick Little, *Parliaments and Politics during the Cromwellian Protectorate* (Cambridge: Cambridge University Press, 2007), and to Christopher Durston, *Cromwell's Major-Generals: Godly Government during the English Revolution* (Manchester: Manchester University Press, 2001).

125 On all of this, see: Robert V. Daniels, *The Conscience of the Revolution: Communist Opposition in Soviet Russia* (Oxford: Oxford University Press, 1960); and Leonard Schapiro, *The Origins of the Communist Autocracy* (London: Macmillan, 1977).

126 The NEP is succinctly summed up by Fitzpatrick, *The Russian Revolution*, 95–6. See also the more detailed discussion in Sergei V. Iarov, "The Tenth Congress of the Communist Party and the Transition to NEP," in Acton, Cherniaev, and Rosenberg, eds., *Critical Companion to the Russian Revolution*, esp. 122–7.

127 This vivid description comes to us from Figes, *A People's Tragedy*, 771–2.

128 Anarchist Emma Goldman is cited in ibid., 771.

129 See, in this connection: Wendy Z. Goldman, "Working-Class Women and the "Withering Away" of the Family: Popular Responses to Family Policy," in *Russia in the Era of NEP: Explorations in Soviet Society and Culture*, ed. Sheila Fitzpatrick, Alexander Rabinowitch, and Richard Stites (Bloomington, IN: Indiana University Press, 1991), 127–8. Refer also to: Kent Geiger, *The Family in Soviet Russia* (Cambridge: Cambridge University Press, 1968), passim.

130 The reader might want to start here with Alexander Erlich, *The Soviet Industrialization Debate, 1924–1928* (Cambridge, MA: Harvard University Press, 1962), and then go on to the subsequent synthesis by Lewis H. Siegelbaum, *Soviet State and Society Between Revolutions, 1918–1929* (Cambridge: Cambridge University Press, 1992). Siegelbaum, in his "Select Bibliography," suggests numerous other important studies as well.

131 Hiroaki Kuromiya, *Stalin's Industrial Revolution: Politics and Workers, 1928–1932* (Cambridge: Cambridge University Press, 1988), 113–5.

132   She makes this point cogently in "The Problem of Class Identity in NEP Society," in Fitzpatrick, Rabinowitch, and Stites, eds., *Russia in the Era of NEP*, 12–33. See also, on this subject: Lynne Viola, *The Best Sons of the Fatherland: Workers in the Vanguard of Soviet Collectivization* (New York: Oxford University Press, 1987).

133   In this connection, see Anne G. Gorsuch, *Youth in Revolutionary Russia: Enthusiasts, Bohemians, Delinquents* (Bloomington, IN: Indiana University Press, 2000).

Chapter 3

1   Thomas E. Kaiser, "Who's Afraid of Marie-Antoinette? Diplomacy, Austrophobia and the Queen," *French History* 14 (2000): esp. 242–3. Among feminists cited by Kaiser are: Joan B. Landes, *Women and the Public Sphere in the Age of the French Revolution* (Ithaca, NY: Cornell University Press, 1988); Elizabeth Colwill, "Just Another *Citoyenne*? Marie- Antoinette on Trial, 1790–1793," *History Workshop* 28 (1989): 63–87; Lynn Hunt, *The Family Romance of the French Revolution* (Berkeley, CA: University of California Press, 1992); and Madelyn Gutwirth, *The Twilight of the Goddesses: Women and Representation in the French Revolutionary Era* (New Brunswick, NJ: Rutgers University Press, 1992).

2   For this definitional discussion, see: https://en.wikipedia.org/wiki/Queen _consort. There is a growing literature on consort queens in old regime Europe. For studies of some *continental* consorts, see: Clarissa Campbell Orr, ed., *Queenship in Europe, 1660–1815: The Role of the Consort* (Cambridge: Cambridge University Press, 2004). English consorts are taken up by Caroline M. Hibbard, "Henrietta Maria in the 1630s: Perspectives on the Role of Consort Queens in Ancien Régime Courts," ch. 5 in *The 1630s: Interdisciplinary Essays on Culture and Politics in the Caroline Era*, ed. Ian Atherton and Julie Sanders (Manchester: Manchester University Press, 2006), 92–110.

3   On the origins and on the practical implications (especially for Cathérine de Médicis) of Salic Law, refer to: Sheila Ffolliott, "Catherine de Médicis as Artemesia: Figuring the Powerful Widow," in *Rewriting the Renaissance: The Discourses of Sexual Difference in Early Modern Europe*, ed. Margaret Ferguson, Maureen Quilligan, and Nancy Vickers (Chicago, IL: The University of Chicago Press, 1986), 227–41; Sharon L. Jansen, *The Monstrous Regiment of Women: Female Rulers in Early Modern Europe* (New York: Palgrave Macmillan, 2002); and Craig Taylor, "The Salic Law and the Valois Succession to the French Crown," *French History* 15 (2001): 358–77.

4   A point made (for instance) by Susan Doran. See Doran, "Elizabeth I and Catherine de Medici," in *The "Contending Kingdoms": France and England 1420–1700*, ed. Glenn Richardson (Aldershot: Ashgate, 2008), 117, n. 2.

5 Fanny Cosandey, "'La maitresse de nos biens': Pouvoir féminin et puissance dynastique dans la monarchie française d'Ancien Régime," *Historical Reflections/Réflexions historiques* 32 (2006), 381–401. My translation here from the French on 381–2 and 399. Cosandey had already discussed these matters at length in: *La Reine de France: Symbole et Pouvoir, XVe-XVIIIe siècles* (Paris: Gallimard, 2000).

6 Katherine Crawford, *Perilous Performances: Gender and Regency in Early Modern France* (Cambridge, MA: Harvard University Press, 2004), 198. Comments about Cathérine, according to Crawford, also "formed an important subtext during the regencies of Marie de Médicis, Anne d'Autriche, [and] Philippe d'Orléans."

7 Doran, "Elizabeth I and Catherine de Medici," 117–8.

8 Mack P. Holt, *The Duke of Anjou and the Politique Struggle during the Wars of Religion* (Cambridge: Cambridge University Press, 1986), 6–7.

9 Hibbard, "Henrietta Maria in the 1630s," 92–3. Hibbard had already addressed some of these issues in her superb monograph *Charles I and the Popish Plot* (Chapel Hill, NC: University of North Carolina Press, 1983), and in "Translating Royalty: Henrietta Maria and the Transition from Princess to Queen," *The Court Historian* 5 (2000): 15–29.

10 Hibbard, "Henrietta Maria in the 1630s," 106.

11 See, in this connection, Malcolm Smuts, "Religion, European Politics and Henrietta Maria's Circle, 1625–41," in *Henrietta Maria: Piety, Politics, and Patronage*, ed. Erin Griffey (Aldershot: Ashgate, 2006), 36–7. Smuts had already explored the religious dimension of this international phenomenon in "The Puritan Followers of Henrietta Maria in the 1630s," *English Historical Review* 93 (1978): 26–45.

12 For this discussion, refer to Michelle Anne White, *Henrietta Maria and the English Civil Wars* (Aldershot: Ashgate, 2006), 106–19.

13 Ibid.

14 This interesting point is emphasized repeatedly by Frances E. Dolan, *Whores of Babylon: Catholicism, Gender, and Seventeenth-Century Print Culture* (Ithaca, NY: Cornell University Press, 1999). As Michelle White has pointed out, by the time civil war erupted in the early 1640s, six (potential) heirs of the couple were alive: three boys and three girls.

15 Refer once again to Cosandey, "La maitresse de nos biens," 381–2, and to her much more detailed analysis of the subject in *La Reine de France: Symbole et Pouvoir*. A very recent scholarly biography of this French queen is: John Hardman, *Marie-Antoinette: The Making of a French Queen* (New Haven, CT: Yale University Press, 2019).

16 I am indebted for this specific insight to Tom Kaiser, who lucidly expatiated upon the issue in an email exchange dating from June 27, 2020. Rumors concerning "debauchery" of one sort or another at the French court during the prerevolutionary years have been recently revisited in: Will Bashor, *Marie*

Antoinette's World: Intrigue, Infidelity, and Adultery in Versailles (Lanham, MD: Rowman & Littlefield Publishers, 2020).

17 Orlando Figes, *A People's Tragedy: The Russian Revolution, 1891–1921* (New York: Penguin Books, 1996), 26–7. Is it, *not,* then, psychologically revealing that a portrait of Marie-Antoinette—*not* of Catherine II—hung over her writing desk in the Alexander Palace at St. Petersburg? Two of the shrewdest testimonies to the empress's personality are: Pierre Gilliard, *Thirteen Years at the Russian Court,* trans. F. Appleby Holt (New York: Doran, 1921); and Bernard Pares, *The Fall of the Russian Monarchy: A Study of the Evidence* (New York: Alfred Knopf, 1939).

18 Refer once again to Hibbard, "Henrietta Maria in the 1630s," 92.

19 Citations from: Allison Heisch, "Queen Elizabeth I and the Persistence of Patrimony," *Feminist Review* 4 (1980): 45–56; and Susan Bassnett, *Elizabeth I: A Feminist Perspective* (Oxford: Oxford University Press, 1988), 124–5.

20 Susan Doran, *Monarchy and Matrimony: The Courtships of Elizabeth I* (London: Routledge, 1988), 8.

21 The geopolitics of this era are analyzed by Ludwig Dehio, *The Precarious Balance: Four Centuries of the European Power Struggle,* trans. Charles Fullman (New York: Alfred A. Knopf, 1982); and by Paul Kennedy, *The Rise and Fall of the Great Powers: Economic Change and Military Conflict from 1500 to 2000* (New York: Random House, 1987).

22 Doran, *Elizabeth I and Foreign Policy, 1558–1603* (New York: Routledge, 2000), 65.

23 For this extended commentary on the early years of Elizabeth's foreign policy, see: R. B. Wernham, *The Making of Elizabethan Foreign Policy, 1558–1603* (Berkeley, CA: University of California Press, 1980), 3–4, 34, and 43–4.

24 See, in this connection: Wallace T. MacCaffrey, *Queen Elizabeth and the Making of Policy, 1572–1588* (Princeton, NJ: Princeton University Press, 1981), 157–60. MacCaffrey continued his history of Elizabethan foreign policy in another monograph eleven years later: see *Elizabeth I: War and Politics, 1588–1603* (Princeton, NJ: Princeton University Press, 1992).

25 See Charles H. Wilson, *Queen Elizabeth and the Revolt of the Netherlands* (The Hague: M. Nijhoff, 1979).

26 Doran, *Monarchy and Matrimony,* 190–1.

27 As cited in MacCaffrey, *Elizabeth I: War and Politics, 1588–1603,* 3–4.

28 See, on all this: Pauline Croft, "'The State of the World is Marvellously Changed': England, Spain, and Europe, 1558–1604," in *Tudor England and Its Neighbors,* ed. Susan Doran and Glenn Richardson (New York: Palgrave MacMillan, 2005), 178–202. Croft also criticizes R. B. Wernham for using the term "armada" too casually, and contends that Philip II abandoned his grand plans for conquest after the *dénouement* of 1588.

29 Refer on this to: P. E. J. Hammer, *Elizabeth's Wars: War, Government, and Society in Tudor England, 1544–1604* (New York: Palgrave Macmillan, 2003).

30 For this judgment, consult again MacCaffrey, *Elizabeth I: War and Politics, 1588–1603*, 573–4.

31 Doran, *Elizabeth I and Foreign Policy, 1558–1603* (New York: Routledge, 2000), 70. Other positive judgments of Elizabeth's foreign policy come from R. B. Wernham, *After the Armada: Elizabethan England and the Struggle for Western Europe, 1588–1595* (Oxford: Clarendon, 1984); and *The Return of the Armadas: The Last Years of the Elizabethan War Against Spain, 1595–1603* (Oxford: Clarendon, 1994).

32 Refer above to n. 19 for the citations from Heisch and Bassnett.

33 See, on all of this: Christopher Haigh, *Elizabeth I: Profile in Power* (New York: Longman, 1988). His scholarship is also revealingly discussed in Charles Beem, *The Lioness Roared: The Problems of Female Rule in English History* (New York: Palgrave Macmillan, 2006), 18–20.

34 See, in this connection: Susan Frye, *Elizabeth I: The Competition for Representation* (Oxford: Oxford University Press, 1993); and Carole Levin, *The Heart and Stomach of a King* (Philadelphia, PA: University of Pennsylvania Press, 1994). Charles Beem analyzes their contributions to the gendered historiography on Elizabeth I in *The Lioness Roared*, esp. 19–23. Susan Doran discusses these issues as well in *Monarchy and Matrimony*, esp. in the Introduction.

35 Beem and Levin, "Why Elizabeth Never Left England," in *The Foreign Relations of Elizabeth I*, ed. Charles Beem (New York: Palgrave Macmillan, 2011). Citation here is from p. 15.

36 Refer again to Doran, *Elizabeth I and Foreign Policy, 1588–1603*, 68. Moreover, as Doran demonstrates again and again in *Monarchy and Matrimony*, many issues in addition to gender—such as domestic factionalism, religion, popular xenophobia, and geopolitical calculations—complicated the marriage negotiations involving Elizabeth I.

37 Beem and Levin, "Why Elizabeth Never Left England," 16–18.

38 See, in this connection: Anna Whitelock, "'Women, Warrior Queen?' Rethinking Mary and Elizabeth," in *Tudor Queenship: The Reigns of Mary and Elizabeth*, ed. Anna Whitelock and Alice Hunt (New York: Palgrave Macmillan 2010). Cited from 184–5.

39 Refer, on this matter, to: Jessica Bell, "The Three Marys: The Virgin; Marie de Médicis; and Henrietta Maria," in Erin Griffey, ed., *Henrietta Maria: Piety, Politics, and Patronage*, 92.

40 The most recent major biography of this consort is Michelle White, *Henrietta Maria and the English Civil Wars* (Aldershot: Ashgate, 2006). It improves on Elizabeth Hamilton, *Henrietta Maria* (New York: Coward, McCann and Geohegan, 1976); Rosalind Marshall, *Henrietta Maria: The Intrepid Queen* (London: Stemmer House Publishers, 1991); and Alison Plowden, *Henrietta Maria: Charles I's Indomitable Queen* (Stroud: Sutton Publishing, 2001).

41 Elizabeth Hamilton has thus expatiated upon this crucial letter of mother to daughter in Hamilton, *Henrietta Maria*, 51. But see also Plowden, *Henrietta*

Maria, 23. Curious readers can also locate it in: Armand Jean du Plessis de Richelieu, *Mémoires du Cardinal de Richelieu, sur le règne de Louis XIII* (Paris: Foucault, 1823).

42　Ann Hughes, *The Causes of the English Civil War*, 2nd ed. (Basingstoke: Macmillan, 1998), 81, 89–90.

43　On all of this, see Hibbard, *Charles I and the Popish Plot*, esp. ch.s 2, 3, and 4. Two additional sources are: Robin Clifton, "The Popular Fear of Catholics During the English Revolution," *Past and Present* 52 (1971): 23–55; and Peter Lake, "Anti-Popery: The Structure of a Prejudice," in *Conflict in Early Stuart England: Studies in Religion and Politics 1603–1642*, ed. Richard Cust and Ann Hughes (London: Longman, 1989), 72–106.

44　As reported in Plowden, *Henrietta Maria*, 70–1. Michelle White has since corroborated this in *Henrietta Maria and the English Civil Wars*, esp. 13–14.

45　Ibid., 17. This issue is also touched upon in L. J. Reeve, *Charles I and the Road to Personal Rule* (Cambridge: Cambridge University Press, 1989), 29; and in Plowden, *Henrietta Maria*, 86.

46　On this matter, see: Smuts, "The Puritan Followers of Henrietta Maria in the 1630s"; Smuts, "Religion, European Politics, and Henrietta Maria's Circle," in Griffey, ed., *Henrietta Maria: Piety, Politics, and Patronage*, ch. 1; and White, *Henrietta Maria and the English Civil Wars*, 16–20.

47　A standard account of anti-Richelieu conspiracies in Louis XIII's France is: William F. Church, *Richelieu and Raison d'Etat* (Princeton, NJ: Princeton University Press, 1973), esp. 197–235. Henrietta was drawn into these intrigues in part because her mother (Marie de Médicis), an inveterate enemy of Richelieu, played so central a role in them.

48　Smuts, "Religion, European Politics and Henrietta Maria's Circle," 36. Refer as well to Hibbard, *Charles I and the Popish Plot*, 19–37, for an excellent analysis of the shifting factional alliances at the English court and their implications for Caroline foreign policy in the late 1630s.

49　Citations from Plowden, *Henrietta Maria*, 164 and 166. Her kinswoman Elizabeth of Bohemia disapprovingly commented that "The Queen is against [any] agreement with parliament but by war." Ibid., 167.

50　White, *Henrietta Maria and the English Civil Wars*, 189–90. At times she would have even had Charles convert (for purely expediential reasons) to Presbyterianism! This, however, was one expedient too far for the king.

51　For these comments, consult: Mary Anne Everitt Green, ed., *Letters of Queen Henrietta Maria* (London: Richard Bentley, 1857), esp. 55, 65, 68, 327, and 336. For a modern commentary on all of this: see Conrad Russell, *The Causes of the English Civil War* (Oxford: Clarendon, 1990), esp. ch. 8, "The Man Charles Stuart."

52　Green, ed., *Letters of Queen Henrietta Maria*, 327.

53　On the impeachment of the queen, refer to Hamilton, *Henrietta Maria*, 197–8; and White, *Henrietta Maria and the English Civil Wars*, 102–4. According to Archbishop William Laud's personal diary, the impeachment was voted in Parliament on May 23, 1643.

54   White, *Henrietta Maria and the English Civil Wars*, 191.

55   The widowed queen consort apparently succumbed to complications from bronchitis and died at Colombes, France, on September 10, 1669, aged fifty-nine. For a brief résumé of Henrietta's life after Charles I's execution, see Ibid., Epilogue, 192–4.

56   Diana Barnes, "The *Secretary of Ladies* and Feminine Friendship at the Court of Henrietta Maria," in Griffey, ed., *Henrietta Maria: Piety, Politics, and Patronage*, 39–56. Citation here from 53–5.

57   Hibbard, *Charles I and the Popish Plot*, 10.

58   White, *Henrietta Maria and the English Civil Wars*, 146. We should also note in this connection that, in her later years, the widowed queen would infuriate members of her own family by trying to Catholicize her youngest surviving children, the Duke of Gloucester and Henriette Anne. See, on this: Plowden, *Henrietta Maria*, 222–3 and 228–30; and Hamilton, *Henrietta Maria*, 242. "These reasons of State are terrible," she also fumed when the French government (reasonably enough) sought a diplomatic *rapprochement* with the Puritan Cromwellian regime during the 1650s. There was, after all, still Habsburg Spain for France to contend with in western Europe.

59   For this chronology, refer back to Doran, "Elizabeth I and Catherine de Medici," in *The "Contending Kingdoms:" France and England 1420–1700*, ed. Richardson (Aldershot: Ashgate, 2008), 117, n. 2. For a brief sketch of her life, consult https://en.wikipedia.org/wiki/Catherine_de_Medici.

60   R. J. Knecht, *Catherine de' Medici* (London: Longman, 1998), xii. All of this, we should point out, despite the fact that her mother, Madeleine de la Tour d'Auvergne, countess of Boulogne, was palpably French!

61   Ibid., 270–1. Verdicts on the Queen Mother have varied wildly over the years. At the negative extreme is J. E. Neale, *The Age of Catherine de Medici* (London: Jonathan Cape, 1966). At the other extreme, Jean Héritier, in *Catherine de' Medici*, trans. Charlotte Haldane (London: Allen and Unwin, 1963), sees her as "a great, national, and moderate statesman, who struggled in isolation, with diplomacy as her principal weapon, against two mutually hostile and armed factions." See also R. J. Knecht, *The French Wars of Religion, 1559–1598* (London: Longman, 1998); and Mack P. Holt, *The French Wars of Religion, 1562–1629*, 2nd ed. (Cambridge: Cambridge University Press, 2005).

62   Knecht, *Catherine de' Medici*, 270–1.

63   N. M. Sutherland, *Princes, Politics and Religion 1547–1589* (London: Hambledon Press, 1984), 50–1. Nicola M. Sutherland has long depicted Cathérine de Médicis's career in largely positive terms—terms that emphasize the interaction in this era between domestic and international affairs. Her other works include: *The French Secretaries of State in the Age of Catherine de Medici* (Westport, CT: Greenwood Press, 1976); and *The Massacre of St.*

Bartholomew and the European Conflict, 1559–1572 (London: Macmillan, 1973).

64 Refer once again to Doran, "Elizabeth I and Catherine de Medici," 117–8.

65 The fundamental source here is: Hector de la Ferrière–Percy and Gustave Baguenault de Puchesse, eds., *Lettres de Cathérine de Médicis*, 10 vols. (Paris: Imprimérie Nationale, 1880–1909).

66 Refer once again to Doran, "Eliabeth I and Catherine de Medici," 117–32, for one of the most thoroughgoing analyses of this question and of other issues as well in the longstanding relationship between the two women.

67 Ibid, 119–21.

68 Ibid., 126–7. We should also recall here that Mary Stuart had (briefly) been married to Francis II—and that, more dangerously, she was the niece of the pro-Spanish Duke and Cardinal de Guise.

69 Consult, in addition to sources already cited, the following: Philip Benedict, "The Saint Bartholomew's Massacres in the Provinces," *The Historical Journal* 21 (1978): 205–25; Barbara B. Diefendorf, *Beneath the Cross: Catholics and Huguenots in Sixteenth-Century Paris* (Oxford: Oxford University Press, 1991); and Denis Crouzet, *Le haut coeur de Catherine de Médicis: Une Raison politique aux temps de la Saint-Barthélemy* (Paris: Albin Michel, 2005).

70 See Ivan Cloulas, *Catherine de Médicis* (Paris: Fayard, 1979); and Marc Venard, "Arretez le massacre!," *Bulletin d'histoire moderne et contemporaine* 39 (1992): 645–61.

71 Sutherland, *The Massacre of St. Bartholomew and the European Conflict, 1559–1572*, 345–6.

72 Sutherland, *Princes, Politics and Religion 1547–1589*, 53.

73 Refer again to Knecht, *Cathérine de' Medici*, xi–xii.

74 Cited from Katherine Crawford, "Catherine de Médicis and the Performance of Political Motherhood," *Sixteenth Century Journal* 31 (2000): 673. Crawford subsequently elaborated on gendered issues in old regime France: see *Perilous Performances: Gender and Regency in Early Modern France* (Cambridge, MA: Harvard University Press, 2004).

75 Crawford, "Catherine de Médicis and the Performance of Political Motherhood," 644.

76 Ffolliott, "Catherine de Médicis as Artemisia: Figuring the Powerful Widow," 241. Refer also to the commentary on all this by Sharon L. Jansen, *The Monstrous Regiment of Women: Female Rulers in Early Modern Europe*, 212–3. Artemisia ruled Caria (a small kingdom in what is now southwestern Turkey) for three years after her husband's death in the fourth century BCE.

77 As Knecht (in *Catherine de' Medici*, 223–5) has duly pointed out.

78 Crawford, "Catherine de Médicis and the Performance of Political Motherhood," 670.

79 For this gendered analysis of Cathérine's diplomatic methods, consult Denis Crouzet, "'A Strong Desire to Be a Mother to All Your Subjects': A Rhetorical Experiment by Catherine de Medici," *Journal of Medieval and Early Modern Studies* 38 (2008): 103–18.

80 Doran, "Elizabeth I and Catherine de Medici," 132.

81 For a quick online biographical sketch, see: https://en.wikipedia.org/wiki/Marie_Antoinette.

82 Refer, in this connection, to: John Hardman, *Marie-Antoinette: The Making of a French Queen* (New Haven, CT: Yale University Press, 2019), esp. the Preface, xix–xx, and 309–10.

83 Consult, in this connection, Kaiser's review of Hardman's *Marie-Antoinette*, in *Journal of Modern History* 93 (2021): 705–7. Thanks also go to Professor Kaiser for allowing me to read his recent paper on this general subject entitled "Marie-Antoinette, a French Queen? Diplomacy and National Identity in an Age of Revolution."

84 Refer again, for this analysis of the Queen's early popularity, to Kaiser, "Who's Afraid of Marie-Antoinette? Diplomacy, Austrophobia and the Queen," esp. 249–51.

85 Ibid., 250–1.

86 This was an event delayed by the fact that—for reasons that specialists are still puzzling over today—the king was unable to consummate his marriage for seven years. Kaiser would additionally argue that this delay in sexual relations—and, hence, in the queen's maternity—created at the time some (invalid) doubts about her fidelity to her husband, and thus, in some circles, about her overall role as France's Queen Consort. I owe this commentary to Tom Kaiser (email exchange of July 23, 2022).

87 See Munro Price, *Preserving the Monarchy: the comte de Vergennes, 1774-1787* (Cambridge: Cambridge University Press, 1995), 24–6.

88 John Hardman, *Louis XVI* (New Haven, CT: Yale University Press, 1993), 128.

89 For this argument, see: Hardman and Price, eds., *Louis XVI and the comte de Vergennes: correspondence 1774–1787*, in *Studies on Voltaire and the Eighteenth Century* (Oxford: Oxford University Press, 1998), esp. 116–8 and 13. Kaiser critically assesses their argument in *Who's Afraid of Marie-Antoinette?* See pp. 254–5.

90 As quoted in Munro Price, *The Road from Versailles: Louis XVI, Marie Antoinette, and the Fall of the French Monarchy* (New York: St. Martin's Press, 2003), 9.

91 Quoted in ibid. from Mercy-Argenteau's secret correspondence with Joseph II and his foreign minister, Prince Anton von Kaunitz.

92 On Maria-Theresa's and Joseph II's generally low estimation of Marie-Antoinette's political abilities, refer again to Kaiser, "Who's Afraid of Marie-Antoinette?," 253. Kaunitz, for his part, was markedly contemptuous in some

of his (to be sure, confidential) comments on the Queen's supposed acumen in
political affairs.

93   Ibid., 254.

94   Ibid., 255. The queen was also damaged in this period, the latest research
indicates, by her compromising ties with the duchesse de Polignac and her
faction at court. On this point, see: Hardman, *Marie-Antoinette: The Making
of a French Queen*, passim.

95   Price, *The Road from Versailles*, 11.

96   A valuable additional source on all of this is: Kaiser, "From the Austrian
Committee to the Foreign Plot: Marie-Antoinette, Austrophobia, and
the Terror," *French Historical Studies* 26 (2003): 579–617. Still, French
statesmen (notably, Vergennes) were probably most concerned about huge,
inaccessible Russia's waxing ambitions from the Baltic Sea to the Balkans.
As Hardman and Price reaffirm (in *Louis XVI and the comte de Vergennes*,
122): "The unavoidable fact of Russian expansion and the steep decline of
French influence were the major eastern European issues that Louis XVI and
Vergennes had to face after 1774." For a similar view, see: Brendan Simms,
Europe: The Struggle for Supremacy, From 1453 to the Present (New York:
Basic Books, 2014), esp. 123–5 and 134–6.

97   The classic study here is: Jean Egret, *The French Prerevolution, 1787-1788*,
trans. Wesley D. Camp (Chicago, IL: The University of Chicago Press, 1977).

98   As cited in Price, *The Road From Versailles*, 29–30. Hardman has recently
endorsed this reading of Louis XVI's mental prostration resulting from these
ministerial setbacks in 1787–88. Hardman, *Marie-Antoinette: The Making of
a French Queen*, 138–9.

99   Kaiser, "From Fiscal Crisis to Revolution: The Court and French Foreign
Policy, 1787-1789," in Kaiser and Van Kley, eds., *From Deficit to Deluge: The
Origins of the French Revolution*. Citation is from p. 30.

100   On all of this, see: Hardman, *Louis XVI*, 149–53; Price, "The 'Ministry of
the Hundred Hours': A Reappraisal," *French History* 4 (1990): 317–39;
and Bailey Stone, "23 June 1789: The Most Crucial Day in the French
Revolution?," Paper Presented at the French Historical Studies in Texas
Meeting, University of Houston, February 23, 2002.

101   Price, *The Road From Versailles*, 59.

102   Ibid., 66. A similar in-depth analysis of the pertinent issues treated at this
séance royale of June 23, 1789, is offered by Stone, *Reinterpreting the French
Revolution*, 82–5.

103   For this damning language, see Hardman, *Marie-Antoinette: The Making of
a French Queen*, 203–4. One of the best modern monographs on the ill-fated
"flight to Varennes" is: Timothy A. Tackett, *When the King Took Flight*
(Cambridge, MA: Harvard University Press, 2003).

104   Citations from Price, *The Road From Versailles*, 210. Hardman
(questionably) has seen the queen's contacts in 1791 with A. P. J. Barnave
in the Legislative Assembly as potentially yielding some sort of compromise

between the royalists and the revolutionaries. Hardman, *Marie-Antoinette: The Making of a French Queen*, 309–10.

105 Price, *The Road From Versailles*, 292 and 293–4.

106 Antonia Fraser, *Marie-Antoinette: The Journey* (New York: Doubleday, 2001), 414. See also Evelyne Lever, *Marie-Antoinette: The Last Queen of France*, trans. Catherine Temerson (New York: Farrar, Straus and Giroux, 1991), esp. 299–302, for a readable (if not exhaustively researched) account of all of this.

107 On this event, refer again to Fraser, *Marie-Antoinette: The Journey*, 424–5. Consult also, in this connection, Kaiser, "From the Austrian Committee to the Foreign Plot," 600.

108 As discussed by Robert R. Palmer, *Twelve Who Ruled: The Year of the Terror in the French Revolution* (Princeton, NJ: Princeton University Press, 1941), 53.

109 As discussed by Fraser, *Marie-Antoinette: The Journey*, 435; and by Kaiser, "From the Austrian Committee to the Foreign Plot," 601–2.

110 Again, refer to Kaiser, "Marie-Antoinette, A French Queen?," esp. 6–9. On the issue of French nationalism in its old regime and revolutionary contexts, refer also to David A. Bell, *The Cult of the Nation in France: Inventing Nationalism, 1680–1800* (Cambridge: Cambridge University Press, 2001).

111 Consult once again the references to their works, detailed in footnote 1.

112 Colwill, "Just Another Citoyenne? Marie-Antoinette on Trial, 1790–1793," 74 and 80.

113 Hunt, *The Family Romance of the French Revolution*, 114, 121–3. Hunt (and other feminists) review specific aspects of this general interpretation: see their essays in Hunt, ed., *Eroticism and the Body Politic* (Baltimore, MD: Johns Hopkins University Press, 1991). Yet Hunt's *Family Romance* has itself been sharply criticized by some of her (feminist) colleagues. Consult, for example, Dorinda Outram's review in *American Historical Review* 98 (1993): 882–3.

114 Colwill, "Just Another Citoyenne? Marie-Antoinette on Trial, 1790–1793," 75.

115 Dena Goodman, "Public Sphere and Private Life: Towards a Synthesis of Current Historiographical Approaches to the Old Regime," *History Theory* 31 (1992): 1–20.

116 Sarah Hanley, "Engendering the State: Family Formation and State Building in Early Modern France," *French Historical Studies* 16 (1989): 4–27.

117 Refer again, in this connection, to Kaiser, "From the Austrian Committee to the Foreign Plot," esp. 603–5.

118 For basic biographical information on Catherine, see: Isabel de Madariaga, *Catherine the Great: A Short History* (New Haven, CT: Yale University Press, 1993), 1–2; and Simon Dixon, *Catherine the Great* (New York: HarperCollins, 2009), "Prologue: The Coronation of a Usurper."

119 Catherine's change of name not only answered to the political demands of the moment—quite urgent in 1762—but also reflected her (at first extremely reluctant) exchange of German Protestantism for Russian Orthodoxy.

120 See, on all of this: David L. Ransel, *The Politics of Catherinian Russia: The Panin Party* (New Haven, CT: Yale University Press, 1975), esp. 1–7, 278, and 288.

121 Refer, for this, to: John P. LeDonne, *Ruling Russia: Politics and Administration in the Age of Absolutism, 1762–1796* (Princeton, NJ: Princeton University Press, 1984), esp. 344–53. See also, by the same author: *Absolutism and Ruling Class: The Formation of the Russian Political Order, 1700–1825* (New York: Oxford University Press, 1994).

122 Paul Dukes, *Catherine the Great and the Russian Nobility: A Study Based on the Materials of the Legislative Commission of 1767* (Cambridge: Cambridge University Press, 1968), 248–9. Other studies of the 1775 and 1785 legislation include: Robert E. Jones, *The Emancipation of the Russian Nobility 1762–1785* (Princeton, NJ: Princeton University Press, 1973); and Dixon, *The Modernisation of Russia, 1676–1825* (Cambridge: Cambridge University Press, 1999), ch. 4.

123 Robert E. Jones, "Runaway Peasants and Russian Motives for the Partitions of Poland," in *Imperial Russian Foreign Policy*, ed. Hugh Ragsdale (New York: Cambridge University Press, 1993). Citation is from p. 106.

124 Cited in M. S. Anderson, *Europe in the Eighteenth Century 1713–1783* (New York: Holt, Rinehart & Winston, Inc., 1961), 166. An updated treatment of all of this is: E. V. Anisimov, "The Imperial Heritage of Peter the Great in the Foreign Policy of his Early Successors," in Ragsdale, ed., *Imperial Russian Foreign Policy*, 21–35.

125 Ibid., 30–1. Madariaga also emphasizes the significance of the 1726 Russo-Austrian alliance in *Catherine the Great*, 11–2.

126 For background on the 1740–8 struggle, see Reed S. Browning, *The War of the Austrian Succession* (New York: St. Martin's Press, 1993).

127 Madariaga, *Catherine the Great*, 12. See also, on this subject: Simms, *Europe: The Struggle for Supremacy, 1453-Present*, 115; and Ragsdale, "Russian Projects of Conquest in the Eighteenth Century," in Ragsdale, ed., *Imperial Russian Foreign Policy*, 75–102.

128 Refer again to Madariaga, *Catherine the Great*, 1–3.

129 John P. LeDonne, *The Russian Empire and the World, 1700–1917: The Geopolitics of Expansionism and Containment* (New York: Oxford University Press, 1997), 239–40. Ludwig Dehio had anticipated this analysis in *The Precarious Balance: Four Centuries of the European Power Struggle*, trans. Charles Fullman (New York: Alfred A. Knopf, 1982).

130 Jones, "Runaway Peasants and Russian Motives for the Partitions of Poland," 106.

131 As cited in Simms, *Europe: The Struggle for Supremacy*, 124. On the First Polish Partition in general, see: Jones, "Runaway Peasants and Russian

Motives for the Partitions of Poland," 103–16; and Herbert H. Kaplan, *The First Partition of Poland* (New York: Columbia University Press, 1962).

132   Cited in D. B. Horn, *British Public Opinion and the First Partition of Poland* (Edinburgh: Oliver and Boyd, 1945), 26 and 36–7.

133   Simms, *Europe: The Struggle for Supremacy*, 149–50. The agony of eighteenth-century Poland is studied in depth by Jerzy Lukowski, *Liberty's Folly. The Polish-Lithuanian Commonwealth in the Eighteenth Century, 1697-1795* (London and New York: Routledge, 1991).

134   Anderson, *Europe in the Eighteenth Century*, 191–2.

135   As cited in Simms, *Europe: The Struggle for Supremacy*, 132–3.

136   T. C. W. Blanning, *The Origins of the French Revolutionary Wars* (London: Longman, 1986), 56–7.

137   Hugh Ragsdale, "Russian Projects of Conquest in the Eighteenth Century," in Ragsdale, ed., *Imperial Russian Foreign Policy*, 82.

138   Simms, *Europe: The Struggle for Supremacy*, 124–5. That Kutchuk-Kainardji alarmed French as well as Prussian and Austrian statesmen is emphasized by H. M. Scott, "The Importance of Bourbon Naval Reconstruction to the Strategy of Choiseul after the Seven Years' War," *International History Review* 1 (1979): 17–35.

139   On Catherine's so-called "Greek Project," see also Ragsdale, "Evaluating the Traditions of Russian Aggression: Catherine II and the Greek Project," *Slavonic and East European Review* 66 (1988): 91–117. Joseph II's coolness toward the whole concept stemmed largely from his concerns about Prussian machinations in central Europe. Karl A. Roider, Jr., *Austria's Eastern Question 1700–1790* (Princeton, NJ: Princeton University Press, 1982), 155ff. Eventually, however, his desire to maintain good ties with Russia—and thus to work for Prussia's isolation—won him over.

140   Ragsdale, "Russian Projects of Conquest in the Eighteenth Century," 97–8, 100.

141   A classic study of this subject is: Isabel de Madariaga, *Britain, Russia, and the Armed Neutrality of 1780* (New Haven, CT: Yale University Press, 1962).

142   Cited in Hans Bagger, "The Role of the Baltic in Russian Foreign Policy, 1721-1773," in Ragsdale, ed., *Imperial Russian Foreign Policy*, esp. 59–60.

143   Cited in Brenda Meehan-Waters, "Catherine the Great and the Problem of Female Rule," *Russian Review* 34 (1975): 293–307. Specific citation is from p. 293.

144   Ibid., 294.

145   For these citations, again, refer to ibid., 294–5, as well as to R. J. White, *Europe in the Eighteenth Century* (New York: St. Martin's Press, 1965), 192; and to Madariaga, *Catherine the Great*, esp. 205–6.

146   Ibid., 216. More recent treatments of this aspect of Catherine's life include: Virginia Rounding, *Catherine the Great: Love, Sex, and Power* (London:

Hutchinson, 2006); and Simon S. Montefiore, *Catherine the Great and Potemkin: The Imperial Love Affair* (London: Orion, 2010).

147 Nicholas V. Riasanovsky and Mark D. Steinberg, *A History of Russia*, 8th ed. (New York: Oxford University Press, 2011), 254–5.

148 Richard Wortman, *Scenarios of Power: Myth and Ceremony in the Russian Monarchy from Peter the Great to the Abdication of Nicholas II* (Princeton, NJ: Princeton University Press, 2006), 53. See also Dixon, *Catherine the Great*, 176–7, for examples of images associating Minerva, "the warlike goddess of wisdom," with Catherine II.

149 On this point, consult Gary Marker, *Imperial Saint: The Cult of St. Catherine and the Dawn of Female Rule in Russia* (DeKalb, IL: Northern Illinois University Press, 2007), esp. 221–5.

150 Citations from Madariaga, *Catherine the Great*, 205.

151 For basic biographical details on Alexandra Feodorovna, see: Orlando Figes, *A People's Tragedy: The Russian Revolution, 1891–1924* (New York: Penguin Books, 1996), 24–7; and M. D. Steinberg and V. M. Khrustalev, *The Fall of the Romanovs: Political Dreams and Personal Struggles in a Time of Revolution* (New Haven, CT: Yale University Press, 1995), esp. the Introduction. A much older, but more intimate, source on the empress is: Pierre Gilliard, *Thirteen Years at the Russian Court*, trans. F. Appleby Holt (New York: Doran, 1921).

152 Alexandra knew German from childhood and Russian fairly well, yet spoke and wrote more naturally, especially in the confines of family life, in English. Steinberg and Khrustalev, *The Fall of the Romanovs*, 27–9.

153 Andrew M. Verner, *The Crisis of Russian Autocracy: Nicholas II and the 1905 Revolution* (Princeton, NJ: Princeton University Press, 1990), 33–4.

154 Wortman, *Scenarios of Power*, 328–33. An equally penetrating analysis of the imperial marriage—and of its dire implications for the reign—comes to us (in strikingly similar terms) from Steinberg and Khrustalev, *The Fall of the Romanovs*, "Introduction: Nicholas and Alexandra, An Intellectual Portrait."

155 Verner, *The Crisis of Russian Autocracy*, 35–6.

156 For this correspondence, see: Gilliard, *Thirteen Years at the Russian Court*, 50 and 83; and Figes, *A People's Tragedy*, 26.

157 Cited in Verner, *The Crisis of Russian Autocracy*, 146–7.

158 Gilliard, *Thirteen Years at the Russian Court*, 54–5. A *staretz*, in the Russian Orthodox tradition, was a sort of ascetic "holy man" usually (but not invariably) associated with a specific monastery.

159 Orlando Figes describes the ill-omened celebrations of 1913 in *A People's Tragedy*, ch. 1. But see also Wortman, "Invisible Threads: The Historical Imagery of the Romanov Tercentenary," *Russian History* 16 (1989), esp. 392–98.

160 A solid study of Russia's role in the coming of the war is: D. C. B. Lieven, *Russia and the Origins of the First World War* (London: Macmillan, 1983). But also see David M. McDonald, "A Lever without a fulcrum: domestic

factors and Russian foreign policy, 1905–1914," in Ragsdale, ed., *Imperial Russian Foreign Policy*, 268–311.

161 Cited in Figes, *A People's Tragedy*, 171–3; and Verner, *The Crisis of Russian Autocracy*, 124.

162 Cited in Abraham Ascher, *P. A. Stolypin: The Search for Stability in Late Imperial Russia* (Stanford, CA: Stanford University Press, 2001), 355. Alexandra had especially hated Stolypin for his opposition to Rasputin. See Bernard Pares, *The Fall of the Russian Monarchy: A Study of the Evidence* (New York: Alfred Knopf, 1939), 142–3.

163 Pares, "Rasputin and the Empress: Authors of the Russian Collapse," *Foreign Affairs* 6 (1927): 22–3.

164 As quoted in Figes, *A People's Tragedy*, 278.

165 Ibid.

166 The words, here, of Pares, "Rasputin and the Empress," 23–4.

167 Two updated treatments of the subject are: Helen Rappaport, *The Last Days of the Romanovs: Tragedy at Ekaterinburg* (New York: St. Martin's Press, 2008); and Bailey Stone, *Rethinking Revolutionary Change in Europe: A Neostructuralist Approach* (Lanham, MD: Rowman & Littlefield, 2020), esp. ch. 3.

168 Steinberg and Khrustalev, *The Fall of the Romanovs*, 27–8. Interestingly, the Imperial tutor Pierre Gilliard also speaks (from *very* close quarters) of Alexandra's apparently incurable Germanophobia in *Thirteen Years at the Russian Court*, esp. 109–10.

169 Citations from Rappaport, *The Race to Save the Romanovs* (New York: St. Martin's Press, 2018), 168–9.

170 Rex A. Wade, *The Russian Revolution. 1917* (Cambridge: Cambridge University Press, 2000), 22.

171 Ibid. See also, on Miliukov's role in all of this: Melissa K. Stockdale, *Paul Miliukov and the Quest for a Liberal Russia* (Ithaca, NY: Cornell University Press, 1996), passim.

172 Orlando Figes and Boris Kolonitskii, *Interpreting the Russian Revolution: The Language and Symbols of 1917* (New Haven, CT: Yale University Press, 1999), 158–64. Figes enlarges upon all of this in *A People's Tragedy*, 284–5.

173 Wortman, *Scenarios of Power*, 330. My emphasis.

174 For this analysis: Figes and Kolonitskii, *Interpreting the Russian Revolution*, 13–17, and 24; and Steinberg and Khrustalev, *The Fall of the Romanovs*, 15 and 30. On attitudes in the army, see also Alan K. Wildman, *The End of the Russian Imperial Army: The Old Army and the Soldiers' Revolt (March–April 1917)* (Princeton, NJ: Princeton University Press, 1980), 110–15; and David R. Jones, "Imperial Russia's Forces at War," in *Military Effectiveness I: The First World War*, ed. Allan Millett and Williamson Murray (Boston, MA: Allen and Unwin, 1988), esp. 284–5.

Chapter 4

1 Richard Stites, *The Women's Liberation Movement in Russia: Feminism, Nihilism, and Bolshevism, 1860–1930*, 1st ed. (Princeton, NJ: Princeton University Press, 1978), 417. See also his subsequent study: *Revolutionary Dreams: Utopian Vision and Experimental Life in the Russian Revolution* (New York: Oxford University Press, 1989).

2 Barbara E. Clements, *Bolshevik Women* (Cambridge: Cambridge University Press, 1997), 18–20.

3 Rochelle G. Ruthchild, "Women and Gender in 1917," *Slavic Review* 76 (2017): 698. Ruthchild had made this same point already in *Equality and Revolution: Women's Rights in the Russian Empire, 1905–1917* (Pittsburgh, PA: University of Pittsburgh Press, 2010). So (subsequently) has Adele Lindenmeyr, in "Writing Women into the Russian Revolution of 1917," *Journal of Modern Russian History and Historiography* 13 (2020): 214–31.

4 Clements, *Bolshevik Women*, 20.

5 Cited from: www.merriam-webster.com/words-at-play/intersectionality--meaning. In our discussions of England, France, and Russia, *race* (*ethnos*) becomes—potentially—a major element in intersectionality most notably in the case of tsarist Russia, where non-Russians constituted nearly 50 percent of the overall population. Here I adopt Melissa K. Stockdale's distinction between *rossiiskie zhenshchiny* (female subjects of the Empire) and *russkie zhenshchiny* (Great Russian women) and focus on the latter. Refer to Stockdale, "'My Death for the Motherland is Happiness': Women, Patriotism, and Soldiering in Russia's Great War, 1914–1917," *American Historical Review* 109 (2004): 80, n. 5. The concentration in most of the literature on "Great Russian women" has necessitated this approach.

6 *American College Dictionary* (New York: Harper and Brothers, 1950), 1181. My emphasis here.

7 Christopher Durston, *The Family in the English Revolution* (Oxford: Basil Blackwell, 1989), 13.

8 Christopher Hill, *The World Turned Upside Down: Radical Ideas During the English Revolution* (Baltimore, MD: Penguin Books, 1972), 306–7, 308, 310.

9 Lawrence Stone, *The Family, Sex and Marriage in England 1500–1800* (New York: Harper & Row, 1977), 240 and 262.

10 Keith Thomas, "Women and the Civil War Sects," *Past and Present* 13 (1958): 42–6. Reprinted in Trevor Aston, ed., *Crisis in Europe 1560–1660* (London: Routledge & Kegan Paul, 1965), esp. (for this citation) 318–9.

11 Margaret George, *Women in the First Capitalist Society: Experiences in Seventeenth-Century England* (Urbana, IL: University of Illinois Press, 1988), 5.

12 Stevie Davies, *Unbridled Spirits: Women of the English Revolution, 1640–1660* (London: Women's Press, 1998), 18 and 16–17.

13 Antonia Fraser, *The Weaker Vessel: Women's Lot in Seventeenth-Century England* (London: Weidenfeld and Nicholson, 1984), 5. Refer also, on this issue, to Davies, *Unbridled Spirits*, 18.

14 Hill, *The World Turned Upside Down*, 308.

15 On women's rights in divorce proceedings, and on their rights in general: see Durston, *The Family in the English Revolution*, 18–20 and 173. Note how Durston—like so many historians of this period—has cast *social* affairs in *constitutional* terms. John Milton (betraying in this his own domestic difficulties) famously initiated a call for the liberalization of English divorce laws as early as 1643.

16 Diane Purkiss, *The English Civil War: A People's History* (London: HarperPress, 2006), esp. 507. Purkiss also discerns literary reflections of such civil war experiences in: *Literature, Gender and Politics During the English Civil War* (Cambridge: Cambridge University Press, 2005). See also Melissa Mowry, *Collective Understanding, Radicalism, and Literary History, 1645–1742* (Oxford: Oxford University Press, 2021) for other thoughts on this subject.

17 Lawrence Stone, *Causes of the English Revolution 1529–1642* (London: Routledge, 1972), 66 and 137. See also, from earlier days: F. S. Siebert, *Freedom of the Press in England, 1476–1776* (Urbana, IL: University of Illinois Press, 1965) and H. S. Bennett, *English Books and Readers, 1558–1603* (Cambridge: Cambridge University Press, 1965).

18 Davies, *Unbridled Spirits*, 25–6.

19 Patricia Crawford, *Women and Religion in England 1500–1720* (London: Routledge, 1993), 132–3. Chidley's association with the Leveller cause is also explored in S. L. Arnoult, "The Sovereignties of Body and Soul: Women's Political and Religious Actions in the English Civil War," in *Women and Sovereignty*, ed. Louise Olga Fradenburg (Edinburgh: Edinburgh University Press, 1992), esp. 237–9.

20 Davies, *Unbridled Spirits*, 25–6.

21 Arnoult, "The Sovereignties of Body and Soul," 233–4. Insofar as religious issues were concerned, Arnoult writes, female (and some male) petitioners had been besieging the Parliament to demand the "suppression of the bishops and reform of the church." For a pioneering (if, unavoidably, severely dated) discussion of these women, and of those petitioners who came after them in the late 1640s, consult: Ellen McArthur, "Women Petitioners and the Long Parliament," *English Historical Review* 24 (1909): 698–709.

22 Crawford, "'The Poorest She': Women and Citizenship in Early Modern England," in *The Putney Debates of 1647: The Army, the Levellers and the English State*, ed. Michael Mendel (Cambridge: Cambridge University Press, 2001), esp. 211–3.

23 Arnoult, "The Sovereignties of Body and Soul," 239.

24 Citation is from Crawford, "'The Poorest She': Women and Citizenship in Early Modern England," 210. This oft-quoted petition (and earlier

pronunciamentos of September 11, 1648, and April 25, 1649) can also be found in Purkiss, *The English Civil War: A People's History*, 507–9. See also the analysis of these petitions in: Patricia Higgins, "The Reactions of Women, with Special Reference to Women Petitioners," in *Politics, Religion, and the English Civil War*, ed. Brian Manning (London: E. J. Arnold, 1973), 190–217.

25 Cited in Crawford, "'The Poorest She': Women and Citizenship in Early Modern England," 210.

26 Higgins, "The Reactions of Women," 209, 218, and 221–2.

27 Ann Hughes, "Gender and Politics in Leveller Literature," in *Political Culture and Cultural Politics in Early Modern Europe*, ed. Susan D. Amussen and Mark A. Kishlansky (Manchester: University of Manchester Press, 1995), 174–5 and 176–7. Hughes has subsequently put such gendered issues (i.e., involving women) in a broader revolutionary context: see Hughes, *Gender and the English Revolution* (London: Routledge, 2012), passim.

28 Brian Manning, *Aristocrats, Plebeians and Revolution in England, 1640–1660* (London: Pluto Press, 1996), 115. Tellingly, too, the women canvassing for signatures for the April 1649 petition discovered that, even in the supposedly most "progressive" sectarian churches, "it [i.e., the petition] was disputed."

29 Crawford, "'The Poorest She': Women and Citizenship in Modern England," 216.

30 See, for example: Rachel Foxley, *The Levellers: Radical Political Thought in the English Revolution* (Manchester: Manchester University Press, 2013); Jonathan Rees, *The Leveller Revolution: Radical Political Organisation in England, 1640–1660* (London: Verso Books, 2016); Gary S. DeKrey, *Following the Levellers: English Political and Religious Radicals from the Commonwealth to the Glorious Revolution, 1649–1688* (London: Palgrave Macmillan, 2018); and Michael Braddick, *The Common Freedom of the People: John Lilburne and the English Revolution* (Oxford: Oxford University Press, 2018). For a discussion of the earlier literature on the Levellers, consult Bailey Stone, *The Anatomy of Revolution Revisited: A Comparative Analysis of England, France, and Russia* (New York: Cambridge University Press, 2014), 294, n. 91.

31 Refer, for all of this, to: G. E. Aylmer, ed., *The Levellers in the English Revolution* (Ithaca, NY: Cornell University Press, 1975), esp. the Introduction, 9–55.

32 Arnoult, "Sovereignties of Body and Soul," 236–8.

33 Cited in Durston, *The Family in the English Revolution*, 15.

34 Quoted in Ibid., 102.

35 See Braddick, *The Common Freedom of the People: John Lilburne and the English Revolution*, 232, 281, and 298. A somewhat more sympathetic (if rather dated) portrayal of Lilburne is that of Pauline Gregg: *Free-Born John: A Biography of John Lilburne* (London: Harrap, 1961).

36 Refer, for this extended analysis, to Hughes, "Gender and Politics in Leveller Literature," esp. 170–1 and 181–2. See also, on gender and masculinity in Stuart England, the following: Anthony Fletcher, *Gender, Sex and Subordination in Early Modern England* (New Haven, CT: Yale University Press, 1996); and Elizabeth A. Foyster, *Manhood in Early Modern England: Honour, Sex and Marriage* (London: Longman, 1999).

37 On the Putney debates of 1647, refer again to the various essays in Michael Mendel, ed., *The Putney Debates of 1647: The Army, the Levellers and the English State*; and also see Samuel Dennis Glover, "The Putney Debates: Popular versus Elite Republicanism," *Past and Present* 164 (1999): 47–80. The Putney Debates had already been reassessed and contextualized masterfully by Austin Woolrych in *Soldiers and Statesmen: The General Council of the Army and Its Debates, 1647–48* (Oxford: Clarendon Press, 1987).

38 Purkiss, *The English Civil War: A People's History*, 506–9.

39 Thomas, "Women and the Civil War Sects," 319–20.

40 Ibid., 320–1.

41 Crawford, *Women and Religion in England 1500–1720*, 129–30. In an aside, Crawford also rhetorically (and somewhat ironically?) comments: "How much freedom women [actually] found in the sects is to be considered."

42 All of this is derived from Thomas, "Women and the Civil War Sects," 320–1 and 323–4.

43 For the Elizabeth Poole incident, see Fraser, *The Weaker Vessel*, 253–4. According to Patricia Crawford (in *Women and Religion 1500–1720*, 135), Poole urged the Grandees to "bring Charles I to trial but spare his life."

44 See, on these (and comparable) individuals, Purkiss, *The English Civil War: A People's History*, 468–9; and Durston, *The Family in the English Revolution*, 19 and 97.

45 Theresa Feroli, *Political Speaking Justified: Women Prophets and the English Revolution* (Newark, NJ: University of Delaware Press, 2006), esp. 15–16, 23, and 32. According to Feroli, both women had been incarcerated by the (Roman?) Inquisition on the Island of Malta from 1658 to 1662.

46 Phyllis Mack, *Visionary Women: Ecstatic Prophecy in Seventeenth-Century England* (Berkeley, CA: University of California Press, 1992), esp. 122–4 and 412. Most of Mack's book (Parts II and III, Chapters 4 – 10) is in fact devoted to the question of women's participation in the Quaker movement *after* the English Revolution.

47 Crawford, *Women and Religion in England 1500–1720*, 179–80 and 182.

48 Fraser, *The Weaker Vessel*, 263–4. As Fraser points out, some of the wildest public disturbances that gave so much notoriety to the "Quaker" movement were associated with the enthusiast and preacher James Naylor. Incidentally, Keith Thomas had anticipated much of the more recent feminist commentary on these issues back in 1958 when he averred that "the more exotic and extravagant of these female prophets and preachers only served to do harm to their own cause, since for most people they illuminated by contrast the virtues of the Marthas who stayed at home." Thomas, "Women and the Civil War Sects," 338–9.

49 Fraser, *The Weaker Vessel,* 263.

50 Crawford, *Women and Religion in England 1500–1720,* 139.

51 This situation is taken up in Davies, *Unbridled Spirits: Women of the English Revolution,* 26–7. See also Mack, *Ecstatic Prophecy,* 122–4, for further discussion of John Roger's ambivalence on these issues.

52 Arnoult, "The Sovereignties of Body and Soul," 242.

53 Ibid.

54 Crawford, "'The Poorest She': Women and Citizenship in Early Modern England," 213–5.

55 Katharine Gillespie, *Domesticity and Dissent in the Seventeenth Century: English Women Writers and the Public Sphere* (Cambridge: Cambridge University Press, 2004), esp. the book's frontispiece and 262. Keith Thomas had in his own way anticipated something of this analysis in "Women and the Civil War Sects," esp. 338–9.

56 Refer, in this connection, to: Paul Ourliac and J. de Malafosse, *Le Droit Familial,* vol. 3 of *Histoire du droit privé* (Paris: Presses Universitaires de France, 1968), esp. 126–59; Marcel Garaud and Romuald Szramkiewicz, *La Révolution française et la famille* (Paris: P. U. F., 1978), esp. 167–76; and J. F. Traer, *Marriage and the Family in Eighteenth-Century France* (Ithaca, NY: Cornell University Press, 1980).

57 Ibid., esp. 139–40.

58 James F. McMillan, *France and Women, 1789–1914: Gender, Society, and Politics* (London: Routledge, 2002).

59 Ibid., esp. 4–8 and 14. James Traer, in *Marriage and the Family in Eighteenth-Century France,* 78, had previously interpreted the Enlightenment's intellectual legacy for women in rather more positive terms.

60 Prominent works in this interpretative vein include: Joan Landes, *Women and the Public Sphere in the Age of the French Revolution* (Ithaca, NY: Cornell University Press, 1987); Madelyn Gutwirth, *The Twilight of the Goddesses: Women and Representation in the French Revolutionary Era* (New Brunswick, NJ: Rutgers University Press, 1992); and Lynn A. Hunt, *The Family Romance of the French Revolution* (Berkeley, CA: University of California Press, 1992).

61 Sarah Hanley, "Engendering the State: Family Formation and State Building in Early Modern France," *French Historical Studies* 16 (1989): 4–27.

62 Dena Goodman, "Public Sphere and Private Life: Towards a Synthesis of Current Historiographical Approaches to the Old Regime," *History and Theory* 31 (1992): 1–20.

63 Olwen Hufton, *Women and the Limits of Citizenship in the French Revolution* (Toronto: University of Toronto Press, 1992), xvii–xviii. See

also, on the twists and turns in this historiography: S. Tomaselli, "The Enlightenment Debate on Women," *History Workshop* 20 (1985): 101–25.

64 On the issue of the salons and their *salonnières*, see: Dena Goodman, "Enlightenment Salons: The Convergence of Female and Philosophic Ambitions," *Eighteenth-Century Studies* 22 (1989): 329–50; her follow-up conspectus *The Republic of Letters. A Cultural History of the French Enlightenment* (Ithaca, NY: Cornell University Press, 1994); and, more generally, Dorinda Outram, *The Enlightenment* (Cambridge: Cambridge University Press, 1995), esp. ch. 6.

65 This cursory discussion of Frenchwomen's activism in prerevolutionary France is drawn from McMillan, *France and Women, 1789–1914*, 20–25. But see also the essays in Harriet B. Applewhite and Darline G. Levy, eds., *Women and Politics in the Age of the Democratic Revolution* (Ann Arbor, MI: University of Michigan Press, 1990).

66 Refer, in this last connection, to: Cynthia Bouton, *The Flour War: Gender, Class, and Community in Late Ancien Régime French Society* (University Park, PA: Penn State University Press, 1993).

67 Hardy's commentary is cited in: Darline G. Levy, Harriet B. Applewhite, and Mary D. Johnson, eds., *Women in Revolutionary Paris 1789–1795* (Urbana, IL: University of Illinois Press, 1979), 34–5. But for October 1789 *in particular*, consult, quite recently, Suzanne Desan, "Gender, Radicalization, and the October Days: Occupying the National Assembly," *French Historical Studies* 43 (2020): 359–90.

68 This chronology of female activism is usefully summarized in McMillan, *France and Women, 1789–1914*, 20–5. Levy and Applewhite delve into the subject in much greater detail in: "A Political Revolution for Women? The Case of Paris," in *The French Revolution: Conflicting Interpretations*, ed. Frank A. Kafker, James M. Laux, and Darline G. Levy, 5th ed. (Malabar, FLA: Krieger, 2002), 317–46. Olwen Hufton had already broached the subject years earlier in "Women in Revolution, 1789–1796," *Past and Present* 53 (1971): 90–108.

69 Dominique Godineau, "Masculine and Feminine Political Practice during the French Revolution, 1793-Year III," in Applewhite and Levy, eds., *Women and Politics in the Age of the Democratic Revolution*, esp. 62–5.

70 Godineau, *The Women of Paris and Their French Revolution*, trans. Katherine Streip (Berkeley, CA: University of California Press, 1998), esp. 52–4.

71 Shirley E. Roessler, *Out of the Shadows: Women and Politics in the French Revolution* (New York: Peter Lang, 1996), 4 and 195–6. See also, along these lines, Sophie Mousset, *Women's Rights and the French Revolution* (New Brunswick, NJ: Transaction Publishers, 2007).

72 Godineau, "Masculine and Feminine Political Practice during the French Revolution," 65–6. Two classic works enlarging upon all these questions of *motivation* are: Albert Soboul, *Les Sans-culottes Parisiens en l'An II* (Paris:

Clavreuil, 1958); and Michel Vovelle, *La Mentalité Révolutionnaire: Société et Mentalité sous la Révolution française* (Paris: Messidor, 1985).

73 Roessler, *Out of the Shadows*, 4 and 195.

74 Hufton, *Women and the Limits of Citizenship in the French Revolution*, 22–3.

75 Consult once again Godineau, "Masculine and Feminine Political Practice during the French Revolution," 68–72. That radicalized women expected, like men, to be held accountable for transgressions against the Revolution is a point advanced by Jennifer N. Heuer, *The Family and the Nation: Gender and Citizenship in Revolutionary France, 1789–1830* (Ithaca, NY: Cornell University Press, 2005), 49–50. See also, in this connection, the evidence cited by Stephanie A. Brown, "Women on Trial: The Revolutionary Tribunal and Gender" (PhD diss., Stanford University, 1996).

76 Godineau, *The Women of Paris and Their French Revolution*, 367–8. Moreover, Katie Jarvis argues that the revolutionaries crafted *economic* (e.g., "useful work") as well as *masculinist* definitions of French citizenship. See *Politics in the Marketplace: Work, Gender, and Citizenship in Revolutionary France* (Oxford: Oxford University Press, 2019).

77 This paragraph's discussion is based on older works cited earlier (in n. 56) but also on: Traer, *Marriage and the Family in Eighteenth-Century France*, 67–8; and Heuer, *The Family and the Nation*, 27.

78 Traer, *Marriage and the Family in Eighteenth-Century France*, 67–8.

79 Consult Ibid., esp. 94–7, 103–4, and 120–36. Heuer also treats these issues in considerable detail, in *The Family and the Nation: Gender and Citizenship in Revolutionary France*. For a provincial "take" on divorce in these years, consult (among other monographs) Roderick Phillips, *Family Break-Down in Late Eighteenth-Century France: Divorces in Rouen, 1792–1803* (Oxford: Oxford University Press, 1981).

80 On all these issues—including the many problems encountered during the 1790s by the "family courts" in the country's provincial municipalities—consult, in addition, Isser Woloch, *The New Regime: Transformations of the French Civic Order, 1789–1820s* (New York: W. W. Norton, 1994), esp. 313–6 and 429.

81 Suzanne Desan, *The Family on Trial in Revolutionary France* (Berkeley, CA: University of California Press, 2004), esp. 68.

82 Ibid., 139–40.

83 For examples of this tendency in the historiography, refer to: Traer, *Marriage and the Family in Eighteenth- Century France*, 103–4; and especially Heuer, *The Family and the Nation*, 27 and 49–50. See also the essays in: Renée Waldinger, Philip Dawson, and Isser Woloch, eds., *The French Revolution and the Meaning of Citizenship* (Westport, CT: Greenwood Press, 1993).

84 On *provincial* Frenchwomen's clubbism and *sociabilité,* see: Martine Lapied, "La Place des femmes dans la sociabilité et la vie politique locale en Provence et dans le Comtat Venaissin pendant la Révolution," *Provence historique*

46 (1996): 83–93; and Laura Talamante, "Political Divisions, Gender, and Politics: The Case of Revolutionary Marseille," *French History* 31 (2017): 63–84.

85 These founding regulations for the Parisiennes are to be found in: Levy, Applewhite, and Johnson, eds., *Women in Revolutionary Paris 1789–1795*, 161.

86 Levy and Applewhite, "Women and Militant Citizenship in Revolutionary Paris," in *Rebel Daughters: Women and the French Revolution*, ed. Sara Melzer and Leslie Rabine (New York: Oxford University Press, 1992), 92–3.

87 Godineau, *The Women of Paris and Their French Revolution*, 121.

88 Desan, "'Constitutional Amazons': Jacobin Women's Clubs in the French Revolution," in *Re-Creating Authority in Revolutionary France*, ed. B. T. Ragin and E. A. Williams (New Brunswick, NJ: Rutgers University Press, 1992), esp. 12–14. Refer also, for additional information on this subject, to the provincial studies cited above (n. 84) by such noted scholars as Martine Lapied and Laura Talamante.

89 Hufton, *Women and the Limits of Citizenship in the French Revolution*, 25–6. Levy and Applewhite say much the same thing in "Women and Militant Citizenship in Revolutionary Paris," 92–3.

90 Ibid., 84. Refer also, on this subject, to Desan, "Gender, Radicalization, and the October Days," 359–90.

91 Amar was speaking on behalf of the Committee of General Security, one of the two most powerful Committees in the Revolutionary Government. As cited in Levy, Applewhite, and Johnson, eds., *Women in Revolutionary Paris 1789–1795*, 215–6.

92 As quoted in Levy and Applewhite, "Women and Militant Citizenship in Revolutionary Paris," 95–6.

93 Desan, "'Constitutional Amazons': Jacobin Women's Clubs in the French Revolution," esp. 30–1 and 34–5.

94 Refer again, in this connection, to the articles by Hanley and Goodman cited earlier, in notes 61 and 62.

95 Hufton, *Women and the Limits of Citizenship in the French Revolution*, esp. 25–6 and 37–9.

96 Godineau, *The Women of Paris and Their French Revolution*, 171–2.

97 Albert Soboul, *The Sans-Culottes: The Popular Movement and Revolutionary Government, 1793–1794*, trans. Rémy Inglis Hall (Princeton, NJ: Princeton University Press, 1980), 252. For additional insights on the popular mentality of the militants in France during the Year II, see: Richard Cobb, "The Revolutionary Mentality in France," *History* 42 (1957): 181–96; and Vovelle, *La Mentalité Révolutionnaire: Société et Mentalités sous la Révolution française*.

98 Godineau, *The Women of Paris and Their French Revolution*, 190–4.

99 The literature on this subject—and on the resultant weakness of the *burzhuaziia* in late Imperial Russia—is truly enormous, and has been reassessed quite recently in Bailey Stone, *Rethinking Revolutionary Change in Europe: A Neostructuralist Approach* (Lanham, MD: Rowman & Littlefield Publishers, 2020), esp. Ch. 2.

100 Refer, in this connection, to William Wagner, "The Trojan Mare. Women's Rights and Civil Rights in Late Imperial Russia," in *Civil Rights in Imperial Russia*, ed. Olga Crisp and Linda Edmondson (Oxford: Clarendon Press, 1989), 65–84. See also Wagner's larger conspectus on the subject: *Marriage, Property and Law in Late Imperial Russia* (Oxford: Clarendon Press, 1994).

101 Most of the foregoing is thoroughly discussed in Wagner, "The Trojan Mare," esp. 66–9. But for some of the historical background to all of this, see also Michelle L. Marrese, *A Woman's Kingdom: Noblewomen and the Control of Property in Russia, 1700–1861* (Ithaca, NY: Cornell University Press, 2002).

102 Again, see Wagner, "The Trojan Mare," 69 on the property question. Significantly, too, Marrese covers this in *A Woman's Kingdom*, esp. for earlier times during which state service tenure loomed large in Imperial affairs.

103 Wagner, "The Trojan Mare," 73 and 79–82. See also, on this subject, his *Marriage, Property and Law in Late Imperial Russia*, esp. ch. 4.

104 Orlando Figes, *A People's Tragedy: The Russian Revolution, 1891–1924* (New York: Penguin Books, 1996), 162–3.

105 See, on all of this: Gregory L. Freeze, "The Soslovie (Estate) Paradigm and Russian Social History," *American Historical Review* 91 (1986), esp. 35–36; Leopold H. Haimson, "The Problem of Social Identities in Early Twentieth-Century Russia," *Slavic Review* 47 (1988): 1–20; and Sheila Fitzpatrick, "Ascribing Class: The Construction of Social Identity in Soviet Russia," *Journal of Modern History* 65 (1993): 745–70.

106 Wagner, "The Trojan Mare," 74–5.

107 Linda H. Edmondson, "Women's Rights, Civil Rights, and the Debate over Citizenship in the 1905 Revolution," in *Women and Society in Russia and the Soviet Union*, ed. Linda H. Edmondson (Cambridge: Cambridge University Press, 1992), 77–100. For a broader perspective on this subject, consult also Linda H. Edmondson, *Feminism in Russia, 1900–1917* (Stanford, CA: Stanford University Press, 1984).

108 Edmondson, "Women's Rights, Civil Rights, and the Debate over Citizenship," 89.

109 For this controversy, see: Stites, *The Woman's Liberation Movement in Russia*, 203–5; Ruthchild, *Equality and Revolution*, 65–6; and Edmondson, "Women's Rights, Civil Rights, and the Debate over Citizenship," 91–2. "Judging from the testimonies of other women at the time," Ruthchild tells us, this debate "replicated in public the kinds of conversations and conflicts occurring in many homes."

110 Stites, *The Woman's Liberation Movement in Russia*, 213–4.

111 Engel, *Women in Russia, 1700–2000*, 122.

112 Ruthchild, *Equality and Revolution*, 192–4. For Ruthchild, this polarization helps enormously to explain why, among liberal politicians like Paul Miliukov, "there were no prominent opponents of women's suffrage" by the time a general war finally broke out in Europe in 1914.

113 Ibid., 193–4.

114 Refer, for instance, to: Alfred G. Meyer, "The Impact of World War I on Russian Women's Lives," in *Russia's Women: Accommodation, Resistance, Transformation*, ed. Barbara E. Clements, Barbara Engel, and Christine Worobec (Berkeley, CA: University of California Press, 1991), 208–24; and Melissa K. Stockdale, *Mobilizing the Russian Nation: Patriotism and Citizenship in the First World War* (Cambridge: Cambridge University Press, 2016). See also the excellent essays in Lindenmeyr and Stockdale, eds., *Women and Gender in Russia's Great War and Revolution, 1914–1922* (Bloomington, IN: Slavica, 2022).

115 On this last point, two modern studies by Laurie Stoff are especially useful: *They Fought for the Motherland: Russia's Women Soldiers in World War I and the Revolution* (Lawrence, KS: University Press of Kansas, 2006); and *Russia's Sisters of Mercy and the Great War: More Than Binding Men's Wounds* (Lawrence, KS: University Press of Kansas, 2015).

116 An early essay on the subject is: Richard Abraham, "Mariia L. Bochkareva and the Russian Amazons of 1917," in Edmondson, ed., *Women and Society in Russia and the Soviet Union*, 124–44. A very similar women's military organization sprang into being at Moscow at roughly the same time. Richard Stites had earlier touched upon the subject in *The Women's Liberation Movement in Russia*, 295–300.

117 Stockdale, "'My Death for the Motherland is Happiness,'" 111.

118 Stoff, *They Fought for the Motherland*, 204.

119 See notably, in this connection, Stoff's discussion in Ibid., 204–6 and 210.

120 Engel, *Women in Russia, 1700–2000*, 134–5.

121 Ruthchild, *Equality and Revolution*, 229–30. The feminist cause also received the powerful support of some nonparty Marxists like E. D. Kuskova, who strove throughout 1917 to bring all parties and factions in the country together in the cause of women's advancement. See Barbara T. Norton, "Laying the Foundations of Democracy in Russia: E. D. Kuskova's Contribution, February—October 1917," in Edmondson, ed., *Women and Society in Russia and the Soviet Union*, 101–23.

122 Stites, *The Women's Liberation Movement in Russia*, 295.

123 Ruthchild, "Women and Gender in 1917," esp. 698–702. For another feminist's revisionist "take" on the term "bourgeois feminism," see: Marilyn J. Boxer, "Rethinking the Socialist Construction and International Career of the Concept 'Bourgeois Feminism,'" *American Historical Review* 112 (2007): 131–58.

124 Stockdale, "My Death for the Motherland is Happiness," 97–8.

125   Engel, *Women in Russia, 1700–2000*, 135–7. The issue of the *soldatki* in 1917 is thoroughly explored by Sarah Badcock, "Women, Protest, and Revolution: Soldiers' Wives in Russia During 1917," *International Review of Social History* 49 (2004): 47–70.

126   As related by Stites, *The Women's Liberation Movement in Russia*, 294–5.

127   Norton, "Laying the Foundations of Democracy in Russia," 117–8. See also n. 121 above on E. D. Kuskova. Significantly, she was expelled from Soviet Russia by the Bolshiviks in 1922, and died in exile. See also Stites, *The Women's Liberation Movement in Russia*, 211, for further details concerning Kuskova's later years.

128   Refer to: William G. Rosenberg and Diane Koenker, "The Limits of Formal Protest: Workers' Activism and Social Polarization in Petrograd and Moscow, March to October, 1917," *American Historical Review* 92 (1987): 296–326. See also their follow-up study: *Strikes and Revolution in Russia, 1917* (Princeton, NJ: Princeton University Press, 1989).

129   Ruthchild, *Equality and Revolution*, 231–2.

130   Engel, *Women in Russia, 1700–2000*, 118–9. Consult also the pioneering study of Rose Glickman, *Russian Factory Women: Workplace and Society, 1880–1914* (Berkeley, CA: University of California Press, 1984).

131   Glickman's research here is cited and summarized in Engel, *Women in Russia, 1700-2000*, 119.

132   Anna Hillyar and Jane McDermid, *Revolutionary Women in Russia, 1870–1917: A Study in Collective Biography* (Manchester: Manchester University Press, 2000), 148.

133   Cited by Steve A. Smith, "Petrograd in 1917: The View from Below," in *The Workers' Revolution in Russia, 1917: The View from Below*, ed. Daniel Kaiser (New York: Cambridge University Press, 1987), 61.

134   Hillyar and McDermid, *Revolutionary Women in Russia, 1870-1917*, 148–50.

135   Ibid., 153–4.

136   Figes, *A People's Tragedy*, 462–4. Crucially, the revolution in the countryside, by largely annihilating the *dvorianstvo* (landed gentry), eliminated one of the last remaining military/administrative pillars of tsarist rule in Russia. See also, in this connection, the pioneering study of Jonathan L. H. Keep, *The Russian Revolution: A Study in Mass Mobilization* (New York: W. W. Norton, 1976), esp. the chapters on the peasantry.

137   As cited in Mark D. Steinberg, ed., *Voices of Revolution, 1917* (New Haven, CT: Yale University Press, 2001), 98.

138   Quoted in Ibid., 105–6.

139   Engel, *Women in Russia, 1700–2000*, 137.

140   Diane P. Koenker, "Moscow in 1917: The View from Below," in Kaiser, ed., *The Workers' Revolution in Russia, 1917*, 86–9. See also Diane Koenker's

larger monograph: *Moscow Workers and the 1917 Revolution* (Princeton, NJ: Princeton University Press, 1981).

141 Orlando Figes and Boris Kolonitskii, *Interpreting the Russian Revolution: The Language and Symbols of 1917* (New Haven, CT: Yale University Press, 1999), 110.

142 Hillyar and McDermid, *Revolutionary Women in Russia, 1870–1917*, 157–8. Two major studies dealing with Aleksandra Kollontai and her writings on class and gender issues are: Barbara E. Clements, *Bolshevik Feminist: The Life of Aleksandra Kollontai* (Bloomington, IN: Indiana University Press, 1979); and Beatrice Farnsworth, *Alexandra Kollontai: Socialism, Feminism, and the Bolshevik Revolution* (Stanford, CA: Stanford University Press, 1980).

143 Hillyar and McDermid, *Revolutionary Women in Russia, 1870–1917*, 154.

144 Wendy Z. Goldman, *Women, the State, and Revolution: Soviet Family Policy and Social Life, 1917–1936* (New York: Cambridge University Press, 1993), 51–2. Refer also to two earlier studies: Anne Bobroff, "The Bolsheviks and Working Women, 1905–1920," *Soviet Studies* 20 (1974): 540–67; and Gail W. Lapidus, *Women in Soviet Society: Equality, Development, and Social Change* (Berkeley, CA: University of California Press, 1978).

145 Goldman, *Women, the State, and Revolution*, 53–6.

146 Refer, here, to: Lewis H. Siegelbaum, *Soviet State and Society Between Revolutions, 1918–1929* (New York: Cambridge University Press, 1992), esp. 149–50.

147 Sources on these developments include: Ralph C. Elwood, *Inessa Armand: Revolutionary and Feminist* (New York: Cambridge University Press, 1992); Clements, *Bolshevik Women* (Cambridge: Cambridge University Press, 1997); and Stites, *The Women's Liberation Movement in Russia*, esp. 336–8.

148 Lapidus, *Women in Soviet Society*, 50–3. See also, on this subject: Clements, "Working-Class and Peasant Women in the Russian Revolution, 1917–1923," *Signs: Journal of Women in Culture and Society* 8 (1982): 215–35; and the long essay on the Russian peasantry by Orlando Figes in Esther Kingston-Mann and Timothy Mixter, eds., *Peasant Economy, Culture, and Politics of European Russia, 1800–1921* (Princeton, NJ: Princeton University Press, 1991).

149 Lapidus, *Women in Soviet Society*, 50–3. The emphasis here is mine.

150 Consult Elizabeth Wood, *The Baba and the Comrade: Gender and Politics in Revolutionary Russia* (Bloomington, IN: Indiana University Press, 1997), esp. 216–8.

151 Clements, *Bolshevik Women*, 18–20.

Chapter 5

1   Refer to Chapter 1, 46–7. For Moghadam's categorization of revolutions, consult once again her 1997 article, "Gender and Revolutions," in *Theorizing Revolutions*, ed. John Foran (London: Routledge, 1997), esp. 143–4 and 152.

2   Cited in Clements, *Bolshevik Women* (Cambridge: Cambridge University Press, 1997), 20.

3   Charles Tilly, *The Vendée*. New Ed. (Cambridge, MA: Harvard University Press, 1976). Cited from the Preface. Elaborating on this insight, Tilly had explained how France's revolutionary leaders "made the unprecedented step of extending the purview of the national government to everyday life at the local scale," and had added that "the substitution of direct for indirect local rule has happened many times and in many places since 1789." How well such a comment would apply (and in such an extreme fashion) to the revolutionary situation in early twentieth-century Russia!

4   *Recusancy*, in this context, refers to those seventeenth-century Englishwomen who (usually, if not always, due to their Catholic faith) rejected the established Anglican service and communion.

5   Refer once again to Chapter 3, 135–9, for a condensed discussion of this subject.

6   Cited in Ann Hughes, *The Causes of the English Civil War*, 2nd ed. (Basingstoke: Macmillan, 1998), 81, 88–90. But see also, on this subject: Robin Clifton, "The Popular Fear of Catholics During the English Revolution," *Past and Present* 52 (1971): 23–55; and Peter Lake, "Anti-Popery: The Structure of a Prejudice," in *Conflict in Early Stuart England: Studies in Religion and Politics 1603–1642*, ed. Richard Cust and Ann Hughes (London: Longman, 1989), 72–106.

7   Michelle Anne White, *Henrietta Maria and the English Civil Wars* (Aldershot: Ashgate, 2006), 33–4.

8   Ibid., 32–3.

9   See, on all these issues: Caroline Hibbard, *Charles I and the Popish Plot* (Chapel Hill, NC: University of North Carolina Press, 1983), esp. 225–6; Anthony Fletcher, *The Outbreak of the English Civil War* (New York: NYU Press, 1983), esp. 332–3; and Malcolm Smuts, "Religion, European Politics and Henrietta Maria's Circle, 1625–41," in *Henrietta Maria: Piety, Politics, and Patronage*, ed. Erin Griffey (Aldershot: Ashgate, 2006), esp. 36.

10   Ibid., 29.

11   Diana Barnes, "The *Secretary of Ladies* and Feminine Friendship at the Court of Henrietta Maria," in ibid., esp. 51 and 54–5. See also, in this connection: Malcolm Smuts, *Court Culture and the Origins of a Royalist Tradition in Early Stuart England* (Philadelphia, PA: University of Pennsylvania Press, 1987). Admittedly, Smuts places somewhat less of an emphasis on gender in this situation than does Barnes, although he does not altogether ignore it.

12 For this fascinating tale, consult: Marie B. Rowlands, "Recusant Women, 1560–1640," in *Women in English Society, 1500–1800,* ed. Mary Prior (London: Methuen, 1985), 149–80. The many *ideological similarities* at this time between English Catholicism and Archbishop Laud's "High Anglicanism" likely made Charles's intervention in such cases all the easier. See, on this subject: White, *Henrietta Maria,* 41–2; and Andrew Foster, "Church Policies of the 1630s," in Cust and Hughes, eds., *Conflict in Early Stuart England.*

13 Refer to Rowlands, "Recusant Women," esp. 160–2. See also Peter Holmes, *Resistance and Compromise: The Political Thought of the Elizabethan Catholics* (Cambridge: Cambridge University Press, 1982). Holmes sees English Catholic families in this era as having held the "two divergent tendencies of accommodation and resistance" in a certain dynamic balance. When the head of the family was *a woman*, argued Holmes, "then the balance could swing towards resistance"—presumably because of the woman's less accountable and, hence, less vulnerable position in the eyes of contemporary English law.

14 Patricia Crawford, *Women and Religion in England 1500–1720* (London: Routledge, 1993), 55.

15 On these points, see: Jeremy Boulton, *Neighborhood and Society. A London Suburb in the Seventeenth Century* (Cambridge: Cambridge University Press, 1987); and Martin Ingram, *Church Courts, Sex, and Marriage in England, 1570–1640* (Cambridge: Cambridge University Press, 1987).

16 Crawford, *Women and Religion in England,* 55–6.

17 Refer once again, in the former connection, to: Diane Purkiss, *The English Civil War: A People's History* (London: HarperPress, 2006), esp. 507; and to Melissa Mowry, *Collective Understanding, Radicalism, and Literary History, 1645–1742* (Oxford: Oxford University Press, 2021), passim.

18 All these "female heroics" are detailed by Antonia Fraser, *The Weaker Vessel: Women's Lot in Seventeenth-Century England* (London: Weidenfeld and Nicholson, 1984), 163 and 171–5.

19 Ibid., 164. Obviously, attitudes were gendered on the Parliamentary side as well: Brilliana Lady Harley, for instance, was said by one source to have defended Brampton Castle, near Hereford, against the Royalists with a veritably "masculine bravery." Ibid., 180.

20 A basic, if somewhat dated, source on this issue is: H. J. Habakkuk, "Public Finance and the Sale of Confiscated Property during the Interregnum," *Economic History Review* 15 (1962): 70–88.

21 Fraser, *The Weaker Vessel,* esp. 205 and 209. Parliamentarians during the Civil War commonly referred to their Royalist adversaries as "malignants."

22 Quoted in Christopher Durston, *The Family in the English Revolution* (Oxford: Basil Blackwell, 1989), 103.

23 Fraser, *The Weaker Vessel*, 209–10 and 210–4. For other examples of indomitable Royalist ladies serving their husbands' interests in the Civil War era, see ibid., 214–21.

24 For details relating to these cases, consult Durston, *The Family in the English Revolution*, 103 and 105.

25 Cited in ibid., 170–1. See David E. Underdown, *Royalist Conspiracy in England* (New Haven, CT: Yale University Press, 1962), 127–58, for a detailed discussion of Penruddock's abortive 1655 uprising against Cromwellian rule.

26 See the basic online reference to her: https://en.wikipedia.org/wiki/Lucy_Hay,_Countess_of_Carlisle. She is also featured in Lita Rose Betcherman, *Court Lady and Country Wife: Two Noble Sisters in Seventeenth-Century England* (New York: HarperCollins, 2005); and discussed by Purkiss, *The English Civil War*, 69, 125, and 565.

27 Ibid., 69 and 125.

28 For a discussion of all this, see: A. B. Worden, *The Rump Parliament* (Cambridge: Cambridge University Press, 1974), esp. 222–3, 226, and 242–8; and Bailey Stone, *The Anatomy of Revolution Revisited* (New York: Cambridge University Press, 2014), 344.

29 Refer, here, to Keith Thomas, "The Puritans and Adultery: The Act of 1650 Reconsidered," in *Puritans and Revolutionaries*, ed. Donald Pennington and Keith Thomas (Oxford: Clarendon Press, 1978), 257–82.

30 Fraser takes this issue up in *The Weaker Vessel*, 233.

31 Thomas, "The Puritans and Adultery," esp. 261–2. As its title implied, the statute dealt as well with issues of incest and "fornication."

32 Refer once again to Sharon L. Arnoult, "The Sovereignties of Body and Soul: Women's Political and Religious Actions in the English Civil War," in *Women and Sovereignty*, ed. Louise Olga Fradenburg (Edinburgh: Edinburgh University Press, 1992), esp. 239–42.

33 Durston has referred to the Barebones Parliament of 1653 as "an unrepresentative assembly which, while no longer considered by historians to have been peopled by a fanatical lunatic fringe, did contain a powerful leaven of revolutionary Fifth Monarchism." (Durston, *The Family in the English Revolution*, 84.) The most exhaustive and persuasive analysis of "Barebones" is still likely that of Austin Woolrych, *Commmonwealth to Protectorate* (Oxford: Clarendon Press, 1982), esp. 165–93.

34 Durston, *The Family in the English Revolution*, esp. 69–72.

35 Consult in this connection E. A. Wrigley and R. S. Schofield, eds., *The Population History of England 1541–1871* (Cambridge, MA: Harvard University Press, 1981), esp. 521.

36 Durston, *The Family in the English Revolution*, 84. The next important word on this agitated question came with Hardwicke's Marriage Act of 1753—not so accidentally, it could be, in the centennial year of the Barebones Parliament's short-lived wedding statute. See, on this controversy: Rebecca

Probert, *Marriage Law and Practice in the Long Eighteenth Century: A Reassessment* (Cambridge: Cambridge University Press, 2009). But see also, by Krista J. Kesselring and Tim Stretton, *Marriage, Separation, and Divorce in England, 1500–1700* (New York: Oxford University Press, 2022), for some of the most recent reflections on how tightly Englishwomen were subordinated to menfolk by the law and practice of early modern marriage.

37 See again, on this subject: Fraser, *The Weaker Vessel*, esp. 253–4; and Crawford, *Women and Religion in England*, 145.

38 *A Treatise of Magistracy: Showing, the Magistrate hath been, and forever is to be, the chief Officer in the Church....out of the Church, and Over the Church.* This extremely long and complicated treatise can be consulted online at https://collections.folger.edu (Folger holdings, ID no. 235969). It is dated simply "in the year 1647."

39 Ibid.

40 Refer again to Arnoult, "The Sovereignties of Body and Soul," esp. 239–42.

41 On the life of Mary Astell, consult https://en.wikipedia.org/wiki/Mary_Astell. The best scholarly treatments of her include: Joan Kinnaird, "Mary Astell and the Conservative Contribution to English Feminism," *Journal of British Studies* 19 (1979): 53–75; Ruth Perry, *The Celebrated Mary Astell: An Early English Feminist* (Chicago, IL: The University of Chicago Press, 1986); Patricia Springborg, *Mary Astell: Theorist of Freedom from Domination* (New York: Cambridge University Press, 2005); and the essays by Hilda L. Smith and Melinda Zook in William Kolbrener and Michal Michelson, eds., *Mary Astell: Reason, Gender, Faith* (Aldershot: Ashgate, 2007).

42 Refer again to Kinnaird, "Mary Astell and the Conservative Contribution to English Feminism," esp. 72–3.

43 As cited from: https://en.wikipedia.org/wiki/Mary Astell. The reference here is to Bridget Hill, *The First English Feminist: "Reflections upon Marriage" and other Writings by Mary Astell* (New York: St. Martin's Press, 1986). In fact, as this online article goes on to say, many a modern feminist scholar has found Astell's reliance upon religious inspiration as difficult to accept as her wholehearted espousal of male dominance within the archetypical family. See above all, in this connection, Katherine Gillespie, *Domesticity and Dissent in the Seventeenth Century: English Women Writers and the Public Sphere* (Cambridge: Cambridge University Press, 2004), 46–7.

44 Kinnaird, "Mary Astell and the Conservative Contribution to English Feminism," 69–70.

45 Perry, *The Celebrated Mary Astell,* 172.

46 The latter citation is drawn from https://en.wikipedia.org/wiki/Mary Astell.

47 Melinda Zook, "Religious Nonconformity and the Problem of Dissent in the Works of Aphra Behn and Mary Astell," in Kolbrener and Michelson, eds., *Mary Astell: Reason, Gender, Faith*, 112–3. Consult Perry, *The Celebrated Mary Astell*, 163–4, for a similar analysis of Astell and her like-minded contemporaries.

48 For a brief profile of her life, consult: https://en.wikipedia.org/wiki/Olympe de Gouges. Scholarly treatments include: Joan Wallach Scott, "'A Woman Who Has Only Paradoxes to Offer': Olympe de Gouges Claims Rights for Women," in *Rebel Daughters: Women and the French Revolution,* ed. Sara Melzer and Leslie Rabine (New York: Oxford University Press, 1992), 102–20; and Sophie Mousset, *Women's Rights and the French Revolution: A Biography of Olympe de Gouges,* trans. Joy Poirel (New Brunswick, NJ: Transaction Publishers, 2007).

49 Refer again to the online article: https://en.wikipedia.org/wiki/Olympe_de_ Gouges. The "Déclaration" can be conveniently perused in Levy, Applewhite, and Johnson, eds., *Women in Revolutionary Paris,* 87–96.

50 The anthology referenced here is: Catherine R. Montfort, ed., *Literate Women and the French Revolution of 1789* (Birmingham, AL: Summa Publications, 1994).

51 Vanpée's essay can be referenced in ibid., 55–79.

52 For Verdier's commentary, see ibid., 189–221. Hence, once again, we see, with the observations of Gabrielle Verdier, the familiar invocation of the postmodernist/feminist concept of *intersectionality.*

53 Scott, "'A Woman Who Has Only Paradoxes to Offer': Olympe de Gouges Claims Rights for Women," 114.

54 For these selections, see: Mousset, *Women's Rights and the French Revolution,* 87 and 88–9. Mousset drew these selections from Olympe de Gouges' voluminous *Écrits politiques,* published in two volumes at Paris in 1793.

55 For these and other details of Olympe de Gouges' literary and political life during the early years of the French Revolution, refer again to the convenient online source: https://en.wikipedia.org/wiki/Olympe_de_Gouges.

56 Annie K. Smart, *Citoyennes: Women and the Ideal of Citizenship in Eighteenth-Century France* (Newark, NJ: University of Delaware Press, 2011), 143–4. Smart correctly points out in this connection that Pierre-Gaspard Chaumette, the Procurator of the radical Paris Commune in 1793, was "willfully misleading" in characterizing de Gouges, not so much as politically "seditious" in the eyes of the government, but as a feminist "invader" of a public "space" ordinarily reserved for male politicians. Obviously, Chaumette's misogyny was on prominent display here.

57 Smart was probably also aware of how Dena Goodman, among others, had earlier challenged the notion of a "public/private dichotomy" so often postulated in feminist writing. Refer again to Goodman, "Public Sphere and Private Life," 1–20. See also, on this point, the more recent study of Jennifer J. Popiel, *Rousseau's Daughters: Domesticity, Education, and Autonomy in Modern France* (Durham, NH: University of New Hampshire Press, 2008).

58 For essential details about her life, refer, online, to: https://en.wikipedia.org /wiki/Madame_Roland. Several important studies are: Gita May, *Madame Roland and the Age of Revolution* (New York: Columbia University Press, 1970); Guy Chaussinand-Nogaret, *Madame Roland: Une Femme en*

Révolution (Paris: Seuil, 1985); and, more recently, Siân Reynolds, *Marriage and Revolution: Monsieur and Madame Roland* (New York: Oxford University Press, 2012).

59 Citations from Mary Trouille's essay: "The Circe of the Republic: Mme. Roland, Rousseau, and Revolutionary Politics," in Montfort, ed., *Literate Women and the French Revolution of 1789*, 81–109.

60 Cited in May, *Madame Roland and the Age of Revolution*, 116. Communication of July 29, 1783.

61 As quoted by Reynolds, *Marriage and Revolution: Monsieur and Madame Roland*, 231–2.

62 May, *Madame Roland and the Age of Revolution*, esp. 228–30. Although Siân Reynolds contends that "there is no evidence that the Rolands shared [J.-P.] Brissot's enthusiasm for the war," she no less quotes Marie-Jeanne as writing that "it seemed to me that . . . our enemies were preparing for it at their leisure, and our inaction would have delivered us up to them without defense." Reynolds, *Marriage and Revolution*, 177, 179, and 295.

63 Consult, in this connection: Susan Dalton, "Gender and the Shifting Ground of Revolutionary Politics: The Case of Madame Roland," *Canadian Journal of History* 36 (2001): 259–82.

64 Reynolds, *Marriage and Revolution*, 231–2.

65 Olwen Hufton, *The Prospect Before Her: A History of Women in Western Europe, vol. 1, 1500–1800* (London: HarperCollins, 1995), 481. Hufton had also discussed these issues at some length in *Women and the Limits of Citizenship in the French Revolution* (Toronto: University of Toronto Press, 1992), esp. 94–5.

66 Harvey Mitchell, "Resistance to the Revolution in Western France," *Past and Present* 63 (1974): 94–131. This specific example of local anti-tax ferment is found on 102–3. Similar complaints emanated from Bangor and Locmaria on Belle-Isle, and at Quiberon—all in the far West of France.

67 Gwynne Lewis, *The Second Vendée: The Continuity of Counter-Revolution in the Department of the Gard, 1789–1815* (New York: Clarendon Press, 1978), 45. The local *juge de paix*, under popular pressure, had eventually to order the release of two ring leaders of these riots—both of them *women*.

68 Timothy Tackett, *Religion, Revolution, and Regional Culture in Eighteenth-Century France: The Ecclesiastical Oath of 1791* (Princeton, NJ: Princeton University Press, 1986), 176–7.

69 Refer, esp. in this connection, to: André Latreille, *L'Eglise Catholique et la Révolution francaise*, 2 vols. (Paris: Hachette, 1946–50), I: 99–116; and John McManners, *The French Revolution and the Church* (Westport, CT: Greenwood Press, 1982), esp. 28–9.

70 See again Tackett, *Religion, Revolution, and Regional Culture in Eighteenth-Century France*, passim; and see also, by the same historian: "The West in France in 1789: The Religious Factor in the Origins of the Counter-Revolution," *Journal of Modern History* 54 (1982): 715–45.

71   Hufton, *Women and the Limits of Citizenship in the French Revolution*,
      94–6. Similar portrayals are offered in Tilly, *The Vendée*, esp. 253; and in
      Tackett, "Women and Men in Counter-Revolution: The Sommières Riot in
      1791," *Journal of Modern History* 59 (1987): 680–704.

72   Tackett, *Religion, Revolution, and Regional Culture in Eighteenth-Century
      France*, 173–4.

73   This incident (along with many others) is discussed in Hufton, *Women and
      the Limits of Citizenship in the French Revolution*, 113ff. Hufton, in fact,
      introduces here a typology of four types of resistance by provincial women to
      religious aspects of the Terror in 1793–94. Ridicule and "low humor" figure
      prominently in that typology.

74   Suzanne Desan, "The Role of Women in Religious Riots During the French
      Revolution," *Eighteenth-Century Studies* 22 (1989): 451–68. Citations from
      460–2. Consult also Desan's subsequent monograph: *Reclaiming the Sacred:
      Lay Religion and Popular Politics in Revolutionary France* (Ithaca, NY:
      Cornell University Press, 1991).

75   Hufton, *The Prospect Before Her: A History of Women in Western Europe*,
      484–5.

76   Refer again to Mitchell, "Resistance to the Revolution in Western France,"
      125–6 and 130–1. Incidentally, Charles Tilly (see *The Vendée*, 253), found,
      like Mitchell, that the birthing-and-baptism functions so important to
      midwifery became a point of heated contention between "juring" and "non-
      juring" priests—as well as their female adherents—in many communities in
      western France during this period.

77   Tackett, *Religion, Revolution, and Regional Culture in Eighteenth-Century
      France*, 173–4.

78   Desan, "The Role of Women in Religious Riots During the French
      Revolution," 452.

79   Tackett, "Women and Men in Counter-Revolution," 686–7. See also, on
      the riots in the South: P. M. Jones, *Politics and Rural Society: The Southern
      Massif-Central, 1750–1850* (Cambridge: Cambridge University Press,
      1985); and the earlier, but still valuable, study of Maurice Agulhon, *La via
      sociale en Province au lendemain de la Révolution* (Paris: Société des Études
      Robespierristes, 1970).

80   Tackett, *Religion, Revolution, and Regional Culture in Eighteenth-Century
      France*, 175–6.

81   Ibid. Another analysis of such gendered attitudes is offered by Desan, "The
      Role of Women in Religious Riots During the French Revolution," 458–60.
      "Revolutionary authorities and Catholic villagers alike," Desan states,
      "shared this pervasive conception of women either as weak malleable souls
      or as uncontrollable furies."

82   Ibid., 459–60. Some men adopted similar tactics in the capital. In 1795,
      for instance, the Convention would be denouncing men implicated in the
      Germinal/Prairial *journées* as "trouble-makers [who] dress as women in the

hope of enjoying impunity." Tackett, we should add, has noted the same phenomenon in connection with men in the far South who had been involved tangentially in the earlier 1791 Sommières religious disturbances.

83 See, for example: Mona Ozouf, *Festivals and the French Revolution*, trans. Alan Sheridan (Cambridge, MA: Harvard University Press, 1988); and Ozouf's pertinent articles in François Furet and Mona Ozouf, eds., *A Critical Dictionary of the French Revolution*, trans. Arthur Goldhammer (Cambridge, MA: Harvard University Press, 1989), 538–70.

84 John McManners has discussed all of this at length in *The French Revolution and the Church*, esp. 120–7. The Thermidorian Convention had officially disestablished the Catholic Church in statutes of September 1794 and February 1795. For the most recent account of the Directory's attempt to *legitimize* itself in religious terms, refer to: Bailey Stone, *Rethinking Revolutionary Change in Europe: A Neostructuralist Approach* (Lanham, MD: Rowman & Littlefield, 2020), 172–3.

85 Hufton, *The Prospect Before Her: A History of Women in Western Europe*, 481–2.

86 Information on these incidents comes from Hufton, "The Reconstruction of a Church, 1796–1801," in *Beyond the Terror: Essays in French Regional and Social History, 1794–1815*, ed. Gwynne Lewis and Colin Lucas (Cambridge: Cambridge University Press, 1983), 21–52.

87 Hufton, *The Prospect Before Her: A History of Women in Western Europe*, 483.

88 Clive Church, "In Search of the Directory," in *French Government and Society, 1500-1850: Essays in Memory of Alfred Cobban*, ed. J. F. Bosher (London: Athlone Press, 1973), 286–7.

89 Desan, "The Role of Women in Religious Riots During the French Revolution," 454, 463. Yet we should also note that, for Desan, female religious protest at times had its *negative* side. "In many instances, religious violence sparked . . . conflicts over political power and cultural control. The inverse side of religion's ability to reinforce female solidarity and to express shared interests was its possible transformation into a realm of bitter political controversy or forced conformity." Ibid., 457–8.

90 Information about this debate in Directorial circles derives from Desan, "Marriage, Religion and Moral Order: The Catholic Critique of Divorce During the Directory," in *The French Revolution and the Meaning of Citizenship*, ed. Renée Waldinger, Philip Dawson, and Isser Woloch (Westport, CT: Greenwood Press, 1993), esp. pp. 204 and 208–9.

91 Ibid., 208–9. On this last point, however, refer also, above, to notes 56 and 57 for differing feminist "takes" in the scholarly literature on the "public/ private dichotomy" issue as it applies specifically to Frenchwomen.

92 Observation by Desan in "Marriage, Religion and Moral Order," 204. Significantly, Timothy Tackett had made a similar argument in *Religion, Revolution, and Regional Culture in Eighteenth-Century France*, esp. 248.

93 The scholarship on these Napoleonic reforms is, obviously, enormous, and cannot be explored here. But the curious reader might want to start with: https://en.wikipedia.org/wiki/Concordat_of_1801; Jean-Marie Leflon, "La paix religieuse," in *Napoleon et l'Empire*, 2 vols., ed. Jean Mistler (Paris: Hachette, 1968), I: 98–107; Nigel Aston, *Christianity and Revolutionary Europe, 1750–1830* (Cambridge: Cambridge University Press, 2002), esp. 255–7 and 311; and Jean-Louis Halperin, *The French Civil Code*, trans. Tony Weir (London: Routledge, 2006).

94 Jennifer N. Heuer, *The Family and the Nation: Gender and Citizenship in Revolutionary France, 1789–1830* (Ithaca: Cornell University Press, 2005), 193–4.

95 Desan, *The Family on Trial in Revolutionary France*, 312–3.

96 Smart, *Citoyennes: Women and the Ideal of Citizenship in Eighteenth-Century France*, 237. Refer also, in this connection, to Popiel, *Rousseau's Daughters*, passim.

97 A brief sketch of her life is offered, online, at: https://en.wikipedia.org/wiki/Ekaterina_Kuskova. The primary effort to rehabilitate Kuskova's reputation in fairly recent times is: Barbara T. Norton, "Laying the Foundations of Democracy in Russia: E. D. Kuskova's Contribution, February—October 1917," in *Women and Society in Russia and the Soviet Union*, ed. Linda H. Edmondson (Cambridge: Cambridge University Press, 1992), 101–23. But see also Figes, *A People's Tragedy*, esp. 148–9, for a discussion of Kuskova's involvement, during the 1890s and early 1900s, in the gradualist Economist movement—an initiative that infuriated Russian Marxist exiles like V. I. Lenin.

98 On all of this, see again the online article cited above; and Norton, "Laying the Foundations of Democracy in Russia," esp. 117–9.

99 The sources for this discussion include: Stites, *The Women's Liberation Movement in Russia*, 295; Rochelle G. Ruthchild, *Equality and Revolution: Women's Rights in the Russian Empire, 1905-1917* (Pittsburgh, PA: University of Pittsburgh Press, 2010), passim.; Ruthchild, "Women and Gender in 1917," *Slavic Review* 76 (2017): 700–2; and Norton, "Laying the Foundations of Democracy in Russia," esp. 103 and 105.

100 Ibid., 117–8. See also, in this connection, the more extended discussion in Edmondson, *Feminism in Russia, 1900–1917* (Stanford, CA: Stanford University Press, 1984), esp. 93–103.

101 The memoirs of Nadezdha Krupskaya are cited by Figes, *A People's Tragedy*, 149. The "Economists," dominant in certain Russian intellectual circles during the time of Lenin's European exile, advocated—like Kuskova and other so-called "Legal Marxists"—the peaceable improvement of workers' conditions *within* the capitalist system.

102 Norton, "Laying the Foundations of Democracy in Russia," 107.

103 Ibid., 108–10.

104 Ibid., 118. Just how intense the forces of *social polarization* along *class* lines were in Petrograd and Moscow during 1917 can be gathered from a major article: William G. Rosenberg and Diane Koenker, "The Limits of Formal Protest: Workers' Activism and Social Polarization in Petrograd and Moscow, March to October 1917," *American Historical Review* 92 (1987): 296–326.

105 Her life is briefly profiled online: see, for example, https://en.wikipedia.org/wiki/Alexandra_Kollontai. Standard studies of Alexandra Kollontai include Barbara E. Clements, *Bolshevik Feminist: The Life of Aleksandra Kollontai* (Bloomington, IN: Indiana University Press, 1979); Beatrice Farnsworth, "Bolshevism, the Woman Question, and Alexandra Kollontai," *American Historical Review* 81 (1976): 292–316; and (once again by Farnsworth) *Alexandra Kollontai: Socialism, Feminism, and the Bolshevik Revolution* (Stanford, CA: Stanford University Press, 1980). But also see, from more recent times: Cathy Porter, *Alexandra Kollontai: A Biography*, rev. ed. (Chicago, IL: Haymarket Books, 2014).

106 Farnsworth, "Bolshevism, the Woman Question, and Alexandra Kollontai," 292–3.

107 See again, on this point: Stites, *The Women's Liberation Movement in Russia*, 213–4; and Engel, *Women in Russia, 1700–2000*, 121–2. Kollontai (and other agitators), we recall, had even appeared at feminist meetings from time to time in the late *ancien régime* to harass their élitist discussion leaders.

108 Farnsworth, "Bolshevism, the Woman Question, and Alexandra Kollontai," 305–6 and 307–8. We will be discussing the 1926 Family Code later in this chapter from the viewpoint of the female peasantry in Russia.

109 Cited from Barbara E. Clements, *Bolshevik Women* (New York: Cambridge University Press, 1997), 227.

110 Mark D. Steinberg, *The Russian Revolution, 1905–1921* (Oxford: Oxford University Press, 2017), esp. 307–9. Other selections from Kollontai's writings in the postrevolutionary years are found in Alix Holt, ed. and trans., *Selected Writings of Alexandra Kollontai* (Westport, CT: L. Hill, 1978).

111 Engel, *Women in Russia, 1700–2000*, 156.

112 A formidable literature on this challenge has emerged in the last few decades. See, for example: James Heinzen, *Inventing a Soviet Countryside: State Power and the Transformation of Rural Russia, 1917–1929* (Pittsburgh, PA: University of Pittsburgh Press, 2004); Tracy McDonald, *Face to the Village: The Riazan Countryside Under Soviet Rule, 1921–1930* (Toronto: University of Toronto Press, 2011); and Hugh D. Hudson, *Peasants, Political Police, and the Early Soviet State* (New York: Palgrave Macmillan, 2012). See also the commentary on this historiography in Stone, *The Anatomy of Revolution Revisited*, esp. 469–70.

113 On all of this, see: Teddy J. Uldricks, *Diplomacy and Ideology: The Origins of Soviet Foreign Relations, 1917–1930* (Beverly Hills, CA: SAGE, 1979); Timothy O'Connor, *Diplomacy and Revolution: G. V. Chicherin and Soviet Foreign Affairs, 1918-1930* (Ames, IA: Iowa State University Press, 1988);

and Jon Jacobson, *When the Soviet Union Entered World Politics* (Berkeley, CA: University of California Press, 1994).

114   Sarah Badcock, *Politics and the People in Revolutionary Russia: A Provincial History* (Cambridge: Cambridge University Press, 2007), 107–8 and 110. Badcock had already studied the attitudes of *soldatki* (i.e., soldiers' wives); see "Women, Protest, and Revolution: Soldiers' Wives in Russia During 1917," *International Review of Social History* 49 (2004): 47–70.

115   Aaron B. Retish, *Russia's Peasants in Revolution and Civil War: Citizenship, Identity, and the Creation of the Soviet State, 1914–1922* (New York: Cambridge University Press, 2008), 203.

116   Donald G. Raleigh, *Experiencing Russia's Civil War: Politics, Society, and Revolutionary Culture in Saratov, 1917-1922* (Princeton, NJ: Princeton University Press, 2002), passim.

117   Barbara E. Clements, "The Effects of the Civil War on Women and Family Relations," in *Party, State, and Society in the Russian Civil War: Explorations in Social History*, ed. Diane P. Koenker, William G. Rosenberg, and Ronald G. Suny (Bloomington, IN: Indiana University Press, 1989), esp. 108. See also, on this subject, her earlier article: "Working-Class and Peasant Women in the Russian Revolution, 1917–1923," *Signs: Journal of Women in Culture and Society* 8 (1982): 215–35.

118   Clements, "The Effects of the Civil War on Women and Family Relations," 108.

119   As cited in Raleigh, *Experiencing Russia's Civil War*, 123–4.

120   Quoted in Retish, *Russia's Peasants in Revolution and Civil War*, 227–8. On the increasingly marginalized status of *Zhenotdel* in the Russia of the 1920s, see also Elizabeth Wood, *The Baba and the Comrade: Gender and Politics in Revolutionary Russia* (Bloomington, IN: Indiana University Press, 1997), 127–39 and 181–93.

121   Retish, *Russia's Peasants in Revolution and Civil War*, 227–8.

122   On religious issues in this period, see: Figes, *A People's Tragedy*, esp. 745–51; and Nicholas V. Riasanovsky and Mark D. Steinberg, *A History of Russia*, 8th ed. (New York: Oxford University Press, 2011), 614–5.

123   Figes, *A People's Tragedy*, 748–9.

124   Farnsworth, "Village Women Experience the Revolution," in *Bolshevik Culture*, ed. A. Gleason, P. Kenez, and R. Stites (Bloomington, IN: Indiana University Press, 1985), 238–60. Citation is from p. 240.

125   Figes, *A People's Tragedy*, 751. For a closer examination of such attitudes, refer also to Figes, *Peasant Russia, Civil War: The Volga Countryside in Revolution, 1917–1921* (Oxford: Oxford University Press, 1989), 147–50.

126   One valuable source on such issues in the Russia of the 1920s is: Victor P. Danilov, *Rural Russia Under the New Regime*, trans. Orlando Figes (Bloomington, IN: Indiana University Press, 1988), esp. 42–4 and 231–43. For educational developments in the countryside in late tsarist times, the classic study is still: Ben Eklof, *Russian Peasant Schools: Officialdom, Village*

Culture and Popular Pedagogy, 1861-1914 (Berkeley, CA: University of California Press, 1986).

127 For the wording of this resolution, see: Farnsworth, "Village Women Experience the Revolution," 245–6. Paradoxically, as Farnsworth points out here, other peasant women—for example, in Tver province—complained that they were not being allowed to punish their own offspring with sufficient severity!

128 Ibid., 246–7.

129 Ibid.

130 Still, according to Figes, *A People's Tragedy*, 790, this decade *did* witness an advance in the literacy rates for rural women in their early twenties. This would indicate, at least, some *generational* change in the localities.

131 Citation (in 1919) is from Figes, *Peasant Russia, Civil War*, 296. Some of the *cultural* reflections of tensions between city and countryside in the Russia of the early—and late—1920s are usefully explored by Katerina Clark, "The City Versus the Countryside in Soviet Peasant Literature of the Twenties: A Duel of Utopias," in A. Gleason, P. Kenez, and R. Stites, eds., *Bolshevik Culture*, 175–89.

132 Farnsworth, "Village Women Experience the Revolution," 242–4. In 1919, Pravda was already reporting that "female antipathy was the chief obstacle to the formation of communes." Ten years later, Soviet leader L. M. Kaganovich would charge that "peasant women were providing much of the resistance to collectivization."

133 Figes, *Peasant Russia, Civil War*, 298–300. The *crèche* referred primarily to nursery facilities for the babies of female laborers in the *kommuny* and other kinds of agricultural collectives.

134 This legislation (and rural reactions to it) are summarized in Siegelbaum, *Soviet State and Society Between Revolutions*, 150–6. For a focused analysis of the subject, see: Farnsworth, "Bolshevik Alternatives and the Soviet Family: The 1926 Marriage Law Debate," in *Women in Russia*, ed. Dorothy Atkinson, Alexander Dallin, and Gail Lapidus (Stanford, CA: Stanford University Press, 1977), esp. pp. 140–1 and 149–52. Wendy Goldman offers a broader context in: *Women, the State, and Revolution: Soviet Family Policy and Social Life, 1917–1936* (New York: Cambridge University Press, 1993).

135 Siegelbaum, *Soviet State and Society Between Revolutions*, 154–5.

136 On *Rabotnitsa* in particular, consult Nancy Vavra, "Rabotnitsa: Constructing the Bolshevik Ideal, Women, and the New Soviet State," PhD diss., University of Colorado, 2002.

137 Citations from Goldman, "Working-Class Women and the "Withering Away" of the Family: Popular Responses to Family Policy," in *Russia in the Era of NEP: Explorations in Soviet Society and Culture*, ed. Sheila Fitzpatrick, Alexander Rabinowitch, and Richard Stites (Bloomington, IN: Indiana University Press, 1991), esp. 128–9.

138 Cited by Stites, *The Woman's Liberation Movement in Russia*, 382.

139   Clements, "The Birth of the New Soviet Woman," in A. Gleason, P. Kenez, and R. Stites, eds., *Bolshevik Culture*, 231–2.

140   Goldman, "Working-Class Women and the "Withering Away" of the Family," in S. Fitzpatrick, A. Rabinowitch, and R. Stites, eds., *Russia in the Era of NEP*, 138–9.

141   Siegelbaum, *Soviet State and Society Between Revolutions*, 188. On Stalin's Revolution, see also: Alexander Erlich, *The Soviet Industrialization Debate, 1924–1928* (Cambridge, MA: Harvard University Press, 1962); James R. Millar and Alec Nove, "A Debate on Collectivization: Was Stalin Really Necessary?," *Problems of Communism* 25 (1976): 49–62; and, perhaps most impressive, R. W. Davies, *The Industrialization of Soviet Russia: The Soviet Economy in Turmoil, 1929-1930* (Cambridge, MA: Harvard University Press, 1989).

142   Helmut Altrichter, "Insoluble Conflicts: Village Life between Revolution and Collectivization," in S. Fitzpatrick, A. Rabinowitch, and R. Stites, eds., *Russia in the Era of NEP*, 192–209. On the *literary* side of this conflict between urban and rural Russia, refer again to Katerina Clark, "The City versus the Countryside in Soviet Peasant Literature of the Twenties," in A. Gleason, P. Kenez, and R. Stites, eds., *Bolshevik Culture*, 175–89.

143   Ibid.

144   Engel, *Women in Russia, 1700-2000*, 168–9. On this last point, Engel notes, rumors circulating among the female peasantry associated collectivization with the arrival of the "Antichrist." On baptism's role as a purported "site of resistance" to statist values, see also David Ransel, *Village Mothers: Three Generations of Change in Russia and Tataria* (Bloomington, IN: Indiana University Press, 2000), esp. 164.

145   Lynne Viola, "Bab'i Bunty and Peasant Women's Protest During Collectivization," *Russian Review* 45 (1986): 189–205. As Viola points out, R. W. Davies had earlier noted that "in the years 1930 and 1931, as a compromise . . . between the state and the peasantry . . . the state was forced to settle for a . . . minimum, in which the peasantry was allowed to maintain a private plot, domestic livestock, and limited direct access to the market." See R. W. Davies, *The Socialist Offensive* (Cambridge, MA: Harvard University Press, 1980), passim. See also, on this general issue: Dorothy Atkinson, *The End of the Russian Land Commune, 1905–1930* (Stanford, CA: Stanford University Press, 1988).

146   Viola, "Bab'i Bunty and Peasant Women's Protest During Collectivization," 199. Consult also, on this subject, the essays found in L. Viola, V. P. Danilov, N. A. Ivnitskii, and Denis Koslov, eds., *The War Against the Peasantry, 1927–1930: The Tragedy of the Soviet Countryside*, trans. Steven Shabad (New Haven, CT: Yale University Press, 2005).

147   Clements, "The Birth of the New Soviet Woman," in A. Gleason, P. Kenez, and R. Stites, eds., *Bolshevik Culture*, esp. 233. For a similar portrayal, see: Barbara Engel, "Transformation Versus Tradition," in *Russia's Women: Accommodation, Resistance, Transformation*, ed. Barbara E. Clements,

Barbara Engel, and Christine Worobec (Berkeley, CA: University of California Press, 1991), esp. 147.

148 Lawrence Stone, *The Causes of the English Revolution 1529-1642* (London: Routledge, 2005), 54–5.

149 See again the commentary of Zook, "Religious Nonconformity and the Problem of Dissent in the Works of Aphra Behn and Mary Astell," 163–4.

150 Figes, *Peasant Russia, Civil War*, 355.

Conclusion

1 This is an issue that I have discussed in some detail in the Conclusion of my latest book, *Rethinking Revolutionary Change in Europe*. See esp. 199–203.

2 Consult, for instance: Carla Pestana, *The English Atlantic in an Age of Revolution, 1640–1661* (Cambridge, MA: Harvard University Press, 2004); and John Donoghue, *Fire Under the Ashes: An Atlantic History of the English Revolution* (Chicago, IL: The University of Chicago Press, 2013). Pestana and Donoghue have in turn drawn inspiration from slightly earlier studies. Examples in point are: Peter Linebaugh and Marcus Rediker, *The Many-Headed Hydra: Sailors, Slaves, Commoners, and the Hidden History of the English Atlantic* (Boston, MA: Beacon Press, 2001); and the essays in David Armitage and Michael J. Braddick, eds., *The British Atlantic World, 1500–1800* (London: Palgrave Macmillan, 2002).

3 Indeed, the essentially "European" nature of the mid-century upheaval in England remains securely fixed in our minds by a formidable corpus of historical research. See, for examples of this: Jonathan Scott, *England's Troubles: Seventeenth-Century English Instability in European Context* (Cambridge: Cambridge University Press, 2000); David Cressy, *England on Edge: Crisis and Revolution, 1640–42* (Oxford: Oxford University Press, 2006); and James Wheeler, *The Making of a World Power: War and the Military Revolution in Seventeenth Century England* (London: Stroud, 1999).

4 Refer in this connection to David Armitage, *The Declaration of Independence: A Global History* (Cambridge, MA: Harvard University Press, 2007); Wim Klooster, *Revolutions in the Atlantic World: A Comparative History* (New York: NYU Press, 2009); Laurent Dubois, "An Atlantic Revolution," *French Historical Studies* 32 (2009): 655–61; Paul Cheney, *Revolutionary Commerce: Globalization and the French Monarchy* (Cambridge, MA: Harvard University Press, 2010); and Pierre Serna, "Every Revolution is a War of Independence," in *The French Revolution in Global Perspective*, ed. Suzanne Desan, Lynn Hunt, and William M. Nelson (Ithaca, NY: Cornell University Press, 2013), 165–82. All such works look back, to some extent, to the mid-twentieth-century syntheses of R. R. Palmer and Jacques Godechot.

5 Dubois, "An Atlantic Revolution," 655–61. See also his *Avengers of the New World: The Story of the Haitian Revolution* (Cambridge, MA: Harvard University Press, 2004).

6 See, on this matter, the essays of Popkin and several of his colleagues in David Geggus and Norman Fiering, eds., *The World of the Haitian Revolution* (Bloomington, IN: Indiana University Press, 2009). See also the critical comments of Gary Wilder in "AHR Forum: Historiographic 'Turns' in Critical Perspective," *American Historical Review* 117 (2012): esp. 734–5. Wilder judiciously evaluates the pluses and minuses of the "Atlanticist school" in French revolutionary studies, but in the end tends to emphasize, as we do, its conceptual (and territorial) limitations.

7 Refer again, above, to Chapter 4, n. 5.

8 Thus Ronald G. Suny, "State-Building and Nation-Making: The Soviet Experience," in *The Russian Revolution: The Essential Readings*, ed. Martin A. Miller (Malden, MA: Blackwell Publishers, 2001), 242. On this balancing of the Great Russian and other ethnic forces within the new Soviet state, see also the pioneering work by Richard Pipes, *The Formation of the Soviet Union: Communism and Nationalism, 1917–1923* (Cambridge, MA: Harvard University Press, 1954). The pertinent issues as of 1924 are recapitulated quite effectively in Siegelbaum, *Soviet State and Society Between Revolutions*, 117–26.

9 See Gregory S. Massell, *The Surrogate Proletariat: Moslem Women and Revolutionary Strategies in Soviet Central Asia, 1919–1929* (Princeton, NJ: Princeton University Press, 1974).

10 Thus Siegelbaum, *Soviet State and Society Between Revolutions*, 155.

11 Massell, *The Surrogate Proletariat*, 232. The *khudzhum* campaign (and resultant controversy) are covered on 226–46. The term "surrogate proletariat" is utilized here by Massell as an alternative to *Zhenotdel* feminists' pejorative description of Muslim women as "the lowest of the low" or as "the oppressed of the oppressed." The issue, all too plainly, has retained relevance in much of the Muslim world in our own twenty-first-century times.

12 Massell discusses and documents this conservative backlash thoroughly in ibid., esp. 266–84.

13 As cited in ibid., 265.

14 Siegelbaum, *Soviet State and Society Between Revolutions*, 156.

15 Citation from Max Weber, *Economy and Society*, 2 vols., 1: 54 (Berkeley, CA: University of California Press, 1978).

16 Skocpol, *States and Social Revolutions*, 29. Refer again to Kimmel, *Revolution: A Sociological Interpretation*, esp. 171–87, for an in-depth analysis of Skocpol's contribution to theories concerning the state's role in major sociopolitical revolutions.

17 See again Goldstone, *Revolution and Rebellion in the Early Modern World*, 5n.

18 For this discussion of the Tudor-Stuart state, consult Michael J. Braddick, *State Formation in Early Modern England, c. 1550–1700* (Cambridge: Cambridge University Press, 2000), 14 and 19–20.

19 As cited in Suzanne Desan, "What's After Political Culture? Recent French Revolutionary Historiography," *French Historical Studies* 23 (2000): 194–5.

20 Steve Smith, "Writing the History of the Russian Revolution After the Fall of Communism," as quoted in Miller, ed., *The Russian Revolution: The Essential Readings*, 275–7.

21 See, for example, his prefatory remarks in Edward Acton, Vladimir Cherniaev, and William G. Rosenberg, eds., *Critical Companion to the Russian Revolution 1914–1921* (Bloomington, IN: Indiana University Press, 1997), esp. 19–20 and 23–4.

22 The reference, specifically, is to Peter B. Evans, Dietrich Rueschemeyer, and Theda Skocpol, eds., *Bringing the State Back In* (New York: Cambridge University Press, 1985).

23 Consult once again Baker and Edelstein, eds., *Scripting Revolution*, 3.

24 Refer again, in this connection, to Parker, *Revolutions in History*, 182.

25 Weber discussed this issue in his celebrated essay "Politics as a Vocation," which first appeared as a lecture at the University of Munich in 1918 and was then published the following year. The full essay is easily accessed in H. H. Gerth and C. Wright Mills, eds., *From Max Weber: Essays in Sociology* (New York: Oxford University Press, 1946), 77–128. Michael S. Kimmel has paraphrased here (freely but accurately) from Weber's essay in his own *Revolution: A Sociological Interpretation*, 35.

26 One proponent of this concept in recent years has been Jack Goldstone, in "Rethinking Revolutions: Integrating Origins, Processes, and Outcomes," *Comparative Studies of South Asia, Africa and the Middle East* 29 (2009): 8–32. Yet Goldstone more recently has reviewed other works on revolutions that might call this emphasis upon so-called "color revolutions" into question. See, again, his review article entitled "The Generations of Revolutionary Theory Revisited." I also owe the reference to "people power" or "color" revolutions—and to their potential relevance for my argument on these final pages of this book—to George Lawson.

27 Refer, again, to Mako and Moghadam, *After the Arab Uprisings: Progress and Stagnation in the Middle East and North Africa* (Cambridge: Cambridge University Press, 2021), passim. Paraphrase is from Goldstone.

SUGGESTIONS FOR FURTHER READING

It would obviously be impossible to provide on these pages an exhaustive discussion of the scholarship on the theorization of gender in revolutionary situations, the major stages of revolution in England, France, and Russia, and specific aspects of women's experiences in those upheavals. My intention in this bibliographical essay is, instead, to direct interested readers toward some of the classic (but, even more, *most recent*) studies that have informed the argumentation in these areas. Pertinent books and articles can be grouped most readily under the chapter headings listed in the Table of Contents. These are not necessarily hard-and-fast categories: readers unable to locate a specific source under one rubric may very possibly find it elsewhere. For the brief documentation supporting the Introduction ("Women in the European Revolutionary Experience") and Conclusion ("Race/Ethnicity and Statism as Women's Revolutionary Problematics"), the reader should refer to the endnotes provided for the first and last sections of the book.

Theorizing Gender in Revolutionary Situations

We can best discuss the critical literature on the theorization of gender (and related issues) in revolutionary situations by viewing it as addressing *three* basic questions: (1) How have scholars dealt in theoretical terms with gender, sexuality, and patriarchy? (2) How does *gender* now figure in today's confrontation between structuralist and postmodernist renderings of revolutionary change? (3) How optimistic—or, it may be, pessimistic— are accomplished feminist authors about prospects for favorable gendered outcomes (i.e., outcomes favorable, specifically, for *women*) in modern revolutionary situations?

Modern scholarship, to begin with, is taking us away from the earlier tendency to distinguish sharply between *gender* as a cultural construct and *sexuality* as a biological construct. The reader can find this change mirrored in the works of Beth Hess and Myra M. Ferree, eds., *Analyzing Gender: A Handbook of Social Science Research* (Newbury Park, CA: Sage Publications,

1987); Joan Wallach Scott, *Gender and the Politics of History*, rev. ed. (New York: Columbia University Press, 1999); and Merry Wiesner-Hanks, *Gender in History* (Oxford: Blackwell, 2001). That radical Marxian feminists had—for their own reasons—been rejecting the notion of an uncomplicated gender/sexuality distinction for years is reflected for the avid reader in the studies of Maria Mies, *Patriarchy and Accumulation on a World Scale* (London: Zed, 1986); and Margaret Randall, *Gathering Rage: The Failure of Twentieth-Century Revolutions to Develop a Feminist Agenda* (New York: Monthly Review Press, 1993). Interestingly, two prominent women's historians of modern France have more recently presented something of a compromise on this issue by trying, conceptually, to preserve both the *separate identities* of gender and sexuality *and* the linkages between them. Read Anne Verjus, "Gender, Sexuality, and Political Culture," in *A Companion to the French Revolution*, ed. Peter McPhee (Oxford: Wiley-Blackwell, 2013); and Karen M. Offen, *The Woman Question in France, 1400-1870* (Cambridge: Cambridge University Press, 2017). Those desiring to move on from the old gender vs. sexuality debates into the realm of "non-binary" theorization should commence with two recent articles: Regina Kunzel, "The Power of Queer History," *American Historical Review* 123 (2018): 1560–82; and Kritika Agarwal, "What is Trans History? From Activist and Academic Roots, A Field Takes Shape," *Perspectives on History* 56 (May 2018): 17–20. Both Kunzel and Agarwal offer the reader a multitude of additional sources.

Any disputation over the relative analytical value of gender and patriarchy clearly assumes an adequate theorization of patriarchy as an historical phenomenon. Two pioneering efforts in this field were: Gerda Lerna, *The Creation of Patriarchy* (New York: Oxford University Press, 1986); and Sylvia T. Walby, *Theorizing Patriarchy* (Oxford: Blackwell, 1990). Walby delved further into this subject in a subsequent article: "The 'Declining Significance' or the 'Changing Forms' of Patriarchy?" found in Valentine Moghadam's invaluable anthology, *Patriarchy and Development: Women's Positions at the End of the Twentieth Century* (Oxford: Clarendon, 1996). The specific meanings to be assigned to "patriarchy" had also been sharply debated by Sheila Rowbotham, Sally Alexander, and Barbara Taylor, *People's History and Socialist Theory*, ed. Raphael Samuel (London: Routledge and Kegan Paul, 1981), 363–73. Carole Pateman also broached this issue in *The Sexual Contract* (Stanford, CA: Stanford University Press, 1988). Widely varying assessments of the relative utility of gender and patriarchy as analytical concepts have been offered over the years. Consult, in this connection, the following: Scott, *Gender and the Politics of History*, esp. 33–4; Tristan Bridges and James Messerschmidt, "Joan Acker and the Shift from Patriarchy to Gender," in *Feminist Reflections* (online article of July 6, 2016); and Joan Acker, "The Problem with Patriarchy," *Sociology* 23 (1989): 239–40.

Specialists disagreeing over the precise theorization of patriarchy and the relative analytical utility of gender and patriarchy have also differed frequently over the *historical origins* of patriarchy. For Friedrich Engels' classic nineteenth-century interpretation of those origins, see his work on *The Origin of the Family, Private Property, and the State* (London: Penguin Classics, 2010), as well as his pertinent reflections in *The Woman Question: Selections from the Writings of Karl Marx, Frederick Engels, V. I. Lenin, Clara Zetkin, Joseph Stalin* (New York: International Publishers, 1977). For Gerda Lerner's countering argument that patriarchy had actually *preceded* private property, class society, and early statist development in world history, consult, once more, her monograph *The Creation of Patriarchy*. Wiesner-Hanks (in *Gender in History*, 12–13) seeks a compromise on the issue by maintaining that "most scholars . . . see the development of patriarchy as a complicated process, involving everything that is normally considered part of "civilization."

But questions dealing with the *universality* and the likely *durability* of gender inequality, or patriarchy, in today's larger world have given rise to even greater argumentation in learned circles. Certainly, feminists of color have frequently clashed over the former issue. See, for examples of this, Beverly Guy-Sheftall and Evelyn M. Hammonds, "Whither Black Women's Studies: Interview," in *Women's Studies on the Edge,* ed. Joan W. Scott (Durham, NC: Duke University Press, 2008), 155–67. Yet many such scholars, by endorsing Kimberlé Crenshaw's notion of *intersectionality*, have helped to reaffirm the concept of patriarchy as a *global* system of "privilege and discrimination" commingling the impacts of race, ethnicity, gender, and other social/ analytical factors. See, in this connection: bell hooks, *Feminist Theory: From the Margin to the Center*, 3rd ed. (New York: Routledge, 1994); and Leslie McCall, "The Complexity of Intersectionality," *Signs: Journal of Women in Culture and Society* 30 (2005): 1771–800. In addition, feminists such as Joan Acker and Laura Lee Downs have differed over whether global patriarchy should be depicted in, primarily, *economic* or *political* colors. Acker argued for an emphasis upon *class analysis* in *Class Questions: Feminist Answers* (Lanham, MD: Rowman & Littlefield Publishers, 2006). Downs, on the other hand, has regarded patriarchy through a suggestively *political* prism— to the detriment of both economics *and* postmodernism—in *Writing Gender History*, 2nd ed. (London: Bloomsbury Academic, 2010). Again, scholars differ in their views of patriarchy's *durability* for the foreseeable future. Both Mihály Simai and Sylvia Walby, writing in Moghadam, ed., *Patriarchy and Development* (Preface and 29–31, respectively) seem markedly pessimistic on the subject, whereas Valentine Moghadam herself has (in the same anthology, 4) attempted to accentuate at least some of the positive aspects of the "development process" as it has come to affect women in various regions of the contemporary world.

Finally, along these theoretical lines, there is the controversy over the continued usefulness of gender as a "category of historical analysis." Joan Scott has been the primary protagonist on this subject, as in her *Gender and the Politics of History*, for example, in the Preface. But she has also (here, as on other topics) had her critics. For one thing, many of the contributors to Moghadam's anthology *Patriarchy and Economic Development*, all too familiar with the glaring disparities between men's and women's status in developing societies all over the world, have had necessarily to insist upon the "staying power" of patriarchy—and, thus, upon the objective reality of "gender" itself—in those far-flung regions. Moreover, academic feminists such as Laura L. Downs, in *Writing Gender History*, and Tristan Bridges and James Messerschmidt, in their online journal *Feminist Reflections*, have rejected Scott's contention that gender has lost its "radical agency" and, thus, its "critical edge."

When we transition from writings on "gender theory" to the scholarship on gender's greater role in European revolutionary theory, we need first to take account briefly of long-standing Marxian and post-Marxian works on revolution and then to concentrate upon the more recent confrontation between structuralist and postmodernist interpretations of this phenomenon. Marxist renderings of revolution, stressing the centrality of *class*, are, of course, legion. Two major commentaries on the subject, insofar as it concerns *Europe*, are: Bailey Stone, *The Anatomy of Revolution Revisited* (New York: Cambridge University Press, 2014), esp. the Introduction; and Ronald Grigor Suny, *The Soviet Experiment: Russia, the USSR, and the Successor States*, 2nd ed. (New York: Oxford University Press, 2011), esp. 1–68. Social scientists who have approached the question of revolutionary change from angles not highlighted that often by Marxists include: Chalmers Johnson, *Revolutionary Change*, 2nd ed. (Stanford, CA: Stanford University Press, 1982); Ted R. Gurr, *Why Men Rebel* (Princeton, NJ: Princeton University Press, 1971), and *Rogues, Rebels and Reformers* (Beverly Hills, CA: SAGE, 1976); and James C. Davies, *When Men Revolt and Why* (New York: Free Press, 1979).

One of the best general yet richly informed introductions to structuralist interpretations of revolution is by Michael S. Kimmel, *Revolution: A Sociological Interpretation* (Philadelphia, PA: Temple University Press, 1990). One can draw from Kimmel's work the impression that this structuralist tendency has split into two chief subtendencies: i.e., capitalism-centered and state-centered structuralism. Outstanding works in the former genre include: Immanuel Wallerstein, *The Modern World-System* (New York Academic Press, 1974), and *The Politics of the World Economy* (New York: Cambridge University Press, 1984); Karl Polanyi, *The Great Transformation* (Boston: Beacon Press, 1957); and Ellen Kay Trimberger, *Revolution from Above: Military Bureaucrats and Development in Japan, Turkey, Egypt, and Peru* (New Brunswick, NJ: Transaction Books, 1978). By far and away the most influential (and most controversial) conspectus in the latter genre is Theda Skocpol, *States and Social Revolutions: A Comparative Analysis of France, Russia, and China* (Cambridge: Cambridge University Press, 1979). She has followed this up with Peter B. Evans, Dietrich Rueschemeyer, and Theda Skocpol, eds., *Bringing the State Back In* (New York: Cambridge University Press, 1989), and Skocpol, ed., *Social Revolutions in the Modern World* (Cambridge: Cambridge University Press, 1994). Perhaps the most recent attempt to review critiques of Skocpol's interpretation by major historians, demographers, and other social scientists is that of Stone, *Rethinking Revolutionary Change in Europe: A Neostructuralist Approach* (Lanham, MD: Rowman & Littlefield Publishers, 2020), esp. the Introduction. Yet still useful (if slightly dated) in this regard are the essays in John Foran, ed., *Theorizing Revolutions* (London: Routledge, 1997).

Critical early reference-points to postmodernism *in general* include Michel Foucault, *The Archaeology of Knowledge*, trans. A. M. Sheridan Smith (New York: Harper & Row, 1972), and *The History of Sexuality*, trans. Robert Hurley (New York: Vintage, 1980). Read also, in this connection, Jonathan Culler's cogent discussion of Jacques Derrida's ideas in *On Deconstruction: Theory and Criticism after Structuralism* (Ithaca, NY: Cornell University Press, 1982). For efforts to see in postmodernism, as some detect in structuralism, a bifurcation into two subtendencies, refer to: Richard J. Evans, *In Defense of History* (New York: W. W. Norton, 1997); Ernest Gellner, *Postmodernism, Reason, and Religion* (London: Routledge, 1992); and Pauline Marie Rosenau, *Post-Modernism and the Social Sciences: Insights, Inroads, and Intrusions* (Princeton, NJ: Princeton University Press, 1992). Beverley Southgate sharply criticized Evans in *Postmodernism in History: Fear or Freedom?* (London: Routledge, 2003), and followed this up with *What Is History For?* (London: Routledge, 2005). Other efforts to champion postmodernist theory (as applied specifically to history) include books by Keith Jenkins, Alun Munslow, and Frank Ankersmit. Historians who, like Southgate, bring a radical postmodernist orientation into their work include Joan Scott, *Gender and the Politics of History*, esp. 200 and 206–7, and Keith M. Baker, most recently in Baker and Dan Edelstein, eds., *Scripting Revolution: A Historical Approach to the Comparative Study of Revolutions* (Stanford, CA: Stanford University Press, 2015). Critics of Scott notably include Charles Tilly, *Roads from Past to Future* (Lanham, MD: Rowman & Littlefield Publishers, 1997); Evans, *In Defense of History*, esp. 185–6; and Laura L. Downs, "If "Woman" Is Just an Empty Category, Then Why Am I Afraid to Walk Alone at Night? Identity Politics Meets the Postmodern Subject," *Comparative Studies in Society and History* 35 (1993): 414–37. Yet Scott also has had her defenders. Examples are Denise Riley, *'Am I That Name?' Feminism and the Category of 'Women' in History* (Basingstoke: Macmillan, 1989); Catherine Hall, *White, Male, and Middle-Class: Explorations in Feminism and History* (New York: Routledge, 1992);

and the essays in Judith Miller and Elizabeth Weed, eds., *The Question of Gender: Joan W. Scott's Critical Feminism* (Bloomington, IN: University of Indiana Press, 2011). The debate goes on!

What remains to suggest vis-à-vis Chapter 1 is good reading on the gendered *consequences* of modern revolutions. It makes sense to begin here with what feminist/Marxian scholars have had to say since the 1970s on this subject. Some of the most obvious sources are Sheila Rowbotham, *Women, Resistance, and Revolution: A History of Women and Revolution in the Modern World* (New York: Pantheon Books, 1972); Margaret Randall, *Gathering Rage: The Failure of Twentieth-Century Revolutions to Develop a Feminist Agenda* (New York: Monthly Review Press, 1993); and the essays in Sîan Reynolds, ed., *Women, State, and Revolution: Essays on Power and Gender in Europe Since 1789* (Amherst, MA: University of Massachusetts Press, 1987). Maxine Molyneux has made her by now famous distinction between "women's interests" and "gender interests" in most revolutionary situations in "Mobilization Without Emancipation? Women's Interests, State, and Revolution," 280–302, in Richard Fagen, Carmen Deere, and José Luis Corragio, eds., *Transition and Development: Problems of Third World Socialism* (New York: Monthly Review Press, 1986). Mary Ann Tétrault, on the other hand, has looked at women's revolutionary prospects from a "Skocpolian" structuralist perspective in her edited anthology: *Women and Revolution in Africa, Asia, and the New World* (Columbia, SC: University of South Carolina Press, 1994). Finally, Valentine Moghadam has classified modern revolutions (and women's prospects in them) from a comparative sociological perspective in her essay "Gender and Revolutions," in Foran, *Theorizing Revolutions*, esp. 142–4 and 152–4.

A Brief Sketch of the English, French, and Russian Revolutions

It might be helpful for those individuals intrigued by the subject of women's experiences in revolutionary England, France, and Russia, but not that familiar with those upheavals in general, to acquire a more specific sense of how events actually unfolded in them. Accordingly, this section of the essay approaches those events under these headings: (1) Developments attending transitions to revolution in the three countries under question; (2) the "honeymoons" of early revolution; (3) the process of radicalization in all three countries; (4) the climactic or "terrorist" phases of revolution; and (5) the "Thermidorian" or post-Terrorist stages of revolution in England, France, and Russia.

Historians covering the transitions to revolution in the countries studied here usually focus on such factors as fiscal/economic issues, constitutional/

political developments, military/strategic questions, and the political-cultural context of events. In the English case, readers might do well to approach fiscal questions by consulting Conrad Russell, *The Fall of the British Monarchies, 1637-1642* (Oxford: Oxford University Press, 1991); Kenneth R. Andrews, *Ships, Money, and Politics: Seafaring and Naval Enterprise in the Reign of Charles I* (New York: Cambridge University Press, 1991); and Andrew Thrush's contribution in Mark C. Fissel, ed., *War and Government in Britain, 1598-1650* (New York: Manchester University Press, 1991). For political/constitutional developments, especially helpful studies include Valerie L. Pearl, *London and the Outbreak of the Puritan Revolution: City Government and National Politics, 1625-43* (London: Oxford, 1961); Robert Ashton, *The City and the Court, 1603-43* (Cambridge: Cambridge University Press, 1979); and Mark Kishlansky, *Parliamentary Selection: Social and Political Choices in Early Modern England* (Cambridge: Cambridge University Press, 1986). That Charles I could not likely expect to engineer any *military coup* against his multiplying enemies in 1639-40 is what readers will gather from Fissel, *The Bishops' Wars: Charles I's Campaigns Against Scotland, 1638-1640* (Cambridge: Cambridge University Press, 1994); Peter Donald, *An Uncounselled King: Charles I and the Scottish Troubles 1637-1641* (Cambridge: Cambridge University Press, 1991); and Allan MacInness, *Charles I and the Making of the Covenanting Movement* (Edinburgh: University of Edinburgh Press, 1991). Yet it was, perhaps, in *political-cultural terms* that the king (and his French and very Catholic queen Henrietta Maria) were most dangerously isolated from the predominantly Protestant population of early-seventeenth-century England. Historians who have most effectively underscored this reality in modern times clearly include Caroline Hibbard, *Charles I and the Popish Plot* (Chapel Hill, NC: University of North Carolina Press, 1983); Ann Hughes, *The Causes of the English Civil War*, 2nd ed. (Basingstoke: Macmillan, 1998); and Jonathan Scott, *England's Troubles: Seventeenth-Century English Instability in European Context* (Cambridge: Cambridge University Press, 2000).

In the French case, the reader should approach statist/financial questions by consulting—in addition to older works by Ernst Labrousse, George V. Taylor, John Bosher, and Robert D. Harris—the following: Eugene N. White, "Was There a Solution to the Ancien Régime's Financial Dilemma?" *Journal of Economic History* 49 (1989): 545–68; David Weir, "Tontines, Public Finance, and Revolution in France and England, 1688-1789," *Journal of Economic History* 49 (1989): 95–124; and Gail Bossenga, "Financial Origins of the French Revolution," Ch. 1 in Thomas E. Kaiser and Dale K. Van Kley, eds., *From Deficit to Deluge: The Origins of the French Revolution* (Stanford, CA: Stanford University Press, 2011). Bossenga's article is especially useful here. On *constitutional* dimensions of the crisis, the classic study, even after all these years, remains: Jean Egret, *The French*

Prerevolution, 1787-1788, trans. Wesley D. Camp (Chicago, IL: University of Chicago Press, 1977). Similarly useful, however, from the constitutional viewpoint of the parlements (i.e. sovereign tribunals) of this Bourbon realm is Bailey Stone, *The French Parlements and the Crisis of the Old Regime* (Chapel Hill, NC: University of North Carolina Press, 1986). But readers should also consult the more recent analysis of prerevolutionary issues by Vivian Gruder, *The Notables and the Nation: The Political Schooling of the French, 1787-1788* (Cambridge, MA: Harvard University Press, 2007). That Louis XVI's government—much like that of Charles I in earlier times, and that of Nicholas II later in Russia—was badly hobbled in its ability to suppress any revolutionary unrest is the likely take-away from studies of tension and poor morale within the French army in the late 1780s. See, in this connection: Egret, *The French Prerevolution*, 47–54; Samuel F. Scott, *The Response of the Royal Army to the French Revolution* (Oxford: Oxford University Press, 1978); and J.P. Bertaud, *The Army of the French Revolution: From Citizen-Soldiers to Instrument of Power*, trans. Robert R. Palmer (Princeton, NJ: Princeton University Press, 1988). It appears equally clear that political-cultural factors—in the form, above all, of Austrophobia and Anglophobia—did as much to isolate Louis XVI (and his Austria-born consort Marie-Antoinette) on the eve of revolution in France as popular fear of Catholicism did to isolate the royal couple in prerevolutionary England. Some of the impressive scholarly works stressing this point include: John Hardman, *Louis XVI* (New Haven, CT: Yale University Press, 1993); Munro Price, *Preserving the Monarchy: The Comte de Vergennes, 1774-1787* (Cambridge: Cambridge University Press, 1995); and, by Thomas Kaiser, "Who's Afraid of Marie-Antoinette? Diplomacy, Austrophobia, and the Queen," *French History* 14 (2000): 241–71.

In the case of Russia, readers interested in fiscal issues might consult Norman Stone, *The Eastern Front 1914-1917* (London: Scribner, 1975); Hans Rogger, *Russia in the Age of Modernisation and Revolution 1881-1917* (London: Longman, 1983); and W. Bruce Lincoln, *Passage Through Armageddon* (New York: Simon and Schuster, 1986). Extremely useful on the *constitutional context* of these events are Orlando Figes, *A People's Tragedy: The Russian Revolution, 1891-1924* (New York: Penguin Books, 1996); and Mark Steinberg and V. M. Khrustalev, *The Fall of the Romanovs: Political Dreams and Personal Struggles in a Time of Revolution* (New Haven, CT: Yale University Press, 1980). On the daunting problems facing Russia's Imperial Army in 1916-17, the reader should start with Allan K. Wildman, *The End of the Russian Imperial Army: The Old Army and the Soldiers' Revolt* (Princeton, NJ: Princeton University Press, 1980), and refer again to Lincoln, *Passage Through Armageddon*, passim. For the political-cultural issues isolating Nicholas and Alexandra from their own court—let alone from Russian society as a whole—consult R. K. Massie, *Nicholas and Alexandra* (New York: Athenaeum, 1967); Andrew M. Verner, *The Crisis of Russian Autocracy: Nicholas II and the 1905 Revolution* (Princeton, NJ: Princeton University Press, 1990); and Orlando Figes and Boris Kolonitskii, *Interpreting the Russian Revolution: The Language and Symbols of 1917* (New Haven, CT: Yale University Press, 1999).

There is abundant scholarship on the "honeymoon eras" of revolution in England, France, and Russia—eras that were marked by both the dynamics of polarization *and* crucial "points of no return." Authoritative sources for polarized relations *within* the English Parliament and between Parliament and Charles I include Conrad Russell, *The Fall of the British Monarchies*, 285–9; Hibbard, *Charles I and the Popish Plot*, 197–8; and also Anthony Fletcher, *The Outbreak of the English Civil War* (London: Edward Arnold, 1981), 35–6. The "point of no return" in the English situation was, of course, the king's bungled attempt to arrest five MPs and one peer on charges of treason and his subsequent flight from London in early 1642. It is carefully studied by Valerie Pearl, *London and the Outbreak of the Puritan Revolution* (London: Oxford University Press, 1961), and by Keith Lindley, *Popular Politics and Religion in Civil War London* (Aldershot: Scholar Press, 1997). On the analogous dynamics of polarization in early revolutionary France, refer to Norman Hampson, *The Constituent Assembly and the Failure of Consensus, 1789-1791* (New York: Blackwell, 1988), and Timothy Tackett, *Becoming a Revolutionary: The Deputies of the French National Assembly and the Emergence of a Revolutionary Culture* (Princeton, NJ: Princeton University Press, 1996). The tale of Louis XVI's "point of no return"—namely, his ill-starred attempt to flee the country in June 1791— is engagingly and convincingly related by Tackett, *When the King Took Flight* (Cambridge, MA: Harvard University Press, 2003). In the Russian case, the dynamics of polarization/radicalization in what turned out to be an exceedingly brief honeymoon phase are best analyzed by Rex Wade, *The Russian Revolution, 1917* (Cambridge: Cambridge University Press, 2000). But see also in this connection Melissa K. Stockdale, *Paul Miliukov and the Quest for a Liberal Russia, 1880-1918* (Ithaca, NY: Cornell University Press, 1993), and Nikolai N. Sukhanov, *The Russian Revolution, 1917* (New York: Harper & Brothers, 1962). On the "April 1917 Crisis" as the "point of no return" in Russia, refer to Wade, *The Russian Revolution*, 80–6; Figes, *A People's Tragedy*, 384; and Sheila Fitzpatrick, *The Russian Revolution*, 3rd ed. (Oxford: Oxford University Press, 2008), 48–9.

There is an equally rich literature on the *phases of radicalization* that extended: in England, from the summer of 1642 to the execution of Charles I in January 1649; in France, from "Varennes" (June-September 1791) to the Jacobin seizure of state power in May-June 1793; and in Russia, from the formation of the First Coalition Government (May 1917) to the Bolshevik seizure of power (late October 1917). Outstanding studies of English radicalization include David Underdown, *Pride's Purge: Politics in the Puritan Revolution* (Oxford: Clarendon, 1971); Robert Ashton, *The*

English Civil War: Conservatism and Revolution (London: Weidenfeld and Nicholson, 1978); Ashton, *Counter-Revolution: The Second Civil War and Its Origins, 1646-48* (New Haven, CT: Yale University Press, 1994); G. E. Aylmer, ed., *The Levellers in the English Revolution* (Ithaca, NY: Cornell University Press, 1975); the essays in Jason Peacey, ed., *The Regicides and the Execution of Charles I* (New York: Palgrave Macmillan, 2001); and Ian Gentles, "The New Model Officer Corps in 1647: A Collective Portrait," *Social History* 22 (1997): 127–44. Comparable works on French radicalization include C. J. Mitchell, *The French Legislative Assembly of 1791* (Leiden: E. J. Brill, 1988); Alison Patrick, "Political Divisions in the French National Convention, 1792-93," *Journal of Modern History* 41 (1969): 421–74; John Markoff, *The Abolition of Feudalism: Peasants, Lords, and Legislators in the French Revolution* (University Park, PA: Pennsylvania State University Press, 1996); Malcolm Crook, *Elections in the French Revolution* (Cambridge: Cambridge University Press, 1996); and Susan Dunn, *The Deaths of Louis XVI: Regicide and the French Political Imagination* (Princeton, NJ: Princeton University Press, 1994). The reader should see, for Russian radicalization, the following: Rex Wade, *The Russian Search for Peace, February-October 1917* (Stanford, CA: Stanford University Press, 1969); Louise Heenan, *Russian Democracy's Fateful Blunder: The Summer Offensive of 1917* (New York: Praeger, 1987); Alexander Rabinowitch, *The Bolsheviks Come to Power* (New York: W. W. Norton, 1978); and John Keep, *The Russian Revolution: A Study in Mass Mobilization* (New York: Norton, 1976).

For reasons that are probably obvious, the climactic "terrorist" stages of revolution in these three polities draw an unusually rapt readership. Classic takes on these "reigns of terror and virtue" are Crane Brinton, *The Anatomy of Revolution* (New York: Prentice-Hall, 1938); and Arno Mayer, *The Furies: Violence and Terror in the French and Russian Revolutions* (Princeton, NJ: Princeton University Press, 2000). On this most radical stage of revolution in the English case, see: David Underdown, *Royalist Conspiracy in England, 1649-1660* (New Haven, CT: Yale University Press, 1960); Norah Carlin, "The Levellers and the Conquest of Ireland in 1649," *Historical Journal* 30 (1987): 269–88; Ian Gentles, *The English Revolution and Wars in the Three Kingdoms, 1638-1652* (London: Pearson, 2007); Austin Woolrych, *Commonwealth to Protectorate* (Oxford: Clarendon Press, 1982); and many essays in J. F. McGregor and Barry Reay, eds., *Radical Religion in the English Revolution* (Oxford: Oxford University Press, 1984). The best statistical analysis of the Terror in France remains by Donald Greer, *The Incidence of the Terror during the French Revolution* (Cambridge, MA: Harvard University Press, 1935). The best study of the Terror from a governmental perspective is still R. R. Palmer, *Twelve Who Ruled: The Year of the Terror in the French Revolution* (Princeton, NJ: Princeton University Press, 1941). Provincial sides of the Terror are analyzed in Paul R. Hanson,

The Jacobin Republic Under Fire: The Federalist Revolt in the French Revolution (University Park, PA: Pennsylvania State University Press, 2003); and Peter M. Jones, *The Peasantry in the French Revolution* (Cambridge: Cambridge University Press, 1988). On Soviet Russia's "Red Terror," the following monographs are of major interest: Richard K. Debo, *Revolution and Survival: The Foreign Policy of Soviet Russia, 1917-1918* (Toronto, ON: University of Toronto Press, 1979); Scott B. Smith, *Captives of Revolution: The Socialist Revolutionaries and the Bolshevik Dictatorship, 1918-1923* (Pittsburgh, PA: University of Pittsburgh Press, 2011); Paul H. Avrich, *Kronstadt 1921* (New York: Norton, 1921); Israel Getzler, *Kronstadt, 1917-1921: The Fate of a Soviet Democracy* (Cambridge: Cambridge University Press, 1983); and Donald J. Raleigh, *Experiencing Russia's Civil War, 1917-1922* (Princeton, NJ: Princeton University Press, 2002).

Finally, the post-Terrorist or Thermidorian stages of these revolutions can be seen, first, as reactions against statist terrorism *as such*, and second, as attempts—successful or unsuccessful, depending on the country in question—to overcome *crises of governmental legitimacy* in turbulent times. For France (which gave "Thermidor" its revolutionary meaning in the first place), the reader should start with Denis Woronoff, *The Thermidorian Regime and the Directory, 1794-1799*, trans. Julian Jackson (Cambridge: Cambridge University Press, 1994), and Bronislaw Baczko, *Ending the Terror: The French Revolution After Robespierre*, trans. Michael Petheram (New York: Cambridge University Press, 1994). Popular aspects of the post-Robespierre era are depicted in François Gendron, *La Jeunesse Dorée* (Québec: Presses de l'Université de Québec, 1979). Isser Woloch has studied the efforts to establish democracy under the Directory in *Jacobin Legacy: The Democratic Movement Under the Directory* (Princeton, NJ: Princeton University Press, 1970). On the attempt (heroic if unavailing) by Cromwell to legitimize his rule in 1650s England, see: Christopher Hill, *God's Englishman: Oliver Cromwell and the English Revolution* (New York: Harper Torchbooks, 1970); Peter Gaunt, *Oliver Cromwell* (Oxford: Blackwell, 1996); Roger Howell, "Cromwell and His Parliaments: The Trevor-Roper Thesis Revisited," in *Images of Oliver Cromwell*, ed. R. C. Richardson (Manchester: Manchester University Press, 1993); David Smith and Patrick Little, *Parliaments and Politics During the Cromwellian Protectorate* (Cambridge: Cambridge University Press, 2007); and Christopher G. Durston, *Cromwell's Major-Generals: Godly Government during the English Revolution* (Manchester: Manchester University Press, 2001). Those interested in constitutional issues arising in early Soviet Russia should start with Robert V. Daniels, *The Conscience of the Revolution* (Oxford: Oxford University Press, 1960) as well as Leonard Schapiro, *The Origins of the Communist Autocracy* (London: Macmillan, 1977), and go on from there. Economic aspects of the era (e.g., involving the NEP) should start with Fitzpatrick, *The Russian Revolution*, 95–6. On *social* aspects of the Thermidorian years in Russia, start with Kent Geiger, *The Family in Soviet Russia* (Cambridge: Cambridge University Press, 1996). On Stalin's industrialization campaign, the reader should start with Lewis H. Siegelbaum's superb synthesis, *Soviet State and Society Between Revolutions, 1918-1929* (Cambridge: Cambridge University Press, 1992), and proceed on from there.

Unsuccessful Consort Queens in the European Revolutions

In this section, the reader will find a brief discussion of scholarly works comparing "queens regnant" and (female) regents at the heart of state power in nonrevolutionary periods with "queens consort" subordinate to male monarchs in revolutionary times. That will be followed by a detailed discussion of works on Elizabeth I and Henrietta Maria in England, Cathérine de Médicis and Marie-Antoinette in France, and Catherine II ("the Great") and Alexandra Feodorovna in Russia.

Continental consort queens are discussed in comparative terms by Clarissa Campbell Orr, ed., *Queenship in Europe, 1600-1815: The Role of the Consort* (Cambridge: Cambridge University Press, 2004). *English* consorts find their historian in Caroline M. Hibbard, "Henrietta Maria in the 1630s: Perspectives on the Role of Consort Queens in Ancien Régime Courts," Ch. 5 in *The 1630s: Interdisciplinary Essays on Culture and Politics in the Caroline Era*, ed. Ian Atherton and Julie Sanders (Manchester: Manchester University Press, 2006). Studies of "regnant queens" in Europe include: Fanny Cosandey, *La Reine de France: Symbole et Pouvoir, XVe-XVIIIe siècles* (Paris: Gallimard, 2000); Sharon L. Jansen, *The Monstrous Regiment of Women: Female Rulers in Early Modern Europe* (New York: Palgrave Macmillan, 2002); and also Katherine Crawford, *Perilous Performances: Gender and Regency in Early Modern France* (Cambridge, MA: Harvard University Press, 2004).

As one would expect, the scholarly literature on Elizabeth I and Henrietta Maria of England is plentiful. It can be divided, roughly, into works stressing their geopolitical and domestic-political roles and those emphasizing their *cultural* and *gendered* roles. Outstanding books on Elizabethan domestic and diplomatic policies include Susan Doran, *Monarchy and Matrimony: The Courtships of Elizabeth I* (London: Routledge, 1988), and *Elizabeth I and Foreign Policy, 1558-1603* (New York: Routledge, 2000); R. B. Wernham, *The Making of Elizabethan Foreign Policy, 1558-1603* (Berkeley: University of California Press, 1980); Wallace T. MacCaffrey, *Queen Elizabeth and the Making of Policy, 1572-1588* (Princeton, NJ: Princeton University Press, 1981), and *Elizabeth I: War and Politics, 1588-1603* (Princeton, NJ: Princeton University Press, 1992); Charles H. Wilson, *Queen Elizabeth and the Revolt of the Netherlands* (The Hague: M. Nijhoff, 1979); and Pauline Croft, "'The State of the World is Marvelously Changed': England, Spain, and Europe, 1558-1604," in *Tudor England and Its Neighbors,* ed. S. Doran and Glenn Richardson (New York: Palgrave MacMillan, 2005). For cultural and gendered "takes" on this regnant queen, consult the following: Allison Heisch, "Queen Elizabeth I and the Persistence of Patrimony," *Feminist Review* 4 (1980): 45–56; Susan Bassnet, *Elizabeth I: A Feminist Perspective* (Oxford: Oxford University Press, 1988); Christopher Haigh, *Elizabeth I: Profile in Power* (New York: Longman, 1988); Susan Frye, *Elizabeth I: The Competition for Representation* (Oxford: Oxford University Press, 1993); and Charles Beem, *The Lioness Roared: The Problems of Female Rule in English History* (New York: Palgrave Macmillan, 2006). See also the essays in Anna Whitelock and Alice Hunt, eds., *Tudor Queenship: The Reigns of Mary and Elizabeth* (New York: Palgrave Macmillan, 2010).

Older biographies of Henrietta Maria, Charles I's consort queen, include those by Elizabeth Hamilton, *Henrietta Maria* (New York: Coward, McCann and Geohegan, 1976); Rosalind Marshall, *Henrietta Maria: The Intrepid Queen* (London: Stemmer House Publishers, 1991); and Alison Plowden, *Henrietta Maria: Charles I's Indomitable Queen* (Stroud: Sutton Publishing, 2001). Such works are, however, superseded by Michelle White, *Henrietta Maria and the English Civil Wars* (Aldershot: Ashgate, 2006). A useful original source for the queen's correspondence with her royal husband is Mary Anne Everitt Green, ed., *Letters of Queen Henrietta Maria* (London: Richard Bentley, 1857). On the irreconcilable demands of English politics and French-style Catholicism imposed from the start of Henrietta Maria's queenship, refer, notably, to Jessica Bell, "The Three Marys: The Virgin; Mary de Médicis; and Henrietta Maria," Ch. 5, *Henrietta Maria: Piety, Politics, and Patronage,* ed. Erin Griffey (Aldershot: Ashgate, 2008). On the interplay between religion, gender, and politics at court during Henrietta's queenship, the curious reader should see the following: Malcolm Smuts, "The Puritan Followers of Henrietta Maria in the 1630s," *English Historical Review* (1978): 26–45, and "Religion, European Politics, and Henrietta Maria's Circle," Ch. 1 in Griffey, *Henrietta Maria: Piety, Politics, and Patronage*; and Diana Barnes, "The *Secretary of Ladies* and Feminine Friendship at the Court of Henrietta Maria," Ch. 2 in Griffey, *Henrietta Maria: Piety, Politics, and Patronage*. Historical background for much of the above is provided by Hibbard, *Charles I and the Popish Plot*, 19–37. More specifically, White, *Henrietta Maria and the English Civil Wars,* passim., is strongest for the *gendered* aspects of this queen's troubled reign.

The scholarship on Cathérine de Médicis and Marie-Antoinette in the case of old regime and revolutionary France is equally formidable. Verdicts on Queen Mother Cathérine have varied wildly over the years. At the negative extreme we find J. E. Neale, *The Age of Catherine de Medici* (London: Jonathan Cape, 1966). At the opposite (very positive) extreme is Jean Héritier, *Catherine de' Medici*, trans. Charlotte Haldane (London: Allen and Unwin, 1963). Somewhere in between, the reader will find R. J. Knecht, *Catherine de' Medici* (London: Longman, 1998) and *The French Wars of Religion, 1559-1598* (London: Longman, 1998); and Mack P. Holt, *The French Wars of Religion, 1562-1629*, 2nd ed. (Cambridge: Cambridge University Press, 2005). At the same time, N. M. Sutherland has played up the interactions between domestic and international affairs during Cathérine's troubled years in power. See, for instance, her *Princes, Politics and Religion 1547-1589* (London: Hambledon Press, 1984); *The French Secretaries of State in the Age of Catherine de Medici* (Westport, CT: Greenwood Press, 1976); and also *The Massacre of St. Bartholomew and the European Conflict, 1559-1572* (London: MacMillan, 1973). Works dealing with the gendered/cultural aspects of Catherine's regency include Katherine Crawford, "Catherine de Médici and the Performance of Political Motherhood," *Sixteenth Century Journal* 31 (2000): 643–73; Sheila Ffolliott, "Catherine de Médicis as Artemesia: Figuring the Powerful Widow," in *Rewriting the Renaissance: The Discourses of Sexual Difference in Early Modern Europe*, ed. Margaret Ferguson, Maureen Quilligan, and Nancy Vickers (Chicago: University of Chicago Press, 1986), 227–41; and D. Crouzet, "'A Strong Desire to Be a Mother to All Your Subjects': A Rhetorical Experiment by Catherine de Medicis," *Journal of Medieval and Early Modern Studies* 38 (2008): 103–18. See also Crawford, *Perilous Performances*, passim, on all these gendered issues.

There is a notable tension in the literature on France's Marie-Antoinette between gendered and more traditional (i.e., political/geopolitical) approaches. In the latter category we might place Evelyne Lever, *Marie-Antoinette: The Last Queen of France*, trans. Catherine Temerson (New York: Farrar, Straus and Giroux, 1991); Antonia Fraser, *Marie-Antoinette: The Journey* (New York: Doubleday, 2001); Munro Price, *The Road from Versailles: Louis XVI, Marie-Antoinette, and the Fall of the French Monarchy* (New York: St. Martin's Press, 2003); and John Hardman, *Marie-Antoinette: The Making of a French Queen* (New Haven, CT: Yale University Press, 2019). The substantial feminist renderings of this consort queen's *ancien régime* and revolutionary years include Elizabeth Colwill, "Just Another *Citoyenne?* Marie-Antoinette on Trial, 1790-93," *History Workshop* 28 (1989): 63–87; Lynn Hunt, *The Family Romance of the French Revolution* (Berkeley, CA: University of California Press, 1992); and Madelyn L. Gutwirth, *The Twilight of the Goddesses: Women and Representation in the French Revolutionary Era* (New Brunswick, NJ: Rutgers University Press, 1992). But for one stimulating critique of this pronounced feminist tendency in historical writing, refer to Dorinda Outram's review in the *American Historical Review* 98 (1993): 882–3. For interpretations of the queen informed both by diplomatic expertise *and* by a sensitivity to gendered analysis, see Thomas E. Kaiser, "Who's

Afraid of Marie-Antoinette? Diplomacy, Austrophobia and the Queen," *French History* 14 (2000): 241–71; and "From the Austrian Committee to the Foreign Plot: Marie-Antoinette, Austrophobia, and the Terror," *French Historical Studies* 26 (2003): 579–617.

Finally, the reader will find bounteous literature on Russia's tsaritsa Catherine II and its last consort empress, Alexandra Feodorovna. In the former case, a heavy stress upon traditional history has been leavened by more recent gendered inquiries. Administrative studies of Catherine include David L. Ransel, *The Politics of Catherinian Russia* (New Haven, CT: Yale University Press, 1975); John LeDonne, *Ruling Russia: Politics and Administration in the Age of Absolutism, 1762-96* (Princeton, NJ: Princeton University Press, 1984); Paul Dukes, *Catherine the Great and the Russian Nobility* (Cambridge: Cambridge University Press, 1968); and Simon Dixon, *The Modernisation of Russia, 1676-1825* (Cambridge: Cambridge University Press, 1999). Studies of Catherinian foreign policy are legion, and include many essays in Hugh A. Ragsdale, ed., *Imperial Russian Foreign Policy* (New York: Cambridge University Press, 1993); Isabel de Madariaga, *Catherine the Great* (New Haven, CT: Yale University Press, 1993); and John LeDonne, *The Russian Empire and the World, 1700-1917: The Geopolitics of Expansionism and Containment* (New York: Oxford University Press, 1997). Innovatory gendered titles on Catherine include: Brenda Meehan-Waters, "Catherine the Great and the Problem of Female Rule," *Russian Review* 34 (1975): 293–307; Simon S. Montefiore, *Catherine the Great and Potemkin: The Imperial Love Affair* (London: Orion, 2010); Virginia Rounding, *Catherine the Great: Love, Sex, and Power* (London: Hutchinson, 2006); and Gary Marker, *Imperial Saint: The Cult of St. Catherine and the Dawn of Female Rule in Russia* (DeKalb, IL: Northern Illinois University Press, 2007).

The reader might first approach Empress Alexandra through contemporary eyes. See, along those lines: Pierre Gilliard, *Thirteen Years at the Russian Court,* trans. F. Appleby Holt (New York: Doran, 1921); Bernard Pares, "Rasputin and the Empress: Authors of the Russian Collapse," *Foreign Affairs* 6 (1927), esp. 22–3, and *The Fall of the Russian Monarchy: A Study of the Evidence* (New York: Alfred Knopf, 1939). For Alexandra's ceremonial coronation, see Richard Wortman, *Scenarios of Power: Myth and Ceremony in the Russian Monarchy from Peter the Great to the Abdication of Nicholas II* (Princeton, NJ: Princeton University Press, 2006). For an incisive analysis of the imperial marriage—and of its dire implications for the reign—consult M. D. Steinberg and V. M. Khrustalev, *The Fall of the Romanovs: Political Dreams and Personal Struggles in a Time of Revolution* (New Haven, CT: Yale University Press, 1995), esp. the Introduction. British journalist/historian Helen Rappaport has quite recently researched the tragic final years of Alexandra Feodorovna and her family: see *The Last Days of the Romanovs: Tragedy at Ekaterinburg* (New York: St. Martin's

Press, 2008), and *The Race to Save the Romanovs* (New York: St. Martin's Press, 2018). Efforts to reinterpret Alexandra's role in *gendered* terms have multiplied, and include Orlando Figes and Boris Kolonitskii, *Interpreting the Russian Revolution: The Language and Symbols of 1917* (New Haven, CT: Yale University Press, 1999), esp. 158–64, and (by Figes alone) *A People's Tragedy*, esp. 284–5. See also Stone, *Rethinking Revolutionary Change in Europe*, Ch. 3, for a detailed synthesis of the scholarship on this last subject.

Women's Emancipatory Roles in England, France, and Russia

Readers especially interested in what Valentine Moghadam has called the "emancipatory" or "modernizing" model of women in revolution will find here a review of scholarship that, for each of our three countries, describes women's disadvantaged legal status in ancien régime times. This will be followed by a discussion of works that focus on women's revolutionary roles and on the ways in which the *gender* dynamic interacted (in each country's upheaval) with *religion, secular ideology, culture, class,* and *revitalized statist authority.*

In the case of England, relatively benign interpretations of women's improved status at law in the revolutionary years include Christopher Hill, *The World Turned Upside Down: Radical Ideas During the English Revolution* (Baltimore: Penguin Books, 1972), 306–10, and Lawrence Stone, *The Family, Sex, and Marriage in England 1500-1800* (New York: Harper & Row, 1977), 240–62. But Keith Thomas waxed less optimistic on the subject in "Women and the Civil War Sects," *Past and Present* 13 (1958): esp. 42–6. Bleak judgments also come from Margaret George, *Women in the First Capitalist Society* (Urbana, IL: University of Illinois Press, 1988); Christopher Durston, *The Family in the English Revolution* (Oxford: Basil Blackwell, 1989); Stevie Davies, *Unbridled Spirits: Women of the English Revolution, 1640-1660* (London: Women's Press, 1998); and Antonia Fraser, *The Weaker Vessel: Women's Lot in Seventeenth-Century England* (London: Weidenfeld and Nicholson, 1984). Women's progressive and radical initiatives during the 1640s–50s, on the other hand, have also attracted a great deal of scholarly attention. Diane Purkiss describes women's radical deeds in the Civil War in *The English Civil War: A People's History* (London: HarperPress, 2006), and their literary activities in *Literature, Gender and Politics During the English Civil War* (Cambridge: Cambridge University Press, 2005). For some women's links with the Levellers in the late 1640s, see Sharon L. Arnoult, "The Sovereignties of Body and Soul: Women's Political and Religious Actions in the English Civil War," in *Women and Sovereignty*, ed. Louise O. Fradenburg (Edinburgh:

Edinburgh University Press, 1992). Patricia Crawford raises gendered issues of citizenship *vis-à-vis* the Putney Debates of 1647: "'The Poorest She: Women and Citizenship in Early Modern England," in *The Putney Debates of 1647: The Army, the Levellers, and the English State*, ed. Michael Mendel (Cambridge: Cambridge University Press, 2001), esp. 211–13. Patricia Higgins studies Englishwomen as petitioners in "The Reactions of Women, with Special Reference to Women Petitioners," in *Politics, Religion, and the English Civil War*, ed. Brian Manning (London: E. J. Arnold, 1973), 190–217. On women's activities as preachers and prophetesses, see: Phyllis Mack, *Visionary Women: Ecstatic Prophecy in Seventeenth Century England* (Berkeley, CA: University of California Press, 1992); Theresa Feroli, *Political Speaking Justified: Women Prophets and the English Revolution* (Newark, DE: University of Delaware Press, 2006); and Fraser, *The Weaker Vessel,* passim. Finally, Katharine Gillespie puts *state* and *civic* issues affecting these women in a broader historical context in *Domesticity and Dissent in the Seventeenth Century: English Women Writers and the Public Sphere* (Cambridge: Cambridge University Press, 2004).

In the case of France, James F. Traer gives us the same general verdict on women's status in *ancien régime* law as we derive from the work on women's legal status in prerevolutionary England. Refer to his *Marriage and the Family in Eighteenth-Century France* (Ithaca, NY: Cornell University Press, 1980). James F. McMillan, in his *France and Women, 1789-1914: Gender, Society, and Politics* (London: Routledge, 2002), accentuates the Enlightenment's "mixed legacy" for all Frenchwomen. Feminist historians have often differed over the matter of this "mixed legacy" in France. Negative "takes" on the subject have come from, among others, Joan Landes, *Women and the Public Sphere in the Age of the French Revolution* (Ithaca, NY: Cornell University Press, 1987); Gutwirth, *The Twilight of the Goddesses;* and Hunt, *The Family Romance of the French Revolution*. A bit of a "correction" on the issue comes from Sarah Hanley, in "Engendering the State: Family Formation and State Building in Early Modern France," *French Historical Studies* 16 (1989): 4–27; and Dena Goodman, "Public Sphere and Private Life: Towards a Synthesis of Current Historiographical Approaches to the Old Regime," *History and Theory* 31 (1992): 1–20. Excellent sources on *Parisiennes'* activism during the Revolution are legion, and include Olwen Hufton, *Women and the Limits of Citizenship in the French Revolution* (Toronto, ON: University of Toronto Press, 1992); Dominique Godineau, *The Women of Paris and Their French Revolution,* trans. Katherine Streip (Berkeley, CA: University of California Press, 1998); and essays in Harriet B. Applewhite and Darline G. Levy, eds., *Women and Politics in the Age of the Democratic Revolution* (Ann Arbor, MI: University of Michigan Press, 1990). On Jacobin women's clubs in Paris (and in the provinces) during these years, see, notably, Levy and Applewhite, "Women and Militant Citizenship in Revolutionary Paris," in *Rebel Daughters:*

Women and the French Revolution, ed. Sara Melzer and Leslie Rabine (New York: Oxford University Press, 1992); and Suzanne Desan, "'Constitutional Amazons': Jacobin Women's Clubs in the French Revolution," in *Re-Creating Authority in Revolutionary France,* ed. B. T. Ragin and E. A. Williams (New Brunswick, NJ: Rutgers University Press, 1992). The best book on family issues in this period is probably by Suzanne Desan, *The Family on Trial in Revolutionary France* (Berkeley, CA: University of California Press, 2004). For the greater long-term question of women's *civic* destiny, as posed in *and after* the Revolution, consult the essays in Renée Waldinger, Philip Dawson, and Isser Woloch, eds., *The French Revolution and the Meaning of Citizenship* (Westport, CT: Greenwood Press, 1993) and Jennifer H. Heuer, *The Family and the Nation: Gender and Citizenship in Revolutionary France, 1789-1830* (Ithaca, NY: Cornell University Press, 2005).

In the case of Russia, the reader will once again find scholarship stressing the inferior status of women at law in prerevolutionary times. William Wagner has led the charge here: see *"The Trojan Mare. Women's Rights and Civil Rights in Late Imperial Russia,"* 65–84, in Olga Crisp and Linda Edmondson, eds., *Civil Rights in Imperial Russia* (Oxford: Clarendon, 1989). Wagner pursues this subject in *Marriage, Property and Law in Late Imperial Russia* (Oxford: Clarendon, 1994). Michelle L. Marrese adds some historical context here in *A Woman's Kingdom: Noblewomen and the Control of Property in Russia, 1700-1861* (Ithaca, NY: Cornell University Press, 2002). Moreover, the strong institutional resistance to furtherance of women's rights in Russia has been well documented. See Gregory L. Freeze, "The Soslovie (Estate) Paradigm and Russian Social History," *American Historical Review* 91 (1986); Leopold H. Haimson, "The Problem of Social Identities in Early Twentieth-Century Russia," *Slavic Review* 47 (1988): 1–20; and Sheila Fitzpatrick, "Ascribing Class: The Construction of Social Identity in Soviet Russia," *Journal of Modern History* 65 (1993): 745–70. On the gradual emergence of a Western-style feminism in the late Imperial era, consult these monographs: Linda Edmondson, *Feminism in Russian, 1900-1917* (Stanford, CA: Stanford University Press, 1984); Richard Stites, *The Women's Liberation Movement in Russia: Feminism, Nihilism, and Bolshevism, 1860-1930,* 1st ed. (Princeton, NJ: Princeton University Press, 1978); and (notably) Rochelle G. Ruthchild, *Equality and Revolution: Women's Rights in the Russian Empire, 1905-1917* (Pittsburgh, PA: University of Pittsburgh Press, 2010). The impact of the First World War on Russian women and on their struggle for equality has also given rise to a formidable literature. See Alfred G. Meyer, "The Impact of World War I on Russian Women's Lives," in *Russia's Women: Accommodation, Resistance, Transformation,* ed. Barbara E. Clements, Barbara Engel, and Christine Worobec (Berkeley, CA: University of California, 1991), 208–24; Laurie Stoff, *They Fought for the Motherland: Russia's Women Soldiers in World War I and the Revolution* (Lawrence, KS: University Press of Kansas, 2006), and *Russia's Sisters of Mercy and the Great War: More Than Binding Men's Wounds* (Lawrence, KS: University Press of Kansas, 2015); and Melissa K. Stockdale, *Mobilizing the Russian Nation: Patriotism and Citizenship in the First World War* (Cambridge: Cambridge University Press, 2016). Russian women's labor issues in late Imperial times are raised by Rose Glickman, *Russian Factory Women: Workplace and Society, 1880-1914* (Berkeley, CA: University of California Press, 1984). On similar issues in the revolution itself, see: Anna Hilyar and Jane McDermid, *Revolutionary Women in Russia, 1870-1917: A Study in Collective Biography* (Manchester: Manchester University Press, 2000); Mark D. Steinberg, ed., *Voices of Revolution, 1917* (New Haven, CT: Yale University Press, 2001); Elizabeth Wood, *The Baba and the Comrade: Gender and Politics in Revolution Russia* (Bloomington, IN: Indiana University Press, 1997); Anne Borbroff, "The Bolsheviks and Working Women, 1905-1920," *Soviet Studies* 20 (1974): 540–67; and Barbara E. Clements, "Working-Class and Peasant Women in the Russian Revolution, 1917-1923," *Signs: Journal of Women in Culture and Society* 8 (1982): 215–35.

Disillusioned and Traditionalist Women Confronting Revolution

Readers who are especially intrigued by what Valentine Moghadam has called "patriarchal" or "woman-in-the-family" models of revolution will find in this final section suggested reading that deals with disillusioned erstwhile female revolutionaries and with those women predisposed from the start to defend settled ways of faith and tradition in revolutionary England, France, and Russia. Once again, a related issue will involve the many ways in which *gendered* considerations affecting all these women interacted with the dynamics of religion, class, *civisme*, and statism.

In the case of England, and commencing with Catholicism, the reader desiring a historical context should check Robin Clifton, "The Popular Fear of Catholics During the English Revolution," *Past and Present* 52 (1971): 23–55; and Peter Lake, "Anti-Popery: The Structure of a Prejudice," in *Conflict in Early Stuart England: Studies in Religion and Politics 1603-1642*, ed. Richard Cust and Ann Hughes (London: Longman, 1989), 72–106. Caroline court Catholicism is aptly discussed by White, *Henrietta Maria and the English Civil Wars*, esp. 32–4; Hibbard, *Charles I and the Popish Plot*, 225–6; and Anthony Fletcher, *The Outbreak of the English Civil War* (New York: New York University Press, 1983), 332–3. For English Catholicism in this connection as a "county" phenomenon, see Peter Holmes, *Resistance and Compromise: The Political Thought of the Elizabethan Catholics* (Cambridge: Cambridge University Press, 1982), passim., and also Marie B.

Rowlands, "Recusant Women, 1560-1640," in *Women in English Society, 1500-1800,* ed. Mary Prior (London: Methuen, 1985), 149–80. On the Civil War heroics of (usually Anglican) Royalist women, see especially Fraser, *The Weaker Vessel,* passim., and Durston, *The Family in the English Revolution,* 103–5. Perhaps the most famous Presbyterian lady involved in the politics of the 1640s and 1650s was Lucy Hay, Countess of Carlisle. She finds scholarly notice in Purkiss, *The English Civil War,* 69, 125, and 565, and in Lita Rose Betcherman, *Court Lady and Country Wife: Two Noble Sisters in Seventeenth Century England* (New York: HarperCollins, 2005). The notorious "Adultery Act" of 1650 is carefully studied by Keith Thomas, "The Puritans and Adultery: The Act of 1640 Reconsidered," in *Puritans and Revolutionaries,* ed. Donald Pennington and Keith Thomas (Oxford: Clarendon Press, 1978), 257–82. Consult also Sharon Arnoult's more general discussion of Puritanism in "The Sovereignties of Body and Soul," esp. 239–42. On marital/divorce matters in revolutionary/postrevolutionary England, see: Durston, *The Family in the English Revolution,* 69–72 and 84, and (just recently) Krista J. Kesselring and Tim Stretton, *Marriage, Separation, and Divorce in England, 1500-1700* (New York: Oxford University Press, 2022). Civil War essayist Mary Pope finds brief mention in Fraser, *The Weaker Vessel,* 253–4, and in Arnoult, "The Sovereignties of Body and Soul," 239–42. Mary Astell, on the other hand, has attracted more considerable notice from historians. See, for example: Joan Kinnaird, "Mary Astell and the Conservative Contribution to English Feminism," *Journal of British Studies* 19 (1979): 53–75; Ruth Perry, *The Celebrated Mary Astell: An Early English Feminist* (Chicago, IL: University of Chicago Press, 1986); Patricia Springborg, *Mary Astell: Theorist of Freedom from Domination* (New York: Cambridge University Press, 2005); and the essays by Hilda Smith and Melinda Zook in William Kolbrener and Michal Michelson, eds., *Mary Astell: Reason, Gender, Faith* (Aldershot: Ashgate, 2007). See also, on issues of gender, *civisme,* and statism: Gillespie, *Domesticity and Dissent in the Seventeenth Century,* esp. 46–7.

In the case of France, readers may wish first to review the literature on Olympe de Gouges and Madame Roland, who—like Lucy Hay in the English Revolution—came to be disillusioned by the course of revolutionary events. In both (French) cases, gendered interpretations have had to compete, increasingly, with political accounts. Scholarly treatments of Olympe de Gouges include Joan W. Scott, "'A Woman Who Has Only Paradoxes to Offer': Olympe de Gouges Claims Rights for Women," in Melzer and Rabine, *Rebel Daughters,* 102–20; essays in Catherine R. Montfort, ed., *Literate Women and the French Revolution of 1789* (Birmingham, AL: Summa Publications, 1994); Sophie Mousset, *Women's Rights and the French Revolution: A Biography of Olympe de Gouges,* trans. Joy Poirel (New Brunswick, NJ: Transaction Publishers, 2007); and Annie K. Smart, *Citoyennes: Women and the Ideal of Citizenship in Eighteenth-Century*

France (Newark, DE: University of Delaware Press, 2011). Studies of Madame Roland that stand out are Gita May, *Madame Roland and the Age of Revolution* (New York: Columbia University Press, 1970); Guy M. Chaussinand-Nogaret, *Madame Roland: Une Femme en Révolution* (Paris: Seuil, 1985); essays in Montfort, ed., *Literate Women and the French Revolution*; and (more recently) Sîan Reynolds, *Marriage and Revolution: Monsieur and Madame Roland* (New York: Oxford University Press, 2012). Several important treatments of provincial Frenchwomen's resistance to successive revolutionary governments on *financial* issues include Hufton, *The Prospect Before Her: A History of Women in Western Europe, vol. 1, 1500-1800* (London: HarperCollins, 1995), 481; Harvey Mitchell, "Resistance to the Revolution in Western France," *Past and Present* 63 (1974): 94–131; and Gwynne Lewis, *The Second Vendée: Continuity of Counter-Revolution in the Department of the Gard, 1789-1815* (New York: Clarendon Press, 1978), 45. For female resistance in provincial France to the Revolution's religious reforms, see, notably: Tim Tackett, *Religion, Revolution, and Regional Culture in Eighteenth-Century France* (Princeton, NJ: Princeton University Press, 1986); Tackett, "The West in France in 1789: The Religious Factor in the Origins of the Counter-Revolution," *Journal of Modern History* 54 (1982): 715-45, and "Women and Men in Counter-Revolution: The Sommières Riot in 1791," *Journal of Modern History* 59 (1987): 680–704. Also valuable in this connection is Desan, "The Role of Women in Religious Riots During the French Revolution," *Eighteenth-Century Studies* 22 (1989): 451–68. Relevant works on the Directory era are Hufton, "The Reconstruction of a Church, 1796-1801," 21–52, in Gwynne Lewis and Colin Lucas, eds., *Beyond the Terror: Essays in French Regional and Social History* (Cambridge: Cambridge University Press, 1983); and S. Desan, "Marriage, Religion and Moral Order: The Catholic Critique of Divorce During the Directory," in Waldinger, Dawson, and Woloch, *The French Revolution and the Meaning of Citizenship*. Readers interested in intersections of *gender*, citizenship and statism in both eighteenth- and nineteenth-century France should again consult Heuer, *The Family and the Nation: Gender and Citizenship in Revolutionary France, 1789-1830*, esp. 193–4, and Smart, *Citoyennes: Women and the Ideal of Citizenship in Eighteenth-Century France*, esp. 237.

In the case of Russia, Ekaterina Kuskova and Alexandra Kollontai fell out with the Bolshevik version of revolution at different times (and for different reasons). On Kuskova, the principal source is Barbara T. Norton, "Laying the Foundations of Democracy in Russia: E. D. Kuskova's Contribution, February-October 1917," 101–23, in Linda Edmondson, ed., *Women and Society in Russia and the Soviet Union* (Cambridge: Cambridge University Press, 1992). But check also Figes, *A People's Tragedy*, 148–9; Stites, *The Women's Liberation Movement in Russia*, 295; and Ruthchild, *Equality and Revolution*, passim., for more details on her career. On Kollontai, the literature is much richer. See Barbara E. Clements, *Bolshevik Feminist: The Life of Aleksandra Kollontai* (Bloomington, IN: Indiana University Press, 1979); Beatrice Farnsworth, *Alexandra Kollontai: Socialism, Feminism, and the Bolshevik Revolution* (Stanford, CA: Stanford University Press, 1980); and Cathy Porter, *Alexandra Kollontai: A Biography*, rev. ed. (Chicago, IL: Haymarket Books, 2014). See also this primary source: Alix Holt, ed. and trans., *Selected Writings of Alexandra Kollontai* (Westport, CT: Hill, 1978). On female peasants' reactions to civil war issues, see the following: Aaron B. Retish, *Russia's Peasants in Revolution and Civil War: Citizenship, Identity, and the Creation of the Soviet State* (New York: Cambridge University Press, 2008); B. E. Clements, "Working-Class and Peasant Women in the Russian Revolution, 1917-1923," *Signs: Journal of Women in Culture and Society* 8 (1982): 215–35; and again Farnsworth, "Village Women Experience the Revolution," pp. 238–60, A. Gleason, P. Kenez and R. Stites, eds., *Bolshevik Culture* (Bloomington, IN: Indiana University. Press, 1985). On the 1926 Marriage Law debate, and on peasant women's reaction to it, see Siegelbaum, *Soviet State and Society Between Revolutions*, 150–6. Material on the subject is also available in B. Farnsworth, "Bolshevik Alternatives and the Soviet Family: The 1926 Marriage Law Debate," in *Women in Russia*, ed. Dorothy Atkinson, Alexander Dallin, and Gail Lapidus (Stanford, CA: Stanford University Press, 1977). Wendy Goldman deals with the historical context of the question in *Women, the State, and Revolution: Soviet Family Policy and Social Life, 1917-1936* (New York: Cambridge University Press, 1993). Siegelbaum sums up the ideological and situational roots of Stalin's coerced industrialization of Russia in *Soviet State and Society Between Revolutions*, 188. The challenges this radical program posed for female (and male) villagers in Russia are discussed in the following monographs: David Ransel, *Village Mothers: Three Generations of Change in Russia and Tataria* (Bloomington, IN: Indiana University Press, 2000); Lynne Viola, "Bab'i Bunty and Peasant Women's Protest During Collectivization," *Russian Review* 45 (1986): 189–205; all the essays found in L. Viola, V. P. Danilov, N. A. Ivnitskii, and Denis Koslov, eds., *The War Against the Peasantry, 1927-1930: The Tragedy of the Soviet Countryside*, trans. Steven Shabad (New Haven, CT: Yale University Press, 2005); and (for historical context) Dorothy Atkinson, *The End of the Russian Land Commune, 1905-1930* (Stanford, CA: Stanford University Press, 1988). On broader *cultural* aspects of the conflict between city and countryside in early Stalinist Russia, consult Katerina Clark, "The City Versus the Countryside in Soviet Peasant Literature of the Twenties: A Duel of Utopias," in A. Gleason, P. Kenez, and R. Stites, *Bolshevik Culture*, 175–89. The impact of Stalin's modernization campaign on women in the Russian countryside is suggested by Barbara Engel, "Transformation Versus Tradition,"in Clements, Engel, and Worobec, *Russia's Women: Accommodation, Resistance, Transformation*, 147.

INDEX